The Government and Politics of India

The Government and Politics of India

Ramesh Thakur

St. Martin's Press   New York

THE GOVERNMENT AND POLITICS OF INDIA
Copyright © 1995 by Ramesh Thakur

St. Martin's Press, Scholarly and Reference Division, 175 Fifth Avenue, New York, N.Y. 10010

First published in the United States of America in 1995

Printed in Malaysia

ISBN 0–312–12718–9 (cloth)
ISBN 0–312–12719–7 (pbk.)

Library of Congress Cataloging-in-Publication Data
Thakur, Ramesh Chandra, 1948–
Government and politics of India / Ramesh Thakur.
p.   cm.
Includes bibliographical references and index.
ISBN 0–312–12718–9 (cloth). — ISBN 0–312–12719–7 (pbk.)
1. India—Politics and government—1947–   I. Title.
JQ231.T43   1995
320.954—dc20   95–8227
                                                      CIP

In loving memory of my father, Shri Awadh Thakur, who left us forever before we could complete our discussions on many of the issues raised in this book

Contents

viii Contents

List of Tables, Figures, Exhibits and Maps

Tables

Figures

Exhibits

Map

List of Abbreviations

AFMC	Armed Forces Medical College
AIADMK	All-India Anna Dravid Munnetra Kazhagam
AIBMAC	All-India Babri Masjid Action Committee
AICC	All-India Congress Committee
BJP	Bharatiya Janata Party
BKD	Bharatiya Kranti Dal
BSF	Border Security Force
CAG	Comptroller and Auditor General
CBI	Central Bureau of Investigation
CME	College of Military Engineering
CPB	Congress Parliamentary Board
CPI	Communist Party of India
CPI(M)	Communist Party of India (Marxist)
CRPF	Central Reserve Police Force
CWC	Congress Working Committee
DM	District Magistrate
DMK	Dravid Munnetra Kazhagam
GDP	Gross Domestic Product
GNP	Gross National Product
HDI	Human Development Index
HIE	*Hindu International Edition*
IA	Indian Airlines
IAF	Indian Air Force
IAS	Indian Administrative Service
ICS	Indian Civil Service
IFS	Indian Foreign Service
IMA	Indian Military Academy
IMF	International Monetary Fund
IOU	Index of Opposition Unity
IPS	Indian Police Service
MLA	Member of Legislative Assembly

MLC	Member of Legislative Council
MP	Member of Parliament
MRTP	Monopolies and Trade Practices Act
NDA	National Defence Academy
NIEO	New International Economic Order
NSA	National Security Act
OECD	Organisation for Economic Cooperation and Development
OHT	*Overseas Hindustan Times*
OPEC	Organisation of Petroleum Exporting Countries
PAC	Public Accounts Committee
PCC	Pradesh Congress Committee
PPP	Purchasing Power Parities
PQLI	Physical Quality of Life Index
PSC	Public Service Commission
PSU	Public Sector Undertaking
RAW	Research and Analysis Wing
RSS	Rashtriya Swayamsevak Sangh
SDO	Sub-Divisional Officer
SGPC	Shiromani Gurdwara Prabandhak Committee
SP	Superintendent of Police
SW	*Statesman Weekly*
TADA	Terrorist and Disruptive Activities (Prevention) Act
TOI	*Times of India*
UK	United Kingdom
UNDP	United Nations Development Programme
UNO	United Nations Organisation
UP	Uttar Pradesh
UPSC	Union Public Service Commission
US	United States
VHP	Vishwa Hindu Parishad

Acknowledgements

I am grateful to the University of Otago for the award of a research grant for a trip to India in 1993–4. Hew McLeod was kind enough to offer helpful comments on the section on Punjab in Chapter 1. My colleagues Chris Rudd and Antony Wood generously read and commented on various parts of the book while it was in progress. I am indebted for some of the information and finer points of analysis to Maj.-Gen. D. N. Banerjee of the Institute for Defence Studies and Analyses, Mr Kalyan B. Chakraborti IPS (ret'd), Mr Sanjay Pande (IPS), Mr Justice Arvind V. Savant of the Bombay High Court, Air Commodore Jasjit Singh of the Institute for Defence Studies and Analyses, and Mr Devesh C. Thakur. The work benefitted from the experience and advice of the series editor Vincent Wright, and the counsel and patience of the press editor Steven Kennedy. I would like to record my appreciation also of the work done by my research assistants Sarah Heal, Jan Preston-Stanley and Christine Wilson. They helped to locate and retrieve information from the library, proofread the manuscript and compile the index. Finally, I am grateful to Macmillan Press Ltd for permission to adapt Figure 11.2 from a chart in Colin R. Patman, 'Economic Planning: Paths to Development', in A. B. Mountjoy (ed.), *The Third World: Problems and Prospects* (Macmillan, 1978), figure 10, p. 48.

RAMESH THAKUR

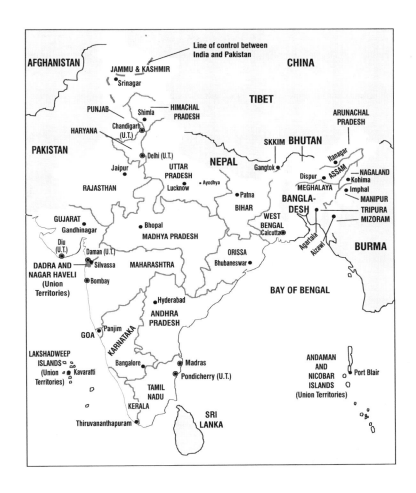

Map of India

1

The Indian Mosaic

The view of India and Indians that persists abroad is narrow and stereotypical. It is derived from an amalgam of the writings of Rudyard Kipling, the mimicry of Peter Sellers and the heart-tugging advertisements of such charitable organisations as World Vision and Oxfam. Personal contacts with the proprietor and family of the neighbourhood dairy store may be leavened with the romanticism of films and television productions like *Heat and Dust*, *The Far Pavilions*, *The Jewel in the Crown* and *Gandhi*. The resulting picture that most Westerners have of India is an odd and contradictory mix of falsehoods, half-truths and fantasies:

- India is a poor country with few resources;
- India has little manufacturing and industrial capacity;
- India's overpopulation causes starvation and hunger on a large scale;
- India is a land of handsome, charming and rich princes and maharajas;
- Indians are heirs to an ancient civilisation that emphasises self-sacrificing asceticism, spiritualism and a stable family life;
- India is full of beggars, child-brides, bride-burners, corrupt officials and self-serving politicians;
- India is chaotic and disordered;
- India's nationhood is fatally flawed by divisions of religion, caste and ethnicity;
- India's defence forces are large in manpower but neither modernised nor well-equipped;
- India is a nuclear power;
- India is a regional bully;
- India has little real influence in world affairs.

As with all cliches and stereotypes, there is of course some truth in most of these images. For example, India's population has doubled in the last generation (Figure 1.1). And not one state of India has so far escaped the poverty trap (Table 1.1). Perhaps a railway journey is not an inappropriate simile of India today. When an express train pulls into the station of a major city, there is a tremendous hullabaloo, confusion reigns supreme as those wishing to detrain jostle noisily with those wishing to entrain, vendors hawk their wares lustily and foreigners can usually be identified by their general air of bewilderment. Yet amidst the chaos there is an underlying order. People do manage to find their allotted seats. They have reliable expectations of arriving safely at their destinations. India's major cities are linked in a vast 62 000 km rail network whose formal rules and informal conventions are reasonably well understood and followed all over the country. And there are regional variations in the 'ground' reality of train travel: computerised seat reservations in Bombay and Delhi give way to the joys of ticketless travel in Bihar.

India's political leaders have taken good care to insulate themselves from the rigours of ordinary train travel. Special VIP quotas are set aside for them. This is but a minor illustration of the misfit between the rhetoric of India's 'socialist' or 'social democratic' people's representatives and the reality of the rarefied existence of the parliamentarians in New Delhi. The MPs are all committed to Gandhian austerity. But they live in magnificent houses in the

FIGURE 1.1
India's population growth, 1961–91

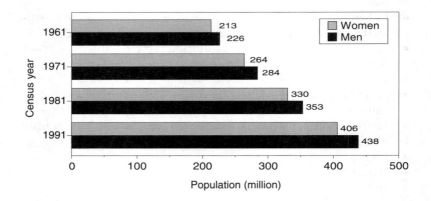

TABLE 1.1

The Union of India, 1991

States	Population (million)	Literacy (%)	Income (US $ per capita)
Andhra Pradesh	66.3	45	280
Arunachal Pradesh	0.86	41	340
Assam	22.3	53	280
Bihar	86.3	39	230
Goa	1.1	77	640
Gujarat	41.1	61	440
Haryana	16.3	55	470
Himachal Pradesh	5.1	64	340
Jammu & Kashmir	6.0		280
Karnataka	44.8	56	340
Kerala	29.0	91	280
Madhya Pradesh	66.0	43	300
Maharashtra	78.7	63	550
Manipur	1.8	61	330
Meghalaya	1.7	48	260
Mizoram	0.69	81	220
Nagaland	1.2	61	310
Orissa	31.5	49	230
Punjab	20.0	57	650
Rajasthan	43.8	39	280
Sikkim	0.40	57	310
Tamil Nadu	55.6	64	360
Tripura	2.7	60	250
Uttar Pradesh	138.7	42	260
West Bengal	67.9	58	390

Union Territories

Andaman & Nicobar Islands
Chandigarh
Dadra & Nagar Haveli
Daman & Diu
Delhi
Lakshadweep
Pondicherry

Total   844 million people   52.1% literacy $330 GNP/capita most exclusive locales in New Delhi whose market rents would be beyond the means of all but the 'filthy rich'. All of this produces a certain formalism in India's politics, adds to the sense of cynicism of ordinary Indians and contributes to an alienation from the political system. The single dominant theme in conversations about the politics of India across the length and breadth of the country is the incompetence, corruption and tyranny of government. One commentator described it as 'a system of governance which is shamelessly unresponsive to the aspirations of its many people in addition to being parasitic and tyrannical' (Kishwar, 1991, p. 2).

Indians are united in their deeply ingrained sense of cynicism towards the culture of corruption. Does India, which undoubtedly has a political structure, also have a common political culture? This is a contested question. It could be argued that shared myths and the operation of a common set of political institutions have created a common political culture. A particular type of institutional experience over a certain period of time has a significant effect on the formation of political attitudes. An all-India sense of the public interest has been formed by the interaction of Hindu modes of thought and modern networks of communication linking the different layers and regions of Indian society in real time in a way that is unique to the second half of the twentieth century.

An alternative interpretation is that the commonality is superficial. Spread over more than six hundred thousand villages and almost four thousand towns, about 80 per cent of Indian society is rural. Most of its people have little contact with one another. The country is subject to unrelenting tension because of the abundance of centrifugal and particularistic forces. While these may be suppressed in times of national crisis, such as war, particularism is the normal condition and universalism the exception. The policy implications of this for any government in New Delhi are that political unity is fragile, can never be taken for granted, but must instead always be assiduously cultivated.

India's physical features exhibit remarkable diversity. The country covers about 3.3 million square kilometres in area. It varies from sub-sea-level desert to the Himalayas, the highest mountain range in the world. The climatic conditions go from tropical heat in the south to near Arctic cold in the north, from perennial drought in some parts of the country to more than a thousand centimetres of annual rainfall in Cherrapunji in Assam. Geological formations range from the 0.5–2 billion years old pre-Cambrian granite of the Indian peninsula to the young Cenozoic mountains in the north which are only about 60 million years old. India may be divided horizontally into three geographical groups: the northern mountain belt, the Indo-Gangetic alluvial plains and the Deccan peninsula. The great Himalayan mountains have formed a natural protective barrier against Arctic winds as much as against invading armies, shielding South Asia from biting frost even more than from alien hordes. About one-quarter of India is forested. Bombay and Calcutta are two of the most densely populated cities in the world; parts of Indian territory along the Himalayas are among the most sparsely populated areas of human habitation.

India's social and demographic characteristics are equally diverse. Its 840 million people (1991 figures) speak more than a thousand dialects. Fifteen languages are important enough to have been specified in the Eighth Schedule of the Constitution (see Table 1.2). English (the language not listed in Table 1.2) is spoken across the country, but is the language of the educated minority. Several of the languages have their own distinctive scripts which are not decipherable to the uninitiated. India's social diversity is so great that there is only an 11 per cent probability that two people picked at random will be from the same ethnic-linguistic group, compared to a 50 per cent probability in the United States (Powell, 1982, p. 45).

Economically, extremes of poverty and opulence are equally mind-boggling. One of the world's industrial giants in aggregate, India also has pockets where time has stood still for centuries: electricity is either unknown or supplied only sporadically, the land is tilled with manual ploughshares, water is drawn from basic wells and firewood is the chief form of fuel. India's major industries are textiles, steel, processed foods, cement, machinery, chemicals, fertilisers, consumer appliances and automobiles. The chief crops are rice, grains, coffee, sugar cane, spices, tea, cashews, cotton, copra, coir, jute and linseed. The major mineral deposits are chromium, coal, iron, manganese, mica, bauxite, gypsum and oil. Livestock include 195m cattle and 55m sheep, and the annual fish catch is 3.6m tonnes. Infrastructural constraints – electricity, telecommunications, transportation, health and education services – continue to retard economic development.

Historically, India is the inheritor of one of the world's great ancient civilisations. Modern Indian society is an amalgam of successive invasions and conquests interacting with indigenous peoples and traditions. The Indus valley civilisation flourished from 4000 to 2500 BC. Classical Indian civilisation was created by the

TABLE 1.2

The major languages, religions and castes of India

Languages			Religions and castes			
	No (m.)	Per cent		No (m.)	Per cent	Per cent
Hindi	251	30	Hindus	699		83.8
Bengali	69	8	of which upper castes		17.6	
Telugu	69	8	of which Brahmins		5.5	
Marathi	65	8	Rajputs		3.9	
Tamil	58	7	Marathas		2.2	
Urdu	43	5	Vaishyas		1.9	
Gujarati	40	5	Kayasthas		1.1	
Kannada	34	4	Jats		1.0	
Malayalam	34	4	Others		2.0	
Oriya	28	4	Backward castes		43.7	
Punjabi	25	3	Untouchables		15.0	
Assamese	13	2	Tribals		7.5	
Kashmiri	4	0.5	Muslims	90		11.2
Sanskrit	1	0.1	Christians	18		2.2
			Sikhs	14		1.7
			Buddhists	6		0.7
			Jains	4		0.5

merger of Aryan invaders from the northwest in about 1500 BC with the earlier Dravidian inhabitants. Arab invaders established a foothold in western India in the eighth century, while Turkic Muslim invaders conquered northern India by the twelfth century. The Mughal dynasty ruled from 1526 to 1857, with the British ruling for less than a century until 1947. The waves of invasions and interminglings throughout history have left their mark on culture, language and literature, religion and social structures. The legacy also includes elements of bitter social cleavages. A useful way of trying to come to grips with the reality of India is to look at the caste, regional, religious and gender divisions. This also enables us to examine some of the major contemporary political controversies in the country.

Snapshot One: Caste

Uneasily together lie the component parts of the Indian mosaic. The caste system, sanctified by centuries of custom, has slowly been permeating the institutions of the modern idiom of parliamentary democracy. It also gives the majority of Indians something in the nature of common beliefs and analogous social structures. It defines a person's hereditary rights and duties with unmatched comprehensiveness, rigidity and thoroughness. It ranks as one of the most complete denials of the principle of human equality, for it places certain groups of human beings in a 'polluting' category in social intercourse. Louis Dumont (1970) has argued that the Hindu caste system rejects the idea of *homo aequlius* and is the apotheosis of the institution of *homo hierarchichus*. At the individual, local and national levels of analysis, caste remains a psychological, social and political phenomenon of the first importance.

The basic unit of the caste system is the *varna*, the fourfold division of Indian society into Brahmin (scholar-priest), Kshatriya (warrior), Vaishya (merchant) and Sudra (peasants and labourers). However, such a simple classification is misleading, for the *yarna* is almost useless as a means of understanding the baffling complexity of 'microcaste' divisions. For example, Brahmins tend to be vegetarians in the south, fish-eaters in Bengal and meat-eaters in Kashmir.

The more meaningful unit of classification is the *jati,* the size of which can range from a few hundred to millions. Unlike the *varna,* which is all-India, the *jati* is geographically and linguistically bounded. The *jati* provides the social identity and a rough-and-ready social security system for village individuals and defines each person's *dharma*. Gandhi popularised the importance of truthful conduct in the Hindu conception of social life. Buddhism stressed the importance of compassion. The notion of *dharma* is common to both Hinduism and Buddhism. A word with no precise equivalent in English, *dharma* is a composite of religion, law, duty and responsibility all rolled into one. Action in accordance with one's *dharma* determines a person's social and inter-species mobility across different lifespans. The moral code embedded in the caste *dharma* thus governs virtually every asp⸀ ⸀ of individual conduct and social relations in India's heartland. Ḱarma is the inevitability of the consequences of action: one can neither be denied the rewards of virtuous conduct in accordance with one's *dharma,* nor escape the punishment due to any departures from such a moral code.

Paradoxically, the rigidity of the caste system in Hindu society is in sharp contrast to the flexibility of Hinduism as a religion. This means that the *jati*, not Hinduism, provides the principle of social cohesion, especially at the local level. As an amorphous and syncretistic religion, Hinduism is itself remarkably diverse in the range of beliefs and across the different regions of India. There is no recognised 'establishment' with a clear priestly hierarchy: there are no archbishops, ayatollahs or chief rabbis. Each Hindu chooses her or his own manifestation of the pantheon of Hindu gods, which scripture to use as the basic prayer text, which sage to follow. The corollary of this is that Hinduism is as much a way of life as a religion. This has made Hinduism peculiarly resistant to change. Buddhists, Jains, Sikhs as well as Hindus have all tried to modify and eradicate the caste system. The system has outlived them all.

Preferential Policies

The Constitution of India adopted in 1950 contained its own provisions to ameliorate the most pernicious effects of the caste system. 'Negative rights' included clauses outlawing discrimination on grounds of caste. 'Positive rights' included constitutional clauses enjoining the state to implement what in the West came to be called 'affirmative action'. The quest for identity, justice and efficiency has led India into policies of positive discrimination mandated by the constitution. Untouchables were given quotas in parliament, state legislative assemblies, public sector jobs and educational institutions.

In 1979, a commission was set up under B. P. Mandal to examine the whole question of quotas for the backward castes. It concluded that although the backward castes comprised 52 per cent of the population, they held only 12.5 per cent of central government jobs, and only 4.7 per cent of jobs at officer level. Its report, issued at the end of 1980, proposed massive discrimination in their favour but was quietly ignored. In August 1990 Prime Minister V. P. Singh decided to implement the Mandal recommendations. He may have done so out of conviction. Or he may have calculated that if he could rally the numerically powerful backward castes to his Janata Dal Party, and perhaps detach the Muslim voting bloc from the Congress, then he would have an unbeatable electoral alliance. Whatever his motivations, the issue aroused strong passions, convulsed Indian society and was instrumental in causing the downfall of the Singh government. It also provoked an intense and lingering debate on the wisdom and justice of preferential policies.

The Case For

Preferential policies have four dimensions: *protective,* where the state strives to achieve equality of protection; *ameliorative,* with the goal of achieving equality of opportunity; *compensatory,* motivated by the desire to achieve equality of outcome; and *participative,* with the goal of achieving equality of empowerment. The belief underlying the policies is that some groups are so far behind in all measurable criteria that their survival and integration into the mainstream of society will not be possible without the government taking an active role to bring them to the same economic, political and social level as the other groups. On all three dimensions – social, political and economic – the outcastes are the most marginalised, disadvantaged and destitute people in Indian society. After centuries of discrimination against them, they require a period of positive discrimination in order to help them make the transition to equal and full participants in modern Indian society.

Socially, preferential policies will help to integrate the castoffs into the mainstream of Indian society. It will restore dignity and self-esteem to the people who find themselves at the bottom of the heap for no fault of their own. The exclusion of outcastes from the social mainstream is one of the biggest causes of the material and spiritual degeneration of the country; the caste hierarchy corresponds to the occupational hierarchy; breaking the link through government-enforced recruitment of outcastes into high-income occupations will sound the deathknell for the caste system.

Economically, affirmative action programmes will help to draw more and more of the formerly excluded groups into the expanding middle classes. The proportion of scheduled castes in India's central government services went up from 3.0 per cent in 1972 to 9.7 per cent in 1992 at the level of under-secretary or higher, and from 4.1 per cent to 11.6 per cent at section officer level (*India Today*, 30 April 1994, p. 32).

Politically, preferential policies will help to absorb the downtrodden into the political mainstream. They might otherwise be alienated from the political process and take to destructive revolutionary means. In terms of the efficiency argument, India's biggest asset is its people. The outcastes and other backward castes comprise more than half of India's population. The country can ill-afford to waste this potential pool of talent by refusing to develop and tap their abilities and skills.

The argument about the adverse effects of such policies on job efficiencies is less than persuasive. Positive discrimination to help the backward castes began in the princely state of Mysore (called Karnataka today) in 1921. In Karnataka, more than 90 per cent of the people belong to groups for whom jobs are reserved. But the quality of government is not noticeably bad in comparison with governments of other states. Similarly, the argument that the benefits of affirmative action are restricted to a minority of individuals or families within the target groups is also specious. The Mandal report had responded to this criticism by remarking that when a backward caste person becomes a senior government official, the material benefits may accrue only to his family. But the psychological spinoff is considerable and extends to the whole community which feels socially elevated by having its 'own man' in the corridors of power. Safeguards against abuse of the programme were set by the Supreme Court in a majority verdict delivered on 16 November 1992: the quotas of reservations may not exceed more than 50 per cent of jobs, preferential treatment may not be extended to promotions, and the 'creamy layer' of target groups are to be excluded from the reserved quotas.

The Case Against

The moral premises and assumptions of preferential policies are themselves open to question (see Thakur, 1993a, pp. 114–20). More seriously, after being in operation for more than four decades, they have produced eight harmful effects in India.

Persistence. Affirmative action programmes are always described as temporary expedients. In India, the rhetoric of transience is negated by the reality of persistence and proliferation.

Triple Expansion. Positive discrimination policies in India have trebled in scope, embracing additional measures for the same target group, extending positive discrimination to newer sectors of society, and incorporating additional target groups into the programmes. The backward castes and tribes already had 22.5 per cent of government jobs, parliamentary seats and university admissions reserved for them. The Mandal Commission recommended the incorporation of another 27 per cent into the reserved quota. But if any member of the target groups succeeded in open competition, then that would not count against the reserved quota. In other words, by definition every one of the quota – almost half of all government jobs – was to be filled by unqualified people. In May 1992, the Minorities Commission recommended that job reservations should be extended to religious minorities as well as the backward castes. After decades of constitutionally sanctioned efforts to protect and promote sectarian preferences, India is caught in an escalating cycle of increasing numbers of groups putting forth expanding claims to entitlements.

Fraudulence. If membership of a particular group confers unequal privileges, and if job markets and prospects for upward mobility are stagnant or shrinking, then fraudulent claims of membership in the target groups will multiply.

Dirigisme. The spiralling cycle of preferential entitlements, and the need to ensure against fraudulent claims, lead to an expanding role for government at a time when India is trying to reduce government intrusion into the economy and society. For example, by the time that the Rao government decided in September 1993 to implement the Mandal Commission recommendations, it was required to establish the following distinctions: membership of the scheduled castes and tribes; meaning and membership of the other backward castes (OBCs) whose status would be decided by the National Commission for the Backward Classes; following a directive from the Supreme Court, the definition and composition of the More Backward Castes (MBCs) from among the Backward Castes (BCs); the apportionment of separate quotas to the two sub-categories of the BCs from within the 27 per cent reservations for them; the definition and determination of the 'creamy layer' within the BCs who are ineligible for reserved quotas.

Capture. Within groups receiving preferential treatment, benefits have been captured disproportionately by the better educated, more articulate and more politically skilled elite among the 'disadvantaged'. On 16 November 1992, the Supreme Court ruled that the government could not reserve an additional 10 per cent for the poor among the 'forward' castes. Its directive on the creamy layer was meant to negate the capture of preferential benefits by the better off. But the court explicitly ruled out the extension of the creamy layer concept to the 22.5 per cent reservations for the scheduled castes and tribes: the concept was to apply only to the 27 per cent quota for the 'other backward castes'.

Divisiveness. Every affirmative action produces an equal and opposite communal reaction. If a government frames public policy in a racially conscious way, then it cannot expect groups suffering relative deprivation to act in a race-blind manner. In 1990, as the Indian government tried to broaden the definition of the under-privileged and to extend the range of reservations for them, Indian society was convulsed. Students took to highly publicised suicides, streets were in flames, and the instrument of sectarian harmony became the path to civil conflict.

Politicisation. Preferential policies are are meant to reduce and eliminate inter-group disparities. Instead, they create and nurture vested interests parasitically dependent upon the dispensing of state privileges. Indian politicians try to calculate sectarian 'vote banks'. Considerable cynicism towards the political process is now evident in India because individual and national interests are widely perceived to have been subordinated to the claims of numerous special interest groups.

Bihar, which may offer a foretaste of what to expect in the rest of India, has seen the rise of a new type of caste. Designed to assert social superiority, caste is now being used as a system for the distribution of political spoils. It is organised for capturing political power and the social and material benefits that flow from it, whether it be a government job, preferential entry into an educational institution or a government licence. As castes identify with parties rather than individuals, caste associations are organised and act as pressure groups. Thus the modern idioms of parliamentary institutions have been absorbed by ancient caste lineages and are being used to serve the ends of the latter.

Counter-productiveness. State dependency undermines the dignity of a collective entity and retards the realisation of human worth of its individual members. Preferential policies foster the working-class values of solidarity instead of the middle-class values of thrift, hard work, self-improvement and property ownership; rest on the assumption of superiority in the non-target group; reinforce the sense of inferiority in target groups; perpetuate their sense of being victims not masters of their destiny; and keep them in ghettos. Thomas Sowell, an eminent black American based at Stanford University, has argued that the above effects are found in almost all countries with such policies (Sowell, 1990).

Snapshot Two: Secularism

If secularism is understood as the gradual displacement of ascriptive ties of religion, caste and ethnicity by achievement-based calculations, then the opposite has happened in India. Far from being confined to the private sphere, caste and religion have come forcefully on to the centre stage of public life. Paradoxically, while almost every religion preaches universal brotherhood, religion has been a constant source of friction throughout human history. The history of the Indian subcontinent has been especially unfortunate in this respect, leading to partition in 1947.

The secular and sacred authority were separated in traditional Hindu social order through the *varnashrama-dharma* system: 'the Indian socio-political norm was characterized by orthopraxy in observance of similar customs and social distance between castes rather than by orthodoxy in terms of identical beliefs held by all individuals' (Mansingh, 1991, p. 297). (*Varnashrama* is the Hindu classification of society and life into four divisions and orders; *dharma* refers to the duty pertaining to a particular caste or order.) This also enabled social cohesion to be maintained within a pattern of diversity; state-enforced orthodoxy was neither necessary nor indeed possible. Islam by contrast is distinctive for uniting the spiritual and temporal aspects of social order. The overriding criterion of state legitimacy is the one propounded by the Ulama of an elected head of the Islamic community, enforcing the Shariah and crushing non-believers by giving them the choice of embracing the faith or being put to the sword. But this does not mean that the Hindu tradition was necessarily one of tolerance. In a challenge to the 'dubious historicity' of this claim, Embree (1990, pp. 25–6) has put forward an 'encapsulation' thesis which differs from toleration, absorption and synthesis. Encapsulation, which precluded dialogue, interaction and integration, provided the basis for the coexistence of the Hindu social order with an Islamic political order from the seventh century onwards. As long as the outsider did not threaten the Hindu paradigm, his beliefs were accorded the same legitimacy. The political centre could neither coerce nor coopt the Hindu hierarchy to its own religious will because there was no such hierarchy. Hindu society was therefore 'able to yield political power without conceding cultural hegemony' (Embree, 1990, p. 82).

Conflicts and alliances between India's rulers were based on political clashes of interests and expediency rather than religious divides and communities. The most important concept was loyalty to the salt (that is, to the ruler as food-provider) and the most despicable betrayal was disloyalty to the salt (*namak haram*). Rulers hoping to found dynasties found it expedient to promote this concept, in return accepting responsibility for guarding all the faiths of their subjects. Loyalty was doubly reciprocal, imposing rights and obligations on both ruler and subject.

As Muslim rule gave way to the British empire, the British policy of divide and rule hardened vertical divisions along sectarian lines. The Government of India Act of 1935 introduced the principle of communal representation throughout the political system, elevating religious identity above all else and providing separate electorates for Hindus and Muslims. Political coalitions began to be built along communal lines; religious leaders acquired vested interests in demonstrating numerically large followings as the surest path to political power; accommodation and consociationalism lost any political utility.

The problem of religious minorities was not solved with partition (a policy of divide and leave). In the riots accompanying partition, up to one million people were killed and up to eight million moved across the new borders. Although Hindus formed more than four-fifths of the population after independence, this still left significant chunks of Muslims, Christians, Sikhs, Buddhists and Jains (see Table 1.2). The dilemma of the Muslims who stayed behind in India was especially acute. Co-religionists in Pakistan, with extensive familial connections, were now foreigners and enemies. Hindus, with whom the Muslims had little social intercourse, were compatriots and in control of political power. Yet the Hindus blamed the Muslims for the partition and doubted the loyalty of those who remained in India. Mutual suspicions and hostility between India's Muslims and Hindus increased with wars with Pakistan.

Increasing communal tension from the second half of the 1980s onwards flared into periodic riots and killings, for example in Meerut (U.P.), Ahmedabad (Gujarat) and Bhagalpur (Bihar). In the 1980s, more than 7000 people lost their lives in some 4500 communal incidents (*India Today*, 15 January 1990, p. 34), almost quadrupling the figure for the 1970s. (From 1954 to 1982 inclusive, there were 6933 communal incidents resulting in a total of 2723 deaths; Brass, 1990, p. 198.) Moreover, there has been a steady geographical spread of the regions affected by such flare-ups. And there are three times as many Muslim victims as Hindus.

The constitutional safeguards given to minorities have to be understood against the backdrop of this social reality in the subcontinent. Secularism is one of the major principles of the Constitution of India that was adopted in 1950. Secularism can mean one or both of two things. It can mean equal and due respect for all religions and faiths, expressed in Sanskrit as *sarva dharma samabhav* (let all religions prosper). Second, it entails separation of the state from the church. But as we have seen, in its second meaning secularism in India militated against the historical relationship between state and church in both the Hindu and Islamic contexts.

The preamble to the constitution declares one of the objectives to be to secure to all citizens of India liberty of faith, belief and worship. The chapter on fundamental rights provided a constitutional guarantee to minority groups that their sensitivities could not simply be overridden in a majoritarian democracy. The framers of the constitution did not believe that this was sufficient assurance to religious minorities that their rights would not be trampled on. They therefore incorporated a separate group of rights in Articles 25–28 of the constitution focusing on the right to freedom of religion.

Article 25 of the constitution provided that all persons are equally entitled to freedom of conscience and the right freely to profess, practise and propagate religion. But the exercise of these freedoms is subject to state control: the Indian constitution circumscribes religious freedom with the three qualifications of public order, morality and health. Infanticide and *sati* (widow-burning) could not be practised, for example, in the name of religious practices sanctified by centuries of custom. Similarly, the state was permitted to enact measures of social reform, for example opening up Hindu religious institutions of a public character to all classes and sections of society. In a sense this was the corollary to the abolition of untouchability, ensuring that social inequalities could not be legally perpetuated under the cloak of religion. The scope of freedoms of religion conferred by the constitution has been widened by judicial interpretation to the effect that they guarantee not just the right to practise and propagate religious faith and belief, but also all rituals and observances that are regarded as integral parts of a religion by its adherents.

Article 28 prohibits religious instruction in any educational institution maintained wholly out of state funds. Moreover, no person attending a state-aided or state-recognised school can be compelled to take part in any religious instruction; prior consent of the parent or legal guardian is required. In other words, educational institutions may be run by religious groups, impart religious instruction and still receive state assistance. This is a good illustration of the attempt in the Indian constitution to combine state secularism with private religious freedoms. All state educational institutions are fully secular; yet private denominational institutions are permitted to maintain their religious character even if receiving state assistance.

The above set of 'positive' religious freedoms is underpinned by a set of 'negative' religious rights. There is no state religion in India. The state is enjoined not to discriminate against any citizen on the basis of religion in any matter, and in particular in regard to access to or use of public places (Article 15), employment (Article 16) and admission into any educational institution maintained wholly or aided by the state (Article 29). The right of any citizen to aspire to and seek the highest office of state embodies secularism in the political realm.

The Babri Masjid Controversy

The Babri Masjid was built in Ayodhya in 1528 during the reign of Babur, founder of the Mughal dynasty – hence the name of the mosque. In the 1850s, more than 70 people were killed in Hindu–Muslim clashes; a Hindu priest built a small altar to Ram inside the Babri Masjid complex; and the British government built a wall to separate the rival places of worship. In the 1880s the courts refused permission for the construction of a temple in the Hindu area of the complex. An idol of Ram was installed by Hindus inside the mosque in a clandestine night-time raid in December 1949. The courts took possession of the complex in 1950 in response to cross-petitions from Hindus and Muslims.

The two chief protagonists in the Ram Janambhoomi–Babri Masjid controversy are the Vishwa Hindu Parishad (World Hindu Council or VHP) and the All-India Babri Masjid Action Committee (AIBMAC). There are two distinct issues entangled in the controversy. The first is whether Ayodhya is the birthplace of the Hindu god Ram. The second dispute is whether the mosque was constructed on the ruins of a temple. The VHP launched a campaign in 1983 for constructing a temple at the Ayodhya site. When courts ordered the opening of the mosque in 1986 so that Hindus could worship at the Ram shrine, Muslims reacted with mourning all over

India. When the lock of the disputed shrine in the Babri Masjid was opened on 1 February 1986, Member of Parliament Syed Shahabuddin took the lead in organising and launching a Muslim agitation in protest. Three years later more than 600 people were killed in communal riots following the performance of *shilanyas* (laying of foundation stone) in 1989.

In May 1991, four historians – three Hindus (R. S. Sharma, Suraj Bhan and D. N. Jha) and one Muslim (Athar Ali) – submitted a report on the Ayodhya dispute to the government stating that there was no historical or archaeological evidence to suggest that any spot in Ayodhya was venerated as the birthplace of Lord Ram prior to the eighteenth century (*HIE*, 25 May 1991, p. 6). The legend of the destruction of a temple at the site of Ram's birth arose only in the second half of the eighteenth century and was not asserted until the nineteenth century. The Babri Masjid became a protected monument under the Ancient Monuments Act in 1904. The historians described the mosque as a significant example of Sharqi architecture built almost five centuries ago and therefore imposing an obligation on the government to protect and preserve it.

On 6 December 1992, the Babri Masjid was destroyed by a 300 000-strong mob in Ayodhya. The demolition of the mosque plunged India into the worst outbreak of communal violence since partition. The casualties included 1700 dead and 5500 injured (*India Today*, 31 January 1993, p. 28). Other costs included serious doubts about the capacity of the political system to cope with the crisis of confidence and the fright given to international investors just when they were beginning to accept the government's commitment to economic liberalisation and reforms. The most serious cost was the shock to India's secular credentials. Yet support for the destruction of the mosque came from only a subset of the Hindu population: the trading, small business and white-collar middle classes; and those old enough to remember the partition of the subcontinent (Chhibber and Mishra, 1993).

Militant Hindus gloated over the avenging of centuries of Muslim rule; the average Indian Muslim became sullen, frustrated and bitter. The international press and the English language press in India reported and reacted to the events in the language of secularism, constitutionalism and the rule of law. The communalisation of politics by the Bharatiya Janata Party (BJP) was the proximate cause of the Ayodhya crisis. But the cataclysmic events of 6 December 1992 and after were also symptoms of a pervasive regime decay that was slowly corroding the Indian state (Thakur, 1993c). As a former cabinet minister comments, a solution to the Ayodhya problem will remain elusive as long as the government is seen to be 'appeasing the minority fundamentalism. Majority fundamentalism cannot be contained by pampering minority fundamentalism' (A. Nehru, 1993).

On the one hand, the Ayodhya controversy demonstrates the difficulty of basing public rules in a plural society on religion. In a society characterised by moral and religious diversity, legal restrictions must be grounded in reasons that everyone can share. The force of religiously based arguments will be rejected by adherents of competing faiths. But the faithful are not prevented from recognising the validity of arguments grounded in secularism. Hence the imbalance in the recognition of religious and non-religious values in the public realm of multicultural societies. On the other hand, 'freedom of religion' means the freedom to live and worship according to one's religious beliefs. Freedom of expression is functionally meaningless if it does not include the freedom to offend. If it is inoffensive, then it does not need safeguarding.

Snapshot Three: Religious Nationalism in Punjab

As a country marked by sharp social and linguistic diversity, India has pronounced regional tendencies. At times regionalism has found expression in demands for autonomy or secession. One of the first major ethnic groups to articulate sentiments for autonomy were the Tamils under the leadership of the Dravid Munnetra Kazhagam (DMK). They were motivated partly by a fear of having Hindi imposed on them, but mainly from a sense of constituting a distinct ethnic identity. Separatist sentiment declined somewhat when the DMK won victory in Tamil Nadu in the state elections of 1967 with C. Annadurai as party leader.

'Regional nationalism' came somewhat later to Assam in the northeast. It was also different in origins, being fuelled by an increasing resentment of the growing influx of migrants and refugees. Although the process began with the partition of the subcontinent in 1947, it intensified after the India–Pakistan war of 1971 and the establishment of Bangladesh as an independent country. The people of Assam developed a feeling of having been marginalised in their own state, and out of this conviction was formed the United

Liberation Front of Assam (ULFA) in 1979. Yet at no point did ULFA seem to threaten the basic integration of Assam with India.

The most serious threat to national integration (outside the issue of Kashmir, which is discussed in Chapter 3) came from the demand for an independent Sikh state of Khalistan. The roots of Sikh terrorism lie in attempts from Mrs Indira Gandhi onwards to exploit rather than address, let alone redress, Sikh grievances. There was little support among Sikhs (with the exception of expatriate Sikhs) for Khalistan as a separate country; there was considerable support for Khalistan as the focus and symbol of Sikh grievances.

Punjab lies atop two historical faultlines: one separating Muslims from Hindus, the second separating Persian empires from Delhi-centred ones. In independent India, local identities were articulated through the politics either of language or regionalism. The nature, intensity and outcomes of demands for linguistic and regional autonomy were in turn affected by the specific conditions of the intergroup competitions. The Nehru 'model' of intergroup conflict resolution rejected religion as a criterion for recognising a political unit and ruled out the option of secession. Concessions to linguistic and cultural groups would be made on the basis of an accommodation among all parties to a conflict. The linguistic reorganisation of states produced a comfortable binational identity: a Bengali, Maratha, Sikh or Tamil identity at the state level, and an Indian identity at the multilingual central level.

The party of regional identity in Punjab is the Akali Dal. Drawing its support mainly from the agricultural Jat Sikhs, the Akali Dal has been continually frustrated in efforts to get control of the state government in its own right. In disputes with the central government, the Akalis shifted the rhetoric from state rights in a federal polity to the rights of a minority religious group in a secular democracy. Hence the emphasis on symbolic demands like bans on sale of tobacco in Amritsar and broadcasting of devotional music from the Golden Temple by monopolistic state electronic media. Rejection of the demands were met by accusations of the 'Hindu' government in New Delhi trampling on the demands of the Sikh community.

In a matching development, the struggle for political power included efforts to control the well-funded gurdwaras (Sikh temples), with the Golden Temple in Amritsar being the most important. The 'defining moment' in Punjab's recent history is the Anandpur Sahib Resolution of October 1973 and its reaffirmation by the Akali Dal in 1982. The resolution brought together under one rubric the range of religious, economic and political demands of the Akalis. The demand for a separate Punjabi state (Punjabi Suba) was voiced in the early 1960s in both linguistic and religious terms by Sant Fateh Singh and Master Tara Singh. Congress dealt with their demands through Prime Minister Jawaharlal Nehru in Delhi and Pratap Singh Kairon in Chandigarh. Master Tara Singh was regarded as a communalist and a possible secessionist. Nehru and Kairon preferred to deal with Sant Fateh Singh instead, for his definition of the Sikh political community and the extent of its goals were set within the context of the Indian union. The role of the Sikhs in the 1965 war with Pakistan heightened consciousness of the strategic importance of a stable Punjab and provided a formal rationale for granting the wish for a Sikh-majority state. By the time that Mrs Gandhi agreed to the creation of a language-based Punjabi Suba in 1966, Sant Fateh Singh was in firm control of the Akali Dal and remained so until his death in 1972.

The creation of Punjab and Haryana in 1966 left the status of Chandigarh unresolved. The joint capital was awarded to Punjab on 29 January 1970 but the decision was not implemented. Sikhs baulked at having to transfer the Abohar-Fazilka tehsils (two rural Hindu Punjabi-speaking areas which would also require a corridor to link them to their new state) to Haryana in recompense for Chandigarh. The sharing of irrigation headworks on the Ravi and Beas rivers and the distribution of the river waters was in dispute between Punjab, Haryana and Rajasthan. The Sikhs also wanted Sikhism to be recognised as a distinct religion (Article 25 of the constitution appears to lump Sikhs together with Hindus, Jains and Buddhists) and Amritsar as a holy city. There was a further demand for setting up a radio station to relay Gurbani from the Golden Temple in Amritsar. Although the Anandpur Sahib Resolution called for virtual autonomy for Punjab – with the central government having responsibility only for communications, defence, external affairs, the currency and the railways – they were not viewed as non-negotiable demands, but as the starting point of bargaining on centre–state relations.

The stakes were raised with the introduction of the fundamentalist Sant Jarnail Singh Bhindranwale as the means of outflanking the Akali Dal. When the Akali Dal lost power in the state elections in 1980, it split in the following year and the militant faction launched an agitation for the creation of a separate Sikh nation called Khalistan and the fulfilment of Sikh demands as expressed in the

Anandpur Sahib Resolution. The agitation became increasingly bitter and violent and Bhindranwale emerged as a genuine firebrand who resorted to indiscriminate terrorism. His fundamentalism appealed especially to male youths, and the success of his movement, aided and abetted by imported arms and ideas, wrecked the law and order situation throughout the Punjab. The All-India Sikh Students Federation (AISSF), led by Bhindranwale's loyal lieutenant Amrik Singh, was especially successful in recruiting Sikh youths to the cause of Khalistan, the land of the Khalsas.

Punjab and the Political Process

The Punjab quagmire illustrates the shortcomings of both procedural and performance legitimacy. The authorities have failed to institutionalise procedures for resolving inter-state differences on territory, sharing of waters (the Cauvrey river continues to be a cause of division between the governments of Karnataka and Tamil Nadu in the 1990s) and so on. Decisions once made can still be overturned by lobbying and agitation, thereby ensuring that no unpalatable decision is treated with finality. Demands are listened to not in terms of their merits but on the basis of political calculations. The pattern of government policy in responding to the challenge of political terrorism was not atypical. Policy drift was mixed with progressive abandonment and alienation of moderate Sikhs on the one hand and a cultivation of Hindu support by playing communal politics on the other.

The Punjab problem is also a salutary reminder of the complexities of religious and regional politics in India. The bases of political partisanship are social and economic as well as communal. The Sikhs constitute about 55 per cent of the state's population. To form a majority government, a political party must therefore seek to appeal to Hindus as well as Sikhs, or else it must capture almost total Sikh support. The Akali Dal's spells in government were brief precisely because of this difficulty. Its support base was concentrated among the Jat Sikhs, the principal agricultural Sikhs of Punjab. The non-Jats tended to ally with the Congress Party. While Congress has drawn support from Hindus and Sikhs, the avowedly Sikh-based Akali Dal has had to seek alliances with the Hindu-based Jan Sangh/BJP. 'Party politics, therefore, have normally tended to moderate Hindu–Sikh political polarization and to work against the entrenchment of communal divisions' (Brass, 1991, p. 177). Bhindranwale was useful to Indira and Sanjay Gandhi, and Giani Zail Singh (a Congress stalwart who was later made President) because of the appeal of his fundamentalism to the rural Jat peasantry who provided the core support for the Akali Dal. Sanjay Gandhi's role in recruiting Bhindranwale to the cause of dividing and weakening the Akali Dal accelerated the criminalisation of Punjabi politics and the politicisation of its police and judiciary.

The fate of Punjabi and Indian politics intersected with that of Sikh politics from the late 1970s onwards. The management of all the Sikh shrines in Punjab is in the hands of the Shiromani Gurdwara Prabandhak Committee (SGPC). The SGPC is also the main source of funds and other resources for the Akali Dal. Control of Sikh affairs has traditionally depended on controlling three key institutions: the SGPC because of the financial and personnel resources it commands, its influence over the chain of gurdwaras linking the Sikhs in one religious network, and its symbolic value as the apex body for managing Sikh religious affairs; the Akali Dal as the repository of Sikh nationalism; and the state government because of the scope for patronage that this provides.

There was a violent clash between militant Sikhs and Sant Nirankaris on 13 April 1978. (The Keshadharis or 'orthodox' Sikhs regard the Sant Nirankaris as a heretical sect.) The extent and nature of Bhindranwale's involvement in this remains contentious. But the incident was used to accuse factional rivals of being soft on the Nirankaris. Chief Minister Darbara Singh, a Sikh rival of Zail Singh within Congress, had Bhindranwale arrested for the murder of Lala Jagat Narain (a Hindu newspaper owner) in September 1981, but Home Minister Zail Singh had him released. SGPC president Gurcharan Singh Tohra allowed Bhindranwale and his men and arms entry into the Golden Temple complex. As the cycle of violence escalated and Hindus became the targets of attacks by Sikh militants (which therefore began to threaten Mrs Gandhi's hold over the populous Hindi heartland), President's Rule was imposed in Punjab in the fall of 1983. Caught between the fundamentalism of Bhindranwale and the Congress, the Akali Dal became increasingly aggressive in its demands. That is, Bhindranwale became the point of reference for agitational politics and symbolic leadership of the Sikh community.

Brass (1991, p. 183) has pointed out the unfortunate reversal of the Nehru model. In the 1960s, Nehru had refused to negotiate on the basis of religion and secession but was prepared to cut deals with moderates. In the 1980s, Mrs Gandhi refused to negotiate with the moderates over their demands for regional autonomy but failed to control the extremists. This forced the Akali Dal to increase the stridency of its demands. In the end the central government conceded the religious demands of the Akalis while resisting their economic and political demands. The reason for this was that with Indira and Rajiv Gandhi, resolution of the Punjab conflict was secondary to achieving political control of the state by dividing and otherwise undermining the Akali Dal. But this is also why in the end the Indira Gandhi government came into conflict with Bhindranwale, for he stressed Sikh solidarity and purity. As Bhindranwale became the most prominent spokesman of Sikh identity, so the Akali Dal was forced to match his extremist demands in order to compete as the defender of the Sikh nationhood against Congress and central government machinations. But the failure of the Akali Dal to win any measurable concessions from New Delhi left the initiative almost exclusively with Bhindranwale. At this point Bhindranwale became a double political threat to Congress. On the one hand, his fundamentalism began to cut into Congress support among scheduled caste voters in Punjab who form the critical 'floating vote' that decides elections. On the other hand, the widespread and horrific killings of Hindus by Sikh terrorists inflamed anger in the rest of the country against the Congress government's apparent helplessness.

In June 1984 Mrs Gandhi ordered the army to flush out the Sikh terrorist headquarters inside the Golden Temple complex. Between 500 and 1000 people were killed in the three-day operation, including Bhindranwale and Amrik Singh. Even though executed with the greatest of care towards the religious structures, 'Operation Bluestar' was interpreted as an assault upon the very essence of Sikhdom by Sikhs throughout the world, including the vast majority who remained opposed to the demands for a separate Khalistan. The fact that four of the six generals involved in Operation Bluestar were Sikhs did little to assuage their sense of sacrilege. To their mind, their holiest shrines had been desecrated as an alibi for failures of government over many years. They held Mrs Gandhi, not the Hindu community, culpable for this. As a news magazine noted in its cover story, 'It's *Not* Sikhs Vs Hindus . . . It's Sikhs Versus Indira Gandhi' (*Surya India*, July 1984, p. 36; emphasis in original). The army operation transformed a fringe struggle for independence into the most serious challenge to the authority of the Indian state in the 1980s. 'Sikhs should apologise for what Bhindranwale did to the

Hindus. And the government for what it did to the Golden Temple', wrote Khushwant Singh (1984, p. 36). His call went unheeded. Instead, Sikh terrorism entered its most virulent phase. The violation of the Sikh community was avenged by two of Mrs Gandhi's Sikh bodyguards who assassinated her on 31 October 1984. As word of her killing spread, innocent Sikhs were humiliated, butchered and burnt alive in the streets of the nation's capital. (Some expatriate Sikhs celebrated her killing by dancing and distributing sweetmeats.) The alienation of many Sikhs was completed by the riots in Delhi. Police were passive spectators to the savagery and humiliations inflicted on thousands of innocent Sikhs, Congress party functionaries organised and participated in the atrocities, and justice was not seen to be done in punishing the wrongdoers.

The fact that the perpetrators of such brazen outrage were allowed to go unpunished did much to undermine Rajiv Gandhi's authority in bringing the Punjab problem to heel. There was a general feeling of alienation, anger and insecurity about the place of Sikhs in India. The sentiment of the Sikh community was left in no doubt in the 1989 general election. In effect the Sikhs turned the election into a referendum on the central government's Punjab policy and voted forcefully against it. Six radical Sikhs were elected to the Lok Sabha, two of whom were in prison during the campaign on charges of complicity in Mrs Gandhi's assassination. The Rajiv Gandhi–Longowal accord of 24 July 1985 (requiring Chandigarh to be transferred to Punjab by 26 January 1986, the establishment of a commission to determine the compensatory transfer of territories to Haryana and the referral of the river waters dispute to a tribunal) failed to be implemented. Longowal himself was assassinated a month after signing the accord for having 'betrayed' Sikh interests. (Opposition groups castigated Gandhi for having capitulated to Sikh extremists.) The Akali Dal government that had been formed after elections in September 1985 (with a 68 per cent turnout) was riven by factionalism and unsuccessful in combating terrorism. Central rule was reimposed in May 1987 (with elections scheduled in the neighbouring state of Haryana for June 1987) followed by the declaration of an emergency in 1988. V. P. Singh began well after becoming prime minister in 1989: he visited the Golden Temple in a much-publicised gesture, convened an all-party meeting, replaced the governor, released many detainees and promised to prosecute those responsible for the anti-Sikh riots of 1984. But then he too reneged on his promise to hold elections in February 1990, President's Rule was extended by means of a constitutional amendment and Punjab returned to its familiar cycle of an escalating stalemate.

It was not until 1993 that the government was able to announce that the back of Sikh terrorism had been broken. The insurgency in Punjab was declared to be at an end in May 1993. Some 20 000 people are estimated to have been killed during the 1983–93 decade (see Table 1.3). At its height in 1990–91, almost 400 people (including civilians, police and terrorists) were being killed each month in Punjab. An Indian journalist (and one frightened into anonymity) wrote at the start of 1991 that the terrorists had completed two stages of a three-stage plan. The first had been the creation of a secure base of operation and finance and the infiltration of the democratic Sikh forces. The second had been the achievement of military superiority over the security forces in the border area. The final phase would be the wresting of power in Punjab through a carefully planned offensive. All the evidence pointed to the Indian state losing the civil war in Punjab (Anon, 1991).

The viciousness as well as the number of killings increased. Whole families were killed. Trains and buses were stopped and Hindu passengers mowed down. Hindus were targeted in a local version of ethnic cleansing so as to frighten most of them into fleeing the state. A second goal was to incite Hindu–Sikh riots in order to polarise the communities beyond redemption. In 1992, the writ of the terrorists was more effective than that of the state or central government. They proclaimed their decrees on wall posters or through newspapers (editors who dared to disobey had cause to fear for their lives), and were obeyed. The consumption of meat, eggs and alcohol declined; lavish wedding ceremonies became memories; the art of cheating in

TABLE 1.3

The killing fields of Punjab, 1986–93

	1986–89	1990	1991	1992	1993
Civilians killed	4937	2849	3161	1520	231
Police killed	399	506	495	251	14
Terrorists killed	1478	720	1494	2109	258
Total	6814	4075	5150	3880	503

Source: Figures from Manoj Joshi, supplied to author by Air Commodore Jasjit Singh, Director of the Institute for Defence Studies and Analyses, New Delhi.

examinations disappeared; all government work was done only in Punjabi; and the state government radio stopped all Hindi broadcasts after the station director of All-India Radio in Chandigarh was killed. All this changed with a suddenness from about September 1992 onwards. In the state assembly elections of February 1992 (the first since 1985), only 28 per cent of voters cast their ballots as the militants threatened to kill voters as well as candidates. (This was the lowest voter turnout ever in any state election in India.) Voter turnout in the municipal elections of September 1992 was 70 per cent, increasing to 82 per cent for the village council elections in January 1993.

There are several reasons for the reversal of the police–terrorists balance of power. Earlier successes of the militants was due to superior firepower (the terrorists armed with AK-47 assault weapons were confronted by police armed with antique bolt action .303 rifles); the historically unsettled nature of the border districts; the large presence of criminal elements such as smugglers; the involvement of Pakistan in financing, training and arming the militants; and the lack of political muscle in the state and central governments. The police force was almost doubled over five years, from 35 000 to 60 000. It was given more sophisticated weaponry. Before, the police force was demoralised by the cycle of suspected terrorists being arrested by the police only to be released by the government. Now it was given more or less complete *carte blanche* by Chief Minister Beant Singh to eliminate the threat of terrorism by any means, and proceeded to do so by ruthless counter-terror. It was able to do so because the terrorists had isolated themselves from the people by resorting to extortion and rape, thereby sullying their previous glamorous image as defenders of the faith. It was determined to do so because the terrorists had begun to kill family members and other relatives of police officers. The singleminded pursuit of terrorists was symbolised in the head of the Punjab police force K. P. S. Gill. He is widely credited with having turned a decrepit and demoralised police force into a real fighting force with a hardened resolve. The army did its part by sealing the border with Pakistan, damming the flow of arms and men.

On most 'objective' measures, Sikhs continue to do quite well in India. The province is the wealthiest in the country (Table 1.1), Sikh farmers are among the most prosperous, Sikh businessmen have flourished all over the country and Sikhs are still over-represented in the armed forces officer corps. The 'subjective' reality is that Sikhs remain resentful that the demand for the Punjabi Suba was the last to be conceded and required two decades of agitational politics, that many Hindu Punjabis lied in claiming Hindi rather than Punjabi as their 'mother tongue' for political purposes, and that Chandigarh is yet to be handed over to Punjab as its capital. To these have been added the stains on the Indian polity of the troubled 1980s decade and the feeling that, despite having shed bled on the battlefield in disproportionate numbers for the defence of India, their loyalty is still suspect.

Snapshot Four: Gender

Women in Development

Women make up one-half of the world's population, perform two-thirds of the world's work, receive one-tenth of its income and own less than one-hundredth of its property (UNO, 1985). If development is defined as the expansion of real choices for the worst-off members of society in the worst-off countries of the world, then women constitute a critical reference group for analysing successes and failures of development. The standard liberal theory sees women and development as part of an overall process of modernisation which is linear, cumulative, expansionist and diffusionist. Traditional societies are viewed as authoritarian and patriarchal (where male dominance is institutionalised over women in society in general and over women and children in the family in particular), modern societies as democratic and egalitarian. Modernisation will liberate women from the traditional constraints on them and transform men's attitudes 'and incline them to accord to women status and rights more nearly equal to those enjoyed by men' (Inkeles and Smith, 1974, p. 26). The functional requisites of industrialisation in particular are supposed to liberate women from the patriarchal extended family, constrictive religious beliefs and menial farm labour.

Feminist analyses of industrial Western societies challenged the basic assumption of modernisation theory of increasing male–female parity (Ryan, 1975; Tilly and Scott, 1978). Modernisation measures 'progress' in the public sphere; women are confined mainly to the domestic sphere. The labour market remains gender-stratified, with women under-represented and concentrated in the low-skilled, low-paid clerical and service clusters. Colonialism and westernisation marginalised women even more by structuring access to education, credit and politics to men only. Urbanisation can also cut women off from kinship support networks and constrict job opportunities for women in the 'modern' sector: women are not transformed into producers but remain reproducers.

The subject of the impact of development on women also ties in to the debate on growth versus equity. Which should be addressed first: eradication of poverty by gender-neutral strategies, or a focus upon specifically gender issues from the very beginning? The mainstream development view is that 'while women were a distinct subset of the poor, with their own characteristics both in the economic as well as in the social field and while their struggles for recognition and empowerment were legitimate and important, the larger or more prior problem or need, was to clear the undergrowth before expressing a specific gender concern' (Jain, 1990, p. 1454).

Development must at a minimum entail the ending of hunger and poverty. If poverty can be shown to have a decisive gender bias, then the tension between poverty-minimising and gender-specific strategies may turn out to rest on a false dichotomy. Sen cites female education in particular as being very efficacious in promoting growth with equity in Sri Lanka and in the state of Kerala in India (Sen, 1981). Many now argue that 'strategies to end hunger and alleviate poverty, if they are to be successful, must include women' (Snyder, 1990: v). For women are increasingly central to growing or purchasing adequate food supplies for their families. Women produce 80 per cent and 60 per cent of the food in Africa and Asia respectively; one in every three households in the world has a woman as the sole income earner (UNIFEM, 1989, p. 13).

Yet development continues to be planned essentially around the idealised or nuclear family concept with a male as the head of the house. The practical effect of this is to make men the beneficiaries of credit programmes, land allocation, rural extension services and cash-earning employment. 'Women's work' is undervalued, discounted and rendered invisible in national accounts as a result of the so-called pipe and pail syndrome: when a man lays a water pipe in a city, it is an economic activity; when a woman fetches water in a pail in the village, it is a household chore. Hence the continuing perception of women as dependants: unproductive objects of welfare.

Liberal feminism is incrementalist, pluralist and reformist (Jaquette, 1982, p. 272). The object is to improve existing institutions and sensitise them to gender relations. The delivery of specially targeted resources will help to offset disadvantages and thereby enable women to share equally in political, social and economic benefits. The cause of women's marginalisation therefore is partly defective conception of development plans to the extent that they are uninformed about women's concerns and needs, and partly defective implementation of plans which might have been sound enough in conception and benign enough in intention. The solution is to improve women's access to new technology, training, skills and labour markets; that is, to integrate women into the process of modernisation and the public sphere of capitalist structures.

Radicals reject the view that women's subordination is due mainly to slippage between the conception and implementation of development plans. Instead, the deepening of gender subordination is held to be integral to the incorporation of women into an exploitative global capitalism. To Marxists and neo-Marxists, the cause of women's oppression is structural. Male domination of social and political relations was a function of their control of production for exchange. Capitalist industrialisation marginalises women still further by isolating production for use from production for exchange. Goods for the marketplace are produced not in the family economic unit but in factories; the family is a consuming unit only; and women are 'specialised' consumers. Dependent development recruits males into the expanding cash economy, displaces women from the labour force and converts them into a reserve army of labour (Saffiotti, 1975).

The other role for women is to prop up international capitalism as unpaid household workers and as reproducers of the labour force. Single young women in Hong Kong, Korea, Taiwan and in Mexico along the US border are said to be particularly appealing to multinational firms seeking the most docile exploitative labour. That is, the fate of women depends not on repressive or enlightened policies of their own governments, but on the mode of articulation of their national economies with international capitalism. In this perspective, the concepts of relations of reproduction, surplus value of female labour and women as sex objects are added to the standard Marxist vocabulary of relations of production, surplus value and women as class.

The solution of the 'woman question' for Marxists and neo-Marxists is also structural: a systemic transformation of relations between nations, classes and genders. Salvation lies in dismantling the three interlocking systems of exploitation: of all workers by capitalism, all Third World people by imperialism, and all women by patriarchy.

Yet in practice, socialist regimes display obvious weaknesses in resolving the 'woman question'. The 'revolutionary' societies of China, Cuba, Vietnam and the Soviet Union remained male dominated. One study concluded that sexual stereotyping with all its attendant consequences had not been eradicated in communist societies. As a group women 'tend to be more apolitical and less visible in positions of political, economic, and social power in the Communist countries . . . than in the West or the developing nations' (Jancar, 1978, p. 207).

The feminist critique of socialism argued that the oppression of women is caused not by capital accumulation as such, but by the sexual division of labour which works to the benefit of men as well as capitalism. Women's unpaid work in the household has the effect of enabling men to live on, and therefore work for, lower wages. So it does help the cause of capitalism by creating surplus value. But it also self-evidently serves the interests of men. Therefore, men as well as capitalism have a vested interest in structuring society in ways that perpetuate the subordination of women (Park, 1993, p. 130). That is, Marxism as an ideology of economic revolution has proven wanting as a conceptual vehicle for feminism. Women continue to serve the patriarchal establishment, whether as supporters of the status quo as in India or as revolutionaries seeking to replace one type of male political order with another as in China.

Women in India

India is a good case study of women in developing countries for a number of reasons. It had a woman as one of the more durable and impressive heads of government of modern times. Mrs Gandhi was a good symbol of the duality of women in India, combining grace and charm with an authoritarian personality and ruthlessness towards rivals from within and outside her own political party. India offers potentially rich rewards for empirical and theoretical explorations of women's questions because of the sheer size of its population: every sixth woman in the world is an Indian. In terms of one of the world's oldest civilisations, how do we understand the emphasis on gender segregation, the subordination of woman to male authority (the woman is dependent on her father during childhood, husband during adulthood and son during old age), the origins and persistence of purdah in Indian society? The family is a source of security for the Indian woman, offering her affection, identity, esteem and a future. But the family's ethos of selflessness also enables the extraction of unequal sacrifices from women, and so produces and perpetuates an enormous inequity in the position of women in traditional Indian society. As well, how is the position of women in the Indian family related to the caste system?

Traditional Indian society has been exposed to several alien influences over the centuries. Western values were introduced into India during the period of British colonial tutelage. This raises the question of the impact of colonialism and westernisation on the position of women in Indian society; in particular, whether it led towards female empowerment or consolidated the subordination of women even more tightly within repressive relations of reproduction. There is also the question of the role played by women in the Indian nationalist struggle. They were active participants in the nationalist movement in the nineteenth and twentieth centuries. But women's issues were not raised as part of the nationalist struggle. Instead, women's role within the family as mothers, wives and daughters was re-emphasised (Mazumdar, 1976, p. 63). Indeed the subordination of women's concerns to the larger nationalist cause was praised as an example of the traditional Hindu ideal of the dutiful, uncomplaining and self-sacrificing woman. Even so, a later generation of Indian feminists could draw upon this tradition of militancy and public activism by women in movements for social and political change (Jayawardena, 1986, p. 108).

Women in India have had the vote since the adoption of the constitution shortly after independence, thereby having formal equality in the political process from the start. The constitution also guaranteed full equality between the sexes and, by the start of the 1990s, India had some of the most advanced legislation in the world proclaiming and guaranteeing equal rights for women. At the same time, India conjures up images of *sati*, child-brides and a host of other women-specific social diseases. Arranged marriages in India in effect treat marriage as an exchange relationship in which a woman is one of the objects of exchange between two groups of men. Widowhood is an unclean status in Hindu society; widows are inauspicious and remarriage for them is taboo (but not for widowers). Indian women who choose not to define themselves as private sexual property still run the risk of others defining them as public sexual property. India is not averse to having tradition invoked by religious leaders (Hindus and Muslims alike), not as an expression of deeply held commitment to long-sanctified values, but as the most efficient means of controlling resources and consolidating social, economic and political power.

It is also true that 'westernisation', 'modernisation' and 'development' in themselves are just as likely to worsen as to improve the position of women. 'If anything . . . the influence of the British on the status of Indian women was negative . . . . The British introduced the alien western notion of women as inferior, and so added a derogatory component to their subjugation' (Hale, 1989, p. 374). The investigations of the Committee on the Status of Women in India (1971–4) demonstrated that after three decades of planned development since independence, women's position had worsened in virtually every sphere and sector with the exception of some educational and employment gains for upper-middle-class women. In general, women's economic participation rates had declined, while the gaps in female–male mortality and life expectancy rates had widened (ICSSR, 1975; see also Desai and Krishnaraj, 1987).

Nothing so explodes the myth of genteel Hindu civilisation as dowry deaths (which refers to women who are killed or commit suicide in disputes over their wedding dowries). The number of dowry deaths in India jumped from 2209 in 1988 to 5582 in 1993. Registering a complaint with the police is the easy part. Coaxing or goading them into action is somewhat more difficult, and securing a conviction in such cases is the major difficulty. The victim's body might have been cremated before the police had an opportunity to examine it for any signs of force or struggle on the part of the dead woman. There is unlikely to be much circumstantial evidence to back up a charge of murder. Dowry deaths are typically family affairs, involving the husband, his parents and brothers and sisters. Family connivance means that there will be few if any witnesses to testify to premeditation or execution of a dowry death. Even an intended victim who survives an attempted murder could be reluctant to give evidence or testimony against her husband or in-laws, for she might see little future for herself unless she can somehow ingratiate herself back into the good books of her husband and his family.

The comparative disadvantage of women in India can be tabulated with the help of World Bank and UN statistics (Table 1.4). The choice of indicators requires some justification. Investment in education is investment in a nation's human capital. Primary enrolment figures give us the minimum educational efforts, adult literacy figures the minimum educational achievements. In develop-

TABLE 1.4

A woman's place in India

	Females as a percentage of males		Maternal mortality rates (per 100 000 live births) (1988)	Contraceptive prevalence rate (percent) (1985–9)
	Literacy (1990)	Parliament (1990)		
Developing countries	69	14	420	41
Industrial countries	100	13	26	70
World		14	370	43
India	**55**	**8**	**550**	**34**

Sources: UNDP, 1992; World Bank, 1993.

ing countries, economic reality compels girls to a childhood of working in the fields, helping in the collection of firewood and in carrying water. Many girls therefore drop out of primary and secondary school not by choice, but because of economic necessity and patriarchal family priorities. Of those who remain, many are compelled to leave as a result of early marriage and pregnancy. For the few who survive such female attrition in the school system, markers are constructed to guide women away from agricultural, scientific and technological subjects.

Literacy is the surest path out of several gender-based difficulties that women face. Education by itself is the most likely means for women to achieve equality of opportunity. Increasing women's access to education will multiply their life choices, expand their productive capacities and enlarge their incomes. Social returns from female literacy are even higher than from male literacy, in the form of reduced fertility, lower population growth, reduced infant mortality and improved family nutrition (UNDP, 1990, pp. 31–2). The female literacy rate is a measure of an ability which includes a number of attendant advantages that can perhaps best be expressed as the most effective means of widening the real choices of women. For example, a Worldwatch Institute study in 1985 reported that more children (17m) die in developing countries each year because of their mothers' ignorance about health care than because of famine and war. Female education, the study concluded, is essential in child immunisation, hygiene, breast feeding and family planning. Moreover, since an increasing number of women are heads of households, failure to remove the impediments to women's education limits family income and retards the wellbeing of many families (Sivard, 1985). 'Education is also the strongest variable affecting women's own sense of well-being' (Snyder, 1990, p. 9). In short, a major transformation could be wrought in the health and nutrition of coming generations by the simple expedient of keeping more girls at school for longer periods.

Some 70 per cent of Indians live in the countryside. In rural India as a whole, about 80 per cent of women are illiterate; in rural Bihar, among the three poorest states in India (Table 1.1), the rate of adult female illiteracy is 90 per cent (*The Economist*, 4 May 1991, 'India Survey', p. 8). Part of the reason for this is that educational stereotypes in India cast boys as intelligent and girls as diligent. Women's groups in India, in a song protesting against the social evil of dowry, urge parents to give their daughters the gift of education. Just four or five years of primary schooling gives a woman a better chance of acquiring the knowledge and gaining the confidence to plan pregnancies, utilise available health services, acquire skills for earning a higher income outside the home and take part in family and community decisions on matters affecting her life.

The contraceptive prevalence rate is important symbolically as well as substantially. Symbolically, it signifies the success achieved by women in controlling the use of their own bodies in one central respect. Substantively, birth control frees women from the endless cycle of involuntary reproduction: the role and status of women are no longer a function of the means and relations of reproduction. It is also a useful shorthand for capturing all sorts of other measures: education, independence, choice, class, etc.

Maternal mortality rates are an important indicator because 'maternal causes' are the leading cause of death for 25–35-year-old women in most developing countries (Grant, 1986, p. 43). Health indicators are a shorthand for the treatment accorded to women in many societies as well. And health and education correlate very strongly (Figure 1.2). The mortality rates for under-5-year-old children in 1988 correlates more strongly with female adult literacy (1985, $N = 111$, $r = 0.83$) than with GNP per capita (1987, $N = 119$, $r = 0.61$) (calculated from figures in UNDP, 1990, tables 4–5).

The index of parliamentary representation captures female political empowerment relative to men. The goal of achieving equality of empowerment is considered desirable in order for target groups to be given increased access to the corridors of power. It is

FIGURE 1.2
Female adult literacy and under-five mortality rates, 1990

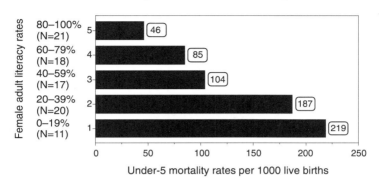

Note: The under-5 mortality rates are simple averages for each of the five literacy cohorts, not population-weighted averages.
Source: Based on data in UNDP, 1992, pp. 134–7.

argued that lack of empowerment leads to alienation; participative democracy encourages social integration. Political empowerment is different from and indeed more than political participation. If politics is all about the authoritative allocation of values and resources, then more equitable representation of women in the key political and decision-making structures is essential. Women's participation in policy-making is considered to be important in developing countries because of women's marginalisation through the development process and the ineffectiveness of constitutional and legal provisions for gender equality. Women are as much the object of laws as men. But the Indian administrative and judicial machinery is alleged to have been insensitive to gender equity. A shift from viewing women as welfare beneficiaries to treating them as actors requires that they be inducted into policy-making and decision-making structures. In an ideal world, the two sexes would show rough parity in their parliamentary representation. A severe under-representation of women in the legislative institutions is a universal shortcoming. India measures poorly on this measure in comparison to all other reference groups (Table 1.4). In the 1991 general election, less than 6 per cent of party nominations went to women; only 36 women were elected to the Lok Sabha.

Further Reading

Brass (1990). An excellent survey of India's political history since 1947.

Dumont (1970). A brilliant and highly influential attempt to theorise the caste system around the concept of status, the separation of status and power, and notions of purity and impurity.

Grewal (1990). A balanced account which examines the gamut of political, economic, cultural and demographic developments over the entire span of Sikh history.

Hasan (1995). Written by a leading Indian Islamic scholar, the book is an account of the history of Indian Muslims, their main currents of thought, their fears and anxieties and the effects of social, economic and legal changes on them.

Jeffrey (1994). A study of the changing nature of Punjabi society, and in particular of the impact of 'modernisation'. The updated second edition also examines the larger themes of ethnic conflict and threats to national unity.

Manushi: A Journal about Women and Society. Essential – but not always pleasant – reading for anyone interested in the subject of women in Indian society.

Phadnis (1989). An influential study of ethnic identities and movements.

Rudolph and Rudolph (1967). An enduring study of the dialectical relationship between tradition and modernity in caste associations, the Indian legal system and the personality of Mahatma Gandhi.

Sowell (1990). An excellent cross-national study of the effects of preferential policies.

Srinivas (1962). An important study of politics and social change by one of India's most distinguished sociologists.

2

Constitutional Government

Indians are surprisingly conscious of constitutional probity. During the staggered 1991 elections which saw the likeliest prime ministerial hopeful Rajiv Gandhi assassinated, Vice-President Dr Shankar Dayal Sharma commented that 'constitutional functionaries must set an example of rectitude and perfect observance of constitutional and legal proprieties' (Datta-Ray, 1991a). In this chapter I propose to deal with the following questions:

1. What do we mean by the terms 'constitution' and 'constitutionalism'?
2. What were the legacies bequeathed to India by British colonialism?
3. What is the structure of government established by the Constitution of India?
4. What is the structure and role of the judiciary in India?

Constitutionalism

A *constitution* lays down the rules of the political game in order to ensure fair competition. It establishes the framework within which rival individuals and groups can engage in the struggle for power in a stable and orderly manner. Every political system needs clearly understood agents and rules for the authoritative allocation of values. The constitution does this by specifying the organs of government; the manner of their creation and organisation; their powers and limits in relation to one another and to the citizens; the procedures for

37

formulating and executing laws and resolving conflicts among members of the political community; and the conditions under which the polity may be defended against internal and foreign enemies. The constitutional relationship between the state and the citizens, it may be noted, contains the key to the organising principle of the political system (Marxism, democratic socialism, liberalism and so on). The Indian constitution has attempted to strike a balance between the liberty of citizens, the authority of the state and the cohesiveness of society.

Constitutionalism is the technique of striking the proper balance between establishing a system of government which has sufficient permissive authority and power to enable it to perform the necessary political tasks, and restricting the scope of governmental authority with a system of restraints to preclude the creation of a tyranny. Constitutionalism may not obtain even where there is a written constitution, if the latter does not act as an effective restraint on the government. In the former Soviet Union, for example, the constitution was a minor inconvenience that could be overcome at the whim of the ruling communist elite. Constitutionalism may in a sense be regarded as the modern political equivalent of *dharma,* that ancient untranslatable Hindu concept which means religion, duty, responsibility and law all rolled into one. The word *dharma* was used often by the great Mauryan emperor Ashoka (269–232 BC), many of whose rock edicts survive. In his 26th year, Ashoka inscribed the following message: 'this is my rule: government by the law, administration according to the law, gratification of my subjects under the law, and protection through the law' (Wolpert, 1977, pp. 66–7).

Legacies of the Raj

Precolonial societies were usually authoritarian; loyalties were concentrated within clans and kinship groups; and systems of peaceful succession had not yet evolved. As the British progressively withdrew from former colonies, the political and economic institutions that they had established were in most cases managed in ways that were a throwback to the earlier social patterns: authoritarian, clique-ridden and corrupt. India did not fit this pattern. An important reason for India departing from the norm for postcolonial societies was the legacies inherited from British India.

Even so, claims of an enduring British heritage should be treated with a tinge of caution. During the early 1950s, social scientists began a comprehensive poll of villagers to determine how many Indians knew that British rule had ended in 1947. The survey had to be aborted when it was realised that a majority of villagers were not aware that the British had ever arrived (Manchester, 1983, p. 856).

The elective principle was introduced into local bodies in India in 1884 and into provincial councils in 1892. The progressive introduction and expansion of the principle was not without controversy in Britain. One group argued that representative government was alien to Indian society, incompatible with the social cleavages dividing Indian people and potentially disastrous for the Muslim community which had been loyal to British rule. Speaking to the Indian Councils Bill in the House of Lords on 23 February 1909, Lord Morley, Secretary of State for India, referred to 'the extremists, who nurse fantastic dreams that some day they will drive us out of India' (Hansard, *Parliamentary Debates*, House of Lords, 23 February 1909, col. 118). British rule ended on 15 August 1947. In a memorable speech that captured the evocative and expectant mood of the infant country in this ancient land, Jawaharlal Nehru declared that 'At the stroke of the midnight hour, when the world sleeps, India will awake to life and freedom. A moment comes, which comes but rarely in history, when we step out from the old to the new, when an age ends, and when the soul of a nation, long suppressed, finds utterance' (Nehru, 1961, p. 13). On 26 January 1950, India adopted a new constitution and became a republic. How new was the constitution?

The British joined the struggle for a commercial foothold in India through the East India Co. which was chartered in London in 1600. As the Mughal empire waned, the British pushed for ever-expanding privileges and territories. By the end of the seventeenth century, the East India Co. was already aiming to establish a locally financed British-based system of civil and military power that would lay the foundation of a secure English dominion in perpetuity. Through the company, the British began to acquire India piecemeal with little regard for their own legal and contractual niceties. But if any of the native princes violated the terms of a contract, then that was sufficient pretext to take over his territory. By the time of the great Indian mutiny/first war of independence in 1857, the company's raj covered more than 60 per cent of the country. In the remaining 40 per cent, there were more than five hundred 'independent' princes.

The East India Co. was replaced by direct crown rule in 1858. A lasting legacy of the manner of the establishment of British rule in India was a deep-seated suspicion in Indian minds of multinational corporations.

The long-term economic consequences of imperialism remain a subject of debate. British imperial policies could be spectacularly cruel. There was a callous destruction of a flourishing textile handicrafts industry through a deliberate policy of favouring metropolitan economic interests. The British markets were closed to Indian textiles while the products of the Lancashire cotton mills were given free entry into India, a policy which led Lord Bentinck to remark in 1834 on 'the bones of the cotton-weavers bleaching on the plains of India' (Hanson and Douglas, 1972, p. 11). The non-reciprocal opening of the Indian market to British goods destroyed the hopes of India emerging as a major manufacturing centre and produced an excessive dependence of the Indian economy on the agricultural sector. Agriculturists increased from 55 per cent of the total occupational workforce in the mid-nineteenth century to 74 per cent by 1939. Yet there was neither a modernisation of agricultural methods nor a growth of rural wealth. The natives provided the revenue for the entire British presence and activity in India as well as the string of military campaigns in and around the subcontinent.

The question of whether on balance British colonial rule retarded or accelerated Indian economic development remains contested and is perhaps inherently unanswerable. For against the exploitative policies must be set the economic, social and administrative infrastructural developments. The reforms introduced by the British, for example land reforms and the development of transportation and communications networks after 1857, were designed mainly to strengthen their rule. The intention may have been self-serving. The result of such activities as building railways, extension of irrigation works and the establishment of plantations brought the advantages of a developing market economy to the Indian merchants as well as to British traders. Still, had the British colonial masters had the interests of their wards as their primary motivation, they would have attempted more positive steps to improve the system of production in India.

The rise of the middle class has been called the most significant creation of the British Raj (Spear, 1957, p. 110). It shifted the correlation of forces in class relations. Professional occupations – legal, medical, engineering, teaching – were Indianised rapidly.

Many of them were sympathetic to the nationalist cause by sentiment and also because colonialism restricted job mobility. At the same time, many of them were government employees and had been exposed to Western values and training. The result was that they effectively constituted a mediating force both between different classes and between the British rulers and their Indian subjects. They were at the cutting edge of the tension between tradition and westernisation. They were also to be the transmission channel for the intellectual legacies of British rule, for example nationalism, Fabian socialism and an evolutionary belief in progress.

The long-term political impact of colonialism is similarly difficult to assess with confidence. The paternalistic view that prevailed at the start of the colonial era held that the entire corpus of Indian literature was less valuable than a shelf of books in an ordinary Englishman's home. Lord Macaulay's justly famous minute of 1835 aimed to create 'a class of persons, Indian in blood and colour, but English in taste, in opinion, in morals, and in intellect' (Hardgrave and Kochanek, 1993, p. 32).[1] English replaced Persian as the official language of government in 1835, and British advances in India continued to be based on assumptions of racial superiority. Thus Forbes, member of the Governor's Executive Council in Madras, wrote in 1906 that

> administration in India will only be good administration so long as it is essentially British; that no intellectual or educational attainments will ever endow the Indian with the qualifications necessary to govern wisely and well . . . and that the Indian will fail in *character*, however brilliant he may be in intelligence or erudition. (in Hanson and Douglas, 1972, p. 16; emphasis in original)

The political legacies of British rule are easier to identify. They include a rise in political consciousness; tools, machinery and experience of government; party politics; and civil disobedience as a legitimate technique of political protest. At the level of beliefs, the experience of the Raj was instrumental in instilling a belief in the importance of a strong and stable government. Hence the pragmatic concessions to 'reasons of state' in the new constitution of independent India: proportional representation, a fairer system of political democracy in such a diverse country, was eschewed in favour of first-past-the-post which promised to deliver more effective government; fundamental rights were conditional, not absolute; the powers of state could be expanded in times of national emergency; and so on.

The British also bequeathed the basic organisational structure of government to independent India. The country inherited a unitary system of government, albeit with strong federal features. The Morley–Minto reforms of 1909 extended the elective principle to the state legislative councils, extended the suffrage and introduced communal electorates. They also initiated a far-reaching debate on three constitutional issues: a further extension of the suffrage, and if so, the principles on which this was to be done; the further extension of the elective principle to all members of legislative bodies; and the appropriate power-sharing arrangements between provincial and national governments.

The Montagu–Chelmsford reforms (1919) had divided authority between central and state governments, and legislative functions between two chambers. The binary principle that infused British Indian rule was evident also in the system of dyarchy or dual government. The provincial governments were given responsibility for 'transferred' subjects such as education, health and local self-government. The governor retained authority over key 'reserved' subjects, including revenue and law and order. The suffrage was still limited to property taxpayers, landholders and men with educational qualifications, who together accounted for under 4 per cent of the population in the countryside and 14 per cent in municipal areas. But at least some power had been devolved and provincial authorities were no longer mere administrative agents of the central government. Even more important, the representation of Indians in provincial councils was increased.

The Government of India Act (1935) of the UK parliament provided the structural link from the 1919 reforms to the 1950 constitution. The 1935 Act retained the federal features with different classes of constituent political units. Legislative functions were apportioned among them according to central, provincial and concurrent lists. The electorate was expanded from six to thirty million, covering about one-sixth of the adult population. On the one hand, there was an essentially conservative orientation to the franchise qualification, for example property ownership. On the other hand, from 1921 onwards, British tutelage gave many Indians direct experience with the conventions, norms, practices and techniques of parliamentary debate and ministerial responsibility. The group that was to guide India through independence led the nationalist struggle by electoral means as well as civil disobedience.

As well as the organising principles, India inherited some of the actual institutions of government. Indeed the legacy that brought the greatest satisfaction to the British themselves is that of the bureaucracy. The elite Indian Civil Service (ICS) was an administrative aristocracy of fewer than 2000 officers. The 'steel frame' of British administration had been largely Indianised by 1947, although not without problems. In theory, the Charter Act (1833) and the ICS Act (1861) outlawed discrimination against Indians. But something else bequeathed by the British, and at which Indians were to prove to be skilled pupils, was how legal requirements could be circumvented in practice. For example, for 'logistical' reasons, the ICS examinations could only be held in Britain. They virtually required studies in Britain. Surendra Nath ('Surrender Not') Bannerjea wrote the examinations in London in 1869 and performed better than most Britons who were accepted into the ICS, but was disqualified by the bureaucracy. He won his legal appeal against the disqualification, was admitted into the ICS, but was subsequently dismissed for a minor infraction of rules. As a result of such sharp practices, the proportion of Indians in the ICS was only 5 per cent in 1913. It had risen to 13 per cent by 1921 and to almost half the total intake by the time of independence. So again, with ill grace or good, in the end the British did leave behind a corps of Indians who had actual experience of administration at the elite level.

The virtues of the ICS were supposed to be many. They were generalist and non-technical and as such surprisingly adaptable. They were recruited from the educated elite by a difficult competitive examination process. Their sense of duty and *esprit de corps* kept them strangers to corruption. Most crucially, their loyalties were pan-Indian rather than regional, provincial or communal. This helped to foster a sense of centralised governance by officers who were widely dispersed all over India. Although assisted by specialised medical, engineering and police personnel, the ICS officers retained overall responsibility at each level of administration. Another distinctive feature was the fusion of judicial and administrative functions and personnel up to the district level.

Yet the ICS legacy was to prove a mixed blessing. The service was the administrative arm of an alien ruling power. After independence, the civil service became an instrument to implement public policies framed by democratically elected governments. Could the transition from master to servant of the people be made successfully without a major overhaul of the structure of administration? The problem was exacerbated by the very *esprit de corps* which had made the ICS such a valuable tool for the Raj. The elitism of the service detached it from the village heartland of India. Exclusiveness was a useful asset when the primary purposes of the ICS were revenue collection and maintenance of law and order. It became a liability when the basic thrust of the service was changed to developmental tasks. The generalist orientation and the air of superiority over specialist personnel was to impede the progress towards functionalised task performance. Similarly, the sense of paternalism was to obstruct the move back from *dirigisme*.

In comparison with the pre-independence history of many other Third World countries, for example the Belgian Congo, India still had cause to be grateful for the legacy of a centralised, cohesive, dedicated and efficient administration which had been opened up significantly to 'the natives' by the time of independence. Another ambiguous legacy was that of civil disobedience, both in regard to the technique and legitimacy of political protest. Mahatma Gandhi launched his first *satyagraha* or civil disobedience movement in 1920. (The literal meaning of the term is urging of truth.) By providing an alternative channel of demand articulation, this has imbued the Indian political system with greater political legitimacy. It has enabled individuals and groups to challenge government policies, for example the planned construction of the giant Narmada dam project. It can be used to put pressure on governments for redressing injustices. On 22 September 1992, Bhanwari Devi, a worker with the Women's Development Programme promoted by the state government of Rajasthan, was raped by two men while three others assaulted her husband. The indifference of the state government to the attacks led women's groups to launch an agitation with the rallying slogan *Nyay Karo Ya Jail Bharo* ('Dispense Justice or Fill the Prisons') (*Manushi*, no. 72, 1992, pp. 18–20). And agitational techniques can be used by opposition parties. On 25 February 1993, the Bharatiya Janata Party (BJP) defied a government ban on a planned rally. BJP leader Lal Krishan Advani was among the many prominent people who were arrested in an unprecedented security operation in New Delhi. Speaking to reporters before his arrest, Advani said that courting arrest had been the traditional way of launching a political protest movement in India since the struggle for independence.

The person most responsible for the adoption and success of non-violent civil disobedience was Mahatma Gandhi. In this as in other respects, Gandhi demonstrated an uncanny ability to synthesise tradition and modernity and harness both towards specifically political goals. The tension between the two – Sanskritisation and westernisation (Srinivas, 1962) – was to transcend the transition to independence. Similarly, many other problems – domestic, regional and international; social, political and economic – survived the shift to independent status. There were two major challenges to national integration: the problem of the independent princedoms, and the communal divide between Hindus and Muslims. There was a powerful communist party that had shown itself singularly insensitive to the nationalist identity. The Congress Party faced difficult choices between gradual change and revolutionary transformation, and between the party-as-organisation and the party-as-government. It also faced an equally painful transition from a nationalist movement to the party of government.

In foreign relations, Indians inherited a healthy scepticism towards the fine phrases of Western leaders. A major fillip to the nationalist movement was given by the massacre at Jallianwalla Bagh. On Sunday 13 April 1919 – the year of Woodrow Wilson's self-determination and idealism in world affairs, of Versailles and formal condemnation of Germans for war crimes – an unarmed crowd gathered in Jallianwalla Bagh square in Amritsar, the holy city of the Sikhs. Brigadier R. E. H. Dyer ordered his troops to fire 1650 rounds into the crowd whose avenues of escape had first been closed. The number of people killed was 379, with more than a thousand wounded. At a subsequent inquiry, Dyer explained that he had ordered 'the least amount of firing which would produce the necessary moral and widespread effect' (Wolpert, 1977, p. 299). In Britain the princely sum of £26 000 was subscribed by the people as a testimonial to General Dyer's devoted gallantry as 'The Saviour of the Punjab'. In the dramatic Atlantic Charter of August 1941, US President Franklin Roosevelt and British Prime Minister Winston Churchill affirmed 'the right of all peoples to choose the form of government under which they will live'. Yet on 9 September Churchill explained in his House of Commons that the Atlantic Charter did not apply to India, Burma and other parts of the British empire (Wolpert, 1977, pp. 333–4).[2]

India also inherited some enduring conflicts in its foreign relations as part of the ambiguous legacies from the Raj. There were border disputes with China and complications of relations with the mountain kingdoms along the Himalayas whose origins go back to certain sharp practices by British colonial authorities. The most important of the conflicts inherited with independence was the problems stemming from the partition of the subcontinent into India and Pakistan, with Kashmir today being both the symbol of the Indo–Pakistan conflict and the major bone of contention between them. The roots of the conflict go back to the desire of the British to protect the political rights of the Muslims against the encroachments of representative government. The Muslims believed that their representation should reflect not merely their numerical strength, but also their contributions to the maintenance of the Raj. They persuaded the British authorities that only communal electorates could assure them effective representation.

The system of communal electorates, in which Muslims could vote for their own candidates, was part of the package of the Morley–Minto reforms of 1909. The effect was to break the dependence of religious politicians on the support of the other community. Hindu politicians would reap maximum political rewards by enhancing their appeal to the Hindus, and Muslim politicians to Muslims. The discipline of moderation and accommodation imposed by the need to cultivate crossover votes from both major communities was thus removed. The impact of communal electorates was to ensure an emphasis on Muslim interests and loyalties; social cleavages were institutionalised in a system of political dualism (Weiner, 1987b, p. 41).

India's Constitutional Structure

The structure of governance under the Indian constitution is shown in Figure 2.1. India is a republic, with no hereditary rulers. It has a representative and parliamentary system of government formed on the basis of periodic elections. Every adult citizen may vote in the elections and seek elective office. In essence, the 1950 constitution completed the democratisation of politics begun by the British. The retention of the basic axioms and structures of the Government of India Act of 1935 generated some criticism that the constitution was 'un-Indian' and democracy was a mere top-dressing. The Constituent Assembly, elected indirectly by the provincial assemblies in 1946, aimed to set up a system of government that would facilitate social change and economic development within a democratic structure. Reflecting the Congress triumphs in the provincial elections of 1945,

FIGURE 2.1
The three levels of government in India

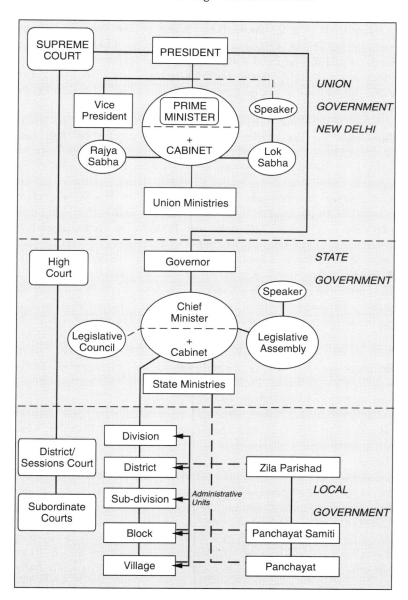

the Constituent Assembly was dominated by the Congress Party. The president of the assembly was Dr Rajendra Prasad, who was later to become the first President of India. The drafting committee was chaired by Dr B. R. Ambedkar. Some of the other influential personalities in the Constituent Assembly were Jawaharlal Nehru, Sardar Vallabhbhai Patel and Maulana Abul Kalam Azad. The new constitution of independent India came into effect on 26 January 1950; the date is celebrated every year with due pomp and ceremony as Republic Day.

At 395 articles and eight schedules, India's constitution was among the longest in the world. (By 1993, the constitution had been expanded to 441 articles and twelve schedules.) There were four main features of the political system set up by it: India is democratic, secular, federal and republican. While some members of the Constituent Assembly had been in favour of a decentralised Gandhian state, most were comfortable with the system of parliamentary democracy that was familiar to them. A federal distribution of powers, again familiar from the colonial heritage, was believed to be the best institutional means of accommodating India's diversity. Secularism was a logical corollary of the Congress Party's passionate rejection of the two-nation theory on which Pakistan had been partitioned off from India. The republican status was an expression of freedom and independence from the British crown. But India was keen to remain a full member of the Commonwealth of Nations if this could be done without proclaiming allegiance to the British crown. The creative formula adopted was to accept the British monarch as the symbol of the free association of the member-nations, and as such the head of the Commonwealth.

India's founding fathers were at best ambivalent in their attitudes both towards Western ideals and Soviet experiments. In Nehru's own pithy assessment, 'all the evils of a purely political democracy are evident in the United States; the evils of the lack of political democracy are present in the USSR' (Nehru, 1960, pp. 562–3). Many influential personalities in the pre-independence Congress Party, while educated in the West, had flirted sentimentally with communism. The philosophy underlying India's constitution reflects this dual attraction. The Preamble declares India to be a sovereign democratic republic and proclaims the following goals: social, economic and political justice; liberty of thought, expression, belief, faith and worship; equality of status and opportunity; dignity of the individual; and unity of the nation.

Tension between Liberalism and Socialism

The simultaneous attraction of Western democracy and Soviet socialism is particularly apparent in the chapters on Fundamental Rights (Part III) and Directive Principles of State Policy (Part IV). In Britain, fundamental human rights are a product of a long political heritage rather than written constitutional guarantees. The chapter on fundamental rights in the Indian constitution essentially gives constitutional status and guarantee to the dignity and worth of individuals that Western liberalism emphasises. In sum, in enumerating the basic rights of Indian citizens, the framers of its constitution were influenced from abroad by the tradition of the English rule of law (for example in Article 14 of the constitution guaranteeing equality before the law and equal protection of the laws), the American Bill of Rights, and the Universal Declaration of Human Rights adopted by the UN General Assembly in 1948. Domestic influences included the caste system and the range of religious, linguistic and cultural minorities whose group rights needed safeguarding against majority encroachments. As a result, some features of the constitution are distinctly Indian.

The 'fundamental rights' are conditional rather than absolute, attempting to strike a balance between individual and community rights. Thus Article 15 of the constitution prohibits discrimination on grounds of religion, caste and gender; yet it also permits the enactment of special provisions designed to improve the lot of such disadvantaged groups as women and the outcastes. Moreover, the state may impose 'reasonable restrictions' on free speech and assembly in the interests of public order and morality (Article 19). Most important, the same article confers the right ('freedom') to acquire, possess and dispose of property, yet permits the state to impose 'reasonable restrictions' in the general interest. Not surprisingly, the state found itself embroiled in a number of court cases in regard to property rights. Several constitutional amendments had to be enacted in pursuit of agrarian reform and the social control of the means of production.

The constitution does not recognise the doctrine of natural rights: no Indian can claim a right outside the chapter on fundamental rights. This contrasts sharply with the American conception, where the enumeration of rights is not to be construed to deny or disparage others retained by the people. Another interesting feature of the fundamental rights in India is that they proscribe individual as well as state behaviour, for instance in an injunction against untouchability. Finally, it is constitutionally permissible in India to suspend various fundamental rights in times of emergency, and to enact preventive detention laws; judicial scrutiny is denied in either case. That is, necessity of state triumphed over due process of law.

Necessities of life, on the other hand, are notably absent for millions of Indians. Many Congressmen at the time of independence were impressed by the argument that freedom is possible only with economic security, and that liberty is an empty abstraction to the hungry. As an influential member of Indian officialdom put it more recently, 'The immediate task [of the less developed countries] is to provide the mass of the people with bread: those finer aspects of human existence which are built on the foundations of a full stomach – and which are really relevant only to those who have one – can afford to wait' (Nehru, B.K., 1979, p. 57).

If the state in India was to restrict itself to the task of maintaining the external conditions of public order, then the civil rights would remain a hollow mockery for a majority of Indians. In the light of India's poverty, 'economic rights' (for example, the right to an adequate means of livelihood) could not realistically be enshrined as a basic right; but they could be and were enshrined as ideals. The constitution accordingly incorporated them as directive principles, as a guideline for future public policy (Articles 36–51). Some of these are in the nature of socioeconomic rights, except that they are not enforceable through the courts, for example the right to an adequate means of livelihood. Others are in the nature of directives to the state on the manner of exercising its legislative and executive powers, for example in regard to promoting prohibition (Article 47). A third category articulated the ideals to be reached for by the state so as to nudge India towards a socialist society.

The directive principles were described as 'fundamental in the governance of the country and it shall be the duty of the state to apply these principles in making laws' (Article 37). But they were not justiciable (that is, not enforceable through the judiciary). There would be instances where the principles came into conflict with the rights. For example, the directive that the ownership and control of material resources be redistributed to subserve the common good (Article 39) cuts across the rights to property (Articles 19, 31). (The right to property under Article 31 was deleted from the chapter on fundamental rights by the 44th Constitution Amendment Act in 1978.) In the event of a clash with directive principles, the courts would necessarily have to decide in favour of fundamental rights. The constitution explicitly provides that laws abridging the fundamental rights shall be void (Article 13). This is why during the Constituent Assembly debates T. T. Krishnamachari described the directive principles as 'a veritable dustbin of sentiment' (in Austin, 1966, p. 75).

Since the constitution was adopted, fundamental rights have been steadily eroded and the balance has shifted markedly in favour of the directive principles. Once described as 'a formidable bulwark of individual liberty, a code of public conduct and a strong and sustaining basis of Indian democracy' (Pylee, 1965, p. 325), they have been diluted and outflanked through such measures as the Preventive Detention Act, the Maintenance of Internal Security Act, the Defence of India Rules, the Unlawful Activities Prevention Act, and so on. The main 'special' laws in force in 1993 were the National Security Act (NSA), 1980; the Jammu and Kashmir Public Safety Act, in force since 1978; the Armed Forces (Jammu and Kashmir) Special Powers Act, 1990; and the Terrorist and Disruptive Activities (Prevention) Act (TADA), 1987.

The Judiciary

If there is to be constitutional government, then a political system must have a judiciary independent of and acting as a check on the arbitrary exercise of legislative and executive power. The functions of rule-making, rule-enforcement and rule-interpretation are separated into the three institutions of the legislature, the executive and the judiciary. The judiciary is also the final arbiter on what the constitution itself means.

State-Level Judiciary

The structure of the Indian judiciary is shown in Figure 2.2. Unlike the US model of a dual federal–state court system, India has a monolithic system. The structural base remains the same throughout the country, although the designations are not uniform from one state to the next. Article 214 of the constitution provides that there shall be a high court in each state. In 1992, there were 18 high courts in India in the hands of more than 500 judges. The state high courts comprise a chief justice and other justices appointed by the president. The number of judges on a high court ranges from 2 in Sikkim to 60 in Allahabad, high court of the country's most populous state of Uttar Pradesh (U.P.). Except in cases where the Supreme Court holds original jurisdiction, high courts exercise full legal powers within their particular state (or group of states).

The district court is the principal civil court of original jurisdiction. It is subordinate to the high court, and every lower-level court is subordinate to the high court and district court. District judges and other subordinate judges in a state are appointed by the governor in consultation with the state high court and public service commission. At the bottom rung of the judicial hierarchy, executive magistrates discharge functions of a criminal court as part of their administrative task of maintaining law and order. While executive magistrates are common to metropolitan and other areas, Figure 2.2 shows the pattern of judicial administration to be quite different in the two categories. City civil courts have been set up in metropolitan cities like Ahmedabad, Bangalore, Bombay, Calcutta, Hyderabad and Madras.

The constitution seeks to protect the independence of high court judges through provisions broadly comparable to those affecting the appointment, conditions of office (except that the age of retirement is 60, not 65) and removal of Supreme Court judges (see below). Although high courts are placed under the jurisdiction of the Supreme Court, the latter does not have any direct administrative control over the former. A high court is the apex body of a state's judicial system. But it is not as sharply separated from the federal government as the state supreme courts in the United States. The union government of India exercises control over high courts through powers of appointment and removal (Article 217 of the constitution), as well as transfer (Article 231). Also under central jurisdiction are the establishment and organisation of high courts; the power to constitute a common high court for two or more states, for example the Punjab and Haryana High Court (the jurisdiction of a high court is normally co-terminous with the territorial boundaries of its state); to extend the jurisdiction of a high court to a union territory (for example the High Court of Calcutta covers the Andaman and Nicobar Islands); or to exclude it therefrom. In addition, the Supreme Court can remove almost any case from a high court and take it up directly. The aim of these provisions was to remove the state judiciary from the realm of provincial politics; their effect is to blur the operation of federalism in the judicial sphere.

FIGURE 2.2
Organisational chart of the Indian judiciary

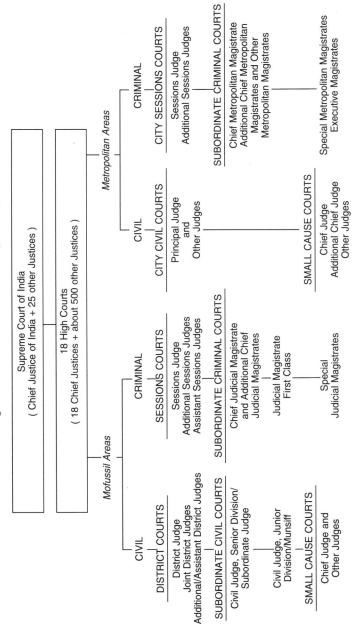

Under Article 227 of the constitution, every high court has a power of superintendence over all courts and judicial tribunals throughout its territorial jurisdiction, with the exception of military tribunals. Interestingly, this power of superintendence includes a revisional jurisdiction to intervene directly in cases of gross injustice, or non-exercise or abuse of jurisdiction, even if the case should not fall within the high court's appellate jurisdiction. That is, the power of superintendence is both administrative and judicial. Furthermore, under Article 228, a high court may transfer a case from subordinate courts to itself if a constitutional interpretation is germane to the disposal of the case. Having decided on the question of law in regard to the correct interpretation of the constitution, the high court may either dispose of the case itself or return the case to the initial subordinate court. The latter is then bound by the high court's finding on the substantial question of law.

Six high courts (Bombay, Calcutta, Delhi, Himachal Pradesh, Jammu and Kashmir, Madras and Patna) exercise original or first-instance jurisdiction in civil matters. The appellate jurisdiction of a high court in civil cases involves questions of fact as well as law. The power of first appeal directly to the high court pertains to decisions of district judges and those of subordinate judges in cases involving amounts above a threshold pecuniary value. In addition, when a court subordinate to the high court decides an appeal from an inferior court, then its decision in turn is subject to a second appeal to the high court. In the high courts of Allahabad, Bombay, Calcutta, Madras and Patna, an appeal to a high court bench may be made against a decision of a single judge of the high court itself. The criminal appellate jurisdictions of high courts is similarly complicated.

There is one further power of high courts that is worth noting. Article 226 of the constitution confers on every high court the power to issue to any person, authority or government within its territorial jurisdiction directions, orders or writs, including writs in the nature of *habeas corpus*, for the enforcement of any of the fundamental rights or for any other purpose. Because this power derives from the constitution, it cannot be abridged or removed other than by a constitutional amendment. Moreover, while the Supreme Court can issue writs only where fundamental rights have been violated, the high courts can issue them even where ordinary legal rights have been infringed, so long as a writ is a proper legal remedy in such cases.

The Supreme Court of India

The Supreme Court of India came into being on 26 January 1950 alongside the adoption of the constitution. In its role as the supreme guardian of the constitution, the Supreme Court is vested with original, appellate and advisory jurisdictions. Moreover, its interpretation is binding on all other courts within the territory of India (Article 141), and all civil and judicial authorities throughout the territory of India are enjoined to act in aid of the Supreme Court (Article 144).

The Supreme Court has original jurisdiction firstly as a federal court. In a federal polity, both units of government derive their powers from and are limited by the same constitution. Differences of interpretation of the federal–provincial distribution of powers, or conflicts between state governments, require authoritative resolution by a judicial organ independent of both levels of government. Under Article 131 of the constitution, the Supreme Court of India is given exclusive original jurisdiction in a dispute between (a) the central government and any one or more states; (b) the central government and one or more state governments on one side, and one or more state governments on the other side; and (c) two or more states, if and insofar as the dispute involves any question about a law or fact on which the existence or extent of a legal right depends. The court also has non-exclusive original jurisdiction as the protector of fundamental rights. Article 32 gives citizens the right to move the Supreme Court directly for the enforcement of any of the fundamental rights enumerated in Part III of the constitution.

The Supreme Court has comprehensive appellate jurisdiction in cases involving constitutional issues (Article 132); civil and criminal cases involving specified threshold values of property or a death sentence (Articles 133 and 134 respectively); and wide-ranging powers of special appeals (Article 136).

The Supreme Court of India has been vested with the power to render advisory opinions on any question of fact or law that may be referred to it by the president (Article 143). In December 1978, for example, an advisory opinion of the Supreme Court upheld the constitutional validity of special courts that had been set up to deal with offences committed during the 1975–7 emergency. This is different from ordinary adjudication in three senses: there is no litigation between two parties, and the advisory opinion of the court is not binding on the government and is not executable as a judgment of the court. The provision is an interesting and conscious departure from the American precedent. The US Supreme Court decided early on against such a role, on the argument that it would encroach upon the legislative function and thereby negate the separation of powers that underpins the US constitution.

The availability of the provision gives a soft option to the Indian government on some politically difficult issues, for example the controversy surrounding the Babri Masjid complex in Ayodhya. The government decided to refer aspects of the dispute to the Supreme Court for an opinion under Article 143 of the constitution. Unfortunately, since there was no legal point as such at issue, there was a danger that referral to the Supreme Court would further politicise the judiciary instead of resolving what was essentially a political problem. The judiciary exists to interpret laws, expound the constitution and ensure that the rule of law prevails. Responsibility for maintaining law and order vests in the executive arm of government. Cabinet can weigh popular opinion in the balance before deciding upon issues of public policy. The judiciary cannot decide upon questions of belief, opinion or political wisdom, nor pronounce upon questions of history, archaeology and mythology. Cabinet cannot 'shift the responsibility to the courts for matters for which the government is too weak, too timid or too confused to decide for itself' (Palkhivala, 1993, p. 9). The judiciary cannot compensate for inadequacies of government or the failure of the political process. In a significant decision on 24 October 1994, a five-member bench of the Supreme Court ruled that the reference to it, of the question of a temple having existed at the disputed site in Ayodhya, was 'superfluous, unnecessary and does not require to be answered' (*India Today*, 15 November 1994, pp. 29–30).

Independence of the Judiciary

The independence of judges is safeguarded in the constitution by several means affecting their appointment, salaries and dismissal. But because a judiciary is formally independent does not mean that it is also socially neutral. Judges tend to be predisposed towards stabilising the social order by upholding the dominant values of society (Hague *et al.*, 1992, p. 281). With few exceptions, India's senior judges have come from the upper strata of society. They are generally held in high public respect. And many of the severest critics of the failings and shortcomings of the judiciary have been members of the legal profession itself.

The framers of the constitution believed it would be unwise to leave the appointment of the judges to the president's discretion. But the alternative of making judicial appointments subject to legislative concurrence was thought to be too cumbersome and vulnerable to political pressures. Instead, a middle course was adopted. The chief justice of India and 25 other justices of the Supreme Court are appointed by the president on the advice of the cabinet and after consultation with other persons. For appointing the chief justice, the president is required to consult such judges of the Supreme Court and high courts as he deems necessary. In the appointment of other judges of the Supreme Court, consultation with the chief justice is mandatory (Article 124). These provisions clearly tried to apply lessons learnt from the American experience of the sometimes unseemly politicisation of the nomination and appointment process.

Despite this, over the years the appointment of high court and supreme court judges, including chief justices, became a focus of political controversy. In 1981, in the case of *S. P. Gupta* v. *Union of India* (more commonly referred to as the *Judges' Transfer* case), the Supreme Court itself conceded the last word on appointments to the executive. In 1992, the lists of recommendations for appointments of judges submitted by Bihar's Chief Minister Laloo Prasad Yadav and Chief Justice B. C. Basak of the Patna High Court held no names in common. The resulting impasse frightened Judge Basak so much that he went to the Law Ministry in New Delhi seeking and being granted extra security (Pathak, 1992, p. 52).

The 1982 verdict was finally overturned in 1993. On 6 October, a special nine-judge bench of the Supreme Court ruled, by a 7–2 majority, that no appointment of a judge to the Supreme Court under Article 124.2 of the constitution, or to any high court under Article 217.1, could be made unless it was in conformity with the opinion of the Chief Justice of India. In the case of conflicting opinions among the respective constitutional functionaries, the judiciary's opinion would also have primacy in regard to the transfer of high court judges, including high court chief justices. The last was important because in fact transfer of high court judges had become a favourite mode of executive influence over judicial decisions. During the 1975–7 emergency period, for example, Mrs Gandhi had transferred sixteen inconvenient judges to irrelevant posts in a largely successful attempt to intimidate the judiciary into submission to her will. The first instances of transferring high court chief justices out of their home states against their wishes occurred in 1981 with the chief justices of the Madras and Patna high courts. A Supreme Court decision on the *Judges' Transfer* case, delivered in December 1981, abdicated judicial responsibility in the appointment and transfer of judges to the executive. The judgment left the government free to hire high court and supreme court judges, fire temporary judges and transfer high court judges (except on a mass scale). By the end of 1983 it was clear that the power to transfer judges had been used to bend the judiciary to the government's will (Chawla, 1983). In 1985 a three-member bench of the Supreme Court itself accused the Rajiv Gandhi government of packing high courts with 'sycophant judges' (*India Today*, 15 June 1985, p. 78). In March 1993 the Supreme Court quashed the appointment of K. N. Srivastava to the Guwahati High Court, holding that he was not qualified to hold that post. This was the first instance since the constitution came into being that the apex court had quashed a presidential warrant on the appointment of a high court judge.

Once appointed, justices hold office until the retirement age of 65 specified by the constitution itself. A judge may of course vacate office voluntarily. A judge may also be removed from office on grounds of proven misbehaviour or incapacity (Article 124.4). But the process of removal is quite rigorous, requiring a majority opinion of the total membership of the two houses of parliament and a two-thirds majority of those present and voting in each house. In this case the precedent was England, where superior court judges are appointed by the crown but hold office on 'good behaviour' rather than 'the pleasure of the crown'. To shield judges from political controversy, the Indian constitution grants them immunity from criticisms against decisions and actions made in their official capacity. While philosophical criticisms are permissible, no motives can be imputed to any Supreme Court decision. The conduct of high court and Supreme Court judges may not be discussed in parliament unless in the context of an address to remove a judge from office (Article 121). To keep judges free of temptation, the constitution further stipulates that retired Supreme Court judges may not practise law in any Indian court (Article 124.7). But the scope for patronage has not been eliminated totally: retired judges are eligible for appointment for such specialised tasks as commissions of enquiry and university vice-chancellorships.

During office, the allowances, leave and pension rights of justices may not be varied by parliament to their disadvantage (Article

125.2). The salaries of the justices are also fixed by the constitution. But the financial protection of the judges can be overridden by the president if a financial emergency is formally in force in the country (Article 360.4). Over the years, the salaries and conditions of judges have not kept pace with those of politicians. The constitution gives the Supreme Court the right to maintain its own establishment and staff independently of parliament. The associated expenses are chargeable on the consolidated fund, and therefore not subject to parliamentary vote.

The first motion of impeachment against a judge was not tabled in parliament until 1991. The case involved Supreme Court Justice V. Ramaswami. An audit report revealed several irregularities committed by him during his tenure as the Chief Justice of the Punjab and Haryana High Court. A three-man committee consisting of one serving and one retired Supreme Court judge and the Chief Justice of the Bombay High Court concluded that there had been wilful and gross misuse of office, purposeful and persistent negligence in the discharge of official duties, intentional and habitual extravagance at the cost of the public exchequer, and moral turpitude by using public funds for private purposes in diverse ways. The committee observed that 'the acts, therefore, constitute 'misbehaviour' within the meaning of Article 124.4 of the Constitution'. Justice Ramaswami maintained that there were procedural irregularities in the notice of the motion, the constitution of the committee and its functioning. He survived the impeachment motion in the Lok Sabha on 10–11 May 1993. Of the 401 MPs in the house, 196 voted in favour of impeachment, not one voted against, but 205 abstained. The Congress Party, with the largest single bloc of votes in the house, issued a verbal whip late in the day calling on its MPs to abstain. The motion therefore failed (details of the case in *HIE*, 22 May 1993, pp. 4, 5 and 8). But, accepting reality, the judge subsequently resigned.

Judicial Review vs Parliamentary Sovereignty

In the United States, the Supreme Court assumed extensive powers of judicial review under 'due process'. By contrast, in India the constitution expressly provides for judicial review of legislation as to its conformity with the constitution. Rights enumerated in the constitution are made justiciable. Indeed, in India the right to constitutional remedy has itself been made a fundamental right

(Article 32). Judicial review has been particularly significant and contentious in regard to constitutional amendments. The stability of the rarely amended American constitution contrasts markedly with the volatility of the amended-at-whim Indian constitution. Broadly speaking, any constitution may be said to have two goals. Positively, it codifies the values of a society and makes the state responsive to the aims and demands of society. Negatively, it erects safeguards which protect citizens from arbitrary actions of the state. That is, a constitution recognises that the state is simultaneously an embodiment of the pursuit of the civic good life by a collectivity and a threat to the pursuit of the good life by the individual. In keeping with the negative goal, a constitution should not be so flexible as to permit easy and constant modifications by an autocratically inclined government. At the same time, in accordance with the first goal, it should not be so rigid as to obstruct the legitimate demands and aspirations of the people. In sum, a constitution that can be amended only with the utmost difficulty risks atrophy, while one that does not differentiate between ordinary legislation and constitutional amendments risks losing credibility.

The Constitution of India laid down four methods for its own amendment. Some provisions may be amended by a simple majority of parliament, in consultation with or at the request of the states. A second class of provisions may be amended by a simple majority in parliament. A third group requires a majority of the total membership of each house plus a two-thirds majority of Members of Parliament present and voting in each house. The final category of clauses require, in addition to the preceding, ratification by half the number of state legislatures. Between 1950 and 1990, the constitution was amended some seventy times, but without altering the basic structure of the system of government established in 1950.

Incontinent tamperings with a constitution on the basis of overwhelming legislative majorities (see Table 2.1), in order to overcome constitutional obstacles, instil cynicism in the populace towards the principle of constitutional government. No constitution so wilfully changed can command the necessary respect. Constitutional checks upon legislative powers are not anti-democratic in the sense of constituting checks upon sovereignty. In the Austinian view sovereignty resides not in the elected body but in the electors, in the case of both the English and the American systems of government. The sovereign electorate may choose to make the legislature free from or subject to legal limitations (Hart, 1961, pp. 72–3). In Britain the

TABLE 2.1

Constitutional amendments in India, 1950–93

	1950–59	1960–69	1970–79	1980–89	1990–1/6/93
No. of amendments	7	15	22	17	13

first method is preferred, and the electorate exercises its sovereignty in electing legislators and thereafter delegates its sovereign power to parliament. By contrast, in democracies with legally limited legislatures, the electorate's sovereignty resides partly in the constitution and partly in parliament. The 'sovereignty of parliament versus constitutional checks' antithesis is a false equation that may, moreover, prove injurious to parliamentary democracy in its consequences. The dangers were well illustrated in the experience of India's parliament during the 1975–7 emergency (Thakur, 1982).

Liberalism as the theory and practice of individual liberty is embodied in the constitutional state. A constitution is thus a formal statement of the liberties valued in society. In addition, however, the constitution is also a method of guaranteeing the liberties through enforcement mechanisms such as judicial review. An independent and powerful judiciary is one of the chief instruments for the attainment of the liberal goal of freedom from unrestricted state authority. The Indian constitution incorporated the principle in conferring substantial scope to the jurisdiction of courts and safeguarding the independence of their positions. As a result, the judiciary has been one of the most effective stabilising elements of democratic government in India.

Nevertheless, the evolution of tacitly recognised and mutually respected spheres of jurisdiction between the executive and the judiciary is an emergent necessity in Third World democracies. The complete insulation of the judiciary from governmental influence is an article of faith for liberal democracy. Yet the concept at best sits ill at ease in countries beyond the affluent West. Given the absence of a liberal society, is not an independent judiciary the most powerful bulwark of the entrenched elite against the democratic demands for equality?

The experience of the Indian emergency offers salutary warning against accepting such simplistic formulations. During the emergency, the Supreme Court effectively succumbed to governmental pressure and abdicated from its role as the guardian of individual rights against the state. In the historic *Golaknath* case (1967), the Supreme Court ruled, by a 6–5 majority, that fundamental rights could not be abrogated by parliament even by means of constitutional amendments. In the landmark *Kesavananda Bharati* case (1973), the Supreme Court enunciated the doctrine that parliament, being a creature of the constitution, lacked the authority to amend 'the fundamental features' or 'basic structure' of the constitution. (Later, in the *Minerva Mills* case in 1980, judicial review was itself held to be an inseparable part of the basic structure of the constitution that could not be amended.) The judgment was delivered on 24 April 1973. Prime Minister Mrs Indira Gandhi's response on the very next day was to supersede three senior judges involved in the case and appoint Justice A. N. Ray as the next Chief Justice of India. This was the first departure from the convention of appointing the seniormost judge of the Supreme Court as the Chief Justice.

During the 1975–7 emergency the same court under Chief Justice Ray's leadership failed to uphold the basic right of *habeas corpus*. Seven high courts had held that, despite the suspension of Article 21 by the declaration of the emergency, *habeas corpus* petitions were maintainable. On 28 April 1976, in a 4–1 majority verdict, the Supreme Court ruled that people detained during the emergency under the Maintenance of Internal Security Act (the notorious MISA) could not ask the high courts to enforce their fundamental rights, including that of personal liberty. *Habeas corpus* petitions were not, therefore, admissible. The noted constitutional expert H. M. Seervai commented that coming 'at the darkest period in the history of independent India', the judgment 'made the darkness complete' (in Kapoor, 1984, p. 96). The lone but celebrated dissenting vote was that of Justice H. R. Khanna, who argued that the state had no power to deprive a citizen of his life or personal liberty without the authority of law. By contrast, Justice M. H. Beg talked about detainees being 'well-housed, well-fed and well-treated' with 'almost maternal care' (in Gupta, 1982, p. 297). In January 1977, after Ray's retirement as chief justice, the seniormost remaining judge was Khanna. He was superseded by Beg as the new chief justice and resigned. (He was elected to parliament as part of the winning Janata coalition in the general election held shortly afterwards.)

In 1980, in the *Minerva Mills* case, the court overturned the 42nd Amendment Act that had sought to confer limitless power on parliament. The 59–clause bill, passed by a pliant parliament during the emergency in 1976, had virtually rewritten significant parts of the constitution. It tried to overturn the *Kesavananda* verdict by declaring that there was no limitation of the power of parliament to amend the constitution, and that no constitutional amendment could be called into question in any court. Thus the power of judicial review would be severely curtailed. Fundamental rights were made subordinate to an expanded set of directive principles. In its verdict on the case in 1980, the Supreme Court held by a 4–1 majority that the Act, by converting a limited amending power into an unlimited one, deprived the courts of the power of judicial review and thereby rendered fundamental rights into a 'writ in water'. In seeking to abrogate rights that give meaning to freedom and democracy, the Act disturbed the constitutional harmony between fundamental rights and directive principles and therefore contravened the constitution (*OHT*, 14 August 1980).

The fact that the emergency was precipitated in 1975 by the decision of the Allahabad High Court finding Mrs Gandhi guilty of corrupt electoral practices showed how the judiciary has sometimes found itself in the eye of the political storm. In 1982 the High Court of Calcutta and the Supreme Court of India found themselves involved in electoral politics. The Marxist state government wanted to hold elections by the due date of June 1982, and the Election Commission was agreeable. The state Congress Party and Mrs Gandhi argued that there were irregularities in the state's electoral rolls which made it impossible to hold free and fair elections. When Justice Sabyasachi Mukherjee of the high court halted the electoral process, the state government appealed to the Supreme Court, one of whose justices had some harsh things to say about the objectivity of the high court judge. (Mukherjee was later appointed to the Supreme Court and is remembered for basing his judgments on the legal merits of each case, regardless of whether they helped or embarrassed the government.) The five-judge constitution bench of the Supreme Court issued a unanimous verdict removing all restraints on the Election Commission from proceeding with the elections (*SW*, 3 April 1982, p. 1).

Laws and Mores

The subject of executive–judiciary demarcation can be subsumed within a wider philosophical discussion of the desirability of a colonially derived judicial system continuing to operate in an independent country. In this regard recent Commonwealth history is a fertile field of study of the embryology of legal systems. As sovereignty over former colonial territories no longer resides in the Westminster Parliament, so the ultimate rule of recognition shifts and develops a local root. An independent legal system emerges. But the composition, mode of enactment, and structure of the post-colonial legal system may still be that prescribed originally by Westminster. As Morris-Jones notes (1971, p. 240), 'The system of law itself in India is basically derived from the "expansion" or "migration" of the English common law.'

A difficulty arises in societies where the imported legal system is not congruent with the indigenous sector of social life. In such circumstances the criteria of validity used in courts will diverge markedly from the criteria of morality in general usage in the wider society. *The* relation between law and morals may not exist; but neither can a legal system be said to exist in anything but a formal sense where there is no habitual obedience to official rules. Law cannot be based merely on power but must rest equally on authority. For law to be authoritative, the criteria of legal validity must include at least an implicit reference to social mores. In fact, even 'judicial decision, especially on matters of high constitutional import, often involves a choice between moral values, and not merely the application of some single outstanding moral principle' (Hart, 1961, p. 200).

The English legal tradition of adversarial proceedings in court operates on the assumption that the one issue at dispute can be isolated from its context of wider controversies, that the evidence presented is the truth, the whole truth, and nothing but the truth, and that in each isolated dispute one party is right and the other wrong in accordance with law and precedent, and the court is duty bound to sift through the facts and find accordingly. Not all societies function within such a tradition, and many have quite different institutions and structures to regulate conflict and its arbitration. In India, thus, villagers recognise that a dispute involves not just one issue but a network of controversies; that each disputant presents only his side of the dispute; that all disputants must continue to coexist and therefore any settlement must satisfy both sides by being a compromise (Weiner, 1965, p. 214).

The adversarial approach in such society in both its legal and political manifestations can appear to be a method for aggravating rather than settling conflicts. An uncritical imposition of one over the other can simply jam the smooth running of society. Alien systems of law can no more hope to be sensitised adequately to the full nuances of local culture, customs, and mores than can foreign political theories. In consequence of the political–legal framework governing their decisions, even judges sensitive to 'progressive' aspirations find their sympathies severely constrained.

It may be the case that such sympathies are misplaced rather than the scope for their expression curtailed. Liberal democracy does not create social and political cleavages. It simply recognises and legitimates the struggle for power in politics, and provides constitutional means of managing it. The Supreme Court of India is undoubtedly a centre of political power, and the judicial process is a subset of the political process. Unlike other centres of political power, however, the Court has no determinate constituency to shield it in times of crisis. Former Justice H. R. Khanna argued at a convention in New Delhi in March 1982 that 'There is no office which is so infinitely powerful and at the same time so frightfully defenceless as that of a judge' (*OHT*, 1 April 1982, p. 11). The Supreme Court is therefore vulnerable to encroachments upon its role as a *de facto* opposition in a political system dominated by one party (see Baxi, 1980). Indeed at times the opposition parties treat it as a court of last *political* recourse. Despite having such a role thrust upon it, the Supreme Court has generally deferred to the government's right to initiate broad socioeconomic reforms. Neither the political nor judicial correlates of liberal democracy pose insurmountable obstacles to either economic growth or egalitarian redistribution.

Problems

In a speech in 1992, P. D. Desai (1992, pp. 2–3), Chief Justice of the Bombay High Court, remarked on the increasing restiveness of the Indian people with their judicial system based on four factors:

- The slowness and inaccessibility (due to the heavy cost of legal services and ignorance of the general public about their rights and obligations and their enforceability) of the judicial process;
- The antiquated nature of court procedures and management practices;
- Flaws in procedural laws, lack of effective control of court proceedings and availability of multiple remedies at different rungs of the judicial ladder which enable dishonest and recalcitrant suitors to abuse the judicial process; and

- The lowered standards of conduct, character and competence of the legal profession and judges (Desai, 1992, pp. 2–3).

Probably the most serious shortcoming of the Indian judiciary is its excruciating slowness. In a speech on 8 May 1982, Justice V. R. Krishna Iyer of the Supreme Court remarked that 'In India law is on fighting terms with justice.' He went on to offer this advice: 'Once you start a litigation, please execute a will, naming the person who will continue the case in court' (*SW*, 8 May 1982, p. 3). In 1993, there were about twenty million cases pending in the courts of India (*TOI*, 13 December 1993). While the Allahabad High Court was disposing of a little over one thousand cases each year, its backlog grew by fifty thousand cases in 1988–9 (Pathak, 1992, p. 56). The Supreme Court itself accepts some 100 000 cases each year (compared with the 100–150 cases of the 5000 filed that are accepted by the US Supreme Court): perhaps it should be more selective so as to minimise the danger of being 'mired in judicial trivia' (Hardgrave and Kochanek, 1993, p. 103). Part of the explanation for the multiplying backlog lies in the politicisation of the judiciary at all levels, part in its corruption at lower levels: justice delayed can mean pockets filled. Is the Indians' fondness for litigation to be explained by the fact that they use courts not to settle disputes but to further them? Is the lag between judicial theory and practice to be explained by the relationship of judicial norms to the social structure of the judicial system or by their incongruity with indigenous values? A more charitable interpretation is that the frequency and number of resorts to the courts is testimony to the people's faith in their judicial system compared with the other institutions of government.

Conclusion

The key to the successful establishment of constitutional democracy in India may lie in the gradualism of the British tutelage. India went through a comparatively long gestation period of democratic institutions. The principle of gradualism informed the widening of suffrage, the extension of elective government from local to national levels and the broadening of power-sharing arrangements between elective and appointive bodies. But if independent India was going to give meaning to the fine sentiments expressed in its constitution – if it was to protect minorities, give content to equality of opportunity, establish that democracy meant that all votes had equal value and that all citizens were answerable in court – then the judiciary, led by the Supreme Court of India, was going to have to provide firm guidance. Despite occasional failures of nerve, by and large it has done so. At times this has meant that the Supreme Court has had to fill a political vacuum. But in general, for the rule of law to prevail, the judiciary must be seen to be universal, impartial and impersonal. Its task is to expand individual rights and state power simultaneously. It is a delicate and challenging task, but not one beyond the capacity of India's learned judges.

Notes

1. The term 'wog' came to be used by Indians too as a derogatory acronym, but to refer to 'western oriented gentlemen'.
2. All of this helps to explain the Indian explanation for why the sun never set on the British empire: because even God would not trust an Englishman in the dark.

Further Reading

Basu (1993). A standard authoritative account that has been constantly revised and updated over several editions.
Baxi (1980). Examines the apex court as a political institution.
Pylee (1992). A clear and accessible exposition of the main features of India's constitution by a leading authority in the field.
Seervai (1990/1991). *The* book on the subject of India's constitutional law.

3

Federalism

In this chapter I wish to address six issues:

1. The origins of India's federalism.
2. The nature of India's federalism.
3. The nature of fiscal federalism in India.
4. The centralising role of party politics in India.
5. The critical role of state governors in federal–provincial relations.
6. The distinctive status of Kashmir in India's federation.

Origins of Indian Federalism

Politics is often defined in terms of the struggle for power. Democracy is a means of coming to terms with political power, taming it and making it subservient to popular wishes. Federalism is a means of bifurcating it territorially. A unitary system of government concentrates all legal power in a central government, with subordinate units of government being the creation of and subject to the will of that central government. In effect the lower units are administrative extensions of and have no legal status independently of the central government. A confederation is an association entered into by a number of sovereign governments which retain most legal powers but cede some, such as defence and foreign affairs, to the newly created confederal authority. A federation is a half-way house in which two sets of governments coexist with separate but not necessarily equal powers within their respective autonomous jurisdictions. A federal arrangement may be the result of an agreement by a number of independent countries motivated by shared attributes and goals, as in Australia and the United States. Autonomous governments cede a defined part of their sovereignty or autonomy to a new central organism. Or it may be the product of a devolution of power from a previously centralised system of government, as in Canada and India. In neither case did provinces have an existence independent of the colonial government; in both cases, a federal arrangement was imposed by British statute. British India comprised a number of provinces and 562 princely states. The latter, accounting for about two-fifths of the subcontinent's territory, were granted internal autonomy under the paramountcy of the British crown in defence and foreign affairs, and were therefore closer to the confederal model. The provinces on the other hand were essentially administrative units, and the colonial regime, serving the needs of the metropolitan rulers, was unitary in nature.

Federalism in India predates the constitution adopted in 1950. Certain legislative powers were delegated to the provinces as early as 1861. The 'nation-building' subjects of health, education, agriculture and irrigation, and public works, along with the financial ways and means appropriate to these subjects, were given to provincial assemblies by the India Act of 1919. The Government of India Act of 1935 set up a union with federal features. Following the Canadian precedent, the act created autonomous units and combined them into a federation. Provincial legislatures were given autonomous jurisdiction in specified subjects and derived their powers directly from the crown. A practical legacy of the 1935 division of powers was the emergence of a group of politicians experienced in running provincial governments and with their power bases located at the provincial level.

A product more of geography and history than inter-unit agreement, federalism was given formal recognition in the 1950 constitution. It retained the tripartite classification of the powers of state and central governments. These are enumerated in the seventh schedule of the constitution. The central government is given exclusive authority in the 97–item Union List, including currency, income tax, foreign affairs and defence. The State List, embracing 66 items, includes health, education, agriculture, land revenue and police. The 47–item Concurrent List gives shared jurisdiction to the state and central governments in such subjects as civil and criminal law, and social and economic planning. However, state rights are qualified even in this list. The governor of a state has the power to reserve a state bill for consideration by the president, who may choose to disallow it (Article 201). Following the Canadian but departing from the US precedent, residuary powers (that is, those not included in the three lists) are given to the central government (Article 248). If there should be a conflict between the union and a state, then the union law shall prevail.

Thus both before and after independence, the solution to India's perennial problem of unity-in-diversity was sought in a modified model of federalism. The federal features were necessary to accommodate the considerable diversity of the country. The structure of government is clearly federal, and the structures and institutions of government in New Delhi have their counterparts in the state capitals. Article 1.1 of the constitution affirms that 'India, that is Bharat, shall be a Union of States'. In 1993, the Union of India comprised 25 States and 7 Union Territories (see Table 1.1). Union territories account for under 1 per cent of India's territory by area. Goa, having been liberated from Portuguese rule in 1961, became India's 25th state in May 1987, and Daman and Diu, the other former Portuguese colonies, were made a union territory.

The very diversity of India, however, generated strong centrifugal pressures, and a powerful central authority was believed to be necessary to counteract them. The constitutional drafting committee preferred the term 'union' to emphasise two main points. First, unlike the American and Australian federations, the Indian federation is not the product of a negotiation by the constituent units. Second, and again conscious of the US civil war, the framers of the Indian constitution wished to make it clear from the outset that the component parts had no freedom to secede from the Indian union. (The 16th amendment of 1963 made even the advocacy of secession an offence.) The need for territorial integrity and political stability was further underlined by the mass carnage of partition, the conflicts with Pakistan, the communist insurrection in Telengana and the requirements of state-led economic development.

These are the reasons why the word 'federalism' does not appear anywhere in the Constitution of India. At the time that the constitution was drafted, debated and adopted, the issue of group rights of different religions and communities was rather more important and urgent than that of states' rights. Partition demonstrated the dangers of subordinating the national identity to parochial loyalties. The movement for India's independence was led by the Congress Party, which was itself highly centralised. Since the political units of the British Raj were constituted on the basis of administrative convenience, there was little opportunity for regional identities to coalesce around the existing political units. This was to change with the reorganisation of states along linguistic and cultural lines. Only then did the Congress Party's monopoly on the authoritative allocation of values come under serious challenge from strong regional parties promoting ethnonationalism. The rise of regional identities in many parts of the country is perhaps the development that has given most concrete expression to state rights. Yet it may also be the case that consciousness of regional identities has in many cases been a reaction to over-centralisation of Indian politics.

Indian Federalism

The constitutional form given to unity-in-diversity has created some confusion among analysts. The system of government adopted by independent India has been described variously as cooperative federalism (Austin, 1966, p. 187), 'quasi-federal' (Wheare, 1951, p. 28), and unitary in both concept and operation (Chanda, 1965, p. 124). The central government is so dominant in the legislative, administrative and financial spheres as to reduce states to being 'glorified municipalities' (Minoo Masani, quoted in Hanson and Douglas, 1972, p. 115). It may be debated as to whether India is a unitary state with subsidiary federal features, or a federal state with subsidiary unitary features.

No consensus exists among political scientists on a precise definition of federalism. However, one school has traditionally chosen the characteristics of the US political system as the measure of federalism in general, and evaluated other polities against this point of reference. On this arbitrary rather than logically derived basis, there are six correlates of federalism:

- The functions of government are divided between two sets of authorities, one exercising jurisdiction over the whole national territory, the other within its provincial borders;
- The legal status of both sets of authorities is co-equal. That is, the invasion of each other's jurisdiction is legally impermissible. Nor may one level of government, in discharging its own duties, override or veto the operations of the other level;
- The operations of each governing authority are usually conducted by its own set of officials;

- There is a written constitution detailing the above elements;
- The federal legislature is bicameral, with one of the chambers representing the constituent states; and
- The constitutional division of powers between the two sets of authorities is interpreted by an apex court.

India satisfies every criterion except the second (although the third is only partially satisfied, as we shall see in Chapter 7). We should remember too that even in the United States, the Supreme Court has progressively enlarged federal jurisdiction at the expense of state rights, for example in civil rights, and that the revenue and expenditure of the federal government are vastly greater than that of state governments. Indeed the federal government gives financial grants-in-aid for specific projects within state jurisdictions, for example the construction of highways.

On the minimalist criteria, of the range of governmental activities being divided and shared between two sets of constitutional authorities, India is a federal state. But it is a flexible rather than a rigid federation, with the balance between the central and state governments varying to suit the changing circumstances. Where a rigid demarcation of powers might have made the Indian state too brittle, flexibility has given it resilience to absorb and overcome periodic strains and stresses. Under normal conditions, the authority of state governments is coordinate with rather than subordinate to the wishes of the central government. For it is derived not from laws made by the central government, but from the very same constitution which creates and legitimates the central government. Under abnormal conditions, the central government can override most state preferences. But it can do so only within constitutional limits and safeguards and for prescribed periods of time. Other than such temporary dispensations, the legislative and executive boundaries separating the federal and state governments cannot be altered unilaterally. The courts may give a broadening construction of existing powers (judicial verdicts have tended to enlarge the scope of central government powers in all federal systems). But even the courts cannot re-assign powers to one set of government that have been explicitly conferred on another.

The federal ideal has been seriously diluted in India by the constitutional bias in favour of the centre in normal times, the constitutionally permissible opportunities to set aside state governments under exceptional circumstances, the substantial state dependence on the centre for operating and capital revenues, the centralised bureaucratic, police and judicial services, and the centralised nature of the major political parties in India. States are subject to the legislative control of the union under exceptional circumstances and administrative control under normal circumstances. A further qualification to Indian federalism include the lack of dual citizenship (although most states distinguish between domiciles and aliens in the conferment of many rights and privileges, for example admission to medical colleges).

The essence of federalism is a territorially-based dual government. The US constitution prescribes the structure and powers of the federal government, leaving the states free to adopt their own constitutions. In India, only the state of Jammu and Kashmir has the right to determine its own constitution. Under Articles 3–4 of the Indian constitution, the union parliament may reorganise the states or alter their boundaries by a simple majority in the ordinary process of legislation. The consent of the states concerned is not necessary. (Consent necessarily connotes the power of veto.) In the Australian and US conception, the union is indissoluble, the states are indestructible. The alteration of existing boundaries or the formation of new states requires the consent of the states concerned. In India, the president is enjoined merely to 'ascertain' their views and may prescribe a time-limit for them to express their views. The States Reorganisation Act of 1956 reduced the number of states from 27 to 14 by means of unilateral legislation by the Parliament of India.

By virtue of the theory of the equality of state rights, every state of the United States has two senators in the US Senate regardless of area or population. Representation in the Rajya Sabha – the second chamber designed to protect the status and interests of states in India – is weighted according to population, with the number ranging from 1 (the minimum for any state) to 34 (for U.P.) (Table 3.1). In addition, 12 of its 250 members are appointed by the president. Of the 238 Rajya Sabha MPs elected by the state legislatures, several can only euphemistically be said to be residents of the states from which they are elected. (In 1993 the Election Commissioner threatened to begin enforcing the residential qualification more stringently.)

Article 249 empowers parliament to enact laws with respect to any matter included in the State List, for a temporary (but renewable) period of one year, if the Rajya Sabha adopts a resolution by a two-thirds majority that it is necessary and expedient to do so for the whole or any part of India in the national interest. This is in addition

TABLE 3.1

State-wise distribution of seats in Parliament of India (1992)

	House of People	Council of States		House of People	Council of States
Andaman & Nicobar Is[a]	1	–	Kerala	20	9
Andhra Pradesh	42	18	Madhya Pradesh	40	16
Arunachal Pradesh	2	1	Maharashtra	48	19
			Manipur	2	1
Assam	14	7	Meghalaya	2	1
Bihar	54	22	Mizoram	1	1
Delhi[a]	7	3	Nagaland	1	1
Goa	2	1	Orissa	21	10
Gujarat	26	11	Pondicherry[a]	1	1
Haryana	10	5	Punjab	13	7
Himachal Pradesh	4	3	Rajasthan	25	10
			Sikkim	1	1
Jammu & Kashmir	6	4	Tamil Nadu	39	18
			Tripura	2	1
			Uttar Pradesh	85	34
Karnataka	28	12	West Bengal	42	16

Note: [a] Union Territory.

to Article 252 which empowers parliament similarly at the request of two or more states. Critics argued that Article 249 was superfluous because of Article 252, and pernicious in conferring unilateral powers on the central government. On the other hand, it is only the Rajya Sabha, the custodian of state rights in the union, that can so empower parliament, for delimited periods and in order to cope with exceptional circumstances. The balance between states and the centre could be redressed by a more even division of powers between the Lok Sabha (embodying the democratic principle) and the Rajya Sabha (representing the federal principle) in New Delhi.

Articles 256 and 257 of the constitution enjoin state governments to exercise their executive powers in conformity with union laws and without impeding union authority. The central government can also assume executive powers under the same two articles in order to issue directives to state governments. If they fail to comply, then the union government can invoke Article 365 and take over the functions of the recalcitrant state government directly. The last point is even more relevant in regard to the vastly expanded powers of the central government when a declaration of emergency is in force. Again, though, the Indian constitution effectively codified trends that had been emerging in other federal systems where courts had interpreted the war and defence powers of federal governments fairly broadly.

In comparison to the United States, the procedure for amending the Indian constitution is weighted in favour of the central government. The US constitution was the product of a voluntary agreement between hitherto autonomous units; it cannot therefore be altered without their consent. Yet the Indian constitution does differentiate between the federal and non-federal features in the amendment procedures. While fundamental rights (which have nothing to do with federalism) can be altered unilaterally by the central government, changing the process for electing the president requires ratification by a majority of state legislatures.

In sum, the framers of the Indian constitution believed that a rigid conception of federalism would not be allowed to negate the national interest. Moreover, the constitution enshrined federalism in a political sense without bureaucratic and judicial correlates. In the United States, 'dual government' is accompanied by a double set of officials and courts. There are two levels of government in India, at the centre and the states. The powers and structures of both are laid out in the constitution. But, as we saw in Chapter 2, the judiciary is integrated into a single hierarchy. Similarly, we shall see in subsequent chapters that the bureaucracy and the police forces are dominated at the district, state and national levels by officers recruited and dismissible by the central government on an all-India basis. The officials administer both state and union laws within the states to which they are deployed. The electoral process too is under the control of a national Election Commission, and the machinery for accounts and audit is similarly integrated.

There has also been some attempt to institutionalise cooperation between states. The States Reorganisation Act of 1956 set up five zonal councils for contiguous states and union territories. A further council was established for the northeastern zone in 1972. Each zonal council comprises the union Home Minister as chairman, the chief ministers and two other ministers of each member-state, and up to two representatives from union territories. Its agenda consists of items of common interest, in particular issues of social and economic planning and border disputes, interstate transport and linguistic, religious or even caste minorities. The zonal councils were given merely advisory roles, and they failed to develop into significant political institutions.

The National Development Council has been a little more visible. It was set up in 1952 for the purpose of promoting cooperation between the centre and the states, as well as among states, in economic planning. It seeks to do so by recommendations on how to achieve plan targets, by a periodic review of the plan, and by debating important questions of social and economic development. It has been suggested that the federal principle could be strengthened if this body, reconstituted on a 1:2 ratio between the central and state governments and including all heads of government at both levels, could replace the Planning Commission as the apex agency for guiding national planning (Paranjape, 1990, p. 2480). Non-planning issues are discussed at the Conference of Chief Ministers with a view to promoting coordination and uniformity.

An analysis of the interstate disputes between Punjab and Haryana on the sharing of river waters or territorial adjustments, or between Tamil Nadu and Karnataka over the River Cauvrey waters, would be grossly distorted if it did not include 'political' calculations as well as the merits of the disputes. The ability of the central government to arbitrate in such interstate disputes is ultimately a function of the respective bargaining assets and skills of the various parties involved in the complex and often protracted negotiations. The constitution confers upon the centre the power to settle interstate disputes, and a favourite mode of interstate dispute-resolution is through the appointment of tribunals. But one result of this is that the centre becomes the focus of demands and grievances from the states involved in the disputes, and the issue is converted into one of centre–state relations.

Financial Relations

The existence of two levels of government in a federal polity makes it necessary to devise an appropriate balance of financial powers between the central and state governments. This is true both for revenue collection and expenditure of the funds raised. That is, the taxing and spending powers have to be divided between the two levels of government to handle public money. The division of powers must be derived from the constitution in order to be authoritative, and must be clear in order to avoid overlap and confusion. At the same time, the existence of two levels of financial authorities exercising separate jurisdictions may impede the creation and growth of an integrated national economy. Litigation between different governments would further retard economic development.

Another problem in India was the imbalance of resources and demands between the centre and the states. The most productive resources – income tax, excise tax, custom duty and foreign aid – are centralised. This was done partly to effect economies in collection and partly to avoid economic distortions. For example, variable excise duties could lead to arbitrary and uneconomic location of industries, while state-based income taxes could bring into conflict the principles of origin and residence. Yet the primary responsibility for fulfilling the demands of a developmental state were vested in the state governments. The asymmetry between the taxing powers and spending responsibilities has led to what is called the problem of vertical fiscal imbalance. For example, although by the mid-1980s the states were spending more than 60 per cent of all tax revenues collected by state and central governments, the share of the total money raised by the states themselves was only about 35 per cent (Mukherjee, 1989, p. 21).

Efforts by state governments to discharge their constitutional obligations with regard to the welfare functions of education, health, agriculture and so on would entail growing expenditure. State governments therefore had to be given adequate finance to enable the proper delivery of these essential public services. There was tension between the centralising requirements of a developing economy and the devolutionary impulse of federalism. India sought to resolve the tension by concentrating revenue-raising powers in the centre, but providing formulas for the transfer of the monies raised to states. The meagre financial resources of the states are supplemented by financial aid from the central government in the form of grants-in-aid. The difficulty with this, however, is the conditions that might be attached to their utilisation, eroding the autonomy of the states.

Taxing powers are divided between the central and state governments by means of specific entries in the union and state lists in the constitution. The most significant taxing powers are given to the union government: income tax, excise tax and customs duty. It was important to maintain a uniform income tax structure throughout the country. Customs duty has to be centrally controlled because of its repercussions for foreign exchange. Excise duty has an impact on the price level, so excise rates required central control in order to facilitate price stability. While sales tax is a state subject, taxes on interstate trade and commerce, as also on imports and exports, are central subjects. Some fine distinctions are made in the entries. While the power to levy estate duties in respect of agricultural lands is vested in state legislatures, that in respect of non-agricultural property belongs to the union parliament. Residuary powers of taxation are also vested in the union parliament. Article 289 of the constitution exempts union and state properties from mutual taxation.

By constitutional amendment and judicial interpretation, central taxes can be classified according to the collection and distribution of their proceeds:

- Some duties are levied by the union, but collected and appropriated entirely by the states, for example stamp duty;
- Some taxes are levied and collected by the union, but their proceeds are distributed entirely within the states in which they have been collected, for example estate duty on non-agricultural property;
- Some duties are levied and collected by the union, and the proceeds are then distributed between the union and the states, for example excise duties.

Even after states have been assigned certain shares in the taxes levied by the central government, their resources may be inadequate to their tasks. The constitution anticipates this contingency and provides for the provision of annual grants-in-aid to such needy states as shall be determined by parliament. The welfare needs of tribal areas are especially underlined. The constitution provides for the establishment at five-yearly intervals of a Finance Commission, an impartial and expert body to recommend what measures should be adopted for the distribution of financial resources between the union and the states. What proportion of income tax should be assigned to the states? In practice, the finance commissions have recommended between 55 per cent and 67 per cent of income tax proceeds as the states' share. What formula should be used to distribute the share assigned to the states among them? Should it be on the basis of financial need and, if so, should this be determined on the basis of population or average income levels? Should it be on the 'source of collection' principle, that is the amounts of taxes collected by the various states, in order to encourage maximum efficiency in revenue collection? Or should it be on a mix of these two criteria? The finance commissions have recommended a mix, with between 75 per cent to

90 per cent of the states' share of income tax proceeds being distributed according to population ratios.

What should be the amounts and distribution of grants-in-aid to the states? Ideally, the allocation of grants-in-aid should be guided by budgetary needs, the capacity to absorb and utilise grants optimally, financial managerial efficiency, fiscal prudence in the tax and expenditure equation, the provision of social services, special circumstances and national priorities. In practice, the primary determinant has been budgetary deficits: which can reward inefficiency and penalise fiscal prudence. Grants-in-aid can be provided under Article 275 (obligatory) or 282 (voluntary). Decisions in the former category are made as per the recommendations of the Finance Commission, and the aid is unconditional. Aid under Article 282 is at the discretion of the Parliament of India and subject to conditions set by it. Similarly, under Articles 270 and 272, the assignment of income tax and excise duties to states is mandatory and discretionary respectively.

A third problem is imbalances between different regions, and the need for the central government to rectify such imbalances. At the time of independence, Maharashtra and West Bengal were more economically advanced than Assam and Bihar. It was feared that the persistence of inter-regional differences would generate political tension and instability. This in turn would pose a threat to the stability of federal arrangements. On the other hand, India is a poor country with limited overall resources and an urgent need for optimum utilisation of all available resources. There was also the fear that some states could slide into financial irresponsibility, the costs of which would have to be borne by the entire nation. So a delicate compromise had to be reached between the competing demands of rapid and balanced development.

The finance commissions have tried to increase the solvency and self-reliance of states by widening the ambit of shared revenues and recommending transfers on an unconditional basis. Paradoxically, however, the states have become increasingly reliant on transfer of funds from the centre, with more than half of all state expenditures being financed through such transfers. The balance would be dramatically altered if India should progressively reduce union-based custom and excise duties, and move instead towards a broad state-based regime of value-added tax. We should note that the shift in the financial centre of gravity towards the central government is not unique to the Indian federation. Every federal system needs some institutional mechanism to oversee adjustments and reallocations of resources between the different units. This has to be done on a flexible basis in order to match the distribution of funds to the changing requirements.

Before leaving this subject, we should note also that efforts by successive finance commissions to allocate grants-in-aid to states, for such basic national purposes as expansion of primary education, have sometimes brought them into jurisdictional rivalry with the Planning Commission. States in turn have not been averse to playing off the two bodies against each other. To the Planning Commission, states will stress their resource-mobilising capabilities in order to persuade the body to sanction prestigious development projects. To the Finance Commission however states will stress the limitations on their resources in order to win a greater share of the revenue being transferred to them from the centre.

Considerable sums of money are given to states by the union government under Article 282 in pursuit of the annual plan objectives which include reductions in regional inequalities. The annual plan allocations are based on a mix of population and economic output of the various states. The Planning Commission has a long tradition of mediating between the central and state governments. But inevitably it was viewed as a creature of the central government, and therefore more deferential to the wishes of those in power in New Delhi than in the state capitals. The political credentials of the Planning Commission were underlined by the frequent changes in its membership with each fresh change of the central government.

The discretionary grants under Article 282 exceed the amounts transferred to states under Article 275. Since the former are based on the recommendations of the Planning Commission, in practice this extra-constitutional body has come to wield a more significant influence on federal–provincial financial relations than the Finance Commission set up by the constitution itself. The convention of appointing one member of the Planning Commission as a member of the Finance Commission helped to provide a link between the two bodies. But it does not rectify the imbalance of the Planning Commission being responsible for about 70 per cent of the total grants disbursed by the centre to the states.

A fourth problem in fiscal federalism relates to emergency measures. If there should be a proclamation of emergency under Article 352 of the constitution because of a threat to national security, then Article 354 provides for the suspension of all provisions relating to the division of tax proceeds between the centre and the states. In addition, a financial emergency can be declared under Article 360 if the president (that is, the union government) is satisfied that the financial stability or credit of India, or any part of the country, is under threat. While a financial emergency is in force, presidential proclamations may order a reduction of salaries of state officials, and require all money bills approved by a state legislature to be reserved for presidential consideration. Interestingly, Article 360 was not included in the draft constitution. Its insertion was prompted in part by the devaluation of the rupee in 1949. Although the article is open to the criticism that it erodes the federal principle even further, its incorporation into the constitution was justified on the argument that the economic structure of the country is one and indivisible, and that the promulgation of a financial emergency would be the exception rather than the norm.

If we move away from an institutional conceptualisation of federalism and examine its operational manifestations, then it becomes clear that India is a cooperative rather than a competitive federation. This is especially evident, for example, in the process of planning that will be discussed in Chapter 11. The formulation of plans is done mainly by the central government, but with an important consultative role for states. The implementation of plans is chiefly in the hands of the states, but with the help of central finances and with an important monitoring and oversight role for the centre. State politicians are particularly interested in those subjects that have the greatest electoral appeal, for example education and agriculture. This has taken on added importance since the existence of different party governments in the centre and the states.

Party-Political Centralisation

The imbalance in favour of the centre in India's federalism has one other interesting consequence. It provides a readier alibi for state governments to pin the blame for their non-performance on a central government controlled by a different party. The Communist Party of India (Marxist) often points to the constraints of federalism in explaining its limited achievements in West Bengal. Since so much power has been vested in the central government, the Congress Party in West Bengal cannot profit as much from the failures of the CPI(M) government in West Bengal. State and national politics are more successfully delinked in other federal systems like Australia and Canada.

India's founding Prime Minister Jawaharlal Nehru was a principal architect of the constitution adopted shortly after independence. During his tenure as head of government (1950–64), he tried to give 'flesh and blood' to the constitutional principles. His government was inclusive, representative of the myriad strands of Indian society, committed to promoting secularism, sensitive to conventions governing relations between the treasury and opposition benches and generally careful not to intrude upon state rights. Yet even Nehru's legacy to Indian federalism was somewhat mixed. On the one hand, he was determined that his Congress Party would rule not only at the centre but in all the states as well. If the people could not see the wisdom of this when electing state assemblies, then the goal could still be achieved by behind-the-scenes manipulation and the use of constitutional tricks for bringing about the downfall of state governments. On the other hand, for most of the Nehru period central and state politics were largely autonomous. Several states were ruled by strong chief ministers from within Congress, and a sort of bargaining model of federalism operated to mediate between a strong government in New Delhi and strong governments in states.

Developments under Prime Minister Mrs Indira Gandhi (1966–77, 1980–4) led to the interlinking of the fates of the central and state governments. The 24th Constitution Amendment Bill abolishing the privy purses of the princes was rejected in the Rajya Sabha in September 1970 when Charan Singh failed to deliver three Bharatiya Kranti Dal (BKD) votes. Mrs Gandhi's response was to break the ruling BKD–Congress coalition in Uttar Pradesh (UP) and bring down the state government. Under Nehru, the centre had functioned as an impartial arbiter of conflicts *internal* to state politics. Under Mrs Gandhi, the stability of state politics became increasingly a function of the struggle for power in the centre. Her position became dependent on having pliant chief ministers; their position was dependent on her pleasure. Before, the surest route to political power at the centre was through building broad-based coalitions at the local and state levels. Henceforth, the competition to occupy a chief minister's chair would be conducted mainly at the prime minister's residence in New Delhi. Power and resources at the state level became a reward for loyalty to the prime minister.

Rajiv Gandhi (1984–9) commented that centre–state relations in India had been reduced to the connection between the Congress

Party's headquarters in New Delhi and its branch offices, with the former exacting obedience in return for largesse (Datta-Ray, 1991b). Congress Party politics became increasingly centralised in candidate selection for state and national elections, cabinet and chief ministerial appointments and distribution of patronage. As the autonomy and influence of state party organisations and leaders was progressively curtailed, and the process of building stable political coalitions was neglected, the need grew for more frequent interventions by the central government in order to cope with chronic instability in the states.

Indian federalism is distinctive for granting the central government the power to dismiss elected state governments and replace them with administrations run directly by the centre under President's Rule. Under Article 356 of the constitution, the president may declare an emergency in a state if satisfied that the government of the state cannot be carried out in accordance with the constitution. President's Rule was imposed infrequently under Prime Ministers Nehru and Lal Bahadur Shastri (1950–66) (Table 3.2). Recourse to it expanded exponentially under Mrs Gandhi (1966–77), generally with partisan motives. The same was true of the Janata government (1977–9), which set the precedent of dissolving nine Congress-ruled state assemblies on the dubious reasoning that the federal elections were a vote of no-confidence in all Congress ministries. When Mrs Gandhi came back to power, she turned the tables by dismissing the assemblies of nine states in which her party had triumphed in the Lok Sabha elections; only Kerala and West Bengal were left untouched.

As democratic government has taken deeper root, political power has been devolved from the centre to the states and districts. As a result, even Congress state politicians have regained some of the

TABLE 3.2

The imposition of President's Rule on States, 1952–92

1952–56	1957–61	1962–66	1967–71	1972–76	1977–81	1982–86	1987–91	1992
4	2	4	16	15	33	6	13	6

Note: The chronology refers to the dates of imposition, not termination, of President's Rule. The total for the 41–year period is 99. There is not one state that has not experienced President's Rule at least once. States to have had President's Rule most often are Kerala (9 times) and Punjab (8 times).

Source: Basu, 1993, pp. 449–51.

bargaining leverage lost during the era of centralisation under Mrs Gandhi. The inability of the central government to bend state governments to its will was demonstrated even during the dominance of both levels by the Congress Party prior to 1967. Some state governments, for example that of West Bengal, were successful in thwarting major union initiatives in land reforms and agricultural income tax. On the other hand, the multiplicity of powerful factions in Congress as well as non-Congress state units leaves considerable room to the central government to play the role of (dis)honest broker. Also, because politics in India has become increasingly distributive along sectarian lines, with politicians attempting to build up vote banks, the centre has acquired an enhanced ability to play patronage politics.

The Sarkaria Commission on Centre–State Relations was set up by Mrs Gandhi in 1983 under the chairmanship of retired Supreme Court judge R. S. Sarkaria. (Mrs Gandhi announced the setting up of the commission shortly after the formation of a regional council of opposition chief ministers of four southern states to buttress the demand for greater state autonomy.) It inquired into the role of the governor, the relationship between state administrations and all-India services, the appointment of high court judges by the centre, the implications of the president's power to withhold assent from bills passed by state legislatures, and state financial dependency on the centre. Its report, published in 1988, recommended the creation of a series of independent federal bodies with constitutional status and advisory functions, such as the National Economic and Development Council and an Inter-Governmental Council, as well as the Planning Commission and the Finance Commission. It sought to reduce the element of arbitrariness in the dismissal of state governments by the centre. The Sarkaria Commission also suggested ways by which the pool of revenue resources shared by the centre and the states could be expanded in order to place the sharing of revenues on a more equitable basis. Overall, although it spoke of 'cooperative federalism', the thrust of its report was in favour of a strong centre that could best preserve the unity and integrity of the country. It may perhaps have been influenced by the exceptional number and strength of challenges to the unity and integrity of India during the mid-1980s. The Sarkaria Report was quietly buried and centre–state relations in the 1990s have settled into the familiar pre-Sarkaria mould of *ad hoc* responses to specific situations.

By the 1990s politicians have gradually become less cosmopolitan and more provincial even as federalism has become steadily more complex, requiring bargaining and accommodation between governments run by various political parties. In 1991, in addition to its good performance at the national level, the Bharatiya Janata Party (BJP) won power in four states: Himachal Pradesh, Madhya Pradesh, Rajasthan and U.P. Ayodhya, site of the disputed Babri Masjid, lies in U.P. The BJP was committed to rebuilding a temple on the site. But the BJP state government, having provoked a Hindu–Muslim polarisation before the 1991 election, realised after it that failure to maintain law and order would invite central government intervention and dismissal of the state government in U.P.

In the Lok Sabha debate on 21 December 1992 Prime Minister P. V. Narasimha Rao argued that Article 356 was too restrictive to have permitted him to dismiss the U.P. government before the Babri Masjid demolition on 6 December, so perhaps it needed to be amended. Students of Indian politics were thus faced by the novel situation of a prime minister justifying non-use of Article 356 to dismiss a state government. Constitutionalists rejected the prime minister's contention that he could not have acted sooner (Noorani, 1993a, p. 11). Under Article 355, the central government can deploy its own security forces to suppress any disturbances without having to impose President's Rule. The central government is charged with the responsibility to protect every state against external aggression and internal disturbance. The deployment of central forces can be ordered in a situation rapidly drifting towards anarchy and, if necessary, against the wishes of the state government. The National Integration Council had met on 23 November. The BJP had boycotted the proceedings. The central government had received intelligence reports warning of specially trained squads being organised for purposes inimical to the security of the Babri Masjid structure.

After the destruction of the Babri Masjid in December 1992, all BJP-run state governments were dismissed and fresh elections held in the four provinces a year later. The fact that the BJP suffered significant reverses in the two important states of U.P. and Madhya Pradesh raised the prospect of the central government dismissing other non-Congress governments before the holding of state elections. Control of the reins of government at the state level gives considerable power of patronage during the holding of elections: incumbency is a decided asset. On the other hand, there is a clear risk of generating sympathy for parties that are seen to have been harshly treated by the centre for purely political reasons. The optimum political strategy therefore is to engineer instability in non-Congress state governments so that they disintegrate about 6–12 months before elections are due, and then impose President's Rule for the interregnum.

The Governor

Of all the constitutional functionaries, the governor has been the most controversial. Probably the most crucial reform in enhancing the confidence of states concerns the role of the governor. Specifically, s/he could be made responsible to the state rather than the central government. Justified originally in terms of providing a much-needed link between the central and state governments as well as a referee in the affairs of states, the office has been misused as an instrument of coercion and manipulation of individuals or parties that are unfriendly to the central government. As a result, the office of the governor has become the focal point of contested federalism. The office is probably one of the best examples of the decay of India's political institutions. At the same time, India is also noted for its resilience and its capacity for political regeneration: not just the rebuilding of enfeebled institutions but the creation of new ones that can cope with the continual pressures and challenges from society.

While every state must have a governor, one person may be appointed the governor of more than one state. For example, the Assam governor has served as the governor of Meghalaya as well. Although no woman has as yet been elected to the presidency, several women have been appointed as state governors. For practical purposes, in most instances the governor is the provincial equivalent of the President of India in ceremonial, executive, legislative and judicial functions. All four functions reflect the tension of the governor's split formal personality as representative of the central government and head of the state government. In the ceremonial functions, for example, the governor is a symbolic representative simultaneously of the President of India and of the state. The legislative functions include summoning, proroguing and dissolving the state legislature. The exercise of these functions can bring into conflict those commanding majority support in the central parliament and state legislature. Like the president, the governor too, acting on advice, may promulgate ordinances that have legislative force while the state legislature is in recess.

There are also some important differences, starting with the manner of coming to office. A state governor is appointed by and holds office at the pleasure of the president (Articles 155–6). Once again the Indian constitution followed the Canadian model while eschewing the Australian and US precedents. The draft constitution had called for an elected governor. An appointed governor cuts across the federal as well as the democratic principle; a governor appointed from outside the state may not be sensitive enough to the local needs and aspirations; and the office could become a point of friction if different parties were in power in a state and at the centre. Yet in the end the Constituent Assembly opted for an appointed governor chiefly to protect national interests against undesirable parochialism. On the one hand, the expense and effort of holding elections would not be justified for a ceremonial post. Yet on the other hand, an elected governor would also be a rival source of authority to the chief minister. Governors are usually appointed to states other than their own in order to minimise partisan involvement with local politics.

In practice, the office of the governor has been merely ornamental if the state government commands a clear majority on the floor of the assembly, and if it is of the same party as the central government. The interesting episodes concern exceptions to these two conditions. As is the case with the president at the centre, the governor can acquire considerable ability to influence the politics of a state if the majority party is immobilised by powerful rival factions, or if there is no single party with a majority in the legislative assembly. This has been only too common in India since the 1967 state elections, in which year five state governments were formed without a clear legislative majority. On these occasions, reflecting the power of patronage conferred by the manner of appointment and dismissal of the governor, the office-holder can become a mere tool of the central government. Even more unsavoury is the practice of dismissing state governments that still command a majority in their assemblies.

The scope for bending the affairs of states to the wishes of the centre through the governor comes from two sources: the discretionary powers of the governor and the emergency powers of the union government. Together, the two ensure that the governor functions as the 'eyes and ears' of the union government. Given the ever-present threat of disorder in several parts of India, the 'constructive contribution' of the emergency powers of the union government to the maintenance of fragile political institutions should not be ignored (Manor, 1991, p. 146).

The governor of a state is required to act in accordance with the aid and advice of his chief minister and cabinet except in those

provisions of the constitution that require him to exercise his functions
'in his discretion'; the question of whether the matter is one requiring
his discretion is in turn at the absolute and unquestionable discretion
of the governor (Article 163). Such discretionary power extends, for
example, to administering the affairs of a union territory adjoining
the state for which the governor is responsible, or to certain areas
(usually tribal or hill areas) for which the governor of a state may be
designated as having special responsibilities (Article 371). The
discretionary latitude of the governor, whose scope is greatly
expanded during President's Rule, is in marked contrast to the
binding requirement that the president must always act on the aid
and advice of the prime minister and the central cabinet. A president
cannot therefore call on gubernatorial precedents to guide his own
actions when making delicate decisions.

Under Article 356, the president may dismiss a state government if
he is satisfied, on the basis of a report from the governor 'or
otherwise', that the constitutional government of the state has broken
down. For obvious reasons, such a report may have to be
communicated against the wishes of the state government.
Similarly, a governor may use her own judgment on whether to
reserve a bill that has been duly passed by the state legislature for
presidential consideration. A governor would be constitutionally
remiss if she did not do so, for example, in the case of a bill seeking to
erode the powers of the state high court.

One set of controversies that have swirled around the office arose
from gubernatorial judgments that have anticipated, and sometimes
even disregarded, the likely vote on the floor of a house rather than
testing the majority of a government. The practice became
commonplace during the prime ministerial reign of Mrs Gandhi
and after the loss of Congress monopoly over state governments from
1967 onwards. Yet the first example of the dismissal of a state by the
central government occurred in 1959 during the Nehru era (although
Mrs Gandhi was party president at the time). The communist
government of Kerala was dismissed by the governor on his
instinctive conclusion that the minds and feelings of the people had
experienced a tremendous shift against the communist ministry. (No
actual or public opinion poll was held to document such a shift of
electoral opinion.) The post-1967 developments institutionalised the
practice of using the governor to pursue the interests of the ruling
party at the centre in installing the government or chief minister of its
choice. Governor Gopala Reddy dismissed the Charan Singh

ministry in U.P. in 1970 without awaiting the assembly vote that was due within a few days. When faced between equally unstable alternatives of divided non-Congress coalitions and a factionalised Congress, governors restricted their options to asking a Congress chief minister to prove a majority on the legislative floor within a generous period or imposing President's Rule. In tandem with the centre, state units of the Congress Party followed the strategy of 'divide or join': divisions would be encouraged within non-Congress coalitions in order to bring about their disintegration, or else an alliance would be formed with one powerful group against another.

We have already discussed the events of 1977 and 1980. In both years, six of the nine dismissed governments commanded a majority in their respective legislatures at the time of their dismissals. On 16 August 1984, Governor Ram Lal would not give Chief Minister N. T. Rama Rao 48 hours to prove his majority in the Andhra Pradesh assembly and replaced him with Bhaskara Rao, a defector from the ruling Telugu Desam Party. Despite all sorts of bureaucratic and police harassment by Bhaskara Rao and physical impediments to rail and air travel by the Congress government in New Delhi, Rama Rao managed to parade a majority of members of the legislative assembly (MLAs) before the President in New Delhi on 21 August, at which point the central government distanced itself from the actions of the state governor.

It is clear then that state governments are dismissed more for party-political reasons than any other. In effect the collective legal responsibility of the state cabinet to its legislative assembly under the conventions of parliamentary democracy has been displaced by the individual political responsibility of the governor to the central government under the imperatives of a centralising federalism. As a corollary, in effect the governor has usurped the constitutional prerogative of the legislature to make and unmake governments in parliamentary democracies.

A second set of controversies has involved the dismissal of state governments independently of reports from the governor recommending such action. One of the most notable of such instances occurred in 1991 in the state of Tamil Nadu (see Tummala, 1992). The Dravida Munnetra Kazhagam (DMK) government was in power after the 1989 elections. In 1990, the National Front central government collapsed. Chandra Shekhar became prime minister because, although he controlled less than 10 per cent of the Lok Sabha MPs, he had the support of Rajiv Gandhi's 197 Congress MPs.

The pro-Congress All-India Anna DMK (AIADMK) opposition in Tamil Nadu began to urge the dismissal of the DMK government. Pressure during 1990 turned to an ultimatum in January 1991. The governor of the state at the time, appointed by the National Front government, was Surjit Singh Barnala, whose own Akali government in Punjab had been dismissed by Gandhi in May 1987. Despite representations from intelligence agencies purporting to show the DMK's entanglements with Sri Lankan Tamil terrorists, Barnala refused to submit a report to the president recommending a dismissal of his state government. The dismissal was effected over his objection on 30 January 1991 on grounds of the state government's inability to maintain law and order – even though New Delhi had earlier declined the DMK government's request for the deployment of central paramilitary forces for assisting with the maintenance of law and order. (Barnala had always argued that President's Rule in Punjab had actually worsened the law-and-order situation there after May 1987.)

A duly elected state government still in command of a majority in its assembly, and with the law-and-order situation considerably better than in many other states, was thus dismissed by an unelected central government. Analysts were divided as to which was the greater violation: of the norms of democracy or federalism. There was a further twist to the strange affair. Governor Mohammed Yusuf Saleem of Bihar resisted pressure from the Chandra Shekhar government to dismiss the state's Janata Dal government. On 10 February 1991, his address to the joint session of the state legislature, written by the state government, included a passage critical of the dismissal of the DMK government in Tamil Nadu. (The governor was physically manhandled by angry opposition legislators during his entry into the assembly building.) He in turn was dismissed by the union government on grounds of 'constitutional impropriety', thereby raising the question of whose rubber the governor should stamp: that of the central or state government? Barnala was offered the Bihar governorship instead. He refused the Bihar appointment and resigned his Tamil Nadu post.

The above comments indicate the degree to which the office of the governor has been politicised into serving the interests of the party in power in New Delhi. The practice has been underlined by appointing party candidates who have been defeated in elections to the office of governor, as well as retiring bureaucrats and military officers who have been loyal to the prime minister or the ruling party. The

Sarkaria Commission recommendation, that a governor should not belong to the party in power in New Delhi in the case of a state with a different party in power, has been ignored by all governments. In 1990, V. P. Singh's National Front government asked 18 Congress-appointed governors to resign. Home Minister Mufti Mohammad Sayeed openly declared that the governor was a representative of the centre and as such should enjoy the confidence of the centre (*HIE*, 27 January 1990, p. 1). This despite a Supreme Court ruling in the *Raghukul Tilak* case that the governor, occupying an independent constitutional office, is not subject to control by the union government. The relationship between the central government and a state governor is not that of employer–employee, said the court in its verdict delivered on 4 May 1979. There was an interesting variant on the theme in 1992. On 27 March, Governor M. M. Thomas of Nagaland accepted his chief minister's advice to dissolve the Legislative Assembly and hold fresh elections, on the ground that no stable government could be formed because of a fluid party situation. The governor's recommendation was taken as proof that constitutional government in the state had broken down, and on 2 April Nagaland came under President's Rule under Article 356 of the constitution.

An insistence on appointing persons who are regarded as unacceptable by state governments can strengthen the suspicion that the governor is an agent of and imposed by the union government. The office of the governor will be less controversial and less politicised if conventions are established that persons appointed to the post should be acceptable to the state governments, and should be continued in office for their full term except for incompetence or proven incapacity to function. The appearance of nonpartisan consensus is vital to the smooth functioning of all non-executive constitutional figureheads. This will also ensure that governors are more sensitive to the need to avoid controversy and to act evenhandedly. For while impartial conduct and devotion to constitutional propriety has been the norm with presidents, the same cannot be said of governors.

The Special Status of Kashmir

Intolerance of provincial governments and recourse to sectarian politics by successive central governments in New Delhi have produced steadily deteriorating problems in the two key states of Punjab and Kashmir. The two together are also a good illustration of the increasing intertwining of religion and politics in modern India (Mansingh, 1991, pp. 308–9).

About two-thirds of the six million people of Jammu and Kashmir are Muslim. Kashmir (as the state is commonly known) has a unique status in the Indian federation conferred on it by Article 370 of the constitution. It is a full-fledged state and part of the 'territory of India' as defined in Article 1 of the constitution. Under the British Raj, it was one of several princely states. While the people were mainly Muslim, the hereditary maharajah, Sir Hari Singh, was Hindu. A popular movement led by Sheikh Abdullah agitated against the maharajah's autocratic rule. Its secular nature attracted support from Congress but opposition from the Muslim League. There was also an embryonic movement to keep Kashmir free of any external attachment. The Kashmir problem thus crystallised into a struggle between three competing versions of nationalism: the religious nationalism of Pakistan, the secular nationalism of India and the ethnic nationalism of Kashmiris (Varshney, 1991).

Attempts by the maharajah to remain independent in 1947 came to nought when the state was attacked by armed tribesmen wishing to force the issue of Kashmir's merger with Pakistan. India made its help in repelling the invasion subject to the accession of the state to India. The maharajah acceded to the Indian Union on 26 October 1947 and Indian troops were flown in on the next day. Pakistani troops crossed the border openly in November and the ensuing first war over Kashmir was ended with a UN-mediated ceasefire on 1 January 1949. Kashmir remains the symbol of the Indo-Pakistan conflict. The military situation in effect partitioned the province between Pakistan and India on a 1:2 basis. The area under Indian control has three parts: Buddhist-majority (51 per cent) Ladakh, Hindu-majority (66 per cent) Jammu, and the Muslim-majority (95 per cent) Jhelum valley. Because of the peculiar history of Kashmir's accession to India, Delhi declared that the Indian government's responsibility would be limited to defence, foreign affairs and communications. Other parts of the constitution would apply to the province only on a provisional basis until such time as the people of Kashmir themselves adopted their own constitution through a constituent assembly. This was done in 1954, embracing the applicability of virtually the entire range of the Indian constitution to the state.

But there were some significant exceptions. The state of Jammu and Kashmir retains its own separate constitution instead of the provisions of Part VI of the Constitution of India which govern the administration of all other states in the union. The state constitution, which was promulgated in January 1957, cannot be suspended under Article 365 on the ground of non-compliance with a union directive. While the Parliament of India has jurisdiction in respect of Kashmir with regard to all matters in the Union List, residual powers are vested in the state government of Kashmir (other than for dealing with terrorism, territorial integrity and secession). Even the power of preventive detention has been vested in the Kashmir legislature. The state's consent is required for any alteration of its name or territory, and for the proclamation of an emergency under Articles 352 or 360 dealing with an internal disturbance and a financial crisis respectively. Rights to employment, settlement and acquisition of property in the state discriminate between 'permanent residents' and non-residents.

Despite a few ups and downs, after 1957 there was a growing web of linkages between Kashmiri nationalism and the Indian political mainstream culminating in a seminal accord between Sheikh Abdullah and Mrs Gandhi in February 1975. In this accord, the 'Lion of Kashmir' accepted the finality of Kashmir's accession to India while the prime minister guaranteed Kashmir's regional autonomy under Article 370. The accord was endorsed by the people in the 1977 elections, generally believed to be the state's first free and fair election. Kashmir became a place of beauty but not a joy forever. Peace and tranquillity lasted until Sheikh Abdullah's death in 1982.

The mantle of leadership of the National Conference Party and the state government was inherited by his son Farooq Abdullah. Mrs Gandhi then subjected the state to her familiar tactics of manipulative politics. She campaigned against the National Conference in the June 1983 elections, and the state unit of the Congress Party refused to accept its loss in the elections. The prime minister began to employ the rhetoric of 'anti-national elements' in Kashmir. She succeeded in splitting the National Conference in 1984 and installing a pro-Congress faction in power, but at the price of the political destruction of her 1975 accord with the Sheikh. Governor Jagmohan proved pliant in dismissing Farooq without giving him the opportunity to prove his majority in the assembly, and so initiated the most serious and sustained period of alienation of Kashmiris from the Indian mainstream.

Moreover, 'by manipulating the removal of an elected Chief Minister who acted as a useful buffer in a State that is of the utmost strategic and demographic importance, the Centre [came] directly to grips with the Kashmir question' (Datta-Ray, 1990, p. 11). By the time that Farooq Abdullah teamed up again with the Rajiv Gandhi-led-Congress in the 1987 elections (which were rigged), Islamic groups were ready to assume the mantle of anti-Delhi militancy. By the end of the 1980s the Indian Army had in effect become an army of occupation, low-intensity insurgency gripped the entire state and the provincial administration had effectively collapsed.

Constitutionally, then, the federal balance is tipped slightly more towards state rights only in the case of Jammu and Kashmir. Kashmir is thus more equal than other states in the Indian union. The delicacy of its situation arises firstly from its geopolitical location at the crossroads of India, Pakistan, Afghanistan, Russia and China; and secondly from the fact that it is India's only Muslim-majority state. Loss of Kashmir would not just deprive India of the fertile and populous Vale of Kashmir; it would also render impracticable Indian claims to the Aksai Chin region of Ladakh and threaten control of Punjab. It attracts the attention of the BJP on both counts. Demands for the abrogation of Article 370 – which was originally described as a temporary and transitional provision – have been voiced most vociferously by the BJP, on the argument that India is one country and Jammu and Kashmir is an integral part of India. A former governor of the province, Jagmohan, pointed to the 'farcical' situation that an Indian could get US citizenship after ten years' residence there, but could not get a similar status (domicile) in Kashmir (*SW*, 26 June 1993, p. 5).

In 1993, the Kashmiri Pandits began to voice a demand for their own union territory, named 'Panun Kashmir', to be carved out of the state. They based their demand on the alleged history of the Muslims' refusal to live in peaceful coexistence with the Hindus of the province. To the Kashmiri Hindus, the Indian government is guilty of failure to protect their lives and property from terrorists. To the Kashmiri Muslims, India is itself the enemy and Indian security forces the perpetrators of the worst outrages that have defiled an entire community. Whatever their religion, most Kashmiris are united in having lost trust in the Government of India.

The fact that Kashmir is the only Muslim-majority state in India, plus the controversial manner of its accession to India, plus the fact that about a third of the erstwhile princely province is under Pakistani occupation, have combined to keep the Kashmiri problem alive as a national, regional and international issue. An armed uprising begun in 1989–90 had claimed some 13 000 lives by the end of 1993. About half a million Hindus (the Kashmiri Pandits) have fled their homes for the safety of Jammu and Delhi. India alleges that the militants are financed, armed and trained by Pakistan, and that without Pakistani complicity the insurgency could be contained. India believes that Pakistan has concluded that it is less costly, safer and more effective to wage a proxy guerrilla war than a real one. The worry in New Delhi has been that in backing terrorist violence in Kashmir (and Punjab), Pakistan was aiming to achieve by means of low-intensity proxy conflict goals that were unattainable by conventional military means.

The patterns of demands by regional, religious and linguistic groups and government responses to them are familiar enough for us to be able to sketch a political profile. The groups' initial demands are couched in moderate language and their goal is usually no more than ensuring the preservation of political space guaranteed to them by the constitution. The state and central governments ignore them: they lack sufficient nuisance value to command the attention of hard-pressed decision-makers. There is no discussion, let alone negotiations. Instead, the mettle of the movements' leaderships is tested by casual repression and harassment. This converts the 'evolution of rising expectations' of the groups into a sense of grievance and arouses them into mobilising wider support for their cause. The government then resorts to the tactic of divide and rule. Intelligence agencies and agents provocateur are used to delegitimise the movements, while new radical leaders are promoted in order to outflank the movements' leaders, possibly to terrorise them and certainly to splinter their followings. Radical leaders promoted into prominence by the government then turn into fanatic secessionists in their own right, or else succeed in driving hitherto moderate leaders into increasingly hardline rejectionists. This is the story of Punjab, Kashmir and Assam as well as a variety of movements within states. The special constitutional rights given to Kashmir could have been used as a healthy precedent for re-establishing centre–state relations with all the other provinces. Instead the central government in New Delhi chose to rule through a series of rigged elections and puppet chief ministers.

Conclusion

The constitution attempts to establish institutions and practices that would permit the preservation of distinct regional identities while maintaining a sense of Indian nationhood: a concurrent list of powers for central and state governments, an independent Finance Commission, and a general institutional framework designed to facilitate voluntary cooperation. Within this framework, efforts have been made to make states realise that they do possess common interests, and that the central government is not a hostile power. In addition to the constitutional framework, there is considerable centre–states and state–state collaboration. That is, while the constitution emphasises demarcation, practical politics place a premium on cooperative bargaining.

Politics is about the control and exercise of power. A political system is about the institutionalised distribution of power. Democracy and federalism are the two great institutions of India's constitutional structure. Democracy seeks to achieve a balanced distribution of power between the state and the citizens. Federalism seeks to strike a satisfactory balance between the central and state governments. A strong government is not inconsistent with democratic governance: the moral authority to govern based on constitutional propriety is more useful than authoritarian powers acquired by stealth and subversion. A strong centre is not incompatible with strong states: there is no reason why a union of strong states should not lead to a still stronger India. Under Indian conditions, excessive centralisation of power will lead to an unnecessary nationalisation of local problems. If the government in Delhi were to try to rule the country as a feudal fiefdom, it would risk displacing the 'politics of accommodation' with the 'politics of manipulation' (Hardgrave and Kochanek, 1993, p. 135).

The most pressing requirement for India since independence has been economic development, pointing to an expansive role for the central government. The contrary permissive and restrictive pulls of democracy generate tensions between majority rule and minority rights; those of federalism generate tensions between central dominance and provincial autonomy. India is effectively a bargaining, cooperative federalism, even though the channels, forums and outcomes of bargaining may change from time to time. The distinction between democracy and federalism is important also in understanding why the crises in Assam, Kashmir and Punjab are more accurately viewed as failures of federalism rather than of democracy. Moreover, the Congress Party, often identified as the key to the stability of the democratic order in India, can itself be a threat to the federal order because of its excessive centralisation.

As a half-way house between a unitary and confederal arrangement, federalism contains an inherent paradox: its units seek national unity but do not wish to lose their own identities. Federalism in India is a particular manifestation of the syncretic impulse in Indian society. People can be proud of their regional identities without any overt or implicit downgrading of their patriotism. The constitution has established institutions to promote a satisfactory blend of regional and national identities. These are buttressed by informal collaboration between the centre and the states, and between the states directly. State ministers sharing particular portfolios – health, education, agriculture, housing–can get together to discuss common problems and map out a common strategy. For example, although education is a state subject, all states have to have knowledge of and confidence in one another's certification process in order to recognise each other's qualifications. Indian federalism should not be evaluated by the standards of competitive, sometimes even confrontational, federalism in Western countries. All in all, India's efforts to preserve unity in diversity have so far successfully – if only just – withstood tensions strong enough to have split apart some other experiments in federalism in developing countries.

Perhaps inevitably, the reorganisation of states along linguistic lines was the prelude to fresh demands for greater autonomy on the one hand, and the subdivision of existing states into newer states on the other. We have already referred to examples of the former: by the communist governments of West Bengal, and the regionalist governments of Tamil Nadu, Andhra Pradesh, Punjab and Assam. A good example of the unsatisfied aspirations for ethnonational statehood within the Indian union is the demand for a separate state of Jharkhand to be carved out of the contiguous tribal districts of Bihar (mainly) and Orissa, West Bengal and Madhya Pradesh. Another example is the periodic demand for a separate Gurkhaland to be parcelled off from West Bengal.

The government has sought to accommodate linguistic diversity with a three-language formula that was recommended by the National Integration Council in 1961. The constitution declared the official language of India to be Hindi in the Devanagari script (Article 343). English, the language of the Raj, was to be retained as the 'language of administration' for no longer than 15 years. States were permitted to adopt languages other than Hindi as their official language(s). The three-language formula required all schools to teach English, Hindi and the regional language of the area; in Hindi-speaking states, the third language would be any other regional language of India. Attempts to 'impose' Hindi on the southern states produced mass protests and agitations against 'Hindi imperialism', and the official languages policy has failed to alter the monolingual status of most Indians. But Hindi did become the official language of India from 26 January 1965, with English becoming a 'subsidiary' official language. It is used for official communication between a non-Hindi state and the union or another state.

Opinion is divided on the cause of the unsatisfactory health of Indian federalism. There are some who argue that the constitutional framework is itself flawed, suited only to the same party being in power in the states and at the centre. The periodic proposal to give constitutional status to the Planning Commission, for example, is part of an overall demand for redefining centre–state relations. Others argue that the constitution as such is sound, but appropriate conventions to underpin it have yet to take root (Palkhivala, 1983, p. 34). It has been argued with reference to Article 356 (permitting the imposition of central rule on states) that 'The powers it confers are freely availed of. The conditions for their exercise are as freely ignored' (Noorani, 1992, p. 12). Clauses that were drafted in order to protect the territorial integrity of the country have been used in so arbitrary and capricious a way that they might well imperil national unity: identity-asserting, separatist and secessionist movements feed on a sense of grievance.

In an important decision on 11 March 1994, the Supreme Court upheld the validity of the dismissal of the four BJP state governments on 15 December 1992. But the court also ruled that presidential proclamations were subject to judicial review, and that the president could be required to submit to the court the material on which he had formed 'requisite satisfaction' in issuing a proclamation under Article 356. Assembly dissolutions could be set aside if the president's proclamation was 'malafide' or based on 'wholly irrelevant or extraneous considerations' (*HIE*, 19 March 1994, p. 2). Applying these criteria, the court held the proclamations of 21 April 1989 and 11 October 1991, dissolving the assemblies of Karnataka and Meghalaya respectively, to have been unconstitutional. The political significance of the verdict is that henceforth, knowing that dismissals of state governments can be set aside by the courts, the central government will be hesitant about abusing Article 356.

There are several long-term trends that favour regionalism, pluralism and decentralisation (Brass, 1982). The best evidence of the reality of a bargaining model of federalism in India is the existence of a variety of parties in power in several states across the country. Brass (1990, pp. 110–18) has classified state party systems into one-party-dominant (the sole remaining example being Maharashtra); one-party-dominant systems with institutionalised opposition; and competitive, where there is some experience and possibility of alternation of government. It is an interesting affirmation of his thesis about the long-term federalising trends that one year after his book was published, the states of U.P., Himachal Pradesh, Madhya Pradesh and Rajasthan moved from the second to the third, competitive, category. An equally dramatic example of the strengthening of 'fiscal federalism' came at the annual meeting of the World Economic Forum of government and business leaders in Davos (Switzerland) in February 1994. There were two delegations from India: a federal, headed by Prime Minister P. V. Narasimha Rao who gave a keynote address on the consolidation of economic reforms; and a state delegation from Maharashtra headed by Chief Minister Sharad Pawar, who tried to present a case for Bombay as an emerging global financial centre.

India can therefore best be described as a cooperative federalism with the paramountcy of the centre being enshrined in the constitution. The elements of cooperative federalism are adminis- trative cooperation between the central and state governments in the implementation of their respective public policies, partial dependence of state governments upon payments from the central government to help finance state projects, partial dependence of the central government on states for the administration of federal programmes, and the use of conditional financial transfers by the central government to shape policies in subjects that are constitutionally within the jurisdiction of states.

Further Reading

Bose (1987). A collection of papers analysing a range of problems in Indian federalism.

Datta (1984). A useful set of readings exploring a range of issues in centre–state relations.

Fadia (1984). A discussion of Indian politics at the state level.

Prasad (1984). Examines the subject from the perspective of a constitutional lawyer.

Sarkaria (1988). The most recent and a comprehensive examination by a government commission of the framework and workings of Indian federalism.

Tummala (1992). A critical examination of the dissolution of the state government of Tamil Nadu in 1991.

4

The President

As Figure 2.1 showed, the President of India stands at the apex of the country's political system. The executive power of government is vested in the president, who is both the formal head of state and the symbol of the nation. Under the Indian constitution, the president has authority and dignity, but no power to rule. Instead, the president performs essentially a ceremonial role. The actual functions of government are carried out by the president only with the aid and advice of the prime minister and cabinet. For a president to use the executive powers formally vested in the office would be to misuse and abuse the trust reposed in the highest dignitary in the land. In this chapter we shall examine:

1. The manner in which the president is elected.
2. The powers of the president.
3. Some of the major controversies that have surrounded the office.
4. The relative merits of presidential and parliamentary government for India.

Choosing the President

Any Indian citizen who is at least 35 years old and qualified for election to the Lok Sabha is eligible to seek the presidency. The president is elected to office for five-year terms, and may be re-elected. In practice, only the first President of India, Dr Rajendra Prasad, was re-elected after the completion of the first term (see Table

4.1). In order to avoid creating a parallel centre of authority in a parliamentary system of government, the president is not directly elected by the people but is chosen instead by an electoral college consisting of the two houses of parliament at the centre and the state legislative assemblies. The system is designed to ensure the election of a truly national candidate following the two principles of uniformity among states and parity between the centre and the states.

The weight assigned to each state elector's vote reflects population ratios: one-thousandth of the total population of each state is divided by the number of elected legislators in the state assembly. (The quotient is rounded to the nearest whole number.) This ensures uniformity among states. For example, if the population of a state is 65 million, and the state assembly has 410 members, then the value of each state elector's vote will be $65m \div (410 \times 1000) = 158.54 = 159$. The aggregate value of the votes of the electors of all states (say 500 000) is then divided by the number of members of the Lok Sabha and the Rajya Sabha (say 750 altogether) to determine the value of the vote of each member of parliament (which in this case would be 667). The aggregate vote of the Lok and Rajya Sabhas combined thus necessarily equals the aggregate vote of all the state assemblies combined, thus satisfying the principle of parity between the centre and the states.

The method of voting is the single transferable vote, with electors casting first and second preferences. To be successful, a candidate must receive an absolute majority of the votes cast by the electoral college. As the lowest polling candidate is eliminated in each round, his or her preferences are transferred to other remaining candidates as per the electors' wishes until such time as one candidate crosses the threshold of 50 per cent of the votes cast. The lack of popular participation robs the choice of excitement and 'tamasha' normally associated with elections in India, but also serves to underline the dignity of the office.

The majority of India's presidents have come from political backgrounds. The first president, Dr Rajendra Prasad (1950–62), was a major personality in the nationalist struggle and also presided over the Constituent Assembly. His successor was the eminent philosopher Dr Sarvepalli Radhakrishnan. The full list of India's presidents is given in Table 4.1.

A serving president may die in office or resign, for example for personal health reasons. A president is also subject to impeachment by parliament for violating the constitution. Either house may prefer

TABLE 4.1

Heads of State of India, 1947–97

Governors General	
Earl Mountbatten	1947–48
C. Rajagopalachari	1948–50
Presidents	
Rajendra Prasad	1950–62
Sarvepalli Radhakrishnan	1962–67
Zakir Hussain	1967–69
Varahagiri Venkata Giri	1969–74
Fakhruddin Ali Ahmed	1974–77
Neelam Sanjiva Reddy	1977–82
Giani Zail Singh	1982–87
R. Venkataraman	1987–92
Shankar Dayal Sharma	1992–97

a charge by a two-thirds majority, which is then investigated by the other house with the president having the right to appear and be represented. For the president to be removed from office the charge must be upheld by a two-thirds majority in the investigating chamber of parliament as well. No president has so far been sought to be impeached. The political powerlessness of presidents suggests that the impeachment provision may be more of a safety-valve than a genuine tool for curbing a renegade head of state. Other than impeachment, the president is not answerable to any court for actions taken in the course of performing official duties.

The president is assisted by the vice-president. The latter is elected for a five-year term by the two houses of parliament in a joint session rather than by an electoral college. Responsibilities include presiding over the sessions of the Rajya Sabha, deputising for the president as necessary and succeeding the president if the latter should die in office, be incapacitated, resign or be impeached.

There is no firm convention of the vice-president succeeding a retiring president. Sarvepalli Radhakrishnan, Zakir Hussain and V. V. Giri did serve an apprenticeship as vice-presidents before being elected to the presidency, but the tradition was broken with the election of Fakhruddin Ali Ahmed in 1974. In July 1992, Vice-President Dr Shankar Dayal Sharma was elected president by 66 per cent of the 4367 state and federal electors against a challenge from lawmaker George Swell, a tribal Christian. In August 1992, Kocheril

Raman Narayanan became the first Scheduled Caste member to be elected Vice-President.

As with all political systems, the choice of presidents and vice-presidents involves political judgment and delicate balancing acts. This is especially true over a period of time. The offices must be rotated between the major regions (in particular between north and south) and between the several constituent groups of the Indian population (especially Hindu and Muslim and, in the 1980s, Sikhs – Giani Zail Singh was a Sikh). The one balance that has not been struck so far is the gender balance: no woman has been president of India.

The 1967 presidential election was the first to be genuinely contested by the opposition. Dr Prasad had won with 84 and 99 per cent of the votes in 1952 and 1957 respectively; Dr Radhakrishnan with 98 per cent in 1962. The Congress candidate in 1967 was Dr Zakir Hussain, the opposition's was former Chief Justice of India K. Subba Rao. There was an unfortunate communal controversy injected into the election because Dr Hussain was a Muslim. In the event, he won by a substantial majority: 56:44 per cent of the electoral college votes. As we shall see, the 1969 presidential election following the death of Zakir Hussain was an especially exciting affair because of the split in the Congress Party.

Powers

Under normal circumstances, the powers of the president of India are merely ornamental, comprising appointive, dismissive, legislative and symbolic functions. Presidential ambitions have been circumscribed too by the method of election: chosen by legislators rather than by direct election, presidents may not challenge those who have been directly elected by the people.

· The president appoints the prime minister and, on the latter's advice, the cabinet; the justices of the Supreme Court and state high courts; the Attorney General and the Comptroller and Auditor General of India; members of special commissions and other high public officials; and the governors of states. The choice of prime minister is not a discretionary prerogative to be exercised by the president but is usually dictated by the party commanding a majority following in the Lok Sabha. When the country's first prime minister Jawaharlal Nehru died in office on 27 May 1964, President

Radhakrishnan had no Indian precedent to guide his actions. He asked the senior cabinet minister, Gulzarilal Nanda, to take on the office until the Congress Party chose a new leader. The procedure was repeated in January 1966 upon the death of Prime Minister Lal Bahadur Shastri, with Nanda once again assuming the mantle of caretaker prime minister until the ruling party chose Mrs Indira Gandhi as its parliamentary leader.[1] In most cases the power to appoint is matched by the power to dismiss: the prime minister formally holds office at the pleasure of the president. In reality the prime minister retains office as long as the confidence of the Lok Sabha can be demonstrated.

The president calls parliament into session, nominates twelve members of the Rajya Sabha, has the right to address both houses of parliament either separately or in joint session and the power to dissolve the lower house. Every bill that has been passed by parliament must be presented to the president for his formal assent before it can become law. Except for money bills, the president may withhold assent and return a bill for clarification, reconsideration or possible amendment by parliament. The presidential 'veto' can however be overridden by both houses of parliament simply passing the bill again. The president of India thus does not have a genuine veto over parliamentary powers, but can refer a matter back to parliament for a second opinion. Some types of bill, for example in respect of state boundaries, can be introduced in parliament only on the president's recommendation.

When parliament is not in session, the president is empowered under Article 123 of the constitution to issue ordinances on the advice of the government if immediate action is held to be necessary. The goal is to ensure that the governmental process does not come to a halt simply because parliament is not in session. The ordinances have the same force and effect as an act of parliament, but they must be laid before parliament for formal enactment within six weeks of parliament reconvening.

The president of India neither reigns nor rules over the country. Nevertheless, the person holding the august office represents and symbolises the nation. The president is the commander-in-chief of the armed services, receives ambassadors from other countries, represents India on state visits abroad and presides on the great national occasions. He has the power to grant pardons. Virtually in all cases, however, presidential powers are exercised only on the advice of the prime minister.

Controversies

Even though executive power is exercised by the prime minister and cabinet, and the president must act on their advice, the prestige of the office confers a measure of influence on the president. Another source of authority is the sworn obligation to preserve, protect and defend the constitution. Arguably, President Fakhruddin Ali Ahmed could have changed the course of recent Indian history if he had overcome presidential diffidence to demand endorsement from cabinet prior to signing the promulgation of the emergency as sought by Mrs Gandhi around midnight on 25 June 1975. For cabinet assent had not been sought, could not have been taken for granted, and indeed was not likely to have been forthcoming for that momentous decision. Once the emergency was a *fait accompli* and political dissenters were already in jail, members of the cabinet had little realistic alternative but to provide retroactive ratification of the decision.

The first president, Dr Rajendra Prasad, tried to break from the British convention that the Head of State is always bound by the advice of the prime minister and cabinet. Dr Prasad was unhappy, for example, with the Nehru government's attempt to reform Hindu personal law. He was prevailed upon in the end to accept the convention even in Indian conditions. As in Britain, therefore, some of the constitutional conventions and practices in India have been defined only as a result of tussles between different parts of the government.

Even so, some powers of the president – appointment of the prime minister, dissolution of parliament – can acquire political significance in a fluid or uncertain environment. This became a pertinent consideration only after the general and state elections of 1967 and the split in the Congress Party in 1969, which together ended the previously dominant stranglehold that the Congress had on the reins of power. The question that arose was: if a general election fails to produce a party with a majority in the Lok Sabha, then who deserves the right of first refusal for the prime ministership?

The answer could be: the leader of the party with the largest number of seats even if still short of a majority, as seems to be the convention in Britain. Such was also the case with the Congress Party's P. V. Narasimha Rao in 1991, the first government to be appointed to office in India without a committed majority in parliament. Of the 507 seats that were declared to be valid, Congress won 226, thereby falling 28 short of a majority. President

Ramaswami Venkataraman invited Narasimha Rao to form a government and prove a majority in parliament. The vote of confidence was sought and given on 15 July. The 241 Congress and allied MPs voted in the affirmative, 111 voted against and 112 abstained.

But there might be a different answer to the question of who deserves the right of first refusal. It could be the leader of a coalition which commands a majority, as was the case with V. P. Singh after the 1989 election. In the latter instance, the task was made easier for the president by the fact that incumbent Prime Minister Rajiv Gandhi interpreted the 1989 result as a failure to endorse his Congress Party and so did not seek to remain in office. It was noted in India and abroad that nothing so became Rajiv Gandhi as the manner of his leaving office. Under different circumstances, someone could retain the office and then use the considerable patronage available to a prime minister to coax wavering MPs to the side of the minority government, at least for a few months. There is a further consideration. India's anti-defection law requires at least one-third of a party's membership to break away, or else the defectors will face disqualification. But the speaker of the Lok Sabha has the sole and absolute power to decide when the law has been broken. The speaker is not chosen until after the Lok Sabha has assembled. There is therefore a crucial time-lag, during a fluid post-election but pre-session interregnum, for playing politics with the calculus of coalition-building.

Even if one party does command a comfortable majority in parliament, it may still be subject to the vagaries of intense intra-party competition for the prime ministership. In July 1979, when Morarji Desai's Janata government collapsed as a result of one faction withdrawing its support from the coalition, President Neelam Sanjiva Reddy asked Y. B. Chavan as the leader of the Congress opposition in the Lok Sabha to explore the possibility of forming an alternative government (see Exhibit 4.1). Chavan informed the president of his inability to form a stable government. Reddy was then faced by two rival claimants to the prime ministership: outgoing prime minister Morarji Desai and Charan Singh, whose defection had brought down the Janata government. For reasons that were never adequately explained, President Reddy gave first right to form a government to Charan Singh. The latter did not survive the first test of confidence in parliament in August. (The whole episode was an adroit political manoeuvre by Mrs Gandhi – de facto Leader of the Opposition – to break up and discredit the Janata coalition.)

EXHIBIT 4.1

Anatomy of a presidential decision to dissolve the Lok Sabha, 1979

11 July	Defections from the ruling Janata party deprive PM Morarji Desai of majority support in Lok Sabha
15 July	Desai submits resignation to President N. Sanjiva Reddy, is asked to carry on as caretaker PM
18 July	President Reddy invites Opposition Leader Y. B. Chavan of the Congress Party to form an alternative government
22 July	Chavan expresses inability to form stable government. Desai and Charan Singh, who led the group of Janata party defectors, assert competing claims to prime ministership
23 July	President Reddy asks Desai and Singh to submit to him lists of their respective supporters in Lok Sabha
27 July	Upon receiving and examining the two lists, President Reddy invites Charan Singh – who has been promised support by the Congress Party – to form a government and to seek a vote of confidence in Lok Sabha by the third week of August
28 July	Charan Singh is sworn in as Prime Minister
20 August	PM Singh is to seek vote of confidence in Lok Sabha when it meets at 10.45 a.m. Congress Party, with 80 MPs in Lok Sabha, decides not to support Singh government. Singh cabinet meets and decides to resign and recommend dissolution of Lok Sabha. At 10.30 a.m. Singh sends letter of resignation to President Reddy and recommends Lok Sabha dissolution
21 August	Jagjivan Ram, having taken over the leadership of the Janata party, writes to President Reddy staking a claim to form a government
22 August	Ram meets President Reddy and claims to have support of 278 MPs in 534-member Lok Sabha. Ram is promised that no precipitate action will be taken by Reddy. Following this meeting, Reddy confers with Chavan, Singh and others and then announces dissolution of Lok Sabha and fresh general election. Singh is to continue until then as caretaker PM. Elections are held in January 1980 and bring victory for Congress Party; Mrs Gandhi returns as prime minister

---

Jagjivan Ram, also of the erstwhile Janata government, now pressed his claims to prime ministership, but was denied the opportunity as the president ordered the dissolution of the Lok Sabha and retained Charan Singh as a caretaker prime minister until fresh elections were held in January 1980. The president was criticised for having accepted the advice to dissolve the house from a person who had never commanded the confidence of the house and for having gone back on an undertaking given to Ram earlier on the same day that no precipitate action would be taken.

Many observers believed that had Jagjivan Ram been given the opportunity, then his considerable parliamentary and political skills would have been sufficient to ensure a reasonable tenure in office. Some argued that Ram was denied the highest prize chiefly because he was a Harijan, the leader of the outcastes. The more widely believed explanation was that President Reddy still harboured old grudges, and remembered how Ram had swung the voting against his candidacy for the presidency back in 1969. A third possible motive might have arisen from the belief that fresh elections would produce a hung parliament, which in turn would expand the influence of the president as power-broker. Whatever the reason, the president's actions in the 1979 crisis were criticised for being partisan and motivated. They generated an immediate political and a lingering constitutional controversy.

Despite the controversy, the president's decisions were not in clear breach of established parliamentary conventions and did not foreshadow an attempt to expand the power available to the president in normal times. Indeed no president has been able to use his position to secure a greater share of day-to-day power.

Discretionary powers of the president can be equally important in regard to dissolving parliament and ordering fresh elections. For example, the V. P. Singh government fell in November 1990. In those circumstances, was President Venkataraman bound by the advice of the defeated prime minister to call fresh elections? Or was it within his discretionary authority to call on Chandra Shekhar to form a government and prove a working majority in parliament even if his faction had only 58 MPs? Was he bound by the latter's advice to order elections upon resignation on 6 March 1991? (see Katyal, 1991, p. 9). A presidential communique explained that the decision of 13 March 1991 to dissolve the Lok Sabha had been taken not because the prime minister had advised it, but because no political party had been prepared to form an alternative government upon the collapse of the existing one.

President Zail Singh created a political stir in early 1987 by withholding his assent to the Indian Postal (Amendment) Bill, popularly known as the 'Snoop Law', despite its having been passed by both houses of parliament. Such an action was unprecedented in independent India. A seasoned politician (he was Home Minister in 1982 before being elected president), Zail Singh was unlikely to overstep the bounds of constitutional propriety if the bill was passed again and sent back to him for assent. But he won public support for himself and for his office by the open expression of displeasure over a bill which would expand enormously the government's power to tamper with private correspondence. Among other things, the bill would have legalised the interception, withholding and destruction of private correspondence, and the raid and seizure of offices and vehicles of private couriers. President Singh suggested that letters should be opened only with a magisterial warrant and in the presence of the intended recipients.

As with other examples, this particular tension was partially a reflection of bad personal relations between the president and the prime minister. Mrs Gandhi had taken great care to observe protocol in being formally deferential to the president, for example by calling on him every week to keep him abreast of government matters. Rajiv Gandhi failed to maintain such habits of communication, and thereby caused offence to a long-time and senior member of the Congress Party who had been instrumental in appointing him prime minister in 1984. At the time of Mrs Gandhi's assassination, Rajiv was not even a member of the cabinet. Instead of asking the number two person in the cabinet, Finance Minister Pranab Mukherjee, to become prime minister, President Singh asked Rajiv Gandhi – the person who, in the president's considered opinion, had the best chance of being elected parliamentary leader of the ruling party.

Rajiv Gandhi defended his record in an address to the Rajya Sabha. He insisted that the president had been kept informed of all important matters of state. Replying by letter on 9 March 1987, President Singh claimed that he had been ignored and slighted by Gandhi and kept in the dark about many important state issues in violation of established constitutional conventions. For example, said the president, he had not been briefed on the prime minister's trip to the United States and a stopover in the Soviet Union. The president's letter was so forthright as to create a credibility gap between the two offices: 'the factual position is somewhat at variance with what has been stated by you', wrote the president to the prime minister (*SW*, 21 March 1987, p. 5). When Speaker Balaram Jakhar refused to permit a discussion of the controversy in the Lok Sabha, opposition parties staged a walk-out on 13 March. A public constitutional crisis like this was quite a departure from the discreet attempts by President Rajendra Prasad and Prime Minister Jawaharlal Nehru to define the roles and jurisdictions of their respective offices.

In the end Rajiv Gandhi decided that perhaps discretion was the better of valour and repaired his relations with Zail Singh. This was fortuitous, for by the end of 1987 the Gandhi government was embroiled in the Bofors arms scandal. President Zail Singh is believed to have held consultations on the possibility of dismissing the prime minister (*India Today*, 15 April 1988, pp. 32–40), but did not in fact proceed to do so.

The president can become embroiled in controversy if the party in power in New Delhi finds itself at odds with a different party in government at the state level. This plumbed fresh depths in 1991 when, as we saw in the last chapter, the state Government of Tamil Nadu was dismissed even when the governor balked at recommending such a course of action.

Sometimes the election of the president can itself become the arena for a power struggle between competing political factions. When President Zakir Hussain died in office in 1969, his deputy V. V. Giri took over as acting President. Constitutionally, the election of a new president was required within six months of the vacancy occurring. It was not until a second ballot that V. V. Giri was elected to the highest office in his own right, for the presidential election had become intertwined with the struggle for political supremacy between Mrs Gandhi and Congress Party stalwarts. The official Congress candidate was N. Sanjiva Reddy, a politician from within the party. Mrs Gandhi let it be widely known that her preferred candidate was V. V. Giri, an independent trade union leader. The latter's election signalled the triumph of Mrs Gandhi in parliament over the established Congress bosses who dominated the party organisation.

The election to the essentially ceremonial office therefore had significant political ramifications. It divided and split the Congress Party. It also underscored the potentially critical position of the president in the aftermath of the 1967 elections which had weakened the dominance of the Congress Party at both central and state levels. In the political uncertainty which prevailed after 1967, the normally routine functions of the president became imbued with political significance because of the discretionary latitude given to the president in making some decisions. Thus the issues were wider than a mere factional fight in the Congress Party between Mrs Gandhi and the so-called Syndicate or old guard which was displeased by her refusal to be a pliant prime minister.

Another debate which perhaps exercised an earlier generation is whether a president could abuse emergency powers granted under the constitution in order to capture real power. This particular concern seems to have abated in recent years, partly because constitutional conventions have become more firmly established, partly because the one example of a substantial abuse of emergency powers involved a prime minister (Mrs Gandhi, 1975–7) rather than a president.

The Indian constitution permits the imposition of emergency rule by the government under specified conditions. While an emergency is in force, the executive can rule under highly simplified procedures and ignore a whole range of constitutional checks on its powers under normal times. The president of India may declare a state of emergency under any one or more of three circumstances:

- Under Article 352 of the constitution, when there is a threat to the security of the country as a result of war or external aggression (as with the invocation of an emergency in 1962 and in 1971) or internal disturbance (as in 1975);
- Under Article 356, when there is a breakdown of constitutional government in a state – the argument that was used to justify the suspension of the communist government of Kerala in 1959 and that became a recurring feature of Indian politics after the end of Congress Party dominance in 1967. In these circumstances the president may assume the functions of government and have these exercised through the state governor, or direct the central parliament to exercise the powers of the state assembly, or make other provisions that may be deemed necessary;
- Under Article 360, when there is a threat to the financial stability of the country or part thereof.

In earlier years, some observers expressed the fear that these wide-ranging powers could be abused by an unscrupulous power-seeking president to launch a constitutional coup and establish a presidential dictatorship. For the powers granted to the president under emergency conditions are in theory extensive and, in combination with a pliant bureaucracy and a diffident judiciary, could destroy the country's parliamentary democracy. The reason for the granting of such wide-ranging powers recalls the dilemma of a fatal weakness inherent in republics that was highlighted by Abraham Lincoln in 1861. 'Must a government, of necessity, be too strong for the liberties of its people, or too weak to maintain its own existence?', he asked (Lincoln, 1919, p. 176). Time has also proven the fears of a presidential dictatorship to have been ill-founded. Experience has confirmed that the ultimate check on governmental excesses – be they by prime minister, cabinet or president – is public vigilance.

Presidential Government for India?

The more intensely debated question in recent times has been whether India would be better advised to switch from a parliamentary to a presidential system of government (see Noorani, 1990). In the Nehru era the question was not seriously addressed precisely because Prime Minister Jawaharlal Nehru held sway over party and parliament. In the mid-1960s the topic was raised, among others, by R. Venkataraman, who was destined to occupy the office himself in 1987. In a letter to the All-India Congress Committee (AICC) on 27 May 1965, Venkataraman, at that time a minister in the Madras government, wrote that 'the presidential system offers the best solution to the chaotic spectrum of splinter parties in India' (Datta-Ray, 1991a).

In a parliamentary system, the government is headed by a prime minister who is a member of the party or coalition commanding a majority in the legislature. A presidential system separates the executive from the legislature and places a directly elected president at the head of the executive branch. The prime minister is first among equals; the president has no equal.

As was noted in Chapter 2, cabinet government was one of the major political legacies of British rule. The debate on a presidential system is predicated on the belief that the performance of parliamentary government has been unsatisfactory. Disillusionment with the state of Indian politics is distilled into a desire to replace cabinet with presidential government. Only the latter, it is argued, can give the country the strong and stable government that the times demand for resolving its many ills. The executive has found the need for a parliamentary majority, in legislatures lacking cohesive and disciplined parties, to be especially debilitating. A fixed-term presidential government would free the executive from the perennial problem of ministerial instability and allow it to concentrate on actually governing the country. The desire for presidential government among some Indians thus betrays a double frustration: with the lack of authority and stability at the centre, and with the weakening of the central government under challenge from a number of states. A presidential type of government, proponents believe, would help to restore order to a troubled country, dilute the corruption of the political system and accelerate the pace of the country's development.

There were many in the Constituent Assembly who supported the American style of executive government for India. Majority sentiment however was in favour of retaining the British model with which both politicians and the people were familiar. Parliamentary institutions in India have evolved over more than a century. Most of the framers of the Indian constitution believed that with independence, Indians would be able to operate responsible government with skill and judgment.

Critics recalled that the parliamentary tradition in India is tainted with colonial authoritarianism. They were less than taken with the idea of adopting a system for independent India simply because the departing British had proclaimed its virtues. In a sense the relationship between the executive and the legislature under the Raj was more reminiscent of presidential systems than of Westminster. The departure of the British left an executive vacuum in India's governance. Collegial cabinets have shown singular incapacity to take decisive action when faced with urgent demands. The end result has been an inefficient, lax and demoralised administration. Even emergency powers vested in the president of India are in fact exercised by cabinet. The latter is incapacitated because it is subject to a multitude of pressures from contrary directions. Indecisiveness of government in India is thus a systemic defect: cabinet government produces policy drift and incoherence. By contrast the American president, it is argued, is more effective because power vests in one person's hands. The executive, being independent of the legislature, can be more single-minded in its pursuit of the national interest free of the debilitating distractions of vested interests.

The picture of the US president in such a critique is somewhat idealised. In many ways the US system can be said to fracture the power of government: it is a system of sharing of powers, not separation of powers among the three branches of the executive, the legislature and the judiciary. The much-vaunted powers of the US president place just as much a premium on the political skills of bargaining, persuasion and manipulation. If firmness of purpose and action is the key criterion, then a decisive and politically skilled head of government has less checks on authority in a parliamentary system than in a presidential one. Conversely, cabinet governments are more likely to have legislative majorities to implement policy programmes.

On the other hand, presidential government would be more stable – or so it is argued. The bane of Indian politics has been defections from ruling parties or ruling coalitions. An executive president (and gubernatorial counterparts at the state level) would be assured of uninterrupted tenure for the full term (if still subject to such other vagaries as death, assassination or impeachment). A directly elected president would have demonstrable popular authority. This has not always been the case with some individuals who have ended up being prime minister of India. Chandra Shekhar, the shortest-serving prime minister of India (November 1990–March 1991), was described as combining a strong personality with a weak party who would have thrived in a presidential system. His own response to this in an interview with an American correspondent was that presidential government promotes stability of administration. But parliamentary democracy is better suited to a country with such wide disparities as India because it ensures greater accountability (Crossette, 1991).

The apparent advantages of the presidential system are especially appealing to the military mind. Former Indian Army deputy chief Lt. Gen. S. K. Sinha wrote in favour of the presidential system in order to rid Indian politics of pettiness and corruption (Sinha, 1991, p. 12). The constitution, he said, had been designed at a time of political leaders with probity; the present crop of politicians lack 'quality, competence and character'. Legislators regard parliamentary tenure as a financial investment and are wont to interfere in the day-to-day running of administration on whim or venality. Presidents would have the freedom to recruit people of talent to their administrations.

Ironically, just a few months after the Indian general's praise of the presidential system, Bangladesh dismantled the presidential system imposed on it by a former military ruler. Bangladesh returned formally to parliamentary democracy in August 1991 to end 16 years of presidential rule and military dictatorship. The ruling Bangladesh Nationalist Party, the main opposition party the Awami League and the Jatiya Party of the deposed president Hossain Mohammad Ershad all supported the change. Introduced in parliament by Prime Minister Begum Khaleda Zia on 2 July, the adoption of the constitutional amendment bill on 6 August by a vote of 307 to nil (with 13 members absent) was greeted by cheers and applause in the house.

Parliamentarians will be predictably pleased with a change from a presidential system to cabinet government. A procedural difficulty in the way of changing to a presidential system in India is how the constitution could be changed to such a drastic extent. Is parliament competent to amend the basic structure of the constitution? If yes, then would it be prepared to abdicate its notional control over the reins of government to a bifurcated executive? Another substantial difficulty would arise from the need to replace cabinet government with presidential-type government at the state level as well, since otherwise there would be general confusion with the operation of two totally unrelated systems at federal and state levels. To replace parliamentary governments with executive governors in the states would weaken central authority. In itself this may not necessarily be such a bad thing; but it does undermine the argument that a presidential system is required in order to strengthen the apparatus of government in New Delhi.

The alternative would be to abandon federalism and transform states into mere administrative units in a unitary system. This would require still more radical constitutional surgery, is unlikely to be supported by state-level politicians who would see their livelihoods disappearing, and would remove politicians from the people still further. In short, changing from a parliamentary to a presidential system of government might turn out to be a case of exchanging one set of problems for another with regard to the stability of the central government, and inviting additional problems with regard to the stability of centre–state relations. Nor would it please the guardians of the Gandhian tradition who continue to press for genuine decentralisation of institutions.

Proponents of presidential politics for India would also do well to remember that the chief goal of the framers of the American constitution was not to create expansive and powerful government, but to limit it. Worries about paralysis of government were subordinate to fears of tyrannical government. The riposte that presidential models other than the US exist – the French system with its combination of a strong executive and a unitary government is especially attractive – still misses the point that institutional arrangements are not self-sustaining: they cannot of themselves generate the necessary support for a democratic yet effective polity.

In any case, the United States is exceptional among presidential systems in the longevity of its constitutional continuity. Many Latin American presidential regimes have been less fortunate, while President Corazon Aquino was no more noticeably decisive and effective in the Philippines than the more ineffectual prime ministers in India. One of the reasons for the lack of effectiveness in presidential systems is dyarchic legitimacy. In presidential systems, the president and the legislature can both invoke the mantle of democratic legitimacy. In the event of a clash between the president and the legislature, there is no democratic means of resolving differences of policy. This can be especially acute if the legislature is controlled by a party different from that of the president's. The latter, claiming independent authority and popular mandate, has no reason to defer to the legislature, and indeed will be perceived as weak for doing so. To the extent that a president can draw upon plebiscitarian authority, there will be a temptation to confuse executive–legislative clashes as a battle between the national interest of the president and the narrower interests of opposition legislators. President Aquino at times attempted to mobilise the people against alleged special interests in the legislature which were frustrating her programmes.

These are particularly striking contrasts to the institutions of votes of confidence in the legislature and the official leader of the opposition in parliamentary regimes. In cabinet systems, the only institution with a democratic legitimacy is parliament. Parliament is nominally supreme over the executive, and the representatives of different interests have constitutional status in the system of government.

The fact that the change of an executive president is accompanied by a wholesale replacement of senior public officials can also be disruptive of the administrative process. From this point of view it is parliamentary systems which provide greater continuity and stability of administration. A prime minister is first among equals in cabinet, with members of cabinet assuming joint ministerial responsibility for all government decisions and having independent power bases which the prime minister may ignore only at political peril. A presidential cabinet consists of appointees who are less likely to be independent-minded.

Another reason for the stability of parliamentary regimes in many European countries might well be the separation of the executive (head of government) and ceremonial (head of state) functions. (Or, in the language of the English writer Walter Bagehot, the 'dignified' and the 'efficient' functions of government.) The former role is made possible as the result of the president being the leader of a particular party and offering a partisan option in public policy. The ceremonial office requires the president (or monarch) to play the role of representing the entire nation and standing above the fray of party politics.

The fixed term of the chief executive makes presidential systems correspondingly more rigid. A president can usually be removed from office only by the uncertain, drastic and divisive process of impeachment. Parliamentary systems confer comparatively greater flexibility through the simpler expedient of votes of confidence on the floor of the house. Governments can be formed and re-formed to reflect changing political realities or alignments precisely because power resides in the office of the prime minister rather than in a popularly elected individual. When the V. P. Singh government lost the confidence of the Lok Sabha by a vote of 346–142 in November 1990, Chandra Shekhar was able to form a minority government with 58 MPs and the promised support of 196 Congress and 11 allied MPs. Superficially, the constant changeover of governments might project an image of volatility and instability. In fact, such flexibility can prevent a crisis of a particular government being converted into a regime crisis: the ouster of a prime minister poses no threat to democracy itself. If a prime minister ceases to enjoy the confidence of the people, party or parliament, then a replacement is possible without the necessity of another national election.

Parliamentary democracy can be more stable especially in societies characterised by deep social and political cleavages (Linz, 1991, p. 22). For in such circumstances, parliamentary regimes have built-in mechanisms for power-sharing, for example through coalition governments. Parliamentary governments have also been found to have a greater ability to rule in multiparty settings (Stepan and Skach, 1993). A presidential system takes a zero-sum game approach to political power with one winner and one or more losers for the entire term of presidential office. Parliamentary regimes place a relatively higher premium on the political skills of bargaining and consensus building. Coalitions can offer effective and continuous representation to a variety of interests which would be excluded from the administration in a presidential regime. Presidential systems in general are thought to have a higher propensity for executives to rule at the edge of the constitution, combined with a lesser ability for the removal of such executives, and a greater susceptibility to military coups (Stepan and Skach, 1993). Parliamentary government is held to be better suited to India's peculiar unity in diversity in particular because 'in contrast to a sort of *individual* presidential executive, the cabinet executive with *collective* responsibility can more adequately reflect the Indian diversities' (M. P. Singh, 1992, p. 361; emphasis in original).

Conclusion

The office of the president of India confers status bereft of power. The 44th constitutional amendment of 1978 changed Article 74 to eradicate the last vestiges of residual discretionary power of the president. Where previously the clause had called for cabinet and prime minister to aid and advise the president in the exercise of his functions, the altered clause specified that the prime minister and cabinet would aid and advise the president who would be obliged to act in accordance with such advice in the exercise of his functions.

In part the occasional controversies that have attended the office in independent India reflect a systemic flaw. The parliamentary model is adapted from Britain with its constitutional monarch. But in Britain the office is hereditary. As such the reigning monarch is not preoccupied with ensuring a further tenure in office and can instead concentrate on acting evenhandedly and avoiding controversy. In India, lacking the tradition of extensive consultation on the election of a president, there has been no bipartisan consensus on the role, functions and discretionary latitude appropriate to the office. Since in effect continuation in office depends on the prime minister's decision to reselect an incumbent president, the latter can sometimes give the impression of deferring to the political sensibilities of the party in power.

As the last comment would suggest, the discretionary latitude available to a president depends less on the office or the incumbent and more on the state of party politics in parliament or cabinet. If a prime minister commands the loyalty of cabinet and the confidence of parliament, and if the government in power is stable, then there is very little scope for independent presidential initiatives. For in the Indian political system, the epicentre of government is the prime minister and the cabinet, not the president. Accordingly, it is to these offices that we shall turn our attention in the next chapter.

Note

1. It has been claimed that President Radhakrishnan lobbied on behalf of Mrs Gandhi. If so, it represented a breach of constitutional propriety: but the matter did not become public until 1989, and so had no effect on the office of the president. See Manor, 1991, pp. 153–4.

Further Reading

Lijphart (1992). A collection of important and influential statements on the respective advantages and shortcomings, by advocates as well as analysts, of the presidential and parliamentary systems of democratic government.

Manor (1991). An examination of the Indian presidency in the context of constitutional heads of state.

Noorani (1990). Examines the parliamentary–presidential debate in the Indian context.

5

Prime Minister and Cabinet

As noted in the preceding chapter, while the president of India may be the head of state, the head of government is the prime minister. Article 74(1) of the constitution provided that 'There shall be a Council of Ministers with a Prime Minister at the head to aid and advise the President in the exercise of his functions'. On 17 March 1971, the Supreme Court judged the requirement to be mandatory, ruling that the president could not function without the aid and advice of prime minister and cabinet. As we saw in the last chapter, Mrs Indira Gandhi made assurance doubly sure by amending Article 74 of the constitution in 1978. In this chapter I will:

1. Examine the role of the prime minister in the Indian system of government.
2. Examine the tenures of the several prime ministers that India has had.
3. Examine the role of the cabinet in the Indian system of government.

Prime Minister

As in all parliamentary systems of government modelled on Westminster, the prime minister of India is the linchpin of the system of government. The convention is by now firmly established in Britain that the prime minister must be a member of the lower house of parliament. At the time of her selection as prime minister in 1966,

Mrs Gandhi was a member of the upper house of India's parliament, the Rajya Sabha. To deflect criticisms of this aspect of her power base, Mrs Gandhi was subsequently elected to the Lok Sabha from Rae Bareilly, which had been her father's constituency in the state of Uttar Pradesh. Rajiv Gandhi maintained the Nehru–Gandhi family tradition of representing Rae Bareilly in the Lok Sabha. Upon his assassination in 1991, there was considerable pressure brought to bear on his widow Sonia Gandhi by sections of the Congress Party to enter parliament from Rae Bareilly. If she was not prepared to do this in her own right, sycophants argued, then she should at least 'keep the seat warm' until daughter Priyanka Gandhi turned of age to enter politics. Their entreaties proved to be in vain.

The constitution defines the duties of the prime minister of India in Article 78, but not the powers of the office. It has fallen to the political scientists to identify the sources, agencies and instruments of the prime minister's power and authority. (Power denotes the capacity to compel or enforce obedience to the dictates of those issuing commands; authority denotes the right to demand obedience to the lawful edicts of the governor; the conceptual link connecting power to authority is legitimacy.) Eight sources of prime ministerial power may be listed: headship of the Council of Ministers, leadership of party, control of parliamentary activities, control of intelligence agencies, control of the bureaucracy, control of foreign policy, emergency powers, and personal charisma.

The prime minister is generally given a free hand in the appointment of members of parliament (MPs) to ministerial posts. In making the selections, the party leader must of course ensure adequate representation to various factions within the ruling party as well as to regional and sectarian interests in the country. For example in 1977, regardless of personal likes and dislikes, Prime Minister Morarji Desai had to include Charan Singh and Jagjivan Ram in his cabinet and give them powerful portfolios (finance and defence respectively). Sometimes public opinion may force certain changes even on dominant prime ministers. After the debacle of the war with China in 1962, for example, Prime Minister Jawaharlal Nehru had to drop his political alter ego V. K. Krishna Menon from the cabinet, for Krishna Menon had become identified in the public mind with the disasters of the whole China policy.

In general, nevertheless, a prime minister can exercise considerable influence on parliamentary colleagues and therefore on the destiny of the country through the prerogative of constituting, reconstituting and reshuffling the ministry – not to mention chairing the meetings. Mrs Gandhi began to assert herself against party elders almost from the start by inducting her own people into the ministry, such as Ashoka Mehta, G. S. Pathak and Fakhruddin Ali Ahmed.

In Western parliamentary governments, there is some tendency to leave particular individuals in charge of particular portfolios for a period of time so that they may develop and use specialised expertise. In India, Mrs Gandhi was prone to continual reshuffling of her ministries. She did this in part to demonstrate her total control, and partly to prevent potential rivals from developing independent power bases by keeping them off balance. But the net effect was to disrupt the smooth and efficient functioning of government. Rajiv Gandhi maintained his mother's tradition.

Playing musical chairs with cabinet choices enlarges the room for manoeuvre of a prime minister who wishes to control the agenda of government. The prime minister is leader of the majority party in parliament and the head of government. A party is elected to office on the basis of a policy platform. The party leader is exceptionally well placed to influence and shape the translation of party manifesto into government policy. The extreme example of prime ministerial control of parliamentary activities was probably the period of emergency rule by Mrs Gandhi (1975–7), when parliament was in effect converted into a personal rubber stamp. All constitutional fetters were removed from the de facto exercise of power by the prime minister, and opposition benches were to be found chiefly in the country's jails.

A recurring debate in India has revolved around the wisdom of fusing or separating the offices of head of party organisation and leader of the parliamentary wing of a political party. Does the combination of the two posts in one person promote streamlining of party affairs or invite authoritarian policy-making in the party? The question might seem strange to those familiar with parliamentary systems in the West which almost invariably separate the functions and the functionaries. It is a genuine enough agony for commentators of Indian politics, where the prime minister has quite often also been president of the organisational wing of the party, and therefore exercised a double source of power and authority. In the early years after independence, Nehru had to learn to live with another person as party president (Purushottam Das Tandon). But Tandon, the protege of the powerful Home Minister Sardar Vallabhbhai Patel, was outmanoeuvred by Nehru after the death of Patel. Nehru's assumption of the post of party president in September 1951 ended the so-called duumvirate, even though in later years he was to relinquish the party post firstly to a weak and relatively unknown person (U. N. Dhebar), and then to his daughter Indira Gandhi. The latter also acted as Nehru's social hostess, and accompanied him on many of his travels around the country and abroad.

Mrs Gandhi was Minister of Information and Broadcasting under Shastri before being catapulted into the prime ministership in 1966 by the party bosses who wanted a pliant woman, young in years and light in experience, at the head of the government. Her streak of independence was demonstrated in the devaluation of the rupee in June 1966, a decision taken without prior consultation with such senior party colleagues as Morarji Desai and party president Kamaraj Nadar. The 1967 general election saw the defeat of many of the party stalwarts: Kamaraj, Atulya Ghosh, S. Nijalingappa, S. K. Patil. With the split in the ruling Congress Party in 1969, Mrs Gandhi became dependent on minor parties of the left for her political survival.

Mrs Gandhi's fortunes revived with the general election of 1971 and the state elections of 1972, which together gave her a commanding position in New Delhi (352 of 518 Lok Sabha seats) and around the country (majorities in 15 states and one Union Territory). Thereafter, she began to dominate all party organs: the All-India Congress Committee (AICC), the Congress Working Committee (CWC), the Congress Parliamentary Board (CPB) and the Central Election Committee. Even in defeat in 1977, when the organisational sections of the Congress Party deserted her, she abandoned them and effectively took the Congress Party with her: as was only too vividly demonstrated with her electoral triumph in 1980. It may not have been entirely accurate to say, as her many sycophants did, that 'India is Indira, and Indira is India'. She did prove the veracity of the saying that 'Indira is Congress, and Congress is Indira'.

The peculiarities of Indian politics give larger scope for prime ministerial control of political life through domination of party processes. Thus Rajiv Gandhi was the final arbiter of the choice of Congress Party candidates for elections from all constituencies. And the party organisation became an instrument for the prime minister of India to control and dominate state politics as well. In 1975, for example, in the context of factional party infighting within the state unit of Congress, Uttar Pradesh Chief Minister H. N. Bahuguna declared that 'Mrs Gandhi is our Supreme Court' (*Statesman*, 25 May 1975). In February 1982 one chief minister (T. Anjiah of Andhra Pradesh) was asked to resign because he had been too effusive in greeting the prime minister (Rajiv Gandhi) during the latter's visit to the state.

Heads of government have also been partial to abusing their control of intelligence services for personal and party-political purposes. Intelligence agencies traditionally come under prime ministerial oversight, not the least because heads of government would mistrust potential rivals in charge of such key operations. The size and complexity of India, combined with a colonial past, saw the emergence of several intelligence agencies: the Intelligence Bureau, including a Research and Analysis Wing (RAW); the Central Bureau of Investigation (CBI); the Criminal Investigation Department (Special Branch); and the Directorate of Revenue Intelligence are some of the more important agencies. Established in 1968 as an external intelligence agency, RAW was separated from the Intelligence Bureau in 1969 and placed under the cabinet secretariat with the prime minister in the chair.

Mrs Gandhi expanded the powers and activities of RAW during the 1975–7 emergency period and gave it an internal surveillance role, with the director of RAW reporting directly to her. The Shah Commission report (withdrawn from sale and circulation by government order on 7 March 1980 after Mrs Gandhi's return to power) documented how the various branches of intelligence succumbed to political pressure and were used to harass, intimidate and imprison political opponents during the two years of emergency rule. RAW was stripped of its internal surveillance functions by the Janata government (1977–9). But in general Mrs Gandhi was not the only prime minister of India to use the intelligence agencies to keep abreast of moves and counter-moves by potential challengers and to harass political opponents.

In addition to using intelligence agencies for maintaining a watching brief over opponents and potential rivals, the prime minister can exercise political control through the regular channels of bureaucracy (including the police). This is especially so in India where the centralisation of the elite administrative and police services facilitates vertical control of their activities. Early in her tenure Mrs Gandhi introduced such phrases as 'committed bureaucracy' in her political vocabulary. Personal loyalty to the prime minister became the most important criterion in determining promotions and assignments of senior officials. At the same time, the scope for career and post-career rewards (e.g. state governorships) was greatly expanded by consolidating centralisation of political authority and of the economy. A bureaucratic command economy was created with government officials in charge, for example, of banks that had been nationalised. The opportunities for rewarding loyal officials were thereby greatly multiplied. The opportunities were fully exploited by the Janata government with their own favoured appointments, postings and dismissals, and the process was repeated when Mrs Gandhi regained power in 1980.

The greatest opportunity for a prime minister of India to exercise total power within the constitution comes during the declaration of a national emergency. It is not an exaggeration to say that the 1975–7 experience was a period of prime ministerial dictatorship (see Thakur, 1976).

The period of emergency rule was an aberration even by Indian standards. Increasingly in the modern world, heads of governments of all countries have begun to play the most visible role in determining their countries' foreign policies. India is no exception to the rule. Nehru was a founding father of nonalignment and the chief architect of independent India's foreign policy. Prime ministerial dominance of foreign policy did not diminish under his successors. No one in India or abroad was in any doubt that the country's foreign policy during Mrs Gandhi's premiership was determined first and foremost by her, regardless of who may have been foreign minister. The same remained true of Rajiv Gandhi. An international role in turn enhances the domestic status and stature of the prime minister. Nehru profited from his image of being a world statesman, and Rajiv Gandhi tried to carve out a niche by such means as the Gandhi–Gorbachev Delhi Declaration of 27 November 1986. All major international conferences, for example the Commonwealth Heads of Governments Meeting (CHOGM) are attended by the prime minister personally. Visits abroad to other countries and to such forums as the United Nations are treated as major political events where the prime minister is on show.

Prime Ministers of India

Both Rajiv Gandhi and Soviet leader Mikhail Gorbachev were to leave office with a higher reputation overseas than in their own countries. In 1991, trying to recapture (with some success) the mystique of earlier years by mingling more freely with the people, Gandhi diluted the heavy presence of the security apparatus around him and paid for it with his life. It remains to be seen whether the magic of the Nehru–Gandhi name will fade or be rekindled by one of Rajiv Gandhi's two children.

As this indicates, the final source of prime ministerial authority is the individual attributes and charisma of the person occupying the office. Nehru, Indira and Rajiv Gandhi did not lack for that intangible yet vital ingredient. Yet of this trinity, only Nehru satisfied the three leadership attributes of diagnosis, prescription and implementation. His vision of progress for the country included an identification of the ills afflicting it, the corrective course of action required to effect a cure, and an appropriate strategy for mobilising the resources needed to bring it about. Mrs Gandhi did not lack in mobilising ability. But her definition of the major problems confronting India tended to be episodic, while her policy recommendations were often just populist measures. Rajiv Gandhi had a clearer blend of diagnosis and prescription, but lacked the political skills and stamina for a sustained implemention of his often worthwhile programmes.

In the initial years, the authority of the first prime minister Jawaharlal Nehru was somewhat tempered by the presence of powerful cabinet colleagues around the decision-making table, for example Sardar Patel. But this did not last, for most of the other leaders of the nationalist movement of pre-independence Congress did not survive very long into independence. Sardar Patel, for example, died in 1950. Prime ministerial leadership was more genuinely collective during Lal Bahadur Shastri's tenure most of the time, although not always. Mrs Gandhi began her reign being reasonably democratic, but ended it anything but. If Morarji Desai of the Janata government came to be widely derided for collective 'non-government', then the comment would be just as applicable to the Janata Front government headed by V. P. Singh.

Jawaharlal Nehru became the first prime minister of India (see Table 5.1) after already having served an exciting and lengthy apprenticeship in party and national politics before independence. An articulate and sensitive intellectual, he was also a shrewd tactician and an international statesman. Wealthy and patrician by birth and upbringing, he was a socialist by conviction who could establish easy rapport with the common folk. He was to leave his mark on the

TABLE 5.1

Prime Ministers of India, 1947–94

Prime Minister	Party	Dates	
Jawaharlal Nehru	Congress	15 Aug 1947–27 May 1964	died
Lal Bahadur Shastri	Congress	9 Jun 1964–11 Jan 1966	died
Indira Gandhi	Congress	24 Jan 1966–24 Mar 1977	defeated
Morarji Desai	Janata	24 Mar 1977–28 Jul 1979	defeated
Charan Singh	Janata	28 Jul 1979–14 Jan 1980	defeated
Indira Gandhi	Congress	14 Jan 1980–31 Oct 1984	died
Rajiv Gandhi	Congress	31 Oct 1984–1 Dec 1989	defeated
V. P. Singh	National Front	2 Dec 1989–10 Nov 1990	defeated
Chandra Shekhar	Samajvadi Janata	10 Nov 1990–21 Jun 1991	defeated
P. V. Narasimha Rao	Congress	21 Jun 1991–	n.a.

constitution of India, on its system of mixed economy, on its identity as a secular parliamentary democracy, and on its place in the world as an independent and nonaligned nation. His personal commitment to rational–scientific 'modernism' may have led him to downplay the importance of traditional factors in Indian society and politics. His imprint on Indian politics will be evident for many years yet.

By contrast, **Lal Bahadur Shastri** was in power for too brief a period to have left a lasting impact. It seems fair to say that he was something of an unknown factor when he became prime minister in June 1964, and died in January 1966 having earned the respect and affection of his countrymen. His modesty and humility sat well with the people, his consensus-building skills were useful in guiding the party and the country through the trauma of Nehru's death, and he was seen to have coped with courage and resolution with the war with Pakistan in 1965.

Upon Shastri's death, the prime ministership reverted to the Nehru family with the election of his daughter **Indira Gandhi**. Of all India's prime ministers, she was the most controversial as well as the most dynamic: perhaps the two are related. She was also to reveal the greatest authoritarian tendencies. Her considerable political talents were most on display in moments of greatest political danger. In ordinary circumstances, she could be guilty of policy drift and incoherence. Under threat, she acted decisively and with little regard for the niceties of democratic politics. In the way she ran her government, Indiraji was often overbearing and secretive. In the way she approached parliament and the opposition, she was hostile and dismissive where patience and subtlety would have won bouquets instead of brickbats. On the positive side, she spoke and acted in defence of India's interests in its foreign relations, and spoke with feeling of the plight of the country's poor. On the debit side, she swept aside democratic norms and parliamentary conventions in pursuit of power for herself and her dynasty, destroying Congress as an organised party with a mass base and holding the country hostage to her authoritarian whims in the 1975–7 years. Yet she accepted defeat at the polls in 1977 with grace, fought her way back into power by means of the ballot in 1980 and was felled by assassins' bullets in 1984. She had no ideology for a Congress Party that was made ruthlessly subservient to her personality and which she split twice for personal survival. She was twice given clear mandates but was guided by no clear mission; that was her tragedy. Yet she was possessed of a certain political tenacity that would have been the greater if harnessed to a larger purpose; that was the nation's hope. The re-election of Mrs Gandhi in 1980 marked a triumph of hope over experience; her assassination in 1984 dashed hopes that the country could at last profit from her considerable experience. A woman who could turf her widowed daughter-in-law out of the family house, when she put her mind to it she could be charm personified. 'An iron fist in a velvet glove' might have been a phrase coined with her in mind.

The orderly transfer of power in 1977 brought **Morarji Desai**, a long-time rival of Shastri and Mrs Gandhi, to the prime ministership at the head of the country's first non-Congress government. A product of Congress culture and the custodian of conservative policies, he could be self-defeatingly self-righteous and inflexible. The achievements of his government in reversing the creeping institution-alisation of authoritarian rule were overshadowed by his coalition disintegrating because of internal contradictions. Some of his supporters proved only too easy prey for Mrs Gandhi's political machinations, while he himself revived memories of her in having a soft spot for his own son.

The collapse of the Desai government, engineered by Mrs Gandhi, promised the fruits of a political deal to **Charan Singh**. Unfortunately, Singh began and remained a regional leader from Uttar Pradesh despite his national ambitions. His most notable impact on Indian politics was to end the Desai government by splitting the Janata coalition.

The real fruits of the 1979–80 crisis were plucked by Mrs Gandhi. With her assassination on 31 October 1984, **Rajiv Gandhi** became India's sixth prime minister. The bearer of a famous name and the beneficiary of the best education that money could buy, he was not particularly attracted to politics but turned instead to flying planes. When his younger brother and Mrs Gandhi's political heir-apparent Sanjay Gandhi died on 23 June 1980 trying to learn to fly as well, Rajiv gave up flying to turn to politics in his mother's hour of need. At the time of his election to the prime ministership, he had little to commend him except his political lineage and the need to reassure a nation distraught with shock and grief. He assumed the mantle of leadership with calm and assurance, but failed to provide leadership in protecting innocent Sikh victims of organised mob fury in search of vengeance for Mrs Gandhi's assassination by Sikh bodyguards. The sympathy wave generated by his mother's death gave him a commanding 415 of the 542 Lok Sabha seats in the general election of December 1984.

Welcomed on the political stage as Mr Clean, Rajiv Gandhi was forced into opposition tainted by the Bofors scandal. The historic but fruitless Punjab and Assam accords of 1985 were precursors to the India–Sri Lanka accord of 1987 which entangled large numbers of Indian troops in a debilitating civil war in a foreign country. While the early years of his term were marked by a drive for modernisation, by 1989 he seemed to have relapsed into the discredited power politics of the old Congress Party. He gradually frittered away the nation's goodwill and became increasingly remote, inaccessible and even arrogant as he grew accustomed to the power and perks of office. Yet he also emulated his mother in accepting defeat in a general election with grace and dignity, and then two years later became a martyr to his belief in a leader being able to reach out to his people.

Rajiv Gandhi proved unable or unwilling to transform Indian politics from an amoral and corrupt pursuit of power and money into the nobler cause of helping the people. **V. P. Singh** came into power at the head of the Janata Front coalition like a knight in shining armour who was going to cleanse and purify Indian politics. He left office a year later with his personal reputation in tatters and the nation in flames. On one front, he tried to defend the Muslim minority from chauvinistic and militant Hindus. On another front, his plans to increase quota reservations for the lower castes to almost 50 per cent led to riots, demonstrations and despair on an unprecedented scale. Widespread respect for a political crusader turned into concentrated hatred for a ruthless political opportunist. Nor was he able to hold together the Janata Front government.

Chandra Shekhar holds the distinction of having served as prime minister for the shortest term. Manipulating his way into office in November 1990 by sabotaging the Janata Front government and entering into a pact with the opposition Congress Party, he resigned in March 1991 to assume a caretaker role until fresh elections were held in May–June. Something of a political recluse (he had never held a cabinet post) and an old-fashioned socialist prior to assuming office, Chandra Shekhar left office with a reputation for forthright common sense and courage. The secret to the Shekhar success seems to have been to act as if he was going to be prime minister for a full term (Padgaonkar, 1991). He simply ignored the many weaknesses afflicting his government: its extremely small size in parliament, the paucity of talent in its thin ranks, the distrust and contempt for it of the intelligentsia, its vulnerability to mischief from within its own ranks and, most importantly, its critical dependence on the Congress Party for survival in office. In the circumstances, Chandra Shekhar could have been expected either to act timidly so as not to alienate Congress, or to go out in a blaze of glory with an unending series of populist measures. In the event, he chose the unexpected third course of thinking, speaking and acting like a long-term head of government. On the pressing issues of the day – the mosque–temple controversy in Ayodhya, the political ferment in Assam, Kashmir and Punjab – he eschewed doctrinaire rigidity and tried to strike a balance between legitimate grievances and the need to uphold constitutional order. In the end (March 1991) Chandra Shekhar resigned and forced a general election rather than subject himself to continual humiliation for the sake of staying in power for a few weeks more. But in the ensuing election, his party paid the price of having betrayed the voters of 1989 and saw its strength collapse from 58 to 5 MPs.

P. V. Narasimha Rao was elected parliamentary leader of the Congress Party at the height of the crisis following Rajiv Gandhi's assassination during the 1991 election campaign. With no power base of his own even in his home state of Andhra Pradesh, contemplating retirement at the age of 70 after a heart by-pass operation, he was expected to be a transitional leader to see the party through the second round of elections. But in part his opponents within Congress neutralised each other, in part he profited from a clean and enemy-free record despite having been in politics for more than four decades.

Once in power, Narasimha Rao demonstrated a hitherto unsuspected desire and flair for leadership. His minority Congress government faced major and immediate policy problems in July 1991. Dwindling foreign reserves and closed lines of credit from overseas aid donors and banks pushed India closer to the brink of defaulting on loan repayments than ever before. The Rao government began immediately to tackle the underlying structural deficiencies behind India's economic difficulties: liberalising the economy, dismantling the apparatus of controls and the culture of subsidies and loss-making public sector enterprises built up over four decades to create a command economy, and opening up the country to foreign investment.

Rao's staying power was helped by a number of factors. No one in the Congress Party wished to assume the burden of prime ministership in such straitened circumstances; no other party wished to risk the reins of government for the same reason; no serving politician wished to court electoral disaster by forcing the country to go the polls so soon yet again, sensing that the mood of the people was for a period of quiet consolidation; the two main opposition combines of the BJP and the National Front–left parties treated each other as political untouchables; and international trends took away realistic alternatives to the Rao government's policy shifts. The collapse of the Soviet Union in particular exercised a sobering influence, for far too many parallels could be drawn between the state of the Indian union and the disintegrating Soviet Union.

To these external factors should be added individual personality traits. Narasimha Rao's plainness and modesty sat well with the Indian people.[1] His directness was quietly reassuring, while his conciliatory and remote presence avoided causing offence to any major party barons. Sonia Gandhi's steadfast refusal to be drawn into politics denied potential opponents the opportunity to rally round a known personality. Political success for Rao in the nation was capped by election to the party presidency in February 1992.

Yet cautious Indians remembered that some of the earlier prime ministers too had demonstrated considerable promise in the early months of their tenure. And by 1993 contradictory assessments of Rao were commonplace in the Indian press. One senior journalist asserted that Rao's performace was sloping downwards with the passage of time: economic liberalisation had failed to deliver, the Ayodhya mosque controversy had been allowed to bubble until it exploded, there was no policy on Kashmir and foreign policy was stagnant (K. Nayar, 1992, p. 7). Another argued that the government had been pulled together after the Ayodhya debacle, the drive to economic liberalisation had been maintained, domestic trouble spots had been tackled in Assam, Maharashtra and Punjab before attention turned to Kashmir, and the foreign policy challenges had been confronted. The 'mixture of courage and caution' had been misinterpreted as vacillation and indecisiveness (Jha, 1993, p. 9). Consensus and decisiveness do not always mix.

Cabinet

India's political system is correctly described as cabinet government. Yet while the Council of Ministers has constitutional status, the cabinet does not get a mention in the constitution. Accordingly, its powers are defined by convention and usage.

The Council of Ministers consists of (in order of precedence):

- Cabinet Ministers
- Ministers of State
- Deputy Ministers
- Parliamentary Secretaries

The total strength of the Council of Ministers can range up to sixty members (the Rao ministry in 1991 was 58 strong), with the number of cabinet ministers averaging between 15 and 20. Theoretically, the full executive is the Council of Ministers, with cabinet being but one of its four components. In reality, cabinet is more important, influential and powerful than the full council. The latter meets rarely, cabinet meets frequently. In some respects ministers of state and deputy ministers are closer to being departmental heads than cabinet ministers. Every minister must be a member of parliament of either house, or become one within six months of appointment either through nomination or by election. A minister may take part in the proceedings of either house of parliament, but voting rights are restricted to the house to which he or she belongs.

In India, cabinet serves three major functions:

- It is the body which determines government policy for presentation to parliament;
- It is responsible for implementing government policy;
- It carries out inter-departmental coordination and cooperation.

We should note however that the cabinet does not consider the budget. The latter is the responsibility not of the cabinet as a whole, but of the finance minister, the prime minister and another one or more allied ministers.

The power and influence of cabinet collectively or cabinet ministers individually depends firstly on the personality of the prime minister of the day, and secondly on how independently powerful and independent-minded cabinet ministers are. For all his commanding stature in the country, even Nehru had to contend with Sardar Patel who was second only to Nehru in influence in cabinet and party and considered to be Nehru's equal in many respects. Other principal members of cabinet with independent power bases of their own were also able to play substantial political roles.

By contrast, Mrs Gandhi established a more personalised and centralised form of prime ministerial government. Efforts by the Janata government to restore the principle and substance of collective responsibility fell victim to internecine warfare within cabinet. Mrs Gandhi reverted to her *durbar* (the royal court) of family and personal advisers after re-election in 1980. Her dominant role in cabinet was reflected also in the expanded size and enhanced status of the prime minister's secretariat (set up by Shastri in 1964), to the extent that it took on some of the characteristics of the American president's executive office. The maintenance of the tradition by Rajiv Gandhi meant that cabinet continued to languish as an institution. Influence was a function not of cabinet office but of the prime minister's patronage. So long as cabinet 'colleagues' could be prevented from developing an independent power base, their services could be dispensed with at the prime minister's pleasure with little risk or cost to the latter.

'Responsible government' ensures that the head of state acts only on the advice of responsible advisers. A trifle confusingly, and as in other parliamentary governments, the Indian cabinet operates on the basis of the two further working principles of cabinet responsibility and ministerial responsibility. The former places individual ministers under the collective cabinet, the latter puts them in charge of government departments.

Firstly, all cabinet ministers accept the principle of collective responsibility. That is, under collective leadership each minister accepts and agrees to share responsibility for all decisions of cabinet. Doubts and disagreements are confined to the privacy of the cabinet room. In that room, decisions are rarely taken by formal vote. Instead, cabinet proceeds by a sense of the meeting after discussion has taken place. If any member of cabinet is unable to support government policy in parliament or in the country at large, then that member is morally bound to resign from cabinet. Foreign Minister M. C. Chagla resigned from cabinet in 1967 because he believed that the government's educational policy was likely to endanger and undermine national unity. A dissenting member may not vote against government policy in parliament or speak out against it in public. Minister of State Mohan Dharia was dismissed from the Council of Ministers in 1975 because of public dissent from government policy on how to handle Jaya Prakash Narayan's people's movement. Open bickering between members of the Janata government on matters of public policy was the prelude to the collapse of the government in 1979. For more than two years the Janata cabinet was less a forum for reaching collective decisions than an arena for factional conflict.

Secondly, each member of cabinet accepts full political responsibility for all acts of commission and omission by officials of the department which falls under her or his portfolio. Officials advise the minister and implement the minister's decisions. The decision itself is a matter for the minister's political judgment, and it is the minister rather than any official who has to be prepared to pay the political price for flawed decisions. Thus the head of Defence Minister V. K. Krishna Menon was the sacrifice paid by the Nehru government for the disastrous performance of the Indian military in the war with China in 1962.

Cabinet ministers accept responsibility for departmental acts because in the system of cabinet government they are expected and required to exercise firm control over the bureaucracy. One of the reasons why Nehru did not abandon the bureaucratic structure inherited from the British colonial administration was that he and his ministers provided crisp and clear policy guidance to their civil servants. Equally, they asserted and established the supremacy of political control over the military: hence the sacrifice of Krishna Menon. Ministers would be responsible for defence policy, soldiers would be left to carry out military operations. Thus ministerial responsibility is the doctrinal assertion of the supremacy of politicians over the machinery of government.

Cabinet is assisted in its tasks by several committees. The most important of these deal with parliamentary, political, foreign, defence and economic affairs. The key cabinet committees are always dominated by the senior ministers, starting with the prime minister: Nehru was chairman of 9 of the 10 cabinet committees during his time. Important issues are usually examined in committee before being taken to the cabinet as a whole for debate and approval or rejection. The committee system can be used by a prime minister or an 'inner cabinet' of powerful ministers to pre-empt decisions and use cabinet chiefly for ratification.

In principle the cabinet is the chief governing authority in the country. It tenders advice to the president for the exercise of all his functions, and it provides legislative leadership in parliament, political leadership in the country and administrative leadership of government departments. It is the final arbiter of India's external relations: from declaration of general principles of foreign policy to decisions of war and peace and negotiations of trade agreements and military alliances. Its central role in government also makes it the focus of most interest- group activity and lobbying, which in turn makes it one of the chief mediators and conciliators of sectoral interests. Yet nominally at least both prime minister and cabinet are subject to control by the parliament, the institution to which we shall turn in the next chapter.

Note

1. 'As an aspiring political analyst and newcomer to the English language put it: "I'm admiring him [Rao] for his shoutlessness"' (Badhwar, 1992, p. 24).

Further Reading

Gopal (1979). An authorised account of the Nehru years based on privileged access to his papers.

Hart (1976). A useful collection of essays on the impact of Mrs Gandhi's prime ministership on India's major political institutions.

Jayakar (1992). An intimate portrait rather than a critical evaluation.

Malhotra (1989). A fine personal and political biography of Mrs Gandhi which is objective, fair and critical while still remaining friendly towards its subject.

Manor (1994). Essays on several dimensions of the prime minister's role and authority.

Pal (1983). Traces the evolution of the role of the prime minister.

Sen Gupta (1989). A critical evaluation by an elder statesman among Indian political commentators.

6

Parliament

The chief means by which the British parliament usurped the monarch's power of rule over subjects was 'responsible government'. Indians were introduced to the novel institution of the legislature by the British. As early as 1833, a conceptual distinction was made between the executive and legislative functions of the Governor-General's Council. After the Indian Councils Act of 1861, there was both a gradual expansion of the legislative tasks entrusted to the legislative councils, and a progressive incorporation of 'natives' into the legislative machinery. The central Legislative Council was enlarged by the Morley–Minto reforms of 1909 at the same time as officials ceased to make up the majority of provincial legislative councils. The belief persisted nonetheless that parliamentary politics was not suited to Indian conditions. Thus Lord Morley, Secretary of State for India, in the House of Lords during the first reading of the Indian Councils Bill on 17 December 1908: if the bill 'were attempting to set up a Parliamentary system in India, or if it could be said that this chapter of reforms led directly or necessarily up to the establishment of a Parliamentary system in India, I, for one, would have nothing to do for it' (Hansard, *Parliamentary Debates*, House of Lords, 17 December 1908, coll. 1985).

Established British opinion had begun to change by the end of the First World War. The Montagu–Chelmsford reforms of 1919 were introduced with the declared aim of gradually developing self-governing institutions leading to the progressive realisation of responsible government in India. Legislative councils were enlarged, made more representative and given more 'nation-building' powers as well as their own sources of revenue (Hanson and Douglas, 1972, p. 95). Many Indians cut their executive and legislative teeth in the period of dyarchy (1919–35). The Government of India Act of 1935 both widened and deepened responsible government. The electorate was expanded by extending the franchise; ministries were made responsible to enlarged provincial legislatures; and dyarchy was abolished as, with a few key exceptions, provincial subjects were handed over to ministries. The Act thus entailed a double shift of political gravity: from appointed officials to elected representatives, and from British to Indian hands. The process was completed with independence and the drawing up of the constitution.

In this chapter, I shall look at:

1. India's lower house of parliament.
2. India's upper house of parliament.
3. The role of committees in facilitating parliament's work.
4. The role of the opposition in parliament.
5. The question of parliamentary sovereignty.
6. State legislatures.
7. The transplant of parliamentary institutions to India.

Lok Sabha

In parliamentary governments, the cabinet is responsible to the parliament. The Parliament of India is bicameral. The lower house is the Lok Sabha or the House of the People. Its members are elected on the basis of universal adult suffrage. Every adult citizen of India is entitled to vote, other than non-residents, the insane, the criminal and those who have been convicted of corrupt electoral practices. The age of qualification was reduced in 1989 from 21 to 18. Some statistical details of the ten general elections held between 1952 and 1991 are given in Table 6.1, while Table 6.2 gives a snapshot of the geographical spread of the Lok Sabha seats across the country. As the latter table shows, of the 543 elective seats, 530 are from the 25 states and 13 are from the seven union territories. The distribution among the states is roughly in proportion to their populations. Of the 543 elective seats in the Lok Sabha, 423 are in the general category, 79 are reserved for scheduled castes (the former untouchables) and 41 for scheduled tribes. In a reserved constituency, only members of the scheduled castes and tribes may run for office, but all adults within the constituency may vote. The two nominated seats are filled by the president with representatives of the Anglo-Indian community.

TABLE 6.1
Lok Sabha elections, 1952–91

	1952	1957	1962	1967	1971	1977	1980	1984	1989	1991
Electorate (million)	173	194	218	251	274	321	364	400	499[a]	520
No of seats	489	494	494	520	519	542	527	542	543	543
Seats contested	479	482	491	515	518	540	526	507	523	524
Candidates	1874	1519	1985	2369	2784	2439	4629	5493	6158	8953
Polling stations	132560	220478	238355	267555	342944	373908	434442	479214	579810	594797
Voter turnout	46.6	67.1	55.4	61.3	55.3	60.5	56.9	63.4	59.6	57.0
Date of dissolution	14/4/57	31/3/62	3/3/67	27/12/70	18/1/77	22/8/79	31/12/84	27/11/89	13/3/91	–

Note: a. The age of voting was lowered from 21 to 18 in 1989, thereby swelling the size of the electorate.
Source: David Butler, Ashok Lahiri and Prannoy Roy, *India Decides: Elections 1952–1991* (New Delhi: Living Media, 1991); *Elections in India* (New Delhi: Ministry of Information & Broadcasting, 1991); Robert L. Hardgrave and Stanley A. Kochanek, *India: Government & Politics in a Developing Nation* (Fort Worth: Harcourt, Brace, Jovanovich, 1993); *India Today*; Myron Weiner, *India at the Polls, 1980* (Washington, DC: American Enterprise Institute, 1983).

TABLE 6.2

Geographical distribution of Lok Sabha seats

North		South	
Haryana	10	Andhra Pradesh	42
Himachal Pradesh	4	Karnataka	28
Jammu & Kashmir	6	Kerala	20
Punjab	13	Tamil Nadu	39
Uttar Pradesh	85	Andaman & Nicobar Islands	1
Chandigarh	1	Lakshadweep	1
Delhi	7	Pondicherry	1
Total	126	Total	132
East		**West**	
Arunachal Pradesh	2	Dadra & Nagar Haveli	1
Assam	14	Daman & Diu	1
Bihar	54	Goa	2
Manipur	2	Gujarat	26
Meghalaya	2	Madhya Pradesh	40
Mizoram	1	Maharashtra	48
Nagaland	1	Rajasthan	25
Orissa	21		
Sikkim	1		
Tripura	2		
West Bengal	42		
Total	142	Total	143

Note: The Lok Sabha has 543 elective seats as distributed above. The remaining two seats are filled by nominations.

The system of voting is the single-member constituency, first past the post. Each constituency is represented by only one member of parliament (MP) in the Lok Sabha. Of those contesting from any constituency, the candidate with the highest number of votes is declared elected, even if the total is well short of a majority. This has produced governments that have substantial majorities in parliament yet lack endorsement from a majority of the voters: in 1984, the Congress captured 77 per cent of seats in parliament with only 48 per cent of the votes cast. With voter turnout in 1984 having been 63.4 per cent, in effect Rajiv Gandhi had a functioning three-quarters majority in parliament with the mandate of less than a third of the electorate. A proportional representation system would have been fairer to opposition parties and more representative in a mathematically defined version of democracy. However, under Indian conditions (size, diversity and complexity) a proportional representation system would always produce utter chaos in each general election.

The conduct of elections is entrusted by the constitution itself to an election commission. The chief election commissioner is an independent official appointed by the president under conditions of service not dissimilar to those of senior judges. The election commissioner's salary is not subject to parliamentary vote, and her or his removal requires a two-thirds majority in each house of parliament. Persons in the office have occasionally produced unhappiness and attracted charges of favouritism towards the Congress as the long-term 'natural' party of government. As with all political systems, the party in government has all the advantages of incumbency when contesting elections. These have not been sufficient to prevent spectacular electoral reverses for the party in power in 1967, 1977, 1980, 1989 and 1991.

By and large, parliament is fairly chosen. While individual seats may have been determined by musclemen or bribes, no general election in India has produced an overall result that was not a fair reflection of voter preferences.

Any citizen of India who is at least 25 years old may seek election to the Lok Sabha from a constituency in which he or she has resided for a minimum period of 180 days. No one person is permitted to be a member of more than one legislative body at the national or state level simultaneously. Individual members of parliament can exert influence more in party forums than in parliament.

The record shows that in the early years, many members of parliament had been prominent in the nationalist campaign for independence. The first parliament (1952–7) was dominated by professionals, especially lawyers. Each successive election has made India's parliament progressively less cosmopolitan and more provincial in character with a lower average level of education. For example, the proportion of lawyers declined from 35 to 20 per cent from the first to the fifth parliament, while the proportion of agriculturists went up from under one-quarter to more than one-third in the same period. That is to say, India's parliament has experienced a certain democratisation. It is the 'people of the land' who now comprise the single largest occupational grouping in parliament. In terms of castes, brahmins are still over-represented and the lower castes remain under-represented. But the general trend once again is towards greater democratisation. So while the Indian parliament remains unrepresentative of the population at large (as is the case with legislatures in other democracies), it does seem to be heading in the right direction.

The term of the Lok Sabha is for a maximum period of five years, although in an emergency this may be extended one year at a time indefinitely. The only occasion on which the Lok Sabha's term was extended was after the 1975 emergency, when the general election that should have been held in 1976 was postponed until the following year. There is no minimum term of parliament. While parliament may be dissolved and fresh elections held because a government has lost the confidence of the house, the more common occurrence is for a prime minister to time a call for fresh elections with the goal of maximising personal or party political gains.

The only time that an Indian government has lost a vote of confidence in the Lok Sabha was in 1990. On 7 November, the House rejected the motion of Prime Minister V. P. Singh seeking its confidence, by a vote of 346 to 142. The vote was the climax of an eleven-hour debate in parliament that was extensive, keenly contested and at times exciting. Newspapers reported that the pace of work in the capital had slowed down considerably as people gathered around radios and newspaper offices to await news of the final vote. The prime minister sent in his letter of resignation to President R. Venkataraman immediately after the defeat of the eleven-month National Front government on the floor of the Lok Sabha.

The Lok Sabha is required by the constitution to convene twice a year, with the maximum allowable period of gap between the two sessions being six months. In practice the Lok Sabha has often met in three sessions per year. The language of parliamentary business is mostly Hindi or English, although a member may use any of the recognised official languages. Many do so by choice, some are forced to it by necessity.

The process of legislation involves three stages corresponding to the familiar three readings of bills in parliamentary systems: the introduction of a bill, its consideration and its enactment into law. The first reading consists of the bill being introduced along with an explanation of its aims and purposes. After the second reading, a bill may be referred to a select committee, circulated for public response or taken up for immediate consideration. The last course is rare and reserved for urgent and uncontroversial items. The second course is the most frequent. The select committee reports back either unanimously or with a majority recommendation and a minority note of dissent. The bill is then considered in the house clause by clause, with members being able to introduce amendments. Once all clauses have been dealt with, the bill has crossed the report stage and is listed for its third and final reading. At this stage only tidying-up amendments are permitted, and the bill is put to a vote. If the speaker authenticates its passing, the bill is sent to the second house where the entire procedure is repeated. When both houses of parliament have passed an identical version of a bill, it is presented to the president for formal assent, and becomes law upon receiving his assent.

'Ordinary' bills may be introduced in either house, must be passed by both houses before being sent to the president, and become law once the latter's assent is signed. 'Money' bills can be introduced only in the Lok Sabha. While they may be taken up for discussion in the Rajya Sabha, the upper house is not competent to refuse assent to money bills. Nor may it frustrate the passage of a money bill by the simple expedient of procrastination: the bill is deemed to have passed if not returned by the Rajya Sabha within fourteen days. A bill which is pending in parliament does not lapse because of the prorogation of the houses. Instead, when a parliamentary session is terminated, a bill which has already been introduced is carried over into the next session.

Although any MP may introduce a private member's bill, most of the Lok Sabha's time is spent dealing with government business. A private bill will have little prospect of enactment, but does help an MP to reassure, appease or deflect criticisms from constituents. The daily and sessional business of government is decided by the cabinet and its parliamentary affairs committee under the chairmanship of the chief whip. (In parliamentary systems, party discipline in the house is maintained by whips for each party.)

Each session of the Lok Sabha is opened with a presidential address. The quorum for the Lok Sabha to be able to meet is one-tenth of its membership. The daily session opens with a question hour which is strongly reminiscent of the British tradition. Some 20 to 25 questions are asked and answered (or successfully evaded) each day that the Lok Sabha is in session. While the form of the initial question is tightly disciplined, supplementary questions are permitted fairly wide latitude by the speaker. As in all parliamentary systems, question-hour can break a minister and make an opposition backbencher.

The Lok Sabha is of course fundamentally akin to other legislative assemblies in parliamentary regimes. Its content can however be quite different, reflecting its own unique sociopolitical environment. For example, members and their modes of conducting business express Indian presuppositions and backgrounds, and many parliamentary practices have evolved in the context of a one-party-dominant political system.

The conduct of the house is in the hands of the speaker who recognises members, keeps order and does other things which are required of presiding officers. Outsiders who are unfamiliar with the Indian political culture wonder how any business gets done in the Indian parliament. To them the speaker of the Lok Sabha appears to lack firmness and direction necessary for running a plenary assembly. While the speaker of the Lok Sabha can indeed have difficulty in maintaining order at times,[1] this is one of the more entertaining spectacles in parliaments in general. The speaker may not vote on an issue before the Lok Sabha, but can exercise a casting vote in the event of a tie on any motion. The speaker is selected by the governing party for formal election by the house but is expected to conduct parliamentary business with fairness and impartiality.

The powers of the Indian parliament may be divided into constitution-amending, procedural, legislative, financial, governmental and constitutive. Under Article 368, parliament is the central forum for amending the constitution. The procedural powers are those which allow parliament to make rules for the conduct of its business.

The legislative powers pertain to the authority and role of parliament in enacting laws for governing the country. Parliament is technically the legislature, the institution which enacts the law of the land with the authority of the people and the assent of the head of state. In reality the legislative agenda is controlled by the government and endorsed by the parliament with the help of tightly maintained party discipline. (See Figure 6.1 for the relationship between the legislature and the executive.) Nor could it be otherwise in a democracy, for only so can the electoral mandate which brought a party into government be implemented. Acting with the government, parliament is all-powerful; if it chose to act independently of the government, parliament would sow confusion and unpredictability in the affairs of state and the minds of the people; if it chose to act against the executive, parliament would bring the business of government to a standstill until fresh elections could be held.

FIGURE 6.1
The structure of parliamentary government in India

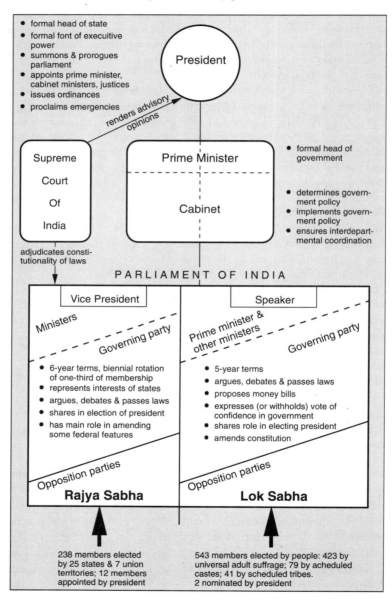

- formal head of state
- formal font of executiive power
- summons & prorogues parliament
- appoints prime minister, cabinet ministers, justices
- issues ordinances
- proclaims emergencies

President

renders advisory opinions

Supreme Court Of India

Prime Minister

Cabinet

- formal head of government
- determines government policy
- implements government policy
- ensures interdepartmental coordination

adjudicates constitutionality of laws

PARLIAMENT OF INDIA

Vice President

Speaker

Ministers

Governing party

Prime minister & other ministers

Governing party

- 6-year terms, biennial rotation of one-third of membership
- represents interests of states
- argues, debates & passes laws
- shares in election of president
- has main role in amending some federal features

- 5-year terms
- argues, debates & passes laws
- proposes money bills
- expresses (or withholds) vote of confidence in government
- shares role in electing president
- amends constitution

Opposition parties

Opposition parties

Rajya Sabha

Lok Sabha

238 members elected by 25 states & 7 union territories; 12 members appointed by president

543 members elected by people: 423 by universal adult suffrage; 79 by acheduled castes; 41 by scheduled tribes. 2 nominated by president

The financial powers of parliament are those empowering it to raise and spend money as it sees fit, including discussion and approval of the annual budget which is usually introduced in mid-February. Only parliament has the authority to levy taxes and spend money from the consolidated fund.

Parliament formally controls the reins of government in the sense that cabinet is required to have the confidence of the Lok Sabha and is collectively responsible to parliament. Under constitutive powers, finally, parliament can legislate to admit or create new states into the union of India; to create a high court for a union territory and to extend the jurisdiction of a high court to or restrict it from a union territory; and to create or abolish a legislative council (an upper house) for a state with the consent of the state's assembly (the lower house).

Rajya Sabha

The Rajya Sabha or the Council of States is the upper house of India's bicameral parliament. It has a strength of 250 members, of whom 238 represent the 25 states and 7 union territories. The distribution of Rajya Sabha seats among states is roughly in proportion to their population strengths, but with some effort at equalisation. Bihar, for example, has 54 seats in the Lok Sabha and 22 in the Rajya Sabha; Himachal Pradesh has 4 in the lower house and 3 in the upper. The remaining 12 seats are filled with members nominated by the president acting on cabinet advice (1) on the basis of their special knowledge or skills in the arts and sciences, (2) in order to rectify a serious under-representation in parliament of any particular group and (3) in an exercise of political patronage to reward party faithfuls or major financial supporters. Members of the Rajya Sabha are elected for six-year terms, with a biennial turnover of one-third of the house. The house is not subject to dissolution. The quorum of the Rajya Sabha is set at one-tenth of the total membership, that is 25, with decisions being made by a majority of members actually present and voting. The presiding officer of the Rajya Sabha is the vice-president of India.

There were three sets of reasons behind adopting a bicameral legislature for the union of India. First, the Rajya Sabha, as its name implies, was to be the chamber for representing and protecting the rights of the states in a federal polity. This is the explanation for giving the Rajya Sabha a role and status equal to that of the Lok Sabha in the electoral college for choosing the president. Members of state legislative assemblies elect Rajya Sabha representatives for their states on a proportional representation system. For example, if the Bihar assembly consists of members from the Congress, Janata and BJP parties in the ratio of 5:5:1, then there would be 10, 10 and 2 MPs from these parties respectively to make up the 22 Rajya Sabha seats for Bihar. (Unlike Australia, Britain and Canada, members of India's upper as well as lower house are called MPs.)

Yet the constitutional position of the Rajya Sabha is not comparable in power, functions or prestige to the US Senate when conceived of solely in terms of state rights. In the event of a deadlock between the two houses of parliament, for example, if reconsideration of a bill fails to achieve a mutually satisfactory resolution, then the president can convene a joint sitting of both houses. Its decisions are made by a simple majority. Since Lok Sabha MPs outnumber their Rajya Sabha counterparts by more than 2:1, in a combined sitting the Rajya Sabha can generally expect to be defeated. Its relative theoretical impotence as the guardian of state rights was underscored by the fact of Congress Party dominance in the central and state governments until 1967, and periodically even after that date.

When the Rajya Sabha did finally assert itself against the Lok Sabha more than thirty years after independence, it do so in defence of party interests rather than state interests. After the general election of March 1977, the two houses of parliament were for the first time controlled by different political groupings. The biennial elections to the Rajya Sabha in March–April 1978 left the new Janata government with 66 members in the 244-strong upper house, still 57 short of a majority. In August 1978, the Rajya Sabha approved a resolution, by a vote of 104 to 78, asking the government to institute an inquiry into the activities of Prime Minister Morarji Desai's family members. The government responded by interpreting the resolution as a recommendation rather than a mandatory directive.

A more serious setback for the government came in the following month when the Rajya Sabha forced a modification of five clauses in the 49–clause 44th constitution amendment bill, jettisoning, for example, the requirement that the basic structure of the constitution could be amended only by referendum. The Janata government decided to accept a dilution of the constitutional amendment bill rather than see it lapse in its entirety. Mrs Indira Gandhi, too, after her return to power in January 1980 had to contend with an opposition majority in the Rajya Sabha for a little while. With different political parties in power in the various states becoming a more frequent occurrence in the 1990s, it is possible that the Rajya Sabha could begin to exercise its proper role as the watchdog of state interests.

The second purpose of establishing a bicameral legislature was to provide an institutional opportunity for second thoughts and wiser counsel even after the passage of a bill by the Lok Sabha. Again, this remained a largely hypothetical role for the Rajya Sabha during the period of Congress Party dominance. As the preceding two paragraphs suggest, this particular function did begin to be served by the upper house after the 1977 general election.

The third function of the Rajya Sabha in the Indian system of governance is to enable a bill to be introduced in parliament even when the Lok Sabha is not in session. Much of the preliminary debate and work on the bill can be completed by the time that the Lok Sabha reconvenes.

We should note that in respect of certain specified federal features of the constitution, the primary amending role has been given to the Rajya Sabha as the custodian of state rights. For example, the powers of the Rajya Sabha itself can be altered only with the consent of a two-thirds majority in the upper house. And the house does provide a few additional jobs. In theory it provides the means to bring in competent or skilled personnel who are not prepared to face the uncertain rigours of political campaigns. They can be appointed to the Rajya Sabha and be inducted into cabinet without having to go through the hurly-burly of elections.

Committees

Plenary sessions of parliament would be too large, cumbersome and unwieldy for the conduct of all parliamentary business. The most substantial consideration of bills takes place in committee. The Lok Sabha operates with the aid of about a dozen committees of between 20 and 25 members. The composition of the committees is determined by the speaker and the chief whip with due regard to respective party strengths in the house. To prevent undue executive influence, no minister who is in charge of a bill being considered by committee is permitted to participate in the deliberations of that committee.

Parliamentary committees help both to expedite parliamentary business and to scrutinise government activities. They may be divided into three broad groups: those that are concerned with the organisations and powers of the houses, for example the rules committee; those that assist the houses in their legislative functions; and those that assist the houses in their financial functions. The third group is generally regarded as the most important. The public accounts committee (PAC), for example, with a lineage going back to 1923, consists of 15 members of the Lok Sabha with another 7 Rajya Sabha members being associated with it. The chairman of the PAC, which has a term of one year, is selected by the speaker of the Lok Sabha. Its task is to ensure that public money is spent in accordance with appropriations as authorised by parliament, and to examine the accounts of state corporations. It does not set or examine government policy so much as the proper implementation of policy. By tradition the PAC is very conscious of its role as the guardian of the public purse and has not been timorous in its investigations in the discharge of its functions. The influence of the PAC is very largely a product of the prestige attached to its published reports. Convention requires a minister to implement PAC recommendations and to report to parliament on follow-up actions.

The committee on estimates consists of 30 members of the Lok Sabha elected each year. The committee selects some government departments and some particular topics for annual examination. It scrutinises specific departmental estimates and recommends economy measures consistent with departmental objectives. That is, it acts pursuant to the twin goals of economy and efficiency. Although it lacks competence to discuss issues of policy, it has traditionally acted with a fairly liberal interpretation of its own terms of reference. The finance minister is under conventional obligation to treat its recommendations for the annual budget seriously, not least because the report of the committee is available to parliament when it votes on demands for grants. During the period of dominance by the Congress Party in particular, the estimates and public accounts committees tended to take on the role normally expected of opposition parties in parliamentary democracies. That is to say, they provided a functional substitute for an effective opposition in keeping a watchful brief on the public purse. The Joint Parliamentary Committee investigating the $1.3 billion securities scam from April 1991 to May 1992 censured Health Minister B. Shankaranand for certain investments made during his tenure as

Petroleum Minister, and Finance Minister Dr Manmohan Singh for failing to check spiralling stock prices. It observed that the scam 'fully exposed' the 'state of the country's governance, adherence to regulations, an alarming decay in the banking system and the questionable viability of some of the nationalised banks'. It concluded that 'a culture of non-accountability has permeated all sections of the Government' (*HIE*, 3 July 1993, pp. 1, 10–11).

The Opposition

The opposition in a parliamentary democracy is expected to play the role of an alternative government. This has not been the case for most of independent Indian history due to the complete dominance of the Congress Party. Because of the multiplicity of political parties in India, the status of the leader of the opposition can be conferred only on the leader of a party with at least fifty seats in the Lok Sabha. After defeat in the 1977 election, Mrs Gandhi's Congress did play that role briefly. But because her return to power was the result of the break-up of the Janata coalition, there was no readily identifiable alternative government on the opposition benches after 1980.

The political landscape was transformed with the defeat of Rajiv Gandhi's Congress in 1989, and from then until 1991 the Congress was clearly a government-in-waiting. Gandhi himself was regarded and acted as the prime-minister-in-waiting. The 1991 election saw a return of Congress as the party with the largest number of seats, but still short of a majority on its own. The erstwhile Janata Front coalition had collapsed, and its various components continued the process of disintegration even after the 1991 election. The largest single party in opposition was the Bharatiya Janata Party (BJP) with 117 MPs. In power by itself in the most populous and politically most important state of Uttar Pradesh, the BJP began to project itself as an alternative government.

Regardless of the numbers or capability to form an alternative government, opposition parties do register and express the diversity of opinions in a country as large and varied as India. The opposition also serves to keep a government on its political toes. The opposition loses when it comes to tallying up the votes on any motion. But its statements in parliament are heard in the country at large and often listened to within the ranks of the Congress Party. For the latter has always been an aggregative party, embracing within its fold many different political philosophies, points of view and preferred policy prescriptions. Opposition arguments therefore often strike a resonance within the Congress Party and can shape public policy by this indirect means.

In turn this makes the opposition parties in India more influential than would be suggested by mere numbers. Jawaharlal Nehru himself was very sensitive to the range of opinion in the ranks of the opposition. In later years, this aspect of opposition MPs was heightened when people sitting on the opposition benches were in many cases former members of Congress with long-standing ties to members of the government. That is, the debate which is ostensibly between the government and the opposition can in effect serve to structure the internal debate within the ruling party. This has been a distinctive feature of Indian politics.

Sovereignty of Parliament

As was noted in Chapter 2 when discussing the judiciary, the parliament of India has at times clashed with the courts over jurisdictional demarcations. In particular, in India governments have not infrequently come into conflict with the Supreme Court over the extent to which parliament may amend the constitution. In the *Golak Nath* case (1967) the court ruled by a 6–5 majority that parliament was not competent to amend the fundamental rights enshrined in Chapter 3 of the constitution. When some of Mrs Gandhi's populist measures, for example abolition of the privy purses of former princes and nationalisation of 14 banks, were struck down by the Supreme Court in 1970, the prime minister set about asserting the supremacy of parliament. She was able to give effect to her wishes after gaining two-thirds majority in the 1971 election. In April 1972, parliament passed the 25th constitution amendment act which allowed parliament to encroach on fundamental rights if it was said to be done pursuant to giving effect to the directive principles of state policy. No court was permitted to question such a declaration. In April 1973, in the *Kesavanand Bharati* case, the Supreme Court ruled that while parliament could amend even the fundamental rights 'guaranteed' by the constitution, parliament was not competent to alter the 'basic structure' or 'framework' of the constitution. The government's response came during the 1975–7 emergency. The 42nd constitution amendment act (1976) unambiguously and unabashedly declared parliament to be competent to amend all provisions of the constitution and the courts to be incompetent to question parliamentary enactments.

The government case in the executive–judiciary dispute began with the assertion that parliament was the repository of the will of the people. Parliament was directly elected by and accountable to the people. Judges were neither elected nor accountable to anyone but themselves and inhabited an ivory tower world. In a related vein, a parliament elected by all adult citizens was more representative of the general will than a constituent assembly which had been elected on a very restricted franchise. Moreover, the courts over the years had delivered contradictory decisions, and inconsistency of judicial verdicts had produced constitutional confusion. Fourth, the constitution was what its clauses said it to be, not what the judiciary interpreted it to be. The concept of the 'basic structure' in particular was nowhere to be found in the constitution itself but was instead an invention of the judges.

By way of a preliminary response, it may be noted that the concept of sovereignty is best understood historically. It originated in the search for a secular basis of state authority in the Europe of the sixteenth and seventeenth centuries. As a theory of politics, sovereignty embodies the notion that in every system of government there must be some absolute power of final decision. The person or body exercising such decision must be legally competent to decide and practically able to enforce the decision. The concept entails a prescriptive and a descriptive element. Contrary to the situation as it ought to be, in reality many states do not possess the unity, clarity and effectiveness of command implied in the concept of sovereignty (Crick, 1968, p. 77). The theory of sovereignty was unknown in the Roman tradition of politics, and in medieval Christendom. The tensions between church and state were not competing claims of sovereignty but struggles for political power.

Seeking to rescue France from its wars of religion, in his *Six Bookes of a Commonweale* (1576) Jean Bodin grounded the authority of the state in a theory of sovereignty. The state's primary concern was with order, not religion, he wrote. In order to discharge the function of government, the sovereign must be above the law. The essence of sovereignty was therefore the power to command. Since the command of the sovereign was law, the obligation to obey followed from the authenticity of the command; it could not be made conditional to the justice of the command. In the *Leviathan* (1651),

Thomas Hobbes made sovereignty more absolute by arguing that the distinction of right and wrong flows from law, and law is the creation of the sovereign. John Austin argued in his *Lectures on Jurisprudence* (1863) that if a determinate human superior received habitual obedience from the bulk of a given society, but was not in the habit of obedience to a like superior, then that determinate superior is sovereign in that society. But sovereignty so defined is a legalistic concept which falls down in the realm of practical politics. For on this conception the prime minister, who receives habitual obedience in parliament, must be sovereign; yet the tenure of the prime minister is subject to the confidence of parliament. Seeking to rescue the theory of sovereignty from this paradox, A. V. Dicey in his *Introduction to the Study of the Law of the Constitution* (1885) introduced the distinction between legal sovereignty vested in parliament and political sovereignty vested in the electorate. We might add that the two are linked inseparably in the processes of the political party.

The origins of parliament itself in Britain lay in the efforts to curb the arbitrary exercise of authority by the executive. That is, the concept of parliamentary supremacy originated in protest against the absolutism of an autocratic monarchy. By contrast, in India parliament is an instrument of the executive. The invocation of parliamentary supremacy is therefore false. From this point of view, the closer parallel today is indeed with the United States and its doctrine of judicial review. Interestingly, in relation to the United States, the doctrine of parliamentary sovereignty destroyed any prospect of conciliation between Britain and the rebellious American colonies. For while the British accepted the doctrine by virtue of tradition, nature and logic, the Americans saw in it the source of tyranny (Crick, 1968, p. 80).

The opposition to government attempts to override judicial restraints began with the simple proposition that in practice parliament meant the executive which in turn was reducible to the prime minister. While in theory the executive is subject to parliamentary control, in reality parliament is malleable to the executive's will. To insist that the constitution could be amended at will by parliament free of judicial oversight would be to reduce the constitution to a private preserve of the prime minister.

Much of the case for parliamentary supremacy evades the central issue in the debate, namely the principle of constitutional government. If the constitution was deemed to be unsatisfactory in its basic structure, then the proper procedure would be to convene another constituent assembly elected on universal adult suffrage with the mandate to draft a new and improved constitution. But thereafter the constitution should be respected by future governments.

As the last comment suggests, the Indian parliament cannot claim original authority, for whatever authority it has is derived from the constitution. Insofar as political theory is concerned, popular sovereignty resides in the parliament of the day in a transient sense and is vested in the constitution in permanent form.

State Legislatures

While in most respects state legislatures are similar to the Parliament of India, there are some important differences. To begin with, the choice of unicameralism or bicameralism was left to states, depending on how they weighed the functions of the second chamber compared to the costs involved in running it. In 1993, five states had second chambers: Bihar, Jammu and Kashmir, Karnataka, Maharashtra and Uttar Pradesh. Any legislative assembly may create or abolish a legislative council for itself by a special majority (a majority of the total membership that is not less than two-thirds of members present and voting), followed by an Act of Parliament (Article 169). Andhra Pradesh created a council by this process in 1957, and then abolished it by the same process in 1985. The size of the council must be no less than 40 and no more than one-third of the total membership of the assembly (Article 171). Like the Rajya Sabha, one-third of a state council's members are elected biennially. Five-sixths of the council members (MLCs) are indirectly elected on a complicated formula involving graduates, educators and members of the legislative assembly (MLAs); and one-sixth are nominated by the governor. But a state council's role is even more circumscribed than that of the Rajya Sabha: it is merely an advisory house that may delay passage of a bill but cannot compel modifications or abandonment.

The legislative assemblies themselves vary in size from a minimum of 40 to no more than 500; their members are chosen for five-year terms by direct election on the basis of universal adult suffrage. As with the Lok and Rajya Sabha respectively in central government, the state assembly is subject to dissolution but not the council. Because of the great difference in size between parliamentary and state legislative constituencies, MLAs are far closer to the people than MPs. MLAs are correspondingly more significant political actors.

Unlike the general decorum of the Lok Sabha, the conduct of business in state assemblies can occassionally resemble street politics. The opening day of the new U.P. assembly in January 1994, for example, was marred by a physical brawl in which several MLAs were bloodied.

Transplant of Parliamentary Institutions in India

Critics decry the slide in standards in the quality of representatives and of their debate in India's parliament. Sceptics argue that parliamentary government was a sham in India before 1967 because of the political dominance of the Congress Party. Since 1967, it has degenerated into farce because of the continual fragmentation and splintering of political parties, unprincipled defections from parties and frequent recourse to 'toppling' governments in power. An apt Indian contribution to the English political vocabulary, toppling refers to the fall of governments as a result of loss of majority in the house when disgruntled members from within the ruling party defect to another faction of the same party or to an entirely different party. The twin roots of toppling therefore are weak party discipline and strong personal ambitions by politicians.

Parliamentary institutions have nevertheless survived in India for more than four decades now. The 543 elective seats attracted a field of almost nine thousand candidates in the 1991 general election. Conventions have been established, and many of the norms of parliamentary democracy are well understood by the people even if not always adhered to by the politicians. Many reasons are proffered in explanation of the successful transplant of parliamentary government in India. The political legacy inherited from the experience of British colonial rule demonstrated both the value and the practicability of parliamentary institutions in India. Further-more, precisely because the legacy was from colonial Britain, it was accompanied by an inherent distrust of authority. The attitude of wariness towards government has acted as a curb on the arbitrary exercise of power by governments for most of independent Indian history even in the absence of an effective opposition.

The fact that the norms of parliamentary democracy have been internalised in the Indian political debates means that all political leaders – yes, even the leaders of the major communist parties – have to profess belief in and commitment to parliamentary institutions and practices, whether or not their professions are genuine. Those whose proclamations of the virtues of parliamentary democracy were based on conviction, for example Jawaharlal Nehru, helped to nurture the institutions from fragile seedlings to relatively sturdy plants.

Nehru's efforts to ensure that parliamentary institutions had taken root firmly in India were helped by the operations of a one-party-dominant system under Congress (Morris-Jones, 1971, pp. 238–40). In order to retain its dominance in the Indian political system, the Congress Party had to work consciously at remaining an aggregative political force. In turn, this meant that a variety of sectional interests was contained within one organisation, thereby reducing the risk of political fragmentation in the country. This contributed to the stability of government as well as ensuring the inclusion of all significant elements of the national community in the political system.

Moreover, the very nature of the Congress as an aggregative party meant that every significant opposition political party had an ideological or sectional counterpart within the Congress. Precisely because the formal opposition parties were so sparsely represented in parliament and posed no threat to Congress as the governing party, their counterparts within Congress claimed and were granted a certain leeway in functioning in effect as the real opposition to majority preferences and policies insofar as substantial debates of issues were concerned. Similarly, the organisation of the Congress had spread far and wide into every corner of the country. Accordingly, the introduction of universal adult suffrage was the prelude to the incorporation of the hinterland into the political system.

Parliamentary democracy is therefore a given value in India by now, not one in need of constant justification. Rather, the onus is on its critics to prove its deficiencies and convince the people of a suitable replacement. The task of opponents of parliamentary democracy is made the more difficult by the distance which now separates the institutions from colonial origins. On the one hand, it is easier to forget the origins of the political model. On the other hand, it is also easier to accept such origins when they cannot be overlooked. When parliamentary democracy was first introduced to India, many expressed scepticism about its prospects in a caste-ridden, cleavage-driven illiterate society. Ironically, in the event the system seems to have been peculiarly suited to the Indians' passion for political debate. To be sure, there are complaints galore about the imperfections and shortcomings of the operation of parliamentary democracy. But broadly speaking it has been a considerable success in

India. It is fallacious today to refer to it as an experiment in an alien setting. Rather, it is an established fact of modern Indian politics.

Note

1. Thus Speaker N. Sanjiva Reddy in the fourth Lok Sabha on 15 April 1969: 'I will see who shouts more. My Goodness! I shout, they shout and all is noise. It is not good' (Gupta, 1982, p. 188).

Further Reading

Morris-Jones (1957). A dated but still useful study of India's parliament.
Panandiker and Sud (1981). Documents an important shift of political power from an urban, lawyer-dominated middle class to the rural agricultural class.

7

The Bureaucracy

In this chapter I shall do seven things:

1. Provide an outline of what a bureaucracy is supposed to be and do.
2. Describe the public service commissions in India.
3. Describe the the all-India and central public services of India.
4. Discuss some of the major problems associated with India's public services.
5. Analyse relations between the civil servants and politicians in India.
6. Discuss the problem and scale of corruption in the public services.
7. Discuss the attempts at reforming India's public services.

The Concept of a Bureaucracy

A stylised (that is, Weberian ideal-type; see Weber, 1957) bureaucracy is an organisation purposefully adapted to attaining a single functional goal. It is organised hierarchically with a clear and strict chain of command from top to bottom. Moreover, the hierarchy is pyramidal in form, with several subordinates carrying out functionally related tasks under one superior at each level. Reflecting this, there is an elaborate division of labour throughout the organisation, with specialist tasks being assigned to appropriately skilled personnel, with the responsibilities becoming increasingly generalised and managerial up the hierarchy. All conduct in the pursuit of official duties is governed by a detailed set of rules and regulations, with 'precedent' being accorded almost mystical reverence. Recruitment into the service is on the basis of competence and specialised training rather than by birth or privilege. And office-holding in the organisation tends to be a life-long vocation; that is, a career.

The stylised version of a bureaucracy is open to the criticism that it overestimates the rationality and efficiency of standard operating procedures of standing organisations staffed by faceless experts. Conversely, it downplays the elements of 'red tapeism', the petty conservatism of officials, and the insidious effects of such processes as exemplified in Parkinson's law that work expands to fill the time available for its completion. (There is also the related Peter principle that each person rises to her or his level of incompetence.) Such objections may well be valid, if to lesser and greater degrees in different bureaucracies. Yet they are also irrelevant to the point at hand. The essential argument is that, under modern conditions, few of the activities entrusted to bureaucracies could be carried out by non-bureaucratic organisations. In the Weberian philosophy, the decisive reason for the advance of bureaucratic organisation was its purely technical superiority over any other form of organisation. 'Bureaucracy-free' structures can indeed achieve collective goals, but only in small, decentralised local communities. That is, if we wish to pursue administrative and productive goals in a large and territorially extensive society, then we need a bureaucratic organisation. The Mughal emperors recognised this and established their own extensive bureaucracy to underpin their administrations; the British introduced the principles of European administration to the subcontinent.

A bureaucracy tenders expert advice to the government so that decisions can be made on the basis of the most informed choices. Once the decisions have been made, responsibility for implementing them is again vested in the bureaucracy. That is, even though a bureaucracy is part of the policy-making structure, bureaucrats are advisers and implementers of public choices made by the policy-makers and decision-makers. The permanence of the career civil servant brings stability and continuity to the task of administration. Moreover, when contrasted with the itinerant nature of many political 'masters' (that is, ministers), the very permanence of the civil servant confers an important measure of political influence over public policy. Information is power, and the bureaucracy is the repository of a vast store of information collected over the course of the years. The minister might call for all relevant information; but the choice of what is all the relevant information, and the retrieval and transmission of that information, is made by the civil servant. The information can be presented in such a manner as to skew the choices towards the option favoured by the bureaucracy. Similarly, civil servants can interpret policy directives in such a manner as to delay and thwart the implementation of government policy that is not to their liking. Bureaucracies act so as to maximise their own budget, for example by increased size of staff and enlarged scope of action. The bigger the bureaucracy, the more significant can be the factors of bureaucratic inertia and slippage.

The permanence of the bureaucracy requires that it be staffed by career civil servants. A person must have professional lifelong tenure, other than for unsatisfactory performance, in order to think of the civil service as a career. Furthermore, the theory of the permanence of the civil service is in contrast to the periodic turnover of politicians and the theory of governments being changed by the ballot box. Yet, in the discharge of official duties, a civil servant cannot discriminate between individual politicians and political parties. Moreover, a civil servant is required to tender advice in the formulation of public policy on the basis of an honest assessment of the best strategy for attaining the goals desired by means of the resources available to the state. Thereafter, once the policy is decided by the political executive (that is, the government), the civil servant is expected to implement it faithfully regardless of support for or opposition to the policy. It is all this which explains the condition of political neutrality of the civil servants and the civil service. A civil servant is not permitted to express personal ideological or party preferences other than in the privacy of the polling booth.

The Public Service Commissions

The Indian constitution is distinctive for including provisions relating to the federal and state public services. The body responsible for the service conditions of civil servants in India is the public service commission: the Union Public Service Commission (UPSC) for the central and all-India services, and a state public service commission for the civil services of that state. Two or more states can be serviced by a joint PSC; a state may also choose to have the UPSC regulate its civil service. The requirement to have a PSC for the union government and for each state, or a Joint PSC for a group of states if so indicated by the legislatures of those states, is mandatory under the Indian constitution. The size, composition and conditions of service of the commissions is determined by governments and formally effected by the president and governors for the union and state PSCs respectively. In 1991 the UPSC comprised ten members plus the chairman. Members are appointed for six-year terms of service, but must retire at the ages of 65 and 62 respectively in the case of the union and state PSCs. Members may also resign or be removed from office on ground of insolvency, paid outside employment, infirmity of mind or body, or misbehaviour as established by the Supreme Court upon reference to it by the president. It is worth noting that even the members of state PSCs can be removed for misbehaviour only with a presidential reference to the Supreme Court. The governor is the formal appointing authority for state PSCs but cannot remove their members other than through the president.

The system of parliamentary government makes the political executive, namely the prime minister and cabinet, responsible to the parliament. In order to work in practice, this has to be buttressed by a permanent administrative executive answerable to, but also protected by, the political executive. The operational requirements of responsible government include (a) the existence of an independent and competent civil service (b) which is staffed by persons capable of giving advice to successive ministers based on long and continuous experience (c) who are secure in their positions as long they do not misbehave officially and (d) carry out the government's policy. In turn this necessitates the framing and administering of rules governing the recruitment and conduct of civil servants, commonly known as the conditions of service.

The Constitution of India contains four safeguards for the independence of the PSCs from the political executive:

- It specifies the manner and grounds for removal as noted above;
- It stipulates that the conditions of service cannot be altered to the disadvantage of an incumbent member of any PSC;
- It makes the expenses of the PSCs chargeable on the consolidated funds of the union and state governments as appropriate; and
- It debars commission members from accepting paid employment after their service on a PSC, except that (a) ordinary members of the UPSC can be appointed as chairman of the UPSC or a state PSC, (b) the chairman of a state PSC can be appointed as

chairman of another state PSC, or as a member or chairman of the UPSC, and (c) ordinary members of a state PSC can be appointed to the UPSC or to chair any state PSC or the UPSC. That is, in effect a member of any public service commission can be promoted within the PSC system but not take any employment outside the system either with the government or in the private sector.

In addition to performing advisory functions in the recruitment and service conditions of all state and union government employees, the union and state PSCs are required by the constitution to submit annual reports to the president and governors respectively (Article 323). The advisory nature of the functions of the PSCs underlines the point that in parliamentary government, responsibility for the proper administration of the affairs of state vests in the cabinet through parliament. Parliamentary oversight is also ensured by requiring the annual reports of PSCs to be laid before each legislature as appropriate. On the administrative side, the relations of the UPSC with the government are under the formal coordination of the Ministry of Home Affairs. But the UPSC also has its own secretariat for conducting its daily business with the various departments.

Constitutional safeguards protect not just the public service commissions but also the civil servants. Rules made by parliament and state legislatures for regulating the conduct of civil servants are subject to judicial oversight vis-à-vis their constitutionality, and the courts have in fact annulled some rules for having contravened particular provisions of the constitution. Action against an official who violates 'good behaviour' can take one of three forms: dismissal, removal or reduction in rank. A dismissed employee is not eligible for re-employment as a civil servant; an officer who has merely been 'removed' is so eligible. The penalty for both categories includes disallowance of pension entitlements for past services. By contrast, 'compulsory retirement' does not entail loss of previously accumulated entitlements.

The constitution provides important procedural safeguards for the civil servant (but not for military personnel) against arbitrary disciplinary measures. A civil servant cannot be dismissed or removed by an authority subordinate to that by which the officer was appointed (Article 311.1). Moreover, no disciplinary action may be undertaken against an official without providing the officer with a 'reasonable opportunity' to rebut the charges (Article 311.2).

Originally, such opportunity had to be provided both at the point of initiating the inquiry into the charges of official misconduct, and at the point of imposing any penalty. The 42nd amendment of the constitution in 1976 took away the second right of an employee to make a representation against the proposed penalty. 'Reasonable opportunity' means that an official must be given the opportunity (a) to deny guilt and establish innocence by being informed of the charges against him and the basis of those charges, (b) for defence against the charges by means of cross-examination of witnesses offering evidence in support of the charges levelled against the employee and (c) for the presentation of evidence and witnesses that will help to establish the employee's innocence.

That is, the government is required:

- To frame specific charges against an officer subject to disciplinary action;
- To inform the officer of those charges;
- To give the officer the opportunity to respond to the charges;
- To come to a decision on the charges only after taking into consideration the officer's response; and
- To follow the rules of natural justice in making any determination against the officer.

The 42nd amendment also took away the right of civil servants to take disputes over recruitment and conditions of service to the civil and high courts, restricting such a judicial recourse to the Supreme Court only (Article 323.A). The provision was implemented with the passage of a law by parliament in 1985 which set up a Central Administrative Tribunal for adjudicating all such disputes regarding all government employees other than defence personnel, officials of the Supreme Court and high courts, and secretarial staff of parliament and the state legislatures.

The Public Services

There are three types of public service in India: the state services, whose officials are recruited, employed and dismissible by a state government; central services, whose officials are recruited, employed and dismissible by the union government for duties throughout the territory of India; and all-India services, whose officials are recruited and dismissible by the union government, but whose services are shared between the central government and that of any one state government. Examples of central services include the defence forces, the Indian Foreign Service (IFS), the Indian Railway Service, the Indian Audits and Account Service, the Indian Customs and Excise Service, the Postal Service and the Indian Revenue Service. Altogether there are more than fifty such services. Of lesser prestige, power and status than the all-India services, the central services are known collectively as the allied services. Of greatest exclusivity and glamour nevertheless is a central service, namely the IFS, the cream of the Indian diplomatic corps. Each of these separate services has a characteristic tendency to develop its own caste-like exclusiveness, with its own grades, salary and promotion structures. Cross-service transfer is very rare.

The Indian Administrative Service (IAS) and the Indian Police Service (which we shall discuss in the next chapter) are the two all-India services listed in the constitution. Article 312 of the constitution empowered parliament to create additional all-India services common to the union and the states if requested by a two-thirds majority of the Rajya Sabha in a resolution stating that it is necessary and expedient in the national interest to do so. Only the Indian Forest Service has been created under this provision. States have resisted attempts to form still more all-India services. The stated reason for their opposition is the additional financial strain that would be imposed on them because of the higher pay scales of the all-India services. The unstated reasons include a reluctance to share the administration of any more services with the central government and to open up still more of the states' public services to non-state civil servants. The recruitment and conditions of service of the all-India services are regulated by rules framed under the All-India Services Act passed by parliament in 1951 under Article 312.

The modern IAS is the direct descendant of the Indian Civil Service (ICS) of the British Raj. We discussed the ambiguous administrative legacy of the Raj in Chapter 2. The ICS was an administrative aristocracy. At a personal level, service in the colonies was sometimes the salvation for gentlemen condemned to mediocrity in their home countries. At the institutional level, the great strength of the ICS officers lay in their remarkable adaptability and dedication. While recruitment into the service placed a premium on liberal education and commonsense intelligence, in-service training emphasised administrative competence and managerial responsibility for a variety of tasks at senior levels of government.

Debutante officers were assigned to subordinate offices in the districts and worked their passage up through senior district and divisional posts in states to the highest rungs of the state and central governments' bureaucratic ladders. An explicit attempt was made to rotate officers from one place to another and from one function to another. ICS officers were the executive arm of the government. As senior executives, their administrative qualities were more important than their specialist skills.

The structure, recruitment, training and ethos of the ICS was retained in the case of the IAS. Like the ICS, the IAS is recruited from among the best and the brightest graduates, its officers trained and required to discharge duties covering a wide range of functions across a number of postings. The 'sanctity' of these all-India services is protected by placing their recruitment, training and service conditions under the supervision of the UPSC as per Part IV of the constitution. The IAS is the only 'multifunctional' government service. The IAS officer is to be found in charge of running steel plants, electricity boards, food corporations, airlines, municipal corporations and even universities. The total number of public sector employees in India is more than 17 million, of whom IAS officers number fewer than 5 000. They are recruited each year on the basis of competitive examinations followed by interviews of shortlisted candidates. Applicants must be 21–28-year-old graduates of recognised universities. (The upper age restriction is relaxed to 31 in the case of scheduled castes and tribes.)

The selection procedure is designed to assess a candidate's overall ability, general knowledge and broad analytical skills. In the 1990s the number writing the examinations is approaching one lakh (the Indian unit of measurement for one hundred thousand). Of these almost one thousand (or 1 per cent of applicants) are taken into the central and all-India services, with the IAS intake numbering around 150 (or 0.15 per cent of the applicants). About one-fifth of the IAS recruits are women, and between one-quarter and one-third come from the scheduled castes and tribes. For a long time the examinations had to be written in English, but since 1978 candidates can choose to write in any of the recognised regional languages. Even so, English remains a compulsory paper, along with general knowledge and an essay composition designed to test powers of reasoning as well as qualities of writing and expression. Probationers are sent for training to the Lal Bahadur Shastri Academy of Administration in Mussoorie. The year in Mussoorie includes courses on the constitutional, economic and social framework of India today, and on public administration. At the end of the year, candidates are required to pass a written examination and qualifying examinations in Hindi and the language of the state to which they have been allotted. The requirement of a riding test has been discontinued. The year in Mussoorie is followed by up to two years of in-field training in the states before confirmation of appointment.

The career of a fresh IAS officer begins with a posting as a Sub-Divisional Officer (SDO) within a district. The IAS officer is a central government employee; the district is the major administrative unit of the state inherited from the colonial system. An IAS officer is normally assigned to one state cadre for her entire professional life, and about 70 per cent of IAS officers are in fact under state postings at any given time.[1] Where possible, the preferences of new recruits are accommodated when making the initial determinations on place-ments into state cadres. Thereafter, an officer may serve stints in the nation's capital, but will be considered to be on assignment to the centre from the state. In both New Delhi and the state capitals, the apex of the bureaucracy is the secretariat. In both units of government, the chief executive of a department is the secretary, and the highest rank in the state civil service is the chief secretary (see Figure 7.1).

The state governments have their own public services which function under the supervision of provincial public service commissions. State officials serve throughout their careers within their state's territorial jurisdictions. State administration is more demanding than central, since it is at this level that the tasks of development are executed, law and order is maintained and most of the interaction takes place between citizens, politicians and civil servants. Yet state services are less prestigious, less well-paid and, therefore, less competently staffed. Their superficial resemblance with the central services is not matched in the quality of recruitment and training. There are also wide disparities between the different states, with Bihar and Maharashtra, for example, representing the poorer and better ends of the spectrum respectively. The latter has a sufficient depth of quality graduates to ensure an efficient state service even after its best are seduced by the central services. The former's pool of talent is so shallow that it is generally under-represented in the central services in proportion to its population.

The peculiar administrative burden-sharing between the union and state governments distinguishes India from other federal systems

FIGURE 7.1
Organisational chart of Revenue Department,
State of Maharashtra, 1993

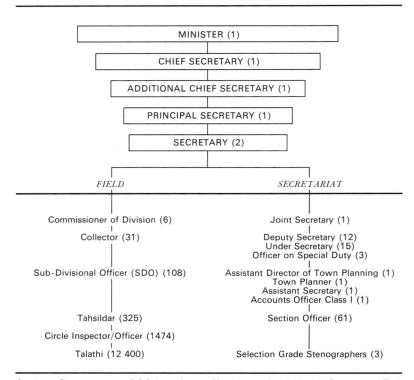

Source: Government of Maharashtra, *Karyakram Andajpatrak (Programme Estimates) 1993–94: Revenue and Forests Department* (Nagpur: Government Publications, 1993), pp. 6, 157.

like the American, Australian and Canadian. Its advantage is that it confers a degree of uniformity of administrative structure and practice throughout the land that would be impossible otherwise. It is also one of the major integrative institutions in Indian politics. The all-India services have in fact been used consciously as a nation-building instrument. The mix of domicile and out-of-state staffing, for example, ensures a spread of talent all around the country and fosters the sense of belonging to one nation. At the same time, there is also an attempt to strike a balance between national integration and localism: at least one-fifth of IAS officers in any state must be recruited from within the state's own administrative service. But no more than half of any state's IAS cadre can be from within the state.

Problems

In the ideal-type bureaucracy that we discussed at the start of this chapter, the official's legal authority rests on technical expertise. In reality, the professional standards of the expert can collide with the administrative requirements of the managerial official (even if the two should be the same person). Organisations today tend to be both professionalised and bureaucratised. We need to distinguish between the two alternative sources of authority if we wish to clarify some of the core issues and conflicts in today's organisations.

Another problem concerns alternative principles of governance. The organising principle of social action can be rooted either in majority rule or in administrative efficiency. The first accepts the freedom to dissent from official decisions, the second demands unquestioning obedience of superiors. Because many organisations, for example political parties, have both principles, they can sometimes experience tension between the two contrary pulls. In pursuit of the second principle, the bureaucracy institutionalised by the British and bequeathed to independent India was designed for administration and stability. Its major requirement was to contain demands. By contrast, the major task of post-independence bureaucracy was to be responsive to citizen demands. The government of independent India faced the difficult task of conversion of a law-and-order and revenue collection apparatus into an instrument of nation-building and development.

It is a cliche to say that independence changed the nature of the administrative tasks. It could be argued that the pre- and post-independence dichotomy is exaggerated. The concern of the British raj was not limited to the maintenance of law and order, but included some nation-building and development goals. Conversely, the requirements of maintaining law and order have if anything increased since independence, starting with the partition-related riots. Yet even while we should not exaggerate the change in the nature of bureaucratic tasks with independence, nor should we deny the substance of the underlying thesis. This is especially so in India because of the ambitious programme of planned economic development that was launched shortly after independence.

Democratisation of the civil services has another aspect to it. Article 335 of the constitution aims to break up the homogeneity of the administrative services by directing that the special claims of scheduled castes and tribes shall be taken into account in appointments to the central and state government services. We touched on the programmes of preferential policies earlier in Chapter 1. The letter and spirit of Article 335 have encountered two difficulties. As regards the letter, the same article stipulates that programmes of affirmative action shall be consistent with administrative efficiency. Possibly because of this rider, the elite services remain disproportionately 'Brahminised'. As regards the spirit, members of the scheduled castes and tribes who do make the transition to the prestigious all-India services are loath to continue to identify themselves with the backward and tribal communities. Instead, they assiduously cultivate the ethos of their new professional identity: which is still almost tangibly elitist.

The elitism of the service in composition and orientation had served the ICS well in ruling over a subject race. This is why, while many British had considered the ICS 'steel frame' one of the finest legacies bequeathed to independent India, many nationalists were contemptuous of an institution that was not Indian, nor civil, nor a service to the people. While democratisation has been attempted and to some extent achieved, by and large the premier administrative services remain elitist. They are narrowly recruited not simply in terms of social strata, but even in terms of educational background. The upper-class, urban families who send their children to the right schools and universities are over-represented; the poor, rural and backward communities are under-represented. In the 1960s, for example, about half of all IAS recruits came from just the four universities of Allahabad, Calcutta, Delhi and Madras. Some 70 per cent came from urban backgrounds, despite only 20 per cent of the population being urban. Only 20 per cent came from agricultural families, with 40 per cent being children of government officials.

We may conclude from this that recruitment on the basis of competitive examinations and interviews has a 'structural bias' in favour of the wealthy, urban and sophisticated graduate. By the mid-1970s, demonstrable progress had been achieved in democratising the services: the majority of IFS, IAS and allied services recruits were from the middle and lower classes (*Hindustan Times*, 6 February

1976). Recruits from a public school (in the English sense of the phrase) background had been pared down to about a fifth of the total intake. The fact remains however that an IAS officer who may be of humble origins quickly becomes elitist in orientation, helped by training, powers, and the perks and privileges of office.

A different kind of problem occurred at the lower rungs of the bureaucracy that were thoroughly bound by routine and precedent. To the lowly functionaries in the vast and labyrinthine bureaucracy of the British Raj, a government job was a comfortable livelihood which could best be safeguarded by pleasing superiors. Almost certainly Indian, the junior bureaucrat preferred regurgitation of his master's views to independent conceptual thinking, the safety of precedents to the frightening prospect of novel challenges. Success lay not in taking initiatives, but in the literal application of the formidable panoply of detailed regulations with which the steel frame had girded the subcontinent.

Another set of problems is generic to the Whitehall model of bureaucracy so well illustrated in the popular British television series *Yes Minister* and *Yes Prime Minister*. The permanence of the career civil servant and the transience of ministerial bosses leaves the latter open to manipulation by the former; there are jurisdictional wranglings between different departments concerning demarcation; and the cabinet, which should ensure coordination in a parliamentary system of government, can itself get entangled in 'turf warfare'. For example food production, which actually takes place within the territorial and legislative jurisdictions of states, is also covered by the Food and Agriculture Ministry, the Planning Commission, the Irrigation and Power Ministry and so on in New Delhi. The 'bureaucratic' rigidity has in some senses been hardened in India by the Whitehall model being transplanted to an entirely different social, economic and political environment. H. V. Kamath of the then-ruling Janata Party described the bureaucratic ethos thus in the Lok Sabha on 25 April 1979: 'If you can, don't move; if you must, move slowly; if pushed, move in circles; and if cornered, appoint a committee' (quoted in Gupta, 1982, p. 402).

India is not immune to the inter-service jealousies and interdepartmental rivalries that afflict all large bureaucracies. This means that officials are hypersensitive to the relativities of salary packages, status and powers of the various ministries. But it also means that any action requires multiple interdepartmental clearances. Part of the reason for this is once again the prevailing norm of safety first: extensive and repeated consultations ensure that responsibility for a mistake cannot easily be pinned on any one official. So no one is prepared to make a decision if it can somehow be passed on to someone else.

Under the regulatory regime established progressively after 1950, India fell victim to a relentless bureaucratic sprawl. Outside India at least, it was generally acknowledged that the country had a hugely bloated, inefficient and parasitically corrupt bureaucracy. A study conducted by the Federation of Indian Chambers of Commerce and Industry concluded that bureaucratic delays had cost the country a staggering Rs 1500 bn in thirty years since 1950. Each file awaiting government clearance for a billion rupee private sector project meant a loss of Rs 250 000 per day to the company concerned, an annual production loss of Rs 2.7m and a revenue loss of Rs 1.6m to the government (*OHT*, 13 May 1982). By the mid-1990s there is widespread sentiment even in India that the country's bureaucracy has become an elephantine, amorphous lump. Its pervasive presence is felt everywhere, its effectiveness or usefulness are apparent almost nowhere.

The Congress government of P. V. Narasimha Rao (1991–) decided to dismantle the heavily interventionist and regulatory state created by successive governments since independence. The dirigiste tendencies of the vast bureaucracy set up to administer the previous licence raj regime proved unsurprisingly resistant to change and demonstrated remarkable ingenuity in devising ways and means of thwarting reform. For example, the government decided on an 'open skies' policy that challenged the monopoly of the state-run domestic carrier, Indian Airlines (IA). Indian entrepreneurs took to the skies with characteristic verve. East West Airways, Jet Airways, Continental Aviation and Modiluft began to offer what IA had signally failed to: transporting passengers to their destinations on time and in comfort. Initial anti-competitive restrictions – IA was given the right to veto routing requests, private carriers were prohibited from charging fares less than 25 per cent below IA fares and from scheduling flights within one hour of IA flights – proved insufficient to dampen commuters' enthusiasm for the private air taxis. IA was compelled to improve its service to woo back customers: a textbook example of the virtues of competition. In addition, however, private airlines were told that they could not legally publish flight schedules and IA pilots were told that they could not switch jobs without a 'no objection certificate' from the IA: textbook examples of anti-competitive behaviour. Captured by the state sector employees, the bureaucracy was being driven by the interests of the people in it and not the public they were meant to serve. (For similar sentiments by a serving civil servant regarding Bangladesh, which emerged from the same British Raj culture, see Ahmed, 1994.)

Civil–Political Relations

Tensions between the bureaucrat and the politician are endemic to all political systems. They are heightened in the case of former colonies because of the transformation of the bureaucracy from a coercive apparatus of the colonial state to a responsive instrument of the indigenous people. Paradoxically, they were particularly acute in India precisely because of the success in socialising Indians into the bureaucratic and parliamentary traditions of the Westminster style of government. Before independence, the civil servant was often the administrator-master confronting the politician as a threat to the colonial law and order. For regardless of personal predilections, the civil servant was an official agent of the colonial state. Independence brought about a reversal of roles, and both sets of people – politicians no less than bureaucrats – had to come to terms with the role reversal. The problems of psychological adjustments were helped by the qualities of both groups of people at the time of independence: the Indians in the pre-1947 ICS (almost half the ICS corps was Indian by then) and the leaders of the nationalist movement were among the best and the brightest of their generation.

The same qualities were helpful also in another sense. On the one hand, Prime Minister Jawaharlal Nehru and his colleagues were confident enough of their own worth that they did not need to demonstrate their superiority by exacting retribution on those who had merely served in their lines of duty. On the other hand, they realised that India was fortunate to have inherited a proven framework of administration and a corps of experienced administrators. Being shrewd enough to recognise this, Nehru resisted calls from within the Congress Party to disband the ICS structure because of its elitist orientation and caste-like exclusivity. Instead, he stressed the ICS as a needed and welcome source of administrative competence and its potential as a nation-building and state-building instrument. He therefore retained it with a changed nomenclature.

Relative to 1947, as the quality of the civil servants and the politicians declined with the passage of time, suspicions between the two groups grew and tensions resurfaced. This was especially the case at the state level where the educational and intellectual calibre of the IAS officers was well above that of the political masters. The state of hostile coexistence spread upwards even to the central government with the propensity of cabinet ministers to shift responsibility for scandals to their departmental secretaries. Not surprisingly, this had a damaging effect on the morale and confidence of the civil servants. In the other direction, attempts at democratic decentralisation deepened the political process down to the village level and exposed the civil servant to politics and politicians as rough and ready as they come. The net result was to politicise the bureaucracy from New Delhi to the villages. Those who were amenable to their master's wishes and biddings began to be rewarded with plum postings and promotions, while those who resisted unwarranted interference with the routines of administration discovered their political independence and professional integrity to be distinctly career-unfriendly. The existence of a thriving private sector and a tradition of lateral mobility between the public and private sectors reduces the costs of resignations and diversifies the sensitivities and loyalties of workers. Lacking this in India, civil servants dare not wear their professional consciences on their dress shirts.

The carrot-and-stick approach gradually wore down the independence and integrity of the entire civil service, culminating in the complete capitulation of the bureaucracy to the excesses of the emergency during 1975–7: the bureaucrats honoured the venerable tradition of obeying orders lawfully issued. Tensions generated by the emergency excesses would have been partly ameliorated by the primacy given to the law-and-order function of the IAS officers, partly by the well-established habit by that date of political interference in bureaucratic affairs, and partly by the equally firmly established centralising tendency of Mrs Indira Gandhi which was 'codified' by the emergency. The other item of interest in the emergency experience was that the quality of administration deteriorated with a centralised authoritarian regime. The lines of bureaucratic authority grew longer while the sensitivity to local needs, conditions and aspirations lessened (Heginbotham, 1976, pp. 88–9).

The emergency period was Mrs Gandhi's darkest hour, and the notion of a committed bureaucracy came to be associated with her reign. At the Congress Party meeting on 16 November 1969, she had attacked the administrative machinery for constituting a stumbling block in the path of progress. The left wing of the party took up the cause and mounted an offensive against the conservative and reactionary leadership of the bureaucracy whose upper-class prejudices were said to be out of tune with the imperatives of progressive social and economic change. They called instead for a new administrative cadre that would be committed to national objectives and responsive to social needs. The concept of a committed bureaucracy provided a cover for increasingly partisan interference by politicians – union and state ministers, MPs and MLAs – in the affairs of administration. In 1993–4 stories circulated in the state of Bihar of an IAS officer having been slapped by a politician in the presence of other people and of having humbly accepted this very public insult. Still, he was more fortunate than Miss Chandralekha, a senior IAS officer in Tamil Nadu. On 19 May 1992, she was badly burnt and disfigured in an acid attack, purportedly for incurring the displeasure of Chief Minister Miss Jayalalitha (*SW*, 21 November 1992). The state government also recommended Chandralekha's suspension on trumped up charges, but the Union Ministry of Personnel declined to oblige.

So the pursuit of a committed bureaucracy had succeeded in producing a class of bureaucrats that was instantly subservient to, if also simultaneously contemptuous of, the politicians. The increasing politicisation of the bureaucracy was only too clear with the attempts by the Janata Government (1977–9) to weed out those guilty of enthusiastically enforcing the emergency regulations, and Mrs Gandhi's follow-up action in punishing such officials as had vigorously helped the Janata Government in its campaign against her. Her son and successor Rajiv Gandhi took prime ministerial disdain of the civil servant still further. He announced the dismissal of Foreign Secretary A. P. Venkateswaran at a nationally televised press conference in February 1987. Venkateswaran, in attendance at the press conference, had received no advance warning of what was to come and was visibly stunned at the announcement.

In the end the civil servant's response to political encroachments was twofold. On the one hand, as a means of promoting self-interest, each officer began to cultivate political patrons, powerful local leaders at each level who could be counted on to return favours through the bureaucrat's career path. On the other hand, as a measure of self-protection, the malaise that had afflicted the lower rungs of the bureaucracy during the British Raj now spread to the top echelons, namely a literal application of the myriad of rules and regulations. For if it could be shown that proper procedures had been followed, then one could not be disciplined. There was a goal displacement from civil service to job security. By the 1990s IAS officers themselves in private conversations referred to their service as 'I Am Safe'. Despite all this, and even though the district officer might now come into contact more with the district and state politicians than with the ordinary folk, the IAS district officer retains the mystical élan and predominance in the scheme of things.

Corruption in the Bureaucracy

The civil servant is to the businessman what the politician is to the bureaucrat. The plethora of controls introduced under the permit-licence raj have vested enormous powers in civil servants over business affairs. The system spawned an inefficient regulatory regime, cripplingly high compliance and transaction costs, a corrupt bureaucratic system and a rent-seeking political system. India's bureaucrats have only too often used red tape to suffocate the private sector. The goals of the Industries Development and Regulation Act of 1951 were help to small industries, prevention of capital concentration and dispersal of industrial expansion across the country. The regulatory regime created in pursuit of these goals discouraged successful firms from growing, encouraged them instead to lose money and, when they failed, forbade them to close. Setting up a new plant, relocating an existing one or expanding it in capacity or range of products could not be decided merely on commercial calculations, but were all subject to licence. They were also subject to the Monopolies and Trade Practices (MRTP) Act. Designed to guard the public interest against private monopolists, the MRTP protected the many public sector monopolies operated by bureau-crats against the public interest.

All of this against the backdrop of the wealth-consuming public servant treating the wealth-creating businessman with scorn and condescension. The prevailing bureaucratic attitude is that the businessman needs to be hemmed in by rules on all sides. Because the government's motive is egalitarian redistribution while that of the businessman is profit, the latter must be curbed by the former, argue the bureaucrats. In more recent times there has also been an element of envy. The official salaries of the civil servants ensure a total divorce between the status and income of bureaucrats. For the bright young person with drive, initiative and self-belief, the private sector offers more attractive salary packages and greater scope for rapid career advancement. Civil servants have suffered relative deprivation of material rewards since independence as businesses have prospered. Because they are in a position to affect private sector decisions worth millions of rupees, most give in to the temptation to transfer some of the freefloating money to their own pockets. In 1993, for example, a young District Magistrate in one of the metropolitan cities was asking and getting one hundred thousand rupees per approval for routine housing construction projects.

Political interference, reduced attractiveness of service and declining morale have all combined to whittle away the bureaucrat's will to remain honest. When politicians above (ministers) and below (party hacks) are both venal, then the IAS officer too gets sandwiched into corruption. India is notorious for its influence-peddling politicians, money-seeking bureaucrats and bribe-dispensing entrepreneurs. A permit-licence Raj creates recurring shortages and multiplies opportunities for illicit profit or 'rent'. Because action depends on bureaucratic and political discretion, the discretionary application of controls makes the rent part-property of the minister and the civil servant making the decision. Bribery is so thoroughly institutionalised that most people engaged in the transactions are aware of the scale of the charges and the lateral and upwards percentage shares in the illicit rent (see Wade, 1985). The market for public office can be quantified, for example, in the marriage market in Bihar: the dowry will reflect the illicit earning potential of the bridegroom's public sector job. Similarly, a state cabinet minister in Bihar will expect a kickback in proportion to the earning potential of the posting of an engineer to a construction project. In turn, squabbles between politicians for portfolios reflect the latter's earning potential rather than policy preferences. In Bihar at least the chief demand on a state cabinet minister is not to make policy but to exercise discretionary authority in exchange for due consideration. The culture of corruption has become deeply embedded in Indian public life.

It could be said that bribes serve to bring the costs of services in line with market prices. Bribery is an efficient mechanism for rationing a good or service which is in short supply. Graft, it has been said often enough, lubricates the wheels of government in India. Yet even from the point of view of economic logic, public corruption is bad because it encourages inefficiency. Managers have built-in incentives to distort and disrupt markets because this increases their market power. It becomes something of a catch-22: rent-seeking is an efficient response to distortions, but distortions are also a logical response to the availability of rent. Special dispensation in order to circumvent bureaucratic or legal hurdles in return for material gain almost certainly occurs in every country. What makes the pervasiveness of corruption in India so distinctive is that graft is necessary to get the lowliest officials to perform their *ordinary* duties for which they are receiving salaries from the public purse.

EXHIBIT 7.1

The tale of the village headmaster, 1975

Ram Pratap Shukla was a 44–year old headmaster in a school in the village of Khatwara in U.P. His salary had not been paid for 11 months. He had already gone thrice to Banda, the district headquarters, from his village before this story begins.

2 June 1975
Ram Pratap and his brother Shiv Pratap travelled from Khatwara to Banda, a distance of about 100 km. The bus fare cost him Rs 15. Arrived in Banda, the two stayed in a dharamsala (charitable dormitory for indigent wayfarers). Because Ram Pratap was asthmatic and looked ill, the manager at first refused them admission but changed his mind when Shiv Pratap explained that they were in some distress.

3 June 1975, 6.00 a.m.
The brothers Pratap went to the offices of the Basic Shiksha Adhikari (Basic Education Officer). (Office hours in the summer are 6.00 a.m.–12.00 p.m.) They knocked on the doors of all, from the Adhikari to the clerks, to no avail. But at the cost of entertaining four clerks to tea, they learnt that the cheque for payment of the salary arrears was ready. The clerks said that money would have to be spent to get the cheque so that all sides gained in the transaction. The brothers returned dejected to the dharamsala, intending to revisit the education office the next morning.

4 June 1975, 4.00 a.m.
Ram Pratap Shukla suffered an asthma attack. By 6.00 a.m., when he was visibly distressed, Shiv Pratap hurriedly summoned a rickshaw and took his brother to the Zila Parishad (District Board) office. Ram Pratap was dead on arrival. His body was placed under a tree outside the Zila Parishad office. Money for the funeral was donated by the local teachers' association and a jeep was arranged to take the body back to Khatwara.

The cheque for Rs 3156.58 owing to Ram Pratap Shukla as accumulated salary was signed on 4 June 1975 after he was dead.

Source: *The Statesman* (New Delhi), 13 June 1975.

The biggest cost is political. Petty corruption is especially endemic at the lower, clerical levels of administration – precisely the point at which the ordinary citizen comes into daily contact with the bureaucracy. People are forced to pay bribes for securing virtually any service connected with the government, even that which is theirs by right and law. People naturally tend to judge the entire structure of government on the basis of direct experiences with the agents of government. It would be difficult to exaggerate the revulsion of ordinary Indians to the ubiquitous and institutionalised venality of public life (see Exhibit 7.1). More than any other factor, corruption of politicians and officials has eroded the legitimacy of dirigiste government at its core. Rajiv Gandhi's biggest political asset in 1984 was his image of being 'Mr Clean'. Hence the importance of the Bofors scandal (involving the purchase of Swedish howitzers for the Indian army) which tainted him and contributed materially to his government's defeat in 1989. In March 1993 Prime Minister P. V. Narasimha Rao too was embarrassed by allegations of corruption. Harshad Mehta, a stockbroker facing charges arising from the $1.6 bn bank-securities scam of 1992, alleged that he paid Rs 10m (about $390 000) in cash to the prime minister at his residence on 4 November 1991 as a means of gaining political patronage. Because of the prevailing culture of corruption, not all Indians were convinced by Narasimha Rao's protestations of innocence.

Reforms

Successive governments have made repeated attempts to reform the administrative structure of the country, but with little visible success. The structure of the all-India services would be instantly recognisable to anyone familiar with their counterparts in British India, but not the quality of the services provided nor the working environment. As well as the Planning Commission, such eminent persons as Paul Appleby, Gopalaswami Ayyangar, A. D. Gorwala and V. T. Krishnamachari have submitted reports on restructuring the administrative services. Although discussion has been plentiful, action has been tardy. In January 1966, the government set up a 5-member Administrative Reforms Commission under the chairmanship of Deputy Prime Minister Morarji Desai to signal its elevated status and firmness of leadership. Its terms of reference included scrutiny of the machinery and procedures of the central government;

the planning machinery at all levels; centre–state relations; financial, economic and personnel administration; and official machinery for the redress of public grievances. It submitted several reports, and the government responded by setting up a Department of Personnel and Administrative Reforms to process and study the reports. This was followed by the setting up of a Committee of Secretaries, and then a Committee of Ministers in 1973. In the meantime, life for the bureaucrats, the politicians and the people carried on as before.

There are several obstacles to substantive reform of the administrative services, starting with the sheer weight of bureaucratic inertia. The administrative tradition may have been inherited from the British, but its scope and reach has expanded enormously under the impact of technology and the explosion of government into economic and social activities. The structure of administration is therefore much more complicated and cumbersome than was the case before 1947. The inertia that is common to any organisation is given extra weight in India because of the size, diversity and federal nature of the country. The 'length of the line' (see Figure 7.1) had caused concern even during the British days. The concerns have become still more acute with the passage of time and the multiplication of tasks and taskmasters. There is a great physical distance between the desk-bound and paper-pushing bureaucrat and the 'average Indian in the village'. This is reinforced by the social distance between the civil servants in the elitist services and the people they are supposed to serve. Together, the social and physical distances ensure that the higher bureaucracy is a self-contained and self-satisfied group.

The bureaucracy has a vested interest in preserving and perpetuating its stranglehold over the nation's affairs, while the bureaucrat has a vested interest in preserving a structure which provides a high-powered job for life to someone who might lack any specialist qualification suited to today's increasingly technocratic job market. The lack of specialist training also produces a dogged devotion to familiar routine. Inertia is encouraged and initiative discouraged by the strong sense of hierarchy and the automatic promotion system.

The need for public sector reform in India is as urgent as the continuing lack of it is surprising. It is possible that the series of economic reforms ushered in by Prime Minister Narasimha Rao and Finance Minister Manmohan Singh since mid-1991 will lead to a progressive retrenchment of the public sector from Indian society and economy and usher in major administrative reforms in its wake.

Conclusion

The modern state is the professional state. Ministers lack both expertise and experience in administration. Professionalism in the art of government requires that policy formulation and policy implementation be placed in the hands of technocrats with the requisite specialist skills and knowledge of the principles of public administration. The total public payroll in India, including the higher state and central civil services as well as the multitude of clerks, peons and assorted hangers-on, has more than quadrupled from four million personnel in 1953 to seventeen million in 1993. The bureaucrats' tentacles reach into the farthest corners of the country and touch the most distant sphere of social activity in India. Their pay and emoluments is a major drain on the public exchequer. Nor is it productive expenditure: India's massive public service can almost be said to represent a vast reserve army of the underemployed. For the bureaucracy below the level of the IAS officers is inefficient and obstructionist rather than competent and facilitative. At the same time, the pervasiveness of government regulations matches the omnipresence of bureaucrats. Both are designed to ensure the delivery of services to the people: agricultural, educational, medical and other. In fact the combination has resulted in the growth of a bureaucratic underclass of 'fixers' and 'brokers' who serve as intermediaries between the people and the bureaucrats (Reddy and Haragopal, 1985). When not even the sound of pencils being sharpened and paper being pushed disturbs the somnolence of secretariat offices in the heat of an Indian summer, the bureaucratic favour-brokers are approached with the request *Jara pairavi kar dijiye* (idiomatically translated from Hindi, 'Please go and lobby on my behalf').

While the structure of the bureaucracy is recognisable as that inherited from the British, the pattern of interactions between the bureaucrat and the minister has been 'fundamentally transformed in the direction of a patrimonial regime in which the political leadership selects officers who are personally loyal, who serve their narrow political interests, and who expect reciprocal preferments in return' (Brass, 1990, p. 52). As this indicates, there is some slippage between the Weberian ideal of a rational–legal bureaucracy and the operational reality of the Indian bureaucracy. The civil servant in India is not guided solely by the formal roles and regulations. Rather, the operational environment is a complex and mutually reinforcing network of rules; personal, kinship, caste and political ties; and financial considerations. Through all this, the principal beneficiaries of the system of patronage that has been established for the production and distribution of benefits and resources are the politicians and bureaucrats themselves. As with so much else in India, the steel of which the administrative frame is constructed has been adulterated with baser impurities.

Note

1. Sometimes this creates interesting situations. In the late 1980s, there was a dispute between the governments of India and Bihar over the fair price for some land that the central government wished to acquire from the state. Intense negotiations were carried on between the two governments by an IAS officer of the Bihar cadre. As a representative of the state government, he would send a formal communication to the central government, and formally receive the same as a representative of the central government; and vice versa.

Further Reading

Dwivedi and Jain (1985). Discusses the tension between the uses and abuses of bureaucratic power.

Heginbotham (1975). Using community development in the state of Tamil Nadu as a case study, explores the tensions created by the pressures of economic development and social change under the direction of a planning bureaucracy.

Jain (1983). A collection of essays examining the dilemmas of a politicised bureaucracy.

Maheshwari (1992). A good account of the recruitment, training and operation of the All-India Services.

Misra (1986). Lucid and well-documented exposition of a controversial thesis, that the 1950 constitution facilitated the emergence of a bureaucracy that is just as self-serving as its predecessor, but neither as honest nor efficient.

Wade (1985). A very good account of the institutionalisation of public corruption.

8

The Security Services

The bureaucracy helps to make and implement laws; the police uphold and enforce them. Every country maintains security services to protect its citizens from lawlessness within and enemies without. Because of their coercive nature, however, the security services can also be misused by governments as an instrument for oppressing their own people. In this chapter, I shall:

1. Describe the police setup in India.
2. Discuss the role of the police in maintaining law and order and solving crimes.
3. Examine the dangers of police politicisation and militancy.
4. Describe the structure of India's defence forces.
5. Speculate on the reasons for the absence of military intervention in India in the context of the literature on military interventions and the state of civil–military relations.

The Police

As Australia's Police Commissioner Peter McAulay puts it, 'Protecting the rights of members of a community to pursue their legitimate interests, peacefully and safely, is fundamental to the political, economic and social wellbeing of any society' (McAulay, 1993, p. 33). The principles of democratic policing are to uphold the rule of law, to uphold the rights of individuals, and to resolve law-and-order incidents with the minimum use of force.

The people of India however regard the police as the protectors of criminals. They perpetrate some crimes themselves, shield criminals, refuse to register complaints against them, fabricate false cases against innocent victims instead, use beatings as their favourite technique of investigation and frequently resort to illegal detentions at police stations. Any contact with the police for the ordinary citizen is an occasion for extortion and bribery. When a foreign oil company executive in New Delhi complained that a technician had demanded a bribe before repairing his phone, 'The police said they'd arrest him – but only for a fee' (*Far Eastern Economic Review*, 23 June 1994, p. 11). Because of the pervasiveness of the police presence throughout the country, the cynicism of the populace towards this very basic state institution is a political fact of the first importance. No analysis of Indian politics will be realistic without a substantial discussion of the police.

The British legacy of the Indian bureaucracy is again obvious in the police services. The basic structure of the police services is in essence still the same as that which was prescribed by the Police Act of 1861. In the division of powers under the Indian constitution, police forces come under the jurisdiction of states. Nevertheless, every state force has a similar structure of organisation, training, command and hierarchy, and functions under similar rules of operation.

The central government also maintains several large police and paramilitary forces (Table 8.1), including intelligence officers and industrial police. Units of the Central Reserve Police Force (CRPF), the Border Security Force (BSF), the Assam Rifles (the grand old unit of the paramilitary forces) and so on are paramilitary rather than police forces. They are well-armed (but not with the heavy weapons of warfare available to the defence forces proper), organised along military lines of battalions and regiments, housed in barracks and subject to military rather than civilian discipline. The CRPF is tasked, with increasing frequency, to assist the state police forces in situations of emergency disturbances, or to substitute for them if they themselves become partisan units in sectarian civil disturbances. The BSF, like the Assam Rifles and Indo-Tibetan Border Police, was created and structured primarily to aid the army along India's long and troubled borders, but can also be called in to lend assistance to state police forces that find themselves over-stretched or otherwise unable to cope. There are also more specialised units like the Defence Security Corps and the Central Industrial Security Force for protecting defence installations and public sector enterprises respectively. The National Security Guards was formed in 1985 (following Mrs Indira Gandhi's assassination) as an elite counter-

TABLE 8.1

Indian military, paramilitary and police forces

Force	Number
Armed Forces (1992)	**1 265 000**
Army	1 100 000
Navy	55 000
Air Force	110 000
Reserves (1992)[a]	**1 305 000**
Army	950 000
Territorial Army	160 000
Navy	55 000
Air Force	140 000
Paramilitary Forces (1992)	**392 800**
National Security Guards	7 500
Central Reserve Police Force (CRPF) (123 battalions)[b]	125 000
Border Security Force (BSF) (149 battalions)[b]	171 000
Assam Rifles (31 battalions)[b]	35 000
Indo-Tibetan Border Police (27 battalions)[b]	29 000
Special Frontier Force	10 000
Rashtriya Rifles[c]	10 000
Coastguard	5 300
Police Forces (1992)	**1 483 000**
Central Industrial Security Force[b,d,e]	84 000
Defence Security Corps[e]	31 000
Home Guard[e]	464 000
Regular Police (1981)	504 000
Armed Police Battalions	400 000

Notes:

a. Indian military specialists claim that the IISS figures on reserves are greatly exaggerated. The correct figures are about 60% of the above.

b. Although under the operational control of the army (except for 5 battalions of the Assam Rifles), these come under the control of the Ministry of Home Affairs for funding.

c. The government has decided to raise the strength of the Rashtriya Rifles to 30 000.

d. The figure of 84 000 is from the Institute for Defence Studies and Analyses in New Delhi. The IISS figure is 74 000.

e. The CISF, DSG and Home Guards are listed by the IISS as paramilitary forces. Indian specialists prefer to place them in the Police Forces category.

Sources: *The Military Balance 1993–1994* (London: Brassey's for the International Institute for Strategic Studies, 1993), pp. 138–40; Paul Brass, *The Politics of India since Independence* (New York: Cambridge University Press, 1990), p. 55.

terrorist force. The Black Cat commandos, so known because of their distinctive uniform, are the country's elite unit for protecting eminent people from terrorist attacks.

The purpose in creating a vast reserve of paramilitary forces was to give the central government an intermediate instrument between the police and the army for deploying force for the maintenance of public order. The breakdown of law and order in Assam, Punjab and Kashmir was dealt with by deploying the paramilitary forces more than the army. The cost of using the paramilitary forces rather than the regular army is that the former, being less disciplined, are more likely to commit atrocities and human rights abuses and thereby exacerbate the problems of communal violence and insurgencies.

Each state, too, maintains armed police battalions. The 'ordinary' police force is responsible for the routine of maintaining public order and carrying out the day-to-day functions of police, including traffic control. Under normal conditions, the armed police is confined to barracks. It is used as a reserve force to handle large-scale threats to law and order. State armed police are of two types. The District Armed Police is usually kept in reserve for riot duty. The mobile units of armed state police forces come in various names: the Provincial Armed Constabulary in U.P., the Military Police in Orissa, the Karnataka State Reserve Police and so on.

The Indian Police Service (IPS) – one of the rods in the British Indian steel frame – was retained alongside the civil service as an all-India service after independence. This ensured continuity in the period of transition from colony to independent country, and uniformity across the country. The IPS is the aristocratic wing of the police force, being to the police what the Indian Administrative Service (IAS) is to the bureaucracy. Recruitment is under the management of the Union Public Service Commission (UPSC), and takes place at the same time and alongside recruitment into the other prestige central services like the IAS and Indian Foreign Service (IFS). Because the latter two are more attractive in terms of status, salary and bureaucratic power, the IPS is generally the second or third preference of hopeful applicants for these services. The police hierarchy argues that the status, salary and career prospects should be broadly similar in the major services in order to facilitate the selection of candidates of comparable qualifications and abilities but job-relevant aptitudes and skills. Despite this, in a world of acute scarcity, all central government careers offer security, power and status. The IPS, IAS and IFS are the three premier services.

After training at the Sardar Vallabbhai Patel National Police Academy in Hyderabad, IPS officers are assigned to a particular state cadre for the rest of their professional lives. An IPS officer begins her or his (as with the IAS, there are several women IPS officers) professional life in a state cadre at the rank of Sub-Divisional Police Officer. The highest rank in a state police cadre is the Director-General of Police. Metropolitan cities like Bombay, Calcutta and Delhi can also have their own police forces independently of their respective state cadres. The British practice of placing the Super-intendent of Police (SP) – the senior police officer in a district – under the control of the district magistrate (DM) has been continued. The DM still exercises control over the district police administration, and the IAS over the state police administration in general (Saha, 1992, p. 11).

State public service commissions are responsible for recruiting officers at the level of Deputy SP. One-third of the IPS cadre is filled by promotion from within a state's police officers. Ordinary police start off as constables after recruitment by the SP of the district; assistant sub-inspectors, sub-inspectors and inspectors too are recruited at the district level. The basic organisational unit of the police is the police station whose officer-in-charge is of inspector rank. The lowest units of administration are the Block Development Officer in civil administration, the Circuit Officer in revenue collection and the Inspector on the police side. But the territorial boundaries of the three branches do not have to be coterminous. In the state of Bihar, there are typically about a dozen police stations per district.

In contrast to the IPS, the rank and file police officers betray abysmal educational standards. The reasons for this include unattractive conditions of service, poor pay and negligible promotion prospects. The able and the enterprising are not, therefore, recruited into the police force at the lower levels. Yet members of the public have the greatest contact with policemen precisely at this level. The common police constable is not held in any high regard, is notorious for petty corruption, and receives little cooperation from the public.

Law and Order

The police play a pivotal role in the country's administrative system through the maintenance of law and order. Their duties have become more onerous and dangerous with escalating sectarian and political violence. The high incidence of group violence has led to the frequent employment of police forces to quell and control political or communal groups, thereby taking away such forces from their primary role of fighting 'ordinary' crime and engaging in routine police duties.

The police can be confronted by five different types of law-and-order problems: sporadic violence, organised violence in the cities, revolutionary violence in the countryside, industrial violence and caste or communal riots.

Spontaneous outbreaks. The easiest to deal with are outbursts of violence caused by the pressures and frustrations of modern urban life: sporadic and isolated outbreaks of violence because, say, someone has been knocked down by a bus in the city. Burning trams in protest against such accidents is common enough in a city like Calcutta, tinged with residual respectability for such actions from the days when the tramways were foreign-owned and therefore legitimate targets of fiery nationalists.

Organised urban protest. Demonstrations, *satyagraha* (fast), *hartal* (strike) and *gherao* (non-violent siege or encirclement) are a staple diet of the Indian political menu. Any or all of these can easily degenerate into violence. Their roots, too, go back to the the pre-independence nationalist movement. They also reflect opposition frustrations in the first-past-the-post system of elections. Opposition parties have consistently won less legislative seats than the proportion of people voting for them in state and national elections. Consequently, with their strength in parliament not reflecting their true political power, they tend to mobilise popular demonstrations as a measure and reminder of their continuing popularity. Protests – especially if they are successful and spectacular – can increase recruitment into a political party through the bandwagon effect. If political leaders are blessed enough to be arrested by the police, then they are assured instant political martyrdom: having been to prison in a political cause is a much sought-after status by hopeful political aspirants in India. The habit of demonstration is most firmly rooted in Bengali political culture, where a Marxist-dominated state government initiated the interesting variant of itself organising a protest strike against the central government in the 1980s.

As the last suggests, the police have to confront a political dilemma as well as a civil disturbance. It is simple enough to control a demonstration and break it up if it turns violent. The difficult task is to gauge firstly the attitude and support of the political authorities, as a safeguard against being made a scapegoat. Secondly, with so many state governments being formed since the 1980s by non-Congress parties, the police also have to be sensitive to the possibility that today's demonstrator at the receiving end of the police *lathi* (bamboo rod) may turn out to be tomorrow's political master. The twin difficulties have taken their toll on police morale, discipline and integrity.

The practice of periodic strikes by assorted elements of the public can be blamed at least partially on government sins of omission and commission. They refuse to pay heed to legitimate demands except when sizeable and violent demonstrations claim their urgent attention. This political error is then compounded by the habit of giving in to demands backed by street power regardless of merits. 'Having so frequently conceded to agitation . . . , Indian governments have made a rod for their own backs, the full force of which is felt by their policemen' (Hanson and Douglas, 1972, p. 159).

Revolutionary rural violence. The third type of law-and-order issue to confront the police in India is violent insurrections in the countryside under the influence of some revolutionary doctrine or another, for example the Naxalite movement. The 'Green Revolution' widened the gap between the rich and the poor in rural society, and sometimes exacerbated unemployment by mechanising agriculture. Forcible occupations of land have become common virtually all across the country. Frequently, this involves clashes between agitating landless labourers and landlords determined to carry through programmes of forcible harvesting. Both sides feel free to take the law into their own hands; landlords have been known to take the law into their pockets too. The police difficulty in this type of agitation is that they are thinly spread on the ground, suffer from defective communications, receive little public cooperation and are perennially apprehensive of not receiving the requisite political backing. The relationship between the political master and the police servant is not one built on mutual trust and respect: perhaps each knows the other only too well.

Industrial disputes. Disputes purely of an industrial type involving professional *goondas* (thugs or rent-a-criminal types) are relatively uncomplicated for the police to deal with. Not so easy have been new forms of protest, e.g. the institution of *gherao*, which pose many problems unfamiliar to the police lexicon. The distinction between ordinary crime and industrial crime has tended to be increasingly blurred, with a corresponding erosion of the distinctions between petty criminals and political wrongdoers.

Sectarian violence.   Communal violence in India is sporadic rather than sustained, with the major exception of the troubles in the Punjab in the 1980s. But the potential for communal violence is ever-present, and the intensity of sectarian violence can easily take on horrifying proportions. Terrorism associated with communal violence has provided both the greatest failure of Indian police – the assassination of Prime Minister Indira Gandhi on 31 October 1984 by her own bodyguards – and one of its moments of greatest triumph – the successful flushing out of terrorists from the Golden Temple in May 1988. The latter success was praised by the influential London *Economist* (28 May 1988, p. 18) as 'one of the most intelligent pieces of antiterrorist police work seen anywhere in recent years'.

Caste violence too has been on a growth spurt in recent years. If we look at a one-year period over 1981–2, we see that there was a backlash against increasing quota seats for the outcastes in the medical colleges of Gujarat. In the ensuing agitation, 30 deaths were reported by mid-March 1981. In April, 14 tribals were killed in a tribal–police clash in the village of Indravalli in the district of Adilabad (Andhra Pradesh). During April–May, 48 deaths were recorded in Biharsharif (Bihar) in fighting between Hindus and Muslims. In July, 18 people were killed in communal clashes in Hyderabad. In August, caste Hindus burnt down 200 *Harijan* (Mahatma Gandhi's word for the outcastes) huts in the South Arcot district of Tamil Nadu. September saw communal rioting and deaths in Baroda (Gujarat), Ahmednagar (Maharashtra), and Dinajpur (West Bengal). The police themselves went on strike in Andhra Pradesh, Bihar and parts of Maharashtra and West Bengal in October. In November, 24 *Harijans* were shot dead in Deoli village, Mainpuri (U.P.). In March 1982, there were outbreaks of communal rioting in Baroda, Aligarh (U.P.), Anantnag (Kashmir), and Kanyakumari (Kerala).

In all such cases, the police have to maintain the fine line between inaction, over-vigorous action, and sectarian partiality and identification with one of the groups engaged in the clashes. *Harijans* mistrust the 'protective forces' comprising upper caste men and officers.

Muslims in general prefer the CRPF to the state police cadres because it is less likely to be aligned with local chauvinism or politics. Sikhs dislike the CRPF in the Punjab because it represents an alien oppressive force; Hindus distrust the state police force because Sikhs predominate.

Solving Crimes

By 1993 there was a widespread sense throughout India that the crime situation was so out of control that it was a threat to the territorial integrity of the country and the very survival of the polity. Terrorists, drug traffickers and organised gangsters were busy stockpiling ever-more sophisticated weapons. They did so with the active (because of bribes) or passive (for fear of their own lives) connivance of police and custom officers. The number and sophistication of the arms and explosives used in the bomb blasts that rocked Bombay in March 1993 could not have been smuggled into the country otherwise.

The procedure for investigation and trials of criminal cases is initiated by reporting a crime to the police. Cognisance of the crime is then taken under section 154 of the Criminal Procedure Code (CrPC). A First Information Report (FIR) is registered and an investigation taken up under sections 156 and 157 of the CrPC. The investigating officer records statements from witnesses under section 161. At this point, however, witnesses are under no legal compulsion to speak the truth, that requirement coming only during trial in the courts. Some senior police officers would like to see this altered on the ground that 'It is human psychology that people speak the truth when examined by the police on the spot' (Verma, 1992, p. 12).

As against this it might be countered that the people are so mistrustful of the police that they are more likely to fear still further coercion and harassment at police hands if the law were to be changed. A Director-General of Police has argued that the criminal law itself helps the criminals to escape justice and encourages corruption in the police force (Verma, 1992, p. 12). Safeguards meant to protect the dignity and person of the innocent are transformed into loopholes for exploitation by the criminals. This results in a lower percentage of crimes being solved. In 'heinous and sensational crimes' the crime solution rate is almost zero. The conviction rate – one of the most effective deterrents against crime – has been slipping steadily, especially in regard to serious crimes. The net result is an erosion of public faith in the institutions of law enforcement. While the central thesis is debatable – all police forces everywhere claim to be handicapped in their fight against organised crime by provisions enacted to protect the civil liberties of citizens – the conclusion regarding the loss of public confidence in the police force is unlikely to be contested.

Police Politicisation

Sociologists and criminologists attribute spiralling acts of individual and group violence to a breakdown in social order and the inability of the justice system to cope with the rising demands made on it by a litigation-prone society. People therefore take the law more and more into their own hands. Certainly no one familiar with India today at even the most rudimentary level will dispute the proposition that the people have lost faith in the ability of government to assure minimal security; justice is a far more distant aspiration. The sensational news reports of many police excesses, for example the much-reported blindings of alleged dacoits in jail in Bhagalpur (Bihar) in 1981, must be put in this perspective. Interviews with some of the senior police officers whose men were responsible for the blindings suggest that the prime motivating cause was frustration with political interference in police efforts to eradicate armed crime. 'Known criminals' would be arrested by the police, only to be released under political influence before going back to terrorising the people. (The politicians resort to the thugs to intimidate opponents between elections, and to 'deliver' votes or 'capture' polling booths during elections.) Pent-up anger and frustration led to the criminals being blinded before the politicians could secure their release yet again.

The incidence also illustrates the point that both police and public recognise that they are trapped in an unjust and insensitive environment which fails to deliver either order or justice. In the words of a BSF Inspector-General, 'The police are feared by the common man, misused by the rich and powerful for their selfish ends, pilloried by the press and made a scapegoat by the party in power' (Sen, 1991, p. 12). This creates a vicious circle which makes individuals resort to self-protection schemes at the same time as tightening the criminal–politician–police nexus even further.

The result is that some section of the political spectrum will always criticise the police for excessive zeal, and another section will attack them for inadequate action. Yet the police cannot be similarly assured of some political defence or support of their actions. The multiplication of protest action has therefore produced a corresponding increase in the need for police officers to cultivate political patrons to protect their backs 'after the fact'.

Gazetted officers and non-gazetted ranks of policemen are only too familiar with political interference in their daily affairs, of being asked to file false charges against political opponents, or drop investigations against political allies. Political patronage has thoroughly infiltrated the justice system. In some parts of the country the practice is strongly institutionalised: the price of recruitment, promotion and transfers for the various ranks is well known to both those seeking and those dispensing political favours. There has grown up in much of India therefore a dual system of justice – the formal channels coexist alongside the political. Indian commentators have long pointed to the unholy nexus between politicians, armed criminals and the police. The bureaucracy and police in India have also long since been politicised at all levels. With a steady criminalisation of politics, there is by now a marked politicisation of crime. Politicians are corrupt, held in general contempt but feared for their ruthlessness in wielding state power. The police are held in private ridicule for their mouse-like timidity towards political superiors and lion-like arrogance in dealings with the general public.

Predictably, whole communities have lost faith in the machinery of the police. In some instances state chief ministers are themselves behind police excesses, with victims being either individual critics or sectarian opponents. In Bihar and U.P. private organisations and groups terrorise the countryside, extracting fat protection money from ordinary law-abiding citizens. The nexus between politicians and criminal gangsters is an established fact, and many policemen end up in the profitable role of middlemen. In the words of a senior Indian journalist, ' "Thanas" (police stations) are on sale. The price depends on the extent of black marketing and illicit trade in the areas they command' (Nayar, 1984). The IPS cadre has been no more immune to politicisation than the IAS, and indeed virtually all the comments about civil servant–politician relations are equally applicable to police officer–politician relations.

Increased political pressures on the Indian police have contributed directly to diminished resistance to personal/petty corruption and brutalisation. In an environment of moral bankruptcy and job scarcity, for a police officer to refuse to do the biddings of his political master is to invite loss of career, material deprivations for family and abandonment of decent schooling prospects for children in the cause of an ideal system of law which is conspicuously lacking. But as the police force becomes more generally corrupted, members of the public in turn are forced into choosing between meting out their own justice or abusing the official machinery for personal ends.

The power of politicians within the district depends on their capacity to dispense favours. Being able to 'influence' the district police, both positively by conferring favours and negatively by obstructing investigations, is a strategic asset in the ability to dole out favours. The local police have also been used with increasing brazenness and frequency to harass, intimidate and otherwise coerce local political or feudal rivals. Recalcitrant police can be 'disciplined' by transfers to remote areas or trivial tasks; pliant officers can be rewarded with plum postings and accelerated upward mobility. Once political control over police transfers and promotions becomes the norm, officers from the rank of Deputy SP upwards require political patronage. The complete subordination of the police and the bureaucracy to the political executive was at its worst during the 1975–7 emergency. Opposition and dissident politicians were kept under surveillance, harassed and arrested in large numbers.

The emergency rule by Mrs Gandhi was the most dramatic manifestation of the politicisation of the police and administrative services of the country. The emergency forced Indian policemen at all levels, but especially senior IPS officers, to confront what Bayley (1983, p. 485) has labelled 'the Nuremberg dilemma': should they execute orders that they believed to be politically motivated, self-serving and possibly illegal? The defeat of Mrs Gandhi in the 1977 election accentuated the rift between officers who had served her cause at personal gain, and those who had refused and been made to suffer. The Shah Commission of Inquiry vividly documented the widespread abuses of official power by administrative and police officers, and some punishment was exacted.

The return of Mrs Gandhi in 1980 began another round of counter-purges and rehabilitations. The most sensational of the former was the midnight arrest and imprisonment of the Central Bureau of Investigation (CBI) officer in charge of the 'Kissa Kursi Ka' case, a satirical film about Indira and Sanjay Gandhi which had mysteriously disappeared. The officer was released in the face of mounting protests, including a petition signed by more than 200 IPS officers. The most spectacular rehabilitation was that of J. S. Bhinder. Prosecuted (but not convicted) of murder under the Janata regime

(1977–80), Bhinder was appointed Police Commissioner of New Delhi by an unrepentant Mrs Gandhi. The country, including officers in various branches of government, drew the conclusion that the age of committed bureaucracy had arrived.

Not surprisingly, political manipulation has sapped police morale and discipline. Inefficient, incompetent, corrupt, brutal and even criminal 'officers of the law' have been shielded from the due processes of the law by powerful patrons. Senior IPS officers admit and decry the fact that in some states they no longer control their own force. An illustration of this was provided in Bihar. On 3 January 1991, two men who had taken part in a fatal attack on Randhir Verma (SP Dhanbad) were killed by the police while in custody. A senior district official explained this away as 'nothing more than a rush of blood'. What he regretted was that through their 'foolishness we have lost some vital clues' (*TOI*, Patna, 13 January 1991).

In 1992 the U.P. police were caught between their legal role of protecting the Babri Masjid in Ayodhya and the political reality of a state government that was committed to destroying the mosque. This, and not the narrower consideration of sympathising with the sentiments of the Hindu mob, was the larger dilemma confronting the guardians of law and order on 6 December. For every senior police officer in India, there is an imbalance today between professional dedication to impartial duty and partial service to the group in power in the state and national capitals. In dealing with a riotous mob without worrying about its relationship with the state government, an officer does little to enhance career prospects and accepts a substantial risk of damage thereto. Cabinet ministers will descend on him not to praise him but to bury him. So in Ayodhya the police, well aware of the BJP state government's politics, stood as silent onlookers to the destruction of a mosque which was under the protection of the Supreme Court of India. The police themselves were alleged to have joined in the massacre of Muslims in the ensuing riots in Bombay.

The Janata government appointed a National Police Commission in 1977 to examine all aspects of the police system. The only other police commissions on a national scale in modern times were in 1860, which created the police structure as we know it in India, and in 1902; the 1977 commission was thus the first in independent India, despite the recommendations of the conference of Inspectors-General since 1953. The National Police Commission completed its work in 1981, and was then disbanded. It died of association with the Janata government. One of the issues that the Commission agonised over was political influence. Its members accepted that democratic government calls for accountability and responsiveness to elected representatives of the people. The requirement therefore was not complete autonomy for the police, but a balance between accountability and professional independence. One means of striking a balance would be the establishment of security commissions at state level to exercise supervisory roles over police forces, with a fixed-term membership whose majority were non-political.

Police Militancy

In addition to politicisation of higher echelons of the police services, there has also occurred a degree of organised police militancy at lower ranks. Unionisation of the police forces is an obviously sensitive issue. The objective conditions explaining and justifying collective police militancy are legion: inadequate pay, allowances, housing, other benefits, and pension; long hours of service; bleak prospects of promotion. The Delhi police took part in a demonstration in 1967; the U.P. armed constabulary mutinied in 1973 and had to be quelled by the army in such major cities as Kanpur, at the cost of about a hundred policemen's lives; more than 20 000 police went on strike in Bombay in 1982 in protest against the Maharashtra government's ban on the police union, and the resulting riots were quelled once again by the army.

Another problem in recent times is tension between state and central government recruits. There is resentment among locally recruited officers that the most important state posts are monopolised by IPS officers. By 1980, 8 states had formally requested that no more IPS officers be assigned to their cadres; Karnataka even began to pay its promoted state officers more than comparable IPS officers (Bayley, 1983, p. 491). Similarly, the practice of sending more than half the IPS recruits into cadres other than their home states was designed to encourage national integration and promote an all-India outlook. But it too has come under strain, with the practice of giving preference to 'home boys' for the seniormost appointments.

The combination of police militancy; politicisation, brutalisation and criminalisation of the police; intensified group violence; and erosion of legitimacy of state authority in virtually all its manifestations: all these have created a state of disorder and the rule of the outlaw. The police performance in the village heartland departs fundamentally from the norms of the instrument of law and order in a democratic society.

Are Police Above the Law?

'I know the mentality of the police from the way they come to the court. Enter court rooms and sit in. They are an irresponsible lot.' – M. N. Venkatachaliah, the Chief Justice of India (*TOI*, 4 February 1994).

The incidence of blinding prisoners in Bhagalpur jail may be explained by the criminalisation of politics. But such episodes also produce their own consequences. In particular, they encourage an attitude and the practice of believing that the forces of order are above the law. There were three sensational cases within a month of one another in 1993–4 which illustrate this very well. In the first case, in December 1993 the Punjab police forcibly tattooed the word *jebkatri* (pickpocket) on the foreheads of three women. (The incident was publicised in the Indian press in January 1994.)

In the second case, on 24 January 1994 the Supreme Court ordered three police officials of the state of Uttar Pradesh to be imprisoned for one month each for beating up an accused person just outside the room of the Chief Justice of India. An SP of the CBI was reprimanded and two other policemen were fined for their role in this unprecedented contempt of the apex court (*TOI*, 25 January 1994).

The third case involves the incident which provoked the chief justice into describing the police as an irresponsible lot. A 20–year old girl Nasrin was married to Shabir in June 1986. Two years later, he reported her to be missing, but would not file a complaint with the police. Five years later, in 1993, Nasrin's mother Shakila Bano spotted her in the red-light area of Kasganj in the district of Etah (U.P.). When she approached the women cell of the Delhi Police for help, a woman police officer demanded a Rs 4000 bribe. Inability to pay the amount led to Shakila Bano being manhandled and thrown out of the Seelampur police station. The National Federation of Indian Women took up her case and obtained a magisterial order to recover Nasrin. By the time of the police raid on the Kasganj house, she had been smuggled elsewhere, presumably with the connivance of the local police. Shakila Bano filed a petition in the Supreme Court and obtained a directive to the U.P. police to produce Nasrin.

Instead, it was the Rajasthan police who produced her in court on 6 January 1994. Shocked and visibly anguished at Nasrin's condition, Mr Justice Venkatachaliah ordered the U.P. police to produce their entire file on her case, including any action taken to try to trace the girl and to prosecute the culprits. The police failed to produce the records. The reasons offered by the state government's counsel were rejected as 'red herrings' by the court, and the chief justice and two other justices ordered the senior SP, SP and former SP of Etah to appear before the court on 7 February. If the officers were found guilty of colluding with Shabir and his family and ignoring judicial orders in such a serious matter, then they would be sentenced to 'substantive prison terms for contempt of the court'. The most telling comment of all from the three judges was that if this was the fate of orders passed by the Supreme Court of India, then they shuddered to think of the plight of mere magistrates and the public at the hands of the police (*TOI*, 4 February 1994). In the event, on 9 February the Supreme Court issued show-cause notices for contempt to the Additional SP (Etah) and the Kasganj police station circle officer. Two others, including the Senior SP, were issued show-cause notices for lying to the court (*TOI*, 10 February 1994).

On 11 September 1991, the Supreme Court of India sentenced six police officers to jail for the arrest and public humiliation of a chief judicial magistrate in the state of Gujarat on 25 September 1989 on 'flimsy charges' (*SW*, 14 September 1991, p. 3). Yet in April 1992, a retired High Court judge and chairman of the Punjab Human Rights Organisation, Mr Justice Ajit Singh Bains, was arrested and publicly humiliated in Chandigarh (*SW*, 18 April 1992, p. 4). A former Director-General of the BSF and National Security Guard pins part of the responsibility for police brutality on the Police Act of 1861 which is still the basic governing act for India's police forces. According to him, the act assigns a 'negative and restrictive role to the police' by enjoining them 'to be a servant of the Government and not the servant of law' (Subramaniam, 1994).

The Military

The line between police, paramilitary and military forces has been increasingly blurred with changing threats to the nation's internal and external security. The terrorist in Kashmir, for example, is just as likely to be an externally trained, externally armed alien as a homegrown product. The overlap was formally recognised with the creation of a new 10 000-strong Rashtriya (National) Rifles by the army in 1991 for tackling terrorist and communal violence. The complementarity of roles and functions is even more apparent in the laws that have been enacted to help the different security forces cope with the myriad threats to law and order (see Mathur, 1992). The government can declare a state or a district to be a 'disturbed area' under the Armed Forces Special Powers Act (1956), empowering army and paramilitary units to search and detain with as much force as they deem necessary. People suspected of endangering national security, public order or essential economic services can be arrested and jailed without warrant or trial, at three-month intervals for up to a year, under the National Security Act (1980). Sixteen essential supplies and services are identified under the Essential Services Maintenance Act (1981) for the purpose of empowering the government to outlaw strikes and lockouts and bring in the army to replace workers. An organisation can be banned by being declared subversive under the Unlawful Activities Prevention Act (1967). The Terrorist and Disruptive Activities (TADA) (Prevention) Act (1985) empowers postal and electronic surveillance and raids on premises in the name of a threat to the unity or sovereignty of the nation. Trials can be conducted in secret and defendants presumed guilty unless they can establish their innocence. The 59th Constitution Amendment Act (1988) authorises the government to declare an emergency for up to two years because of 'internal disturbance'. While such an emergency is in force, Article 21 of the constitution, guaranteeing the fundamental right to life and liberty, can be suspended.

The net result is that for many Indians, the 'government' in effect is the local army or paramilitary commander. The practical consequences of the vast array of laws and instruments available to the state have been felt most brutally in Kashmir and Punjab. The situation in Kashmir has begun to attract the attention of a number of foreign governments (not just Pakistan) and non-governmental organisations like Amnesty International and Asia Watch (Noorani, 1994). In a formal report in April 1994, India's own National Human Rights Commission severely criticised the BSF firing in Bijbehara in Kashmir on 22 October 1993 in which 37 people were killed and another 73 injured (*HIE*, 30 April 1994, p. 2). Again, therefore, an analysis of the government and politics of India takes us into a discussion of the country's defence forces.

The Indian defence forces are one of the largest in the world (Table 8.1), and one of the most powerful and sophisticated among the developing countries. Officers receive pre-training, regimental level and advanced training throughout their professional careers (see Banerjee, 1989). Pre-commission training is imparted at three sets of institutions. The National Defence Academy (NDA) near Pune provides a combined three-year training to potential regular officers of all three services. About 600 cadets are chosen each year on the basis of written tests administered by the Union Public Service Commission (UPSC), followed by interviews by the Services Selection Board. NDA graduates are considered to be equivalent to university graduates in their academic attainments. They then proceed to one further year's training at specialist institutions, for example the Indian Military Academy (IMA) in Dehradun for the 1000 army cadets. (The navy and air force have their own academies.) Short-service commission is offered at a separate Officers Training Academy in Madras. The officer is initially placed in a unit of his service or arm for about six months and then sent on a Young Officers Course at his service school for about five months.

For fifteen years after commission, an officer will undergo about three months of training every second year. Regimental training courses include the Infantry School at Mhow in central India, the High Altitude Warfare School at Gulmarg in Kashmir, the Counter Insurgency and Jungle Warfare School in Mizoram, the Armoured Corps School in Ahmednagar in Maharashtra, the School of Artillery at Deolali in Maharashtra, and technical training institutions like the Armed Forces Medical College (AFMC) in Pune, the College of Military Engineering (CME) near Pune, the Military College of Telecommunications Engineering at Mhow and the Military College of Electrical and Mechanical Engineering at Secunderabad in Andhra Pradesh. (About 10 per cent of Indian Army officers have an engineering degree.)

Advanced training is imparted at the Defence Services Staff College in Wellington in southern India to about 400 officers for 45 weeks each year. The aim is to train them for higher command and staff functions. Army officers need further training before promotion to colonel. The College of Combat at Mhow offers junior, senior and higher command courses, the last being of around 40 weeks' duration. The College of Defence Management in Secunderabad offers four courses, the most important of which is the 42-week-long Defence Management Course for 60 Lieutenant-Colonels/Colonels and equivalent. The highest military training institution in India is the 46-week National Defence College (NDC) in New Delhi for Colonels, Brigadiers and equivalent. Of the 64 members of the NDC each year, 36 are from the Indian military, 12 from the Indian bureaucracy and 16 from friendly foreign countries (mainly Afro-Asian, but including also Australia and Britain).

The defence forces are an effective and powerful lobby group in the competition for scarce resources. Defence expenditure (about $8 bn in 1991) accounts for about one-fifth of central government expenditure and 3–4 per cent of GNP. The figures probably understate the true extent of India's military expenditure and personnel, for many mainly defence-related activities are scattered across several departmental budgets. A question worth raising at this stage is the direct and opportunity costs of military expenditure. UN experts believe that the long-term benefits of disarmament would be substantial. Defence expenditure is considerably more resource-intensive than the social services sector. As resources are reallocated to the civilian sector, there will be increased production of civil goods and services. On the other hand, such a fundamental reallocation will also inflict short-term costs through unemployment or underemployment of labour, capital and other resources (Hartley *et al.*, 1993).

India's military has been called into action for a variety of internal and external tasks:

- In defence of the territorial integrity of the country against external aggression, as against Pakistan in 1947–8, 1965 and 1971, and against China in 1962;
- As the liberator of land occupied by a colonial power, as with the forcible reintegration of Portuguese-ruled Goa, Daman and Diu in 1961;
- As a regional policeman, as with the dispatch of the Indian Peacekeeping Force to Sri Lanka in 1987 and the defeat of the attempted coup in the Maldives in 1988. The former ended in humiliating failure at the hands of Tamil militants 'whose nucleus was covertly armed, equipped, trained and nourished by India' in the words of Lt. Gen. (retd) M. L. Thapan (1993, p. 10). The Maldives operation was a stunning demonstration of political will and rapid-reaction, long-range air insertion capability of the Indian Air Force (IAF);
- As an instrument of international authority, as with participation in a multitude of UN peacekeeping operations;

- As an instrument of national authority, as with the airlift of Indians stranded in the Gulf after the Iraqi invasion of Kuwait in 1990;
- To deal with sporadic outbreaks of large-scale violence in support of civil authorities, as in the wake of the Hindu–Muslim riots after the demolition of the Babri Masjid in Ayodhya in December 1992;
- To deal with persistent low-intensity insurgency, as in Assam and Kashmir;
- To deal with armed rebellion by police and paramilitary forces; and
- To assist with disaster relief operations, as with the massive earthquake in Latur (Maharashtra) in 1993.

The last type of assistance to civil authorities gives much satisfaction to the defence personnel, for it puts their training and skills to the use of the people in an hour of need. But aid to civil authorities to cope with large-scale public violence, let alone with mutinous police, is not welcome. For in effect it amounts to circumventing the inadequacies of the police and paramilitary forces and the political process. And if an entire community should be involved in a struggle against the writ of the central government, then the army can become an instrument for imposing the authority of New Delhi by force, as seems to be the case with Kashmir in the 1990s. All such uses place the army in an invidious position. By training and temperament, soldiers go into action with the goal of applying maximum force at the earliest moment in order to achieve the desired result as quickly and efficiently as possible. By contrast, the requirements of maintaining public order are the use of minimum force as an instrument of last resort (Chari, 1977, p. 19). To expect political sensitivity of the military when coping with an internal threat is to risk politicising the military.

Military Coups

The list of military interventions in Third World countries is long. Valid generalisations about the causes and consequences of military coups attempt to make inferences from a number of case studies where the military has taken over the central institutions of government. Yet many variables cannot be subjected to detailed analysis because of the wall of secrecy that surrounds military affairs, combined with attempts at disinformation designed to discredit the ousted regime and justify its forcible overthrow. The explanatory validity of the generalisations would be strengthened if the same conclusions were reinforced by an examination of countries where the military has stayed out of politics. Like Sherlock Holmes's interest being drawn to the dog that did not bark, students of military interventions might be attracted to India by surprise for its lack of military intervention.

Bearing these comments in mind, five questions can be asked with regard to military interventions:

1. What are the organisational characteristics which impel the military to intervene?
2. What are the background conditions that facilitate or impede military intervention?
3. What are the motives and immediate causes behind any particular coup?
4. How effective is military rule, especially in developing countries?
5. How does the period of military rule shape the post-military political contest?

Organisational characteristics.   In answer to the first question, it is clear that the monopoly of force and coercive power eases the assumption of political rule by the military. Even the weakest army is the strongest coercive institution in a country and possesses enough firepower to displace a civilian regime. Secondly, the professional traits of the military are conducive to taking over control. The structure is hierarchical and centralised, emphasising discipline and obedience to rank and office rather than to individual persons. Channels of communication stress clarity and rapidity of message transmission. Yet, simultaneously, internal secrecy is both a requirement and a habit. The professional aloofness of the military is helped by its separation from civilians. Troops wear distinctive uniforms, live and work in segregated residential communities and office premises, and are indoctrinated into the traditions of their regiment and army. Third, arising from the last point, the military may acquire a distinctive value system. Modern military training and weapons may produce impatience with traditional attitudes and structures in the rest of society, including the political process.

All of the above three characteristics apply to India. Indian Army officers come increasingly from within military families, so that they are part of the military culture 'from cradle to funeral pyre' (Cohen, 1988, p. 107). Reflecting its powerful position in the country's public sector, India's military has, by developing-country standards, a formidable capacity to deploy force. There is a balance between the three service wings of the army, navy and air force; between the requirements of strike and interdiction; and between the capacities for land power, coastal defence and regional force projection with the help of a surprisingly heavy airlift capability. Moreover, all this is backed by a vast defence–industrial establishment of a complexity and sophistication that allows India to manufacture its own range of short and intermediate range missiles. The final element in India's military equation is the nuclear industry. Justified with reference to peaceful applications in the energy sector, its dual-use nature confers at least the capacity to produce nuclear weapons. India is more accurately described as a threshold nuclear-weapon-state than as a non-nuclear-weapon-state.

But the Indian military does not exhibit the fourth organisational characteristic which leads to coups, namely a lack of professional ethics when an officer corps may not have internalised the norms of political inertness.

There are additional organisational features that inhibit the prospects of military intervention in India. The Indian military is so big and diverse that a major civil war would be a very real danger if a coup were to be attempted without advance coordination of the top military commanders: India is not Fiji where a handful of soldiers can enter parliament and take over the country (see Thakur and Wood, 1989). Yet the very size and dispersal of the military makes it virtually impossible to achieve unity of purpose and action by means of a military conspiracy. There is no equivalent of an overall supreme commander of the defence forces or chairman of joint chiefs of staff to bring the three service wings together on a routine basis. The military is also geographically scattered over a wide area. The army is split into five regional commands (northern with HQ in Udhampur, eastern with HQ Calcutta, southern with HQ Pune, western with HQ Delhi, and central with HQ Lucknow). There are also five air commands and three naval commands. The top brass of the Indian Army is distributed between Army Headquarters in New Delhi and the five regional commands.

The Indian military is not dominated by any one ethnic group which can step in when it perceives its vested interests to be under threat from other groups. Departing from the martial races theory of the British, the government of independent India began to broaden the social base of the Indian Army. For example, Sikhs have declined from about one-quarter to about one-tenth of the army. This has been one of the resentments of the Sikhs towards the central government, along with the notable fact that no Sikh has been made army chief, despite the Sikh domination of the upper officer ranks. The cohesiveness of the 35 000-strong officer corps, far from increasing the probability of a coup, in fact dampens it by averting intergroup conflicts within the armed forces. The officers are *Indian* by outlook.

Background conditions. Contextual variables that can spur military intervention include concentration of political, financial, industrial, transport and communications networks; low institutionalisation; economic underdevelopment; permeability of the military to political conflicts; and regional, sectarian and tribal cleavages. India emphatically does not satisfy the first condition. It has several major cities with their own distinctive identities; the political capital is New Delhi but the financial capital is Bombay; even politically, we should include the state capitals; and industrial enterprises are widely dispersed. It is not possible to execute a coup in India by mobilising troops from barracks in the environs of Delhi, occupying government, communications and broadcasting buildings there and broadcasting declarations of national liberation interspersed with patriotic music.

The contextual variables helping to underpin civil society in India include the richness of the institutional heritage. Indians absorbed from the British the principles and structures of government for regulating the struggle for political power, a sophisticated system and network of civilian administration and a mass political party that attracted the politically ambitious. Had the Indian Army taken the lead or even played a major supporting role in the nationalist struggle, it would have been a repository of Indian nationalism independently of other institutions. This happened, for example, in Indonesia. But in fact in India it was people like Jawaharlal Nehru and, more important, the Congress Party as an institution that wore the mantle of having fought the struggle for independence. The Congress Party, not the Indian Army, has also been the most efficient route to political power. It has successfully recruited a large number of individuals and groups into the political process. Participatory democracy in turn has further strengthened the institutions of government and enhanced its legitimacy. At the individual level,

Nehru both symbolised and helped to shape the values of humane liberalism tempered with social justice. India's emergent political culture was turbulent, colourful and exciting, but free of any military influence.

Yet the same army, with shared social and organisational characteristics and military traditions, took over the reins of government in Pakistan not long after independence, while in India it has remained under civilian control. In Pakistan, the military and bureaucratic elites joined forces against the politicians. In India, the political and bureaucratic elites joined forces against the military. Army Chief Ayub Khan let it be known in the early 1950s that he was unhappy at having to report to the Defence Secretary of Pakistan and at being under the control of the civilian Ministry of Defence. Instead, he began to bypass both the Defence Secretary and Ministry, and then also the cabinet, before dispensing with the civilian government altogether. The Indian Army Chief shared the sentiments in regard to the counterpart institutions in India. Defence Secretary H. M. Patel stood firm on the protocol of civilian control and was backed by Home Minister Sardar Vallabbhai Patel and Prime Minister Jawaharlal Nehru (Kapur, 1993, p. 11). The Commander-in-Chief of the Indian defence forces was removed from his position in the Indian cabinet prior to the abolition of the post itself, so that the president is the only overall commander of all the armed forces over and above the three service chiefs. All three of the latter are under the control of the Defence Minister and his Secretary. A number of other changes were also made after independence in terms of the military–civilian relationship whose effect was to downgrade the status of senior military officers relative to civilian and ministerial counterparts (see Cohen, 1990, pp. 172–3).

Cohen (1990, p. 227) also points out a number of other differences between Pakistan and India inhibiting intervention by the military in the latter relative to the former. In Pakistan, the army has been the guardian of Punjabi as well as national interests, whereas no one group dominates the Indian military. India is less strategically exposed than Pakistan, and its soldiers have been prevented from establishing direct ties with foreign defence suppliers. India's political system has developed deeper roots than Pakistan's. It is also more complex and labyrinthine, which would pose serious obstacles to effective governance by the military. The frequent assistance to civil authorities in law-and-order tasks has made the Indian Army conscious of the difficulty of government by force alone. It has also sensitised the army to the ease with which it could become an object of popular hatred as an instrument of coercion.

Moving to economic and social criteria, it is difficult to establish a simple, linear relationship between the level of economic development and propensity to military intervention. Overall, the Indian defence forces have been successfully insulated from the caste, class and religious conflicts that are so common in India today. The rebellion by about two thousand Sikhs after the army's storming of the Golden Temple in 1984 was notable for being the sole such incident since independence.

There are also additional contextual variables reinforcing civilian control over the military in India. Free and fair elections conducted at periodic intervals bestow legitimacy on the government. There is widespread corruption in civil society, but this seems insufficient of itself to trigger a coup. Conversely, India's democratic and federal political setup provides multiple channels of access and institutions for conflict mediation and management (and sometimes even conflict resolution). Not only has the Indian Army not abandoned its apolitical identity despite contrary examples in the neighbouring countries of Pakistan and Bangladesh: it has also remained depoliticised despite the contrary examples of the bureaucracy and the police within India. Equally in contrast to the civil services and the police, the defence forces have remained by and large free of corruption.

Military coups can sometimes serve the geopolitical interests of foreign powers. India's policy of nonalignment provided the doctrinal underpinning to the country maintaining a distance between its defence forces and those of other powers. By the 1970s India was sourcing most of its defence supplies and weapons from the Soviet Union. But Soviet military advisers and staff planners were no more acceptable in India than Western ones. India's officers were not subjected to Soviet indoctrination, its defence doctrines were largely indigenous, and its officer corps was probably more Western than Soviet in outlook and lifestyle (see Thakur and Thayer, 1992, ch. 4).

Causes and motives. The immediate causes and motives of interventions tend to be social class interests, distinctive perceptions of the national interest, corporate interests, individual gain or career ambitions, and a major crisis of government. India does not have a homogeneous ruling class or elite from whose ranks come the bulk of the officer corps. The wars that India has fought have had the important political consequence of forging a bond between the military's and government's definitions of the national interest. They focused the attention of the defence forces on a direct threat from the outside. They eased the military's bureaucratic battles for a larger share of government expenditure. They helped to convince bureaucrats and politicians of the military imperatives of India becoming a regional power, and this in turn gave a focus of modernisation to the military. The sustained expansion of the defence forces helped to ease the bottlenecks to promotion that have generated restiveness in some other armies and led them into launching coup attempts. The continuing modernisation of India's defence forces ensured that its officers kept their professional pride intact. The wars have given ample opportunity to individual officers to earn glory as soldiers defending the nation's borders. In short, the wars have channelled the professional energies of India's defence forces and ensured that its officers are interested in the application of military power rather than the exercise of political power. Even while ensuring that the military stays firmly under civilian control, successive governments have emphasised by words and deeds the vital importance of a strong defence force that can sustain India as a united and respected country in world affairs.

The record of military rule.   A coup is just the initiating point of a military's involvement in politics. The more interesting question concerns the impact of military rule. How effective is it for political and economic development: is it progressive, reactionary or regressive? In general, several potential pitfalls can be identified. To begin with, every dictator likes in due course to convert military dictatorship into legitimate political order. But once it has taken over the reins of government, the military finds it difficult to establish and implement the conditions and timing for its retreat into barracks. In particular, there is the fear of punitive measures against officers responsible for the coup, including death for treason. This can cause policy paralysis and governmental *immobilisme*. The burden of unpopularity for the tough decisions of government fall directly on the shoulders of the generals. The military also ends up progressively collapsing the larger national interest into narrower corporate interests, which in turn erodes the legitimacy of the military institution itself. Escalating policy differences over difficult policy choices and rising unpopularity pose threats to the unity of the military. For all these reasons, the most potent weapon that a military has for securing compliance may well be the threat of potential intervention if it does not get its way. Conversely, distaste for rule by generals grew with greater awareness of the excessive brutality of military rule from Argentina and Chile in Latin America to Burma in Asia.

With regard to the implications of military rule for development, contradictory hypotheses can be found in the literature. The military is held by some to be more developmental because it is more nationalistic, being above the divisions of caste, religion and tribalism that divide Third World societies. Its attitude and behaviour are more likely to be characterised by the 'modern' pattern variables (Pye, 1962). This is said to result from professional training and norms of the military, the emphasis placed on career advancement through achievement, the requirements of military technology and modern weapons systems, and the segregation of the military from the civilians. Generals can make firm and far-reaching decisions without being constrained by the need for political compromise. And they possess the coercive and organisational means to enforce 'right', if unpopular, decisions and so provide the vital stability to the political process without which development is impossible (Janowitz, 1977).

If these putative advantages were genuinely present, then we would expect the beneficial results to be readily apparent in the record of development under military regimes. Yet in fact in most cases little progress is visible over the record of the ousted civilian regimes. In a metaphor suited to the process, the drivers of development may change, but the cars remain the same (Palmer, 1989, p. 252). According to Huntington (1968, p. 221), the impact of military rule on social change varies with the level of development. In an oligarchical society, the soldier is a radical; in a middle-class society, he is a participant and an arbiter; but in an industrial mass society, he is a conservative guardian of the existing order. If true, such a correlation would justify 'progressive' military interventions in 'backward' societies but condemn them in advanced societies for being reactionary. But the conclusion is not accepted uncritically. A body of empirical research shows that any particular military intervention exerts a unique influence on social change, regardless of level of economic development.

Consequently, the civilian–military distinction is of little use in explaining social change (Jackman, 1976; McKinlay and Cohan, 1976). Indicators of direct governmental allocation are affected by regime type, for example the balance of sectoral expenditures between social welfare and law and order. But the indicators of overall system performance are not similarly affected by regime type. Military governments can be just as prone to policy incoherence and instability. Generals in power have to resolve a fundamental tension between the military as the government and as an institution, between the conflicting demands of political legitimacy and corporate security. A preoccupation with preserving its own security generates important discontinuities, repression and self-isolation (Stepan, 1974; Wolpin, 1986).

By contrast, in India the military has played an important role as an agent of modernisation without hindering the growth of political competitiveness (Bopegamage, 1971). Not only does the Indian military serve as a training ground for technical and administrative skills for soldiers; it also helps others acquire such skills. In remote frontier regions, for example, the army has helped with sowing and harvesting by giving technical advice for improving cultivation with modern implements, high-yield seeds and fertilisers. And it has been an effective channel for upward mobility of Indians from modest backgrounds.

After military rule.   The most consistent consequence and legacy of military intervention for post-military politics would appear to be a tendency to produce a patrimonially-dominated political system. A military that has taken over the government once finds it difficult to restore 'normal' relations with a civilian government. Military regimes invariably place restrictions on organised political activity, with the result that no cohesive alternative political structures exist when the military is prepared to return to barracks. In the institutional vacuum, non-organisational means of political relationships dominate, for example personal charisma, feudal followings and sectarian affinities. These retard the process of political development and increase the probability that the post-military state will be patrimonial (Heeger, 1977).

In sum, empirical studies have failed to confirm clear links between military interventions and socioeconomic and organisational variables. The probability of a coup is not linked to the size of an army, its level of professionalism and the career paths of officers leading a coup. Coups may be carried out by large or small and cohesive or fragmented armies, under the leadership of junior or senior officers, in competitive multiparty or one-party systems. Nor is there a firm relationship between coups and social characteristics. Motives vary in the initial decision to intervene, and they often shift during the course of a coup. Nor do military regimes enjoy clear-cut advantages as governments. They face the same economic constraints and the same social cleavages. Finally, civilian and military regimes do not matter for the important outcomes of economic development and political stability (Bienen, 1978). Instead of a society taking on the military virtues of order and discipline under a spell of military rule, the soldiers themselves may acquire the politicians' vices of drift, strife, factionalism and corruption.

Civil–Military Relations

The relationship of the military to the political process is more complex than that presented by a direct seizure of political power. The latter may indicate inability of the armed forces to achieve political goals by other means; it may indicate the nature of the political system; it may indicate the nature of the relationship between the political system and international politics. It is more accurate to speak of the range of political influence of the military – from direct assumption of complete political control to total subservience to the civilian authorities. Intermediate stages include the power of replacing one civilian government by another or acting as the chief political supporter of a particular government, for example in Pakistan, to acting as a powerful pressure group as in the Philippines. The dominance of the civil over the military lacks the sharpness of focus provided by a coup. The latter is an event; the former a set of relationships. It is a less exciting field of inquiry, as attested to by the comparative dearth of literature on civilian control of the military compared to military interventions in developing countries. Yet the successful institutionalisation of such civilian control is at once more significant, subtle and complex than the overthrow of fragile regimes by military coups.

India inherited from the British a large defence force, the pattern of military organisation, the tenets of military doctrine and the convention of subordination of the military to the civilian authorities. The British instilled into their officers the discipline of political neutrality. There were occasions for friction between the civilian and military branches of the British Indian administration, but the principle of the military being under civilian control was never under threat (Chari, 1977, p. 5). Political passivity was both internalised, as part of the personal memories of India's senior military officers at independence; and institutionalised, as part of the corporate memory of the army. Even the Indianised element of the British Indian army was so politically apathetic that it was not infected by the nationalist virus. Conversely, those who had been politicised – for example soldiers who chose to fight alongside Subhas Chandra Bose in the Indian National Army (see Fay, 1994) – were quietly excluded from the army of independent India. This avoided a potential rift and hostility between 'loyalist' and 'nationalist' officers, eased the process of adjustment of the former to the new realities and so helped to cement their loyalties to the new regime. It also underscored the primacy of the professional over the political in the new army. The patriotic credentials of the army were established almost immediately with the war over Kashmir, and confirmed beyond question with the wars in 1962, 1965 and 1971.

The pattern of the civilian–military relationship is shown in Figure 8.1. Prudence and a sense of self-preservation suggest to the government that the military should be allowed to participate in the policy process. For if the military was to be excluded totally, it would be more likely to resort to its power of ultimate veto or compellence. In India, constitutional inhibitions and bureaucratic structures have constricted the advisory and representational functions of the military to the defence–security sector. The military establishment retains control of command and operational matters. Military policy-making is firmly in the hands of the civilian Ministry of Defence and cabinet. The Indian defence forces are not an independent political constituency whose corporate interests have high priority in policy debates. Size for size, the Indian defence forces must be one of the least influential in the world in the policy process.

The chairmanship of the Chiefs of Staff Committee falls on the chief with the longest seniority on the committee. The service chiefs are members of the Defence Minister's Committee, which is the highest collective professional adviser to the government. But the highest policy-making body is the Political Affairs Committee of cabinet, to which service chiefs may be invited but of which they are not members. Even such matters as where to locate particular defence industries, and what weapons and ordnance to produce in which factories, are decided not by the military but by the Ministry of Defence. Ministry officials are specialists in bureaucratic and budgetary matters, but not in strategic affairs. The military would like to have a united voice either through a chief of the defence force in the British Commonwealth tradition or through a chairman of the

FIGURE 8.1
The Structure of India's civil–military relationship

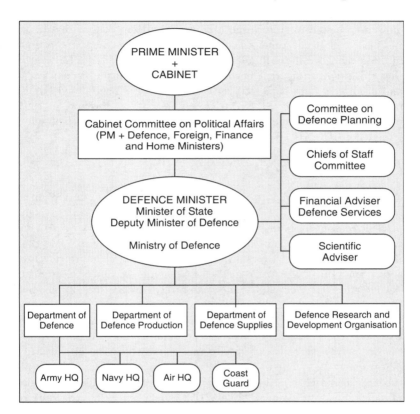

joint chiefs of staff as in the United States, to coordinate operations in wartime and provide integrated advice in peacetime.

The military leadership may sometimes question the extent of civilian–political control of defence matters, but they have never questioned the right of such control. The participation of the military in the policy process is limited to interest group activity, for example lobbying for increased resource allocation. Their unhappiness stems more from a perceived lack of strategic knowledge by the bureaucrats and politicians when making decisions, for example on force modernisation and weapons acquisitions. There has also been periodic restiveness in the armed forces at lack of promotion opportunities, and at deteriorating pay and service conditions in comparison with civilian counterparts (whose material prosperity is often augmented in substantial amounts by illegal commissions).

There has been some unease in India caused by some retired military officers joining the Bharatiya Janata Party (BJP). The fear is that this might indicate a new correlation between the armed forces and a political landscape that is in flux because of heightened Hindu militancy with which the BJP is closely identified. A report in 1991 identified six lieutenant-generals and a major-general as having joined the BJP (*SW*, 6 July 1991, p. 7).

Prospects of Military Intervention in India

The military in India is apolitical and professional, and civilian control is firmly established. Despite this, we can postulate eight possible reasons for being worried that the Indian military might take over the reins of government directly. The first is the simple fact that the actual mechanics of executing a coup are quite elementary. Only a tiny fraction of the army needs to be involved. Once a coup has been carried out successfully, the rest of the army has little choice but to acquiesce, at least in the short term.

Second, the military may step in because of increasing frustrations with the career paths of its officers. The Indian Administrative Service (IAS) cadre is only about one-seventh the size of the army officer corps. Yet while the army has only one general, IAS officers fill the approximately one hundred secretary-level posts that are at the same level as a full general. Every IAS officer will reach the rank of commissioner or collector in 20 years and be equal to a major-general in formal protocol; an army officer can be guaranteed only the rank of lieutenant-colonel after 24 years (Cohen, 1988, p. 106). The uniformed officers' disgruntlement is increased when the army is called in to assist civil authorities and senior officers end up in a subordinate relationship with civilian officers who are their 'juniors' in age and experience. In recent times, there has been a spate of early retirements from the army and navy in particular (Sharma, 1994, p. 3).

Third, a crisis of government resulting from a paralysis of the political and administrative machinery may confront the military with a difficult choice between supporting a government in trouble, withholding support, or taking over the reins of government directly.

So far at least India has escaped general political instability caused by a total breakdown of government.

Fourth, a crisis of identity may arise when the apolitical institution becomes the prop on which a government survives. Should the army remain aloof from the political process and preserve its neutral identity at the cost of the collapse of government, or should it step in to the benefit of the ruling regime? The only occasion on which rumours circulated of the army having possibly been asked to prop up a regime that had lost its democratic legitimacy was in 1977. Defeated at the polls, Mrs Gandhi was thought by some to have sounded out the army about continuing in office. Such stories were never substantiated.

Fifth, a crisis of conscience arises when soldiers trained physically and psychologically to defend a people against foreign enemies are required to turn their firepower on their own citizens. The professional duty of the military is to resist foreign aggression, not to perpetuate an unpopular regime in the face of internal disorders. Alternatively, if it is the legitimate function of an army to shore up a tottering regime, then why not also to change it? Excessive reliance on the army for the maintenance of domestic order is probably the most likely scenario for military intervention. The more often that this is done, the greater will be the probability of direct military rule. Prior to Operation Bluestar in Amritsar in 1984, the uniform of the Indian Army was a badge of honour throughout the Punjab. Afterwards it became a target of Sikh terrorist attacks.

In an interview published on 12 March 1992, Army Chief General S. F. Rodrigues described 'the siege within' (referring to the thesis by M. J. Akbar, 1985) as posing as great a danger to India's security as Pakistan. Consequently, he said, 'good governance' was of concern to the army (*SW*, 21 March 1992, p. 3). This provoked a storm of critical comments in parliament. Yet the army has been called out to help the civil authorities in the restoration of law and order with increasing frequency. By the 1990s, troops were required in an internal security role on average around fifty times per year. Army Chief Gen. B. C. Joshi told the *Eyewitness* newsmagazine (September 1993) that rising ethnic and sectarian unrest had led to more than half the army troops being committed to internal security operations. He acknowledged that this was hurting troop training and war preparedness.

The choice of units is dictated by two apparently contradictory principles. In most cases, neutral regiments are used to quell civil disturbances: Gurkha and Maratha regiments in Kashmir, Rajput and Sikh in Assam and so on. But sometimes 'home' regiments may be used in order to stress an underlying unity. The army assault on the Golden Temple in Amritsar in June 1984 was under the command of Sikh generals in order to make the point that the action was against terrorists, not against the Sikh people. (After the operation, Mrs Gandhi insisted on retaining Sikh bodyguards, despite security advice to the contrary, in order to make the same political point. She paid for her principled stand with her life.)

Sixth, the military may act to displace a civilian regime of which it is contemptuous. Derisive and dismissive attitudes towards Third World politicians resemble those held by the bureaucratic–military elite in Pakistan which was instrumental in rejecting the parliamentary path in that country. Thus after his coup in 1958, 'The image that Ayub soon created about himself was that he was a colossus of justice bestriding the corrupt world of Pakistan' (Sayeed, 1967, pp. 93–4). Lt. Gen. M. L. Thapan (1993, p. 10) wrote contemptuously of the Indian politicians' 'lust for power', the civil servant–politician nexus 'in blatant disregard of the public interest', the 'unacceptable damage to the social and economic order' caused by active misgovernment and the dangers of 'Mandalisation' of the army. If a highly decorated general can write of such matters openly, then it is likely that his views are commonly shared among the top brass of the army. If that is so, then the psychological barrier to a coup – the legitimacy of the political order – has already been corroded.

Seventh, increasing corruption and criminalisation of politics will increase the temptation for the military to take control of the affairs of state. When the political, bureaucratic, police and paramilitary institutions have decayed, the military marks the difference between territorial integrity and national disintegration. In the words of Stephen Cohen (1990, p. 231), 'in all nations, the army operates at the margin of moral behavior'.

Eighth, the military may step in if there is a general perception that the profession is being unduly politicised. In May 1983, Lt. Gen. S. K. Sinha, vice chief and one of the ablest officers of the army, was passed over for promotion as chief in favour of Lt. Gen. A. S. Vaidya. The abandonment of the seniority principle and the appointment of a serving general who had issued statements praising the electoral alliance between Congress and another party during state elections in Tripura raised uncomfortable political questions (*OHT*, 16 June

1983, p. 4; General Sinha took early retirement). Additional tools in the hands of government for 'playing politics' with generals include post-retirement appointments to governorships and ambassadorships. But the combination of sycophancy among generals and corruption among politicians carries its own risks of officer alienation.

Frequent use of the army in support of civil authorities does increase the permeability of the military–political boundary. Yet the Indian military shies away from politicisation because of unhappy experiences that are easy to recall. Within India, memories have not dimmed of the national security disasters that befell the country during Krishna Menon's tenure as defence minister (1957–62). He took a hands-on approach to military matters that included interfering in senior appointments and promotions and tactical decision-making. The dangers of such meddling and consequent tensions within the defence forces compounded the organisational, doctrinal and operational flaws exposed by the Chinese invasion in 1962. Menon's tenure was the only abandonment of civilian control in favour of political control of the military (MacMillan, 1969).

The lessons from within have been reinforced by those from without, in Bangladesh to the immediate east and Pakistan to the immediate west. In neither case did bouts of military rule help to infuse the political order with the efficiency and discipline of the armed forces. In both, the costs to the military included substantial public hostility to the military institution itself. The Indian military is proud of its standing with the people of India, and unlikely to jeopardise it lightly.

This is important because a country of India's size, diversity and complexity could not be governed effectively without general political support. It will be recalled, for example, that the Indian federation is underpinned by the union and state governments deriving their authority from the constitution. The occasional deployment of the army by the centre is in defence of that same constitutional order. An army that had displaced civilian government would be in power but would lack authority. A central government shorn of constitutional legitimacy could not expect habitual obedience from a number of state governments asserting separate regional identities. Moreover, the army's occasional involvement in the maintenance of law and order has exposed it to the reality of the 'ungovernability' of India by coercive means alone. In other countries, the military has sometimes stepped in to play its role as the guardian of national honour and unity. The Indian military is not likely to precipitate a series of events that would pose a serious threat to the political and territorial integrity of the nation. South Asia itself offers an instructive and sobering example: Pakistan broke asunder in 1971 under a military regime.

Conclusion

India conforms to the liberal model of civil–military relations in which government is firmly in the hands of civilian politicians. The commander-in-chief is the president. The use of the military is controlled by the political executive. Responsibility for military action lies with the government. If citizens do not like the uses to which their military is put, they can vote the government out at the next election. By contrast, the police in India do not conform to the liberal model of being 'citizens in uniform' or impartial custodians of the public order. Instead, they are 'the state in uniform' (Hague *et al.*, 1992, p. 380), or agents of state power. Where liberalism views police as the servants of the people, the Indian police behave like masters over the citizens. On 10 February 1994, for example, about 200 troops of the CRPF went on a rampage in Bhubaneswar, the state capital of Orissa, destroying shops and injuring about 30 people (*SW*, 19 February 1994, p. 4). The disjunction between the efficiency, competence and relative integrity of the elite IPS cadre and the rest of the police forces is even more massive than between the IAS and the rest of the civil service. Not because the IPS officers are superior to the IAS, but because the lower echelons of the police possess means of physical coercion that are not available to the bureaucrats. The demoralisation and ill-discipline of the police forces is matched by the public's distrust and fear of them. The police forces are corrupt, inefficient, distrusted and everywhere; the paramilitary forces are brutal, ruthless, feared but called out of barracks only periodically; the armed forces are disciplined, efficient, respected and generally insulated from the public.

The deployment of the military to help in the civil defence tasks of emergency relief assistance is uncontroversial. It serves to raise the profile of the military as the protectors of the people. The dangers of a praetorian state (one in which the military either forms or dominates the political executive) would come from increasing politicisation of the military either directly, or indirectly through frequent and extensive use of the military to maintain civil order. For a politicisation of the military would generate a matching militarisation of politics. Alternatively, if India were to slide into social chaos and political instability, then the numbers of Indians seduced by the vision of the authority, discipline and order of a military dictatorship would multiply. Already by December 1993, more than 60 per cent of metropolitan Indians were professing a preference for a dose of military dictatorship for India.

Further Reading

Bayley (1969). An intensive analysis of civilian–police relationships in India as they affect both the efficiency of the Indian police and the development of a democratic polity.

Bayley (1983). Argues that frustrated by inability to satisfy the public's demand for order and demoralised by politically inspired management, the Indian police have become deeply involved in partisan politics.

Cohen (1990). A very good account of the development of the professional officer in British and independent India.

Kukreja (1991). A major comparative study of three armies with common origins but differing degrees of involvement in the political process.

Nayar, V. K. (1992). Discusses the internal security threats to India.

Thomas (1986). A balanced and informative account of the shifts in India's strategic environment and the problems of internal security, and also of security decision-making.

9

Party Politics

In this chapter, I shall do five things:

1. Look briefly at what a political party is supposed to be.
2. Discuss in some detail the Congress Party of India.
3. Examine the Janata Party and the Bharatiya Janata Party.
4. Describe the main class-based and regional parties.
5. Note the lack of significant pressure group politics in the Indian party system.

Political Parties

A political party is an organised group that seeks to gain political power either by itself or in coalition with others. To the extent that political organisation is essential to the functioning of modern political systems, it is difficult to conceive of realistic alternatives to political parties. Competition between parties gives practical meaning to democracy. In a system of competitive elections, the parties also play an important educative role through the promotion of principles and alternative conceptions of the good life by argument and debate. They are the most important two-way link between society and government. They give national dimension to local politics and translate public opinion into public policy. By performing the function of interest aggregation, political parties convert a number of different individual and social demands into collective goals. They are also the channel for recruiting and socialising elites into the political process and mobilising the populace for the tasks of nation-building and state-building. Yet even while the political party modernises society, it is in turn 'indigenised' and imbued with traditional features like caste calculations. In modern parliamentary democracies, parties also effectively usurp the powers of parliament.

A recurring subject of scholarly inquiry is the relationship between social groups and political parties. Parties may be cohesive in terms of one or more social characteristics such as occupation, religion, region, language or ethnicity. Or they may be 'catch-all' parties without cohesiveness in terms of any major social variable. The durability of *parties* rests on their links with social segments. The stability of *a party system* rests on the strength of the relationship between social cleavages and partisanship (that is, loyalty to a party). If two or more parties have secure bases of support in one segment of society each, then the core support of the parties will structure the competition between them on an enduring basis.

The Lipset–Rokkan three-stage model of links between social cleavages and party systems postulates the first stage as a centre–periphery conflict (Lipset and Rokkan, 1967). The centralising and rationalising nation-builders are pitted against the regional, linguistic and cultural minorities. The second stage in the Lipset–Rokkan model, of state–church conflict, is irrelevant to India because of the absence of an authoritative church hierarchy in Hinduism. The third stage is the emergence into party politics of the urban–rural divide, a conflict between the primary producers in the countryside and the merchants and entrepreneurs in the towns. While the first stage is the product of a national revolution, the third stage is the product of an industrial revolution. So too would be the emergence of the owner–worker cleavage.

In a substantial sense, India has generally had one national party in Congress, and many opposition parties with core support in one state or region only. In formal terms, the country has several national parties. The experiences of coalition governments in 1977–9 and 1989–91 show that a major political problem for India is the creation of cohesive parties out of loose anti-Congress alliances. Instead of disciplined parties organised around distinctive ideological or group interests, the country has had several 'taxicab' parties full of members who hop in and out while the parties drive around in circles. Formal recognition is granted on a state-by-state basis if a party meets criteria specified by the Election Commission. If a party is recognised in four states or more, it is accorded the status of a national party. Nine parties were given national status by the Election Commission in

1991, and another 38 were recognised as state parties. Parties to have received recognition as national parties include the Jan Sangh/BJP, with its support base concentrated in the Hindi-speaking states; the two communist parties with their strengths chiefly in Kerala and West Bengal; a couple of socialist parties rooted mainly in Bihar, U.P. and Maharashtra; and offshoots of the Congress and Janata parties.

How does India compare with regard to the nature and strength of links between social cleavages and party systems? The inquiry is of particular fascination in India because of its social heterogeneity and the variety of its salient differences. The salient cleavage in Kashmir and Punjab is religion; in Bihar, caste; in the northeast, ethnicity (Mizos, Nagas, Gurkhas); in Tamil Nadu, language; and in some of the industrial cities as well as parts of the countryside, class. Moreover, while parties reveal ideological differences, the party system is not characterised by an ideological cleavage.

The Indian National Congress

The Congress Party, one of the oldest political parties in the world, has been the pre-eminent national party in India in terms of the capacity and will to field candidates the length and breadth of the country. The unevenness of its success in voter support was previously masked by the substantial majorities that the party managed to obtain in parliamentary representation due to the vagaries of India's single member, simple plurality electoral system.

The Indian National Congress was founded in 1885 from a number of groups representing the interests of the new urban middle class. From the start, the Congress movement was divided between the moderates and the radicals, the reformers and the revolutionaries, the social liberals and the social conservatives. Much of the early debates concerned tactics: the best means of achieving greater equality of Indians with the British, the risks and rewards of participating in elective bodies, and so on. As the elective principle was introduced and then progressively extended in the late nineteenth century and early twentieth century, Congress began to acquire the trappings of a political party: dues-paying members, fund raising, preparation of election platforms, internal elections for the organisation as well as for electoral candidates, and district offices to act as conduits between party leaders and voters. The elections of 1936–7, following the

Government of India Act (1935), were a major milestone in the development of India's political parties. Congress contested the elections on the basis of a detailed political and economic programme, with the demand for a constituent assembly being a major item. It won almost half the elected legislative seats and formed ministries in seven of the eleven provinces.

In the so-called one-party-dominant system that operated in India from 1947 until 1967 (Kothari, 1964; Morris–Jones, 1978, pp. 196–232), Congress exercised a commanding influence on Indian politics with substantial majorities in the central parliament as well as continuous control of virtually all states. The legislative superiority rested on the party's organisational dominance which gave it an unmatched might and reach throughout the country (Manor, 1988, p. 64). The system of politics was genuinely competitive. But Congress was the centre of political gravity as a centrist, aggregative and pragmatic party which embraced a surprisingly wide range of India's diversity. This meant that the party was internally divided among various factions. But the existence of many factions competing with one another made the party sensitive to social groups and responsive to their demands. Often, the demands would be articulated by opposition parties. The net result was to make the Congress the 'party of consensus' and the opposition groupings the 'parties of pressure' (Kothari, 1964, p. 1162). The opposition parties exercised their greatest influence on public policy at the margins of internal Congress debates.

Kochanek (1968) has explained the success of the Congress Party in moving from being a nationalist movement to a party of government in organisational rather than personal terms. More important than Jawaharlal Nehru's charisma was the effective performance of the function of interest aggregation by the collective leadership of the party. Despite the breadth of its appeal to a diverse set of interests, the party maintained internal cohesion and so preserved myriad loyalties. With the extension of the franchise to every adult citizen after independence, the party deepened its roots and widened its appeal. Moreover, it produced national policies which worked, even if not very well. Congress under Nehru became the embodiment of a remarkable consensus, for such a diverse country, on social, economic and foreign policies.

As the appeal of the nationalist mantle faded, Congress enhanced its attractiveness as the party of patronage. In the process, Congress governments moved away from a concern with social transformation to specialise in the delivery of services. Legislators and party functionaries could be approached to allocate funds for the building of a school, the extension of the railway line, the admission of a child to a college or the appointment of one to a sought-after government job. For this reason, elections for party positions at the local, district and state levels were keenly contested. (The party structure follows administrative rather than constituency boundaries.) Since these were elective positions, aspiring politicians were compelled to mobilise individuals and groups with ever-increasing intensity. Congress became skilled at forging a winning electoral coalition of diverse castes and classes in several regions of India. This is why factional linkages were more important than formal structures in determining the key relationships within the party.

The organisational structure of the Congress Party is shown in Figure 9.1. Any Indian citizen aged 18 or more can become a primary member of the party, but cross-membership of another political party is not permitted. The biennial subscription is a modest one rupee only. Any primary member can become an active member on enrolling 25 primary members biennially. The Indian National Congress includes the plenary and special sessions of the party and the Congress Working Committee (CWC), the All-India Congress Committee (AICC), the Pradesh/Territorial Congress Committees (PCCs), the District/City Congress Committees and the Block or other subordinate Congress Committees. The term of every Congress committee and its officeholders is 'ordinarily' for two years. The apex party body at the state level is the PCC. In 1994 the party had 26 PCCs (the 25 states plus Delhi), and 6 Territorial CCs (the remaining six union territories). All PCC members are party 'delegates'. The key party institutions at the national level are the AICC and the CWC. The AICC is required to meet at least biannually and has the power to frame rules that are binding on all subordinate party committees (Article 13 of the party constitution). The CWC is 'the highest executive authority of the Congress', responsible to the AICC, with the power to execute party policies and programmes (Article 19). There is also a Congress Parliamentary Board comprising the party president, the party leader in parliament and six other members. Its purpose is to regulate and coordinate the parliamentary activities of the party in all legislative bodies (Article 25). The party is required to meet once every two years, but a special session may be convened by the AICC or a majority of PCCs. Since the 1980s the party has had around five General Secretaries who are in

FIGURE 9.1
The organisational structure of the Indian National Congress, 1993

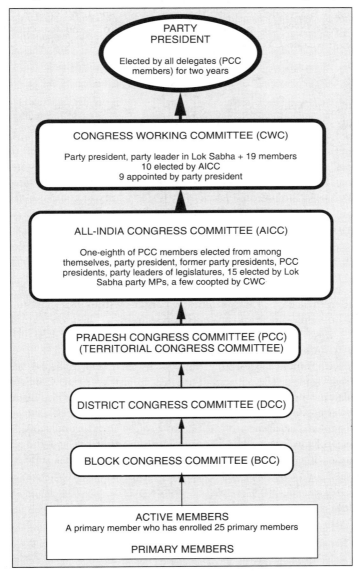

Source: Constitution of the Indian National Congress (New Delhi: AICC, August 1991).

charge of the AICC 'subject to the general control of the president' (Article 21). At the head of the party organisation is the president, elected by party delegates on the basis of a single transferable vote.[1] The president presides over the Congress sessions and exercises the functions of the CWC when it is not in session (Article 18).

Congress System

During the Nehru era (1947–64), the Congress machinery operated mainly at the state level in the hands of powerful party bosses playing the politics of patronage. Factional fighting within Congress took the form of struggles over nominations to the state and central legislatures and of contests for party offices. In the struggle for power at the various levels of party organisation, the biggest prize was control of the PCC. At the national level, Nehru was firmly in control of policy as well as politics. At all other levels, the key to success was mobilisation: of the masses, of the party functionaries on the lowest rung, of members of the legislature. Party bosses had to learn to manipulate loyalties and popular opinion, to appeal to sectarian interests without antagonising any major group, to reward the loyal yet tempt the potential defector, to use governmental patronage to broaden their base of support and to bargain within party channels to maximise the allocation of central resources to their own state. In short, those leaders survived and prospered who knew best how to forge winning electoral and political coalitions.

The alignment of social groups with particular political parties differed from state to state. The Jats might vote for Congress in Rajasthan, the Akali Dal in Punjab, and the Lok Dal in Haryana and U.P. The sum of Congress votes at the national level showed a consistency of support from different groups (urban and rural, high castes and low castes, Hindus and Muslims) that masked the strong identification with particular segments at the district and state levels. Because state and national elections were held simultaneously from 1952 to 1967 inclusive, it was not commonly realised that the seeming national mandate in each election was based on support from quite different, and sometimes even antagonistic, social segments.

The 'Congress system' based on this particular combination – socially segmented factional alliances within states producing big victories at the national level – meant that most opposition parties had their direct counterparts inside Congress. Class-based socialist parties, for example, would establish channels of communication with socialist Congress MPs. The measure of influence of opposition parties was provided, therefore, not just by their numbers in the legislative bodies, but by their ability to exert pressure on the margins of Congress policy debates. And if an opposition party began to acquire too much influence, then Congress proved capable of absorbing either their programmes or their leaders. For example, the Praja Socialist Party lost its major ideological platform when Congress formally adopted the goal of a socialistic pattern of society in 1955. Opposition parties could exploit links with factions inside Congress to exert an influence on public policy out of all proportion to their numerical strength in the central parliament. But state-specific regional parties with significant electoral support in their own right could challenge Congress for control of the state government. This is why the first major challenge to Congress emerged in the context of regional politics rather than national.

Yet the very breadth of special-interest support for Congress exacerbated the difficulties of the party in controlling internal differences. With the death of Nehru in 1964, Congress lost a leader whose personality had dominated independent India's politics. His successor Lal Bahadur Shastri died within two years. When Mrs Indira Gandhi was elected parliamentary party leader and hence prime minister in 1966, Congress was still under the control of powerful state chief ministers. The political landscape was changed fundamentally in the state and national elections of 1967. Inflation, severe scarcities, the threat of famine and mass agitations combined to produce a certain intensity in the politically charged atmosphere of the 1967 elections. The results were stunning for their mould-breaking effects. At the centre, Congress lost almost 80 seats and was reduced to a simple 54 per cent majority in the Lok Sabha. In a further humiliation, the party failed to win majorities in eight states. The Dravida Munnetra Kazhagam (DMK) formed a majority government on its own in Tamil Nadu, while united front or coalition governments were formed in Bihar, Kerala, Orissa, Punjab and West Bengal. In some other states Congress itself entered into coalition arrangements in order to retain power. An equally spectacular feature was the defeat of many Congress stalwarts, including party president Kamaraj Nadar. There was almost a palpable sense of euphoria in many parts of the country at having broken the stifling stranglehold of Congress.

Centralisation and Personalisation

After the state reverses of 1967, the political management skills of the Congress Party bosses were seriously discredited. Alternative parties, singly or in coalition, could credibly offer the prospect of state patronage. As the old-style party bosses came into increasingly open conflict with Mrs Gandhi for control of the party apparatus and government policy, Mrs Gandhi shifted the contest to the populist arena. Her leftist slogans gave her decisive electoral victories against the 'syndicate' of party bosses, and her electoral triumphs handed the levers of state patronage to her. Concluding that state party bosses had lost the ability to deliver votes, Mrs Gandhi began to centralise the party. She used her finely honed skills of party infighting and manipulation to establish an unquestioned supremacy in the state as well as central party machineries. In the process, she hastened the institutional decline of the party. Congress was transformed from a well-organised but decentralised party machine into a collection of sycophantic functionaries whose chief task was to perpetuate the rule of the Nehru–Gandhi dynasty.

The party organisation was split in 1969 and again in 1978 to this end, with success for Mrs Gandhi, atrophy for the party organisation and frailty for Congress-run state governments. The appellation Congress(I) (for Indira) symbolised the transformation of the party from an independent political organisation into a family patrimony. Subservient apparatchiks were appointed (internal party elections rapidly declined) to state cabinets and key party bodies like the AICC and the CWC.

During Nehru's time, the CWC played 'an important role in providing policy leadership to the party organization, in coordinating party–government relations, and in accommodating the conflicting demands of Congress leaders representing the broadening base of the party' (Kochanek, 1968, p. 307). Under Mrs Gandhi, party structures lost their role as two-way communication channels. State chief ministers were hand-picked by Prime Minister Indira Gandhi. State-level cross-cleavage coalitions were dispensed with in favour of rallying calls directly from New Delhi. It was on this basis that in 1971 national elections were for the first time held without simultaneous state elections. In appealing directly to the people and campaigning on national issues, Mrs Gandhi bypassed the intermediary structures and escaped the need for the politics of patronage. She put her faith in her own abilities rather than in the capacity of party bosses in charge of 'vote banks' (another Indian contribution to English). She won her massive majority and consolidated her hold even in states in March 1972 on the crest of victory in the Bangladesh War (1971), winning more than two-thirds of the assembly seats. But the price was the destruction of the Congress system that had served the party so well for so long. 'The de-linking of national from state elections marks the death of the classic Congress system, as does the curtailing of the powers of the Congress chief ministers' (Hewitt, 1989, p. 160).

The results of the 1971–2 elections gave unquestioning power to Mrs Gandhi. She asserted and exercised her authority ruthlessly at the national as well as state level. Not just state chief ministers, but the central cabinet and party posts were frequently shuffled. The goal of such rapid turnover was not to improve organisational or administrative efficiency, but to prevent the institutional consolidation of power by a potential political rival (Kochanek, 1976). She succeeded in that. But the musical-chairs phenomenon of Congress party politics also ensured that there was no administrative competence and political continuity even at the cabinet level. Hence the sense of policy drift that came to characterise Mrs Gandhi's years in power. Yet another adverse consequence of the centralised–personalised style of Congress politics was that more and more of the prime minister's time and energy had to be expended on dealing with state problems to the neglect of pressing national issues. President's Rule was imposed in four states and chief ministers replaced in six within 18 months of the 1972 state elections.

Other parties took up the slack in forming broader coalitions, mobilising the voters and providing avenues for the advancement of politically ambitious elites. Mrs Gandhi was in power but in effect not in office. Her cabinet failed to perform the tasks of government in New Delhi, and her party stopped performing the functions of interest articulation, interest aggregation and social conflict resolution through authoritative policy outputs. Centralisation of power in the hands of the prime minister in New Delhi meant that state party units, with their organisations in disarray, could neither represent local interests nor implement national policies. Congress gradually became an inverted pyramid with its base getting narrower and narrower.

One of the major causes of the periodic debacles suffered by the Congress Party in recent times has been the destruction of democratic processes in the internal affairs of the party. After splitting the

Congress Party in 1969, Mrs Gandhi steadily refashioned the party as a tool to serve her political ends. Her son and successor Rajiv Gandhi saw no need to change her winning ways. During the years of Rajiv Gandhi too (1984–9), Congress remained more a coterie around the prime minister than a party whose organisation reached into the deepest hinterland. Electoral successes masked organisational atrophy. Astonishingly, no elections were held in branches of the Congress Party between 1972 and December 1991. Not surprisingly, therefore, the 1991 party elections were far from models of democratic choices. Party bosses in some states put their faith in the familiar tactics of musclemen, fake membership lists and bureaucratic–police harassment of rivals.

Candidate selection takes account of a number of variables. A person may seek Congress nomination on the basis of loyalty and service to the party over a long period of time or of having rendered a service of particular value. Or the aspiring candidate might point to affinity with the local community in the electorate. Then the different party organs need to be balanced, for example the Youth Congress. The basic conflict usually is between the centralising tendency of the national party leadership and the localising pulls of the district and state units. The tension was best reflected in the change during the Rajiv Gandhi era. As the government, Congress was committed to modernising India. Yet as a party concerned above all to win elections, Congress had to be attuned to traditional values and idioms. The relative influence of district, state and national levels of the party organisation has varied from one election to the next.

Rajiv Gandhi had done well enough in the general election at the end of 1984. He also began his prime ministership promisingly, with accords in Assam and Punjab, a drive towards economic liberal-isation, a commitment to cleansing the party and the government of corruption and hopes of open and consensual government. But the promise of the accords remained unfulfilled, liberalisation was stalled, the government got mired in the major Bofors corruption scandal (involving an illegal $50m commission in the $1.3 bn sale of 155mm howitzers) and Rajiv retreated into a centralised, imperious and distant style of functioning. The cabinet was reshuffled several times a year, always with the promise of further adjustments to follow. At the state level, chief ministers of Congress-ruled states were changed by Rajiv Gandhi on average about every three months between 1985 and 1989. With a progressively narrowing base of support and the party organisation in shambles, Congress lost several states to a variety of mainly regional opposition parties. As Rajiv withdrew into an ever-decreasing circle of close political confidantes for policy advice, increasing numbers of party members found themselves on the outside.

Rajiv Gandhi became aware of the party's organisational malaise in the year following his election defeat in 1989. Acknowledging that he had lost touch with the people, he undertook several journeys in June–July 1990 to the farthest reaches of the country. The trips boosted the morale of party workers. But the journey into the villages of Bihar and U.P. also brought home to him the reality that Congress had ceased to be an effective party machine (N. Chakravarty, 1990). The abject dependence of a once-great party on the personal vote winning abilities of Indira, Sanjay and Rajiv Gandhi reached a climax when, after the assassination of Rajiv in 1991, Congress offered the leadership to his Italian-born widow Sonia (which she declined). Instead, the leadership passed to P. V. Narasimha Rao. It fell to him to depart radically from the Nehruvian legacy in economic and foreign policies. Almost immediately after taking office in 1991, his government launched a major reorientation of economic policy to make it more market-oriented, liberal and open to global trade. Confronted with the end of the cold war and the collapse of the Soviet Union, he also had to refashion external relations that had been built around these 'certainties' in international relations (see Thakur, 1992).

Factional Politics

In a one-party-dominant system, the role of opposition is in many ways performed by factions within the ruling party. This has been taken to such an extent in the case of Congress that its most innocuous moves are scrutinised minutely for their relevance to the party's internal politicking rather than their national implications. The faction was the basic unit of political activity in India during the traditional Congress system. Factions were loose coalitions built around leaders at the local or district level and connected to one another at the state level by political interest rather than ideology or sectarian solidarity. In many respects the faction was a source of strength, not weakness. Vertical in structure, the faction, by cutting across horizontal ties of ascriptive loyalties, served to politicise social and religious groups in secular terms. It performed several integrative functions (Brass, 1965): factional leaders engaged in the competitive drive to political recruitment, the bases of political participation were broader than sectarian cleavages, the relative autonomy of each factional unit tended to insulate the state and national units of a party from personal conflicts at the local level and it channelled conflict and hostility without endangering a party. However, the faction was disintegrative in undermining the basis of the modern political party. It inhibited the emergence of parties aligned along social or ideological lines, encouraged the phenomenon of 'defections' to persons and thus impeded the development of a stable party system.

Japan is another prominent example of a one-party-dominant system (see Hoffmann, 1981). Unlike Japan, India is a federal polity. This has two interesting consequences for party politics in a one-party-dominant system. With the same political party ruling in states and at the centre, the essence of federal bargaining takes place within the ruling party rather than between state and central governments. Such was the case in India until 1967. The breakup of the Congress monopoly on political power after that date has meant that the party has ceased to play this mediating role in India's federal structure. But it has had a second consequence. In the 1989 general election, Congress governments in states where the party suffered electoral reverses for the union parliament submitted their resignations as though they had been defeated on a vote of no-confidence. Chief ministers were replaced by their factional opponents within the Congress Party.

Moreover, the label of one-party-dominant system is somewhat misleading when applied to Congress in India. The party was dominant in national politics by virtue of its strength in the central parliament. But this disguised the reality of substantial opposition from other political parties on a state-by-state basis (Table 9.1). They were not, therefore, peripheral to the political process. Indeed the dominance of a communist party in West Bengal has been such that that state could probably be described as a communist one-party-dominant system. Congress had a distinctive pattern of relationships with other political parties from one state to the next, reflecting its different social base in each state separately.

Earlier studies (for example, Goel, 1974) had found that the social bases of support for the Congress Party were evenly spread across all social groups. Even so, it was somewhat more popular among the elderly (that is, those who had been socialised into politics during the independence struggle), the less educated, the religious and ethnic

TABLE 9.1

Votes for Congress and its closest competitor by states, 1991 Lok Sabha elections (percent)

| State | Congress | | Closest competitor | | |
	Seats	Votes	Seats	Votes	Party
Andhra Pradesh	24	45.8	13	33.2	Telugu Desam
Assam	8	39.3	1	18.0	Asom Gana Parishad
Bihar	1	22.5	28	32.4	Janata Dal
Gujarat	4	28.8	20	52.1	BJP
Haryana	9	41.1	0	28.2	Samajvadi JanataParty
Karnataka	22	43.7	4	28.1	BJP
Kerala	13	38.1	3	22.3	CPI(M)
Madhya Pradesh	27	47.3	12	43.7	BJP
Maharashtra	37	46.0	5	19.5	BJP
Orissa	12	44.4	6	34.7	Janata Dal
Rajasthan	13	45.0	12	41.9	BJP
Tamil Nadu	28	43.5	11	18.5	AIADMK
Uttar Pradesh	5	19.9	50	35.3	BJP
West Bengal	5	36.6	27	36.0	CPI(M)

Note: States with fewer than 5 seats in the Lok Sabha have been omitted from this table. Punjab and Jammu and Kashmir have been left out because elections were not held there in May–June 1991.

minorities and those living in rural areas. Support for the opposition parties was relatively stronger among the young, the educated, the Hindus and the urban dwellers. A major factor contributing to the defeat of Mrs Gandhi's Congress in 1977 was the desertion of the minorities who had suffered the most at the hands of unrestrained officials during the 1975–7 emergency. The westernised middle-class intellectuals may have opposed the emergency in principle; the scheduled castes and tribes and the Muslims opposed it after experiencing its excesses.

The Janata Coalitions

The centrality of Congress in national politics has meant that the major principal theme for other parties has been the appropriate stance towards Congress. Congress has been defeated in national elections only twice, in 1977 and in 1989. In both instances, a loose coalition of other parties came together to form a government for brief interludes, united only in a common opposition to Congress. Of necessity, the two terms of non-Congress governments too have been characterised by 'catch-all' coalitions rather than one-dimensional cohesive parties. Like the Congress, the Janata (1977–9) and National Front (1989–90) governments tried to broaden their appeal to diverse groups. In particular, they tried to woo the many minority and peripheral groups into their all-embracing folds. In terms of the Lipset–Rokkan model discussed above, therefore, the party system in India works in the opposite direction from that predicted by the model. The conflict is not between centralising, nation-building parties, on the one hand, and others catering to centrifugal, peripheral groups on the other. For like Congress, the Janata was a national, centrist party. Rather, the main electoral competition has been between alternative broad-based aggregative or coalition parties that have to attract substantial support from minority groups in order to win office.

In 1977, a diverse group of opposition parties and dissident Congress members who were unhappy with Mrs Gandhi's authoritarian leadership came together to fight the general election on the overriding issue of the emergency. But the glue of government was not strong enough to hold together the constituent units and mutually suspicious leaders, in particular the troika of Morarji Desai, Jagjivan Ram and Charan Singh at the top of the coalition. The component units retained their separate organisations and social bases of support, and were divided over economic policy and political tactics and goals.

By 1979 the Janata government was clearly adrift and rudderless, lacking a programme, *weltanschauung* or grand design informing its actions. Bereft of a frame, the government failed to shape events and instead lurched from near disasters to eventual collapse. In some respects the Janata government died a victim of its prime minister. Morarji Desai proved too rigid and self-righteous to lead a heterogeneous team. Other members of the coalition were concerned more with self-aggrandisement than the collective good. Charan Singh, for example, emerged as egotistical and self-centred, too narrowly involved in the interests of his own and allied castes, much too consumed by a blinding ambition to be prime minister to settle for anything less. Jagjivan Ram completed the triumvirate of prime ministerial contenders.

The strength and cohesiveness of a political faction has traditionally depended on the ability of the leader to distribute material benefits to followers. In this task the contradictions of the Janata coalition proved irreconcilable. Divergent interests represented by the constituent units of the Janata were soon at odds. Charan Singh with his middle peasants, Jagjivan Ram with his harijans, the Jan Sangh with its militant Hinduism and Desai with his old-fashioned Congress secularism and interest aggregation represented constituencies that were not merely separate but also in competition for the same scarce rewards of office. Defections from the Desai government began in earnest after 7 July 1979, and on 17 July Charan Singh resigned as deputy prime minister. With deft political needlework, Mrs Gandhi split the Janata at the seams: Charan Singh's pretensions to government lasted a mere 24 days.

The 1989 coalition had its origins in unhappiness with Rajiv Gandhi. V. P. Singh emerged as the focus of opposition unity. He had been chief minister of the pivotal and populous state of U.P. and Finance and Defence Minister under Rajiv Gandhi. The impression was conveyed that he had lost the finance ministry in January 1987 when his liberalisation drive took him into efforts at cracking down on wealthy tax evaders. His tenure at the defence ministry was terminated when he proved too energetic in trying to uncover the illegal Bofors kickbacks. His resignation from the cabinet and expulsion from the party in 1988 gave him national prominence while tarnishing Rajiv's image of 'Mr Clean'. V. P. Singh's electoral appeal was confirmed with the massive majority of his victory against the Congress candidate in the Allahabad by-election in 1988. With V. P. Singh at the helm, a united opposition group could offer a credible prime minister. Elections were due by the end of 1989. In July 1988, four national (Congress (S), Janata, Jan Morcha and Lok Dal) and three regional (Asom Gana Parishad, DMK and Telugu Desam) parties held discussions on a coordinated strategy. The four national parties merged into the Janata Dal under the leadership of V. P. Singh. The three regional parties retained their separate identities but agreed to cooperate with the Janata Dal in a National Front.

The Janata Dal's strengths were in northern India. Its prospects were brightened when the BJP, with strengths in the west as well as the north, and the Left Front, which was strong in the northeast and Kerala, agreed to work out electoral adjustments with the National Front in about 400 constituencies. After the general election of November 1989, Congress was still the largest single party in parliament, but it was well short of a majority. On 2 December,

V. P. Singh was sworn in as prime minister at the head of the National Front to form a minority government which depended for its survival on the 85-strong BJP and the 52-strong Left Front.

The 143-strong Janata Dal was full of former Congress people, and in many ways offered the familiar Congress vision with a slightly more populist tinge. But its programme of government remained unfulfilled as the National Front was afflicted by *immobilisme*. Chandra Shekhar from U.P. had been outmanoeuvred for the prime ministership and bided his time to launch a challenge for the top prize. Devi Lal from Haryana settled for the deputy prime ministership but unsettled the government with a continual series of questionable decisions and deals in Haryana as well as New Delhi. He quickly acquired a reputation for electoral violence and fraud, and so became a political liability in the public opinion stakes yet an indispensable power broker in the government's survivability stakes. As the Singh government was paralysed by personality clashes, policy incoherence and general drift, in August 1990 V. P. Singh staked out a political constituency by announcing that, on top of the 22.5 per cent quota for the scheduled castes (former untouchables) and tribes, another 27 per cent of all government jobs would be reserved for the backward castes. This violated the BJP plan to unite all Hindus within one movement. The BJP was incensed even more when V. P. Singh decided to court the Muslim vote by projecting himself as the champion of minorities against threats to secularism. When BJP leader L. K. Advani was arrested in Bihar on 23 October 1990 en route to Ayodhya, the BJP withdrew its support from the government. V. P. Singh lost the vote of confidence in the Lok Sabha by 142 to 346 and tendered his resignation.

Chandra Shekhar was sworn in as prime minister on 10 November with a rump group of some 50-odd MPs, but with the support of almost 200 Congress MPs. Totally dependent on Rajiv Gandhi's support for staying in office, Chandra Shekhar proved pliant to Congress demands in rescinding a decision to permit US warplanes to refuel at Bombay en route to the Gulf War and in dismissing National Front state governments in Assam and Tamil Nadu. The latter was especially humiliating, for the excuse of a breakdown of law and order was too thin to be credible in the context of the situation in many other states. On 5 March 1991, Congress MPs staged a walk-out from parliament to protest against the surveillance of Rajiv Gandhi by Haryana state government agents. On 6 March, Chandra Shekhar resigned on grounds of being unable to function as prime minister, and advised the president to call fresh elections. Thus ended India's second attempt to form a Janata coalition government, in ignominy as bad as the first attempt but with an accelerated process of disintegration. The people had their revenge in the 1991 elections, trimming V. P. Singh's Janata Dal to 56 seats and Chandra Shekhar's Samajvadi Janata Party to a mere 5 seats.

The Bharatiya Janata Party (BJP)

The biggest beneficiary of the resulting public disenchantment with the implosion of the Janata Dal was not Congress but the BJP. The party has profited also from the progressive attenuation of secularism. The origins of the BJP go back to a process of competitive ethnic–linguistic nationalism. The Hindu Mahasabha was formed in reaction to the Muslim League and Indian liberals. Set up in Punjab in 1907 and reorganised as an all-India party in 1915, the Hindu Mahasabha foreshadowed the opposition to the import of Western secularism that was to become more familiar around the world from the 1970s onwards. But the party failed to win more than 1 per cent of the vote at its peak in the first general election and rapidly disappeared into oblivion. Similarly, the Ram Rajya Parishad did not make much of an electoral impact as a Hindu revivalist party. Hinduism lacks both a tradition of exclusivity and a hierarchical religious order in which a papal equivalent can pronounce authoritatively on religious dogma.

The closest approximation to a Hindu party in Indian politics was the Bharatiya Jan Sangh. Formed in 1951, it drew much of its organisational strength from the Rashtriya Swayamsevak Sangh (RSS, or National Volunteer Corps). The RSS was formed in 1925 with a militant commitment to the regeneration of India as a Hindu nation. Banned as a communal organisation after the assassination of Mahatma Gandhi in January 1948, some of its leaders entered the electoral arena by forming a new political party called the Jan Sangh. Like most religious movements that draw their vitality from a reaction to the perceived evils of Western cultural imperialism, the Jan Sangh adopted policies that were symbolically important to its Hindu constituency: advocacy of Hindi language and Ayurvedic medicine, protection of the cow and a hawkish stance on defence, including the acquisition of nuclear capability. The party was committed to 'four fundamentals': one country, one nation, one culture and one law.

TABLE 9.2

Votes for the Jan Sangh/BJP, 1952–91

1952	1957	1962	1967	1971	1977	1980	1984	1989	1991
3.1	5.9	6.4	9.4	7.4	*	*	7.4	11.4	19.9

Note: * The party was called Jan Sangh for the 1952–71 elections, formed part of the Janata party in the 1977 and 1980 elections, and contested the 1984 election as the Bharatiya Janata Party.

Source: *India Today,* 15 April 1991, pp. 52–3 and 15 July 1991, p. 20.

As Table 9.2 shows, the progress of the Jan Sangh, renamed BJP for the 1984 election, was steady rather than spectacular until the 1989 general election, and dramatic in the 1991 election. Although popular explanations focused on the BJP's exploitation of majority Hindu sentiment, its 1989 and 1991 successes were built on eight factors:

1. It offered collective leadership within a hierarchical party leadership as against the Congress cult of personality. The BJP has been cultivating an image of cohesion and clarity, contrasting its self-assurance with the fractious uncertainty of other opposition parties.
2. It made an effort to project an image of a party that was internally disciplined and based on conviction and values.
3. It ran a systematic and methodical election campaign.
4. Its front-rank leaders were skilful orators when speaking to mass audiences.
5. It had an effective plan for mobilising grass-roots cadre support. The BJP's most vigorous campaign canvassers during elections are the disciplined members of the RSS.
6. It became home to the expanding middle class that had abandoned Rajiv Gandhi when his economic liberalisation stalled and he retreated into the familiar socialism of Congress.
7. It offered a clear-cut, unapologetic identity based on nationalism and patriotism. According to the Hindutva (revivalist Hinduism) doctrine, Hindus have a distinctive cultural identity and social ethos which should be the dominant and unifying basis of the nation's polity. Many nationalists had previously stood by the Congress because they believed that only Congress could provide a stable and powerful source of authority to guarantee national security. As Rajiv Gandhi's inability to cope with the myriad

internal and external challenges to the Indian state became increasingly clear, so the BJP promise of strength and stability gained more adherents.

8. It exploited religious sentiments by mobilising nationwide to rebuild a putative temple at the site of Lord Ram's birthplace and kingdom in Ayodhya.

Religious Nationalism

The first five factors had proved insufficient to catapult the Jan Sangh/BJP into a major political force until the 1980s. The Jan Sangh participated in five coalition governments in the Hindi cowbelt in northern India between 1967 and 1971. It played a major role in the formation of the Janata Party in 1977, and was an important constituent unit of the Janata government. The Janata foreign minister from 1977 to 1979 was the veteran Jan Sanghi Atal Behari Vajpayee. The party also won control of state governments in Himachal Pradesh, Madhya Pradesh and Rajasthan as well as Delhi. From an ideological point of view, the Jan Sangh, with strong links to the paramilitary RSS, was the symmetrical equivalent to the communist parties. The latter appealed to the young with its commitment to social transformation by an attack on the capitalists, feudalists and bourgeoisie domestically and on the United States internationally. The Jan Sangh appealed to the youth with its vision of a Hindu *rashtra* (nation) through religious revivalism, opposition to the Muslims domestically and confrontation with traditional foreign enemies like China and (especially) Pakistan on the basis of armed strength. In economic policy the BJP is a fierce critic of traditional Congress socialism and supports liberalisation. But it is also opposed to foreign investment.

The blurring of the seventh (patriotism) and eighth (religion) factors was to prove decisive in the 1989 and 1991 elections. In its own version of liberation theology, the BJP decided to liberate Lord Ram in Ayodhya. BJP leader L. K. Advani launched his movement for the construction of a temple to Ram in Ayodhya in October 1990. He engaged in a 10 000 km long *Ratha Yatra* (chariot journey) in a jeep painted to look like a war chariot, calling upon the people to demonstrate *Ram Bhakti* (Ram worship) and *Lok Shakti* (people power). The slogan adopted by the party was *mandir wohin banayenge* (we will build the temple there, and only there). In contemporary newspeak, the programme for building the temple was justified on grounds of maintaining national unity and integration (the collapsing of the seventh and eighth factors in the list above). In reality, when the 100 000–strong gathering of *kar sevaks* (holy volunteers) tried to storm the Babri Masjid in September 1990, about 30 were killed by police in the attempt and hundreds more died in communal riots which ensued. The V. P. Singh government collapsed immediately after as the BJP withdrew support in parliament.

The BJP had contested 226 seats in 1989, and increased its parliamentary strength more than fortyfold to 85 seats. Congress spokesmen dismissed the gains as marginal and ascribed it to seat adjustments with the Janata Dal (Gupta, 1990, p. 12). Two years later the BJP fielded candidates in 479 seats. Voters returned to the Congress fold to some extent because of the sympathy generated by the assassination of Rajiv Gandhi between the two rounds of voting (to be discussed in the next chapter). This produced a collapse of votes for the BJP in comparison to pre-election expectations. The significance of the dramatic increase in the BJP's parliamentary representation from 85 to 119 in just two years was somewhat lost as a result. The BJP performed especially well in the Lok Sabha elections from the following states (with the bracketed figures being the percent of votes for the BJP): Gujarat (51.4), Karnataka (28.8), Madhya Pradesh (42.0), Rajasthan (41.0) and U.P. (33.0). The party also did very well in Delhi, winning 40.1 per cent of the votes there.

In addition to its good performance at the national level, the BJP won power in four states in 1991: Himachal Pradesh, Madhya Pradesh, Rajasthan and Uttar Pradesh (U.P.). The BJP improved on its performances even in several states where it failed to win many seats. It won almost a third of the popular vote in Karnataka, but only 4 of the 27 seats. In the Marxist stronghold of West Bengal, the BJP failed to win a single seat; but it captured more than 10 per cent of the total vote in the state. Nationwide, as well as winning in 119 constituencies, the BJP came second in another 158. The BJP was the only political party to increase its share of the popular vote from 1989 to 1991, from about 11 per cent to almost 20 per cent (Table 9.2). The net outcome undermined the theory that the BJP had fared well in 1989 chiefly because of seat adjustments with other opposition parties. It also vindicated the party's claim to be a truly national party.

The most encouraging aspect of the 1991 results for the BJP was that its votes increased (generally by a factor of two) among virtually all the cohorts with the exception of the Muslims and the scheduled castes and tribes. By contrast, the Congress vote declined slightly in virtually all cohorts except for the same two groups again (Table 9.3). Most notably, the BJP received 27.3 per cent support of the new voters (those aged 18–21 years), only a little less than the 32.2 per cent support in this cohort for the Congress. The table would seem to indicate that the Congress is a party of the past, and the BJP the party of the future. But there are three qualifications to this. Firstly, Table 9.3 is generally consistent with earlier studies about the social bases of party support for Congress. Yet the party has been able to maintain a dominant position for more than two decades since the trends were mapped. Secondly, India is predominantly a rural country. The BJP's strength remains concentrated in urban strongholds. Thirdly, the BJP is most attractive to upper caste Hindus who in fact constitute a minority of voters. If the BJP is to exploit political opportunities in the future, therefore, it may need to broaden its appeal without losing its core support. And the party has given every indication of wishing to increase its representation both in the Lok Sabha and in an expanding circle of state assemblies. It is the only opposition party starting to approach the Congress in the will and capacity to field candidates all over the country.

Attempts to Broaden Support Base

But the BJP has failed to win significant numbers of seats in the east and south. Table 9.4 shows that the BJP won only 5 per cent of the votes in the eastern states, and less than 4 per cent in the south. The table also shows the limitations of such regionally confined electoral strengths. There are 545 seats in the Lok Sabha in total. Of these, 543 are filled by election. To command a majority in the house, a party needs to win 273 of the 543 elective seats. Even if the BJP won every seat in the north (126 seats) and west (143 seats) – an unlikely eventuality – it would still win only 269 seats, four short of the magic threshold. It must try to achieve a substantial breakthrough in the larger eastern (Assam, Bihar, Orissa and West Bengal) or southern (Andhra Pradesh, Karnataka, Kerala and Tamil Nadu) states. One scholar concluded after the 1991 general election that 'The BJP has not yet established itself as a remotely credible proactive force anywhere in south India' (Manor, 1992, p. 1272). Dravidian India is distinctive in its languages, temple architecture, customs, caste divisions, skin colour and history. Despite being more Hindu than

TABLE 9.3

Congress and BJP voting cohorts, 1989 and 1991

	Gender		Age				Location		Caste and religion			
	M	F	18–20	21–30	31–50	50+	Urban	Rural	Upper	Backward	SC/ST	Muslim
Congress												
1989	37.8	41.5	37.5	37.8	39.9	41.2	41.6	38.6	32.2	30.6	44.2	45.8
1991	36.6	37.9	32.2	35.8	38.0	40.1	36.1	37.3			44.1	46.3
BJP												
1989	11.9	10.9	13.2	12.1	11.6	9.8	20.5	8.0	36.4	20.8	9.5	3.9
1991	20.9	18.3	27.3	22.4	17.7	16.3	27.7	17.5			11.4	–

Source: *India Today*, 15 April 1991, pp. 52–3; 15 July 1991, pp. 34–5.

TABLE 9.4

Congress and BJP performances in the 1991 Lok Sabha elections by region

Region	Seats declared	Congress			BJP		
		No	% of region	% of party total	No	% of region	% of party total
North	102	18	17.6	8.0	56	54.9	47.9
South	130	90	69.2	39.8	5	3.8	4.3
East	135	34	25.2	15.0	7	5.2	6.0
West	140	84	60.0	37.2	49	35.0	41.9
Total	507	226	44.6	100.0	117	23.1	100.0

Note: For the breakdown of the four regions into their component states, see Table 6.2 above.

the north, it is also anti-centre, anti-Hindi and anti-Brahmin (Austin and Lyon, 1993, p. 45). On the other hand, by October 1993 the party itself was feeling more buoyant about its growth prospects 'south of the Vindhyas'. (In popular lore, the Vindhyachal ranges are the dividing line between north and south India.) Party leaders were more optimistic than a year earlier about their prospects in Andhra Pradesh, Karnataka, Tamil Nadu and Kerala (*HIE*, 9 October 1993, p. 16).

This leaves the east. In the 1991 general election, the BJP won 5 of Bihar's 54 Lok Sabha seats on the basis of about 17 per cent of the votes. Adjacent to U.P., Bihar is susceptible to the Hindutva crusade. Any additional increase in the share of the popular vote there will produce exponential gains in seats for the BJP.

The party has also tried to make political headway further east by exploiting fears of Muslim refugees from Bangladesh swamping Hindu-majority West Bengal, Assam and other northeastern states. In the 1950s and 1960s, most of the migrants from the then East Pakistan were Hindus seeking refuge in India. Those who came to India before the 1971 Bangladesh War have become Indian citizens. Most migrants since 1971 have been economic refugees: Bangladeshis poor and desperate enough to seek a better life in somewhat less poor India. In December 1991, the Indian government said that there were about 100 000 illegal Bangladeshi migrants in New Delhi and another 587 000 in West Bengal (*The Economist*, 14 November 1992, p. 33).

Few believe the BJP's claims of up to 30 million illegal Bangladeshi migrants. But few doubt that the true figure is much higher than the official count. Anyone with a local address can register as a voter in most parts of India. The ruling parties of Assam and West Bengal have a history of turning a blind eye to the problem of illegal immigrants because the new voters support them at election time. Like right-wing parties in some European countries, the BJP too has made political profit in Assam and West Bengal by exploiting the issue of immigration. To the BJP, a Hindu migrant from Bangladesh is a refugee, a Muslim is an infiltrator.

The BJP also tried to make political capital out of the Tin Bigha dilemma. Partition in 1947 left some unresolved border problems between India and Pakistan. Some Hindus found themselves in enclaves inside East Pakistan, while some Muslims ended up in enclaves in India. An agreement in the 1950s on a mutual transfer of enclaves fell victim to deteriorating relations between India and

Pakistan. With the emergence of Bangladesh as an independent country, Prime Ministers Indira Gandhi and Mujibur Rahman reached a fresh agreement on an exchange of enclaves. But the Muslim enclave of Dahagram–Angrapota was to remain with Bangladesh. In order to connect the enclave to the rest of Bangladesh, India agreed to lease a strip of territory to Bangladesh in perpetuity. The Tin Bigha corridor is only 180 metres by 85 metres. But leasing it to Bangladesh created a 50 000-strong Hindu enclave of Kuchlibari cut off from the rest of India. The Hindus would have the right to move across the Tin Bigha corridor at designated times. Dissatisfied with this, they succeeded in delaying implementation of the Gandhi–Rahman agreement through a succession of legal challenges. The Supreme Court of India finally cleared the lease in 1990. The lease was effected on 26 June 1992, despite BJP objections, amidst heavy security precautions.

The national challenge for the BJP will be to preserve the loyalty of its niche Hindu support and yet reach out to a broader coalition of social forces. Otherwise the BJP will risk remaining the party of opposition, especially if Congress should succeed in revitalising its party organisation. The imperatives of two-party competition may compel the BJP to follow broadly aggregative, and consequently moderate policies in order to win majority support. The dynamics of a two-party system may therefore create centrist and inclusive drives and increase the responsiveness of parties to individual and group demands. In the 1977 election, a major factor in the Congress defeat was the desertion of the party by the Muslims and scheduled caste groups who had suffered disproportionate bureaucratic and police excesses during the 1975–7 emergency rule. They cast their lot with the Janata in that year. By contrast, in the 1980 election, Congress won a majority of votes in Sikh-dominated Punjab and the Christian-dominated constituencies of Kerala; and a plurality of seats in constituencies in which Muslims formed at least one-fifth of the population (Weiner, 1987b).

That is, Congress normally prevails when it successfully mobilises minority groups to its cause. Conversely, it is displaced when a single opposition coalition manages to exercise a nationalising influence through party and programmatic inclusiveness. If the BJP wishes to displace Janata-type coalitions as the main challenger to Congress in a functioning two-party system, it will have to shift from a posture of extremism to one of centrism. Some fear that the BJP may be the Trojan horse of Hindu fascism. The BJP, the RSS, the Hindu

Mahasabha, the youth-based Bajrang Dal (Bajrang is a popular alias for the Hindu monkey god Hanuman) and the Vishwa Hindu Parishad (VHP or World Hindu Council) are known collectively as the *Sangh Parivar* (the Sangh Family). In English they are also referred to as the saffron brotherhood. Saffron is the holy colour of Hinduism, and the Sangh Parivar has adopted it as its colours. Similarly, the BJP's lotus symbol too appeals to traditional Hindus. Others hope that the BJP has exhausted the political potential of Hindu chauvinism and will become a sober party of the centre–right.

The fears of the first group are fed by the vitriolic hatred directed at Muslims by many BJP supporters. Their speeches are widely circulated on easily available audiocassettes. The hopes of the second group rest on the tradition of tolerance of Hindus and the need for the BJP to moderate its image if it wishes to capture the vast middle ground: the restrictions of respectability. The record of BJP governments at state level is inconclusive as to whether the experience of administration will soften the rough edges of BJP or make the party even shriller as a means of hiding its shortcomings in office.

What is clear is that the BJP has successfully moved to occupy the centre of India's political agenda. It has thrown down the gauntlet not just to the Congress Party but to the Nehru vision of a secular–democratic state. The dominant issue by 1993 was not support or opposition to Congress, but to the BJP. This because the BJP's Hindutva vision held the prospect of remoulding the pattern of Indian politics *since* independence. This much was clear even in the crucial elections that were held in November 1993 (see Table 9.5) in those states where BJP governments had been dismissed after the demolition of the Babri mosque in December 1992. The pace, the terms of reference and the political idiom for the elections were dictated by the BJP. It suffered significant electoral reverses in Himachal Pradesh, Madhya Pradesh and U.P. Gains in Delhi and Rajasthan were not sufficient to compensate for the losses in the cradle of the *Sangh Parivar's* cultural nationalism. The Congress did very well in Himachal Pradesh and Madhya Pradesh, improved its position consideraby in Rajasthan, but declined still further in U.P. In the last, it was the combination of the Samajvadi Party (SP) led by Mulayam Singh Yadav, and the Bahujan Samaj Party (BSP) led by Kanshi Ram, that increased its tally from 42 to 176 and went on to form the government. The coalition's votes came mainly from the Harijans (outcastes), Yadavs (a backward caste) and Muslims, who make up 21 per cent, 17 per cent and 19 per cent of the state's

TABLE 9.5

Congress and BJP performances in state elections, 1993

	Seats declared	Congress	BJP
Delhi	70	14	49
Himachal Pradesh	68	52	8
		(9)	(46)
Madhya Pradesh	316	173	114
	(320)	(56)	(220)
Rajasthan	199	76	95
	(200)	(50)	(85)
Uttar Pradesh	422	28	177
	(425)	(46)	(211)

Note: Figures in brackets indicate previous party positions.
Source: *India Today,* 15 December 1993.

population respectively. The Janata Dal, which had previously drawn support from these groups, fell from 91 seats in the 1991 election to 27 in 1993.

Despite all this, three points should be borne in mind. First, even in U.P., while the number of seats for the BJP declined, its share of the vote rose from 31 per cent in 1991 to 33 per cent in 1993. Second, the political polarisation in all five sets of elections was in terms of the BJP and opposition to it. In U.P., for example, the Muslims ignored the Delhi Shahi Imam's *fatwa* in favour of the Janata Dal and decided that the SP–BSP coalition was the safer bet to defeat the BJP. (The Muslim turnout in U.P. was around 75 per cent, compared with the state average of 57 per cent.) In other words, it is no longer Congress but the BJP that has to be defeated by the other parties forming an electoral coalition against it. Third, the party has been issued another reminder of the need to broaden its programme if it wishes to expand its support base. A single-issue platform has taken it thus far, but is not enough for any more gains. As party General Secretary K. N. Govindacharya noted, 'From Ram mandir, we should turn to Ram Rajya based on concrete socio-economic policies' (*India Today*, 15 December 1993, p. 34).[2]

The question for political scientists is whether the rise of the BJP reflects the emergence of a new middle class, the restlessness of a post-independence generation, the lack of visionary leadership in Congress or the institutional decay of the Congress Party. The BJP may be hoping to ride into power after P. V. Narasimha Rao has presided over the liquidation of Congress. Or it may falter as it fails to make the transition from a religious pressure group outside the established political framework to a party of government. BJP state governments too have been faulted for their ineptitude and corruption. It is internally divided in regard to economic policy. Its general image of being more business-friendly than the old socialist Congress has become irrelevant with the shift towards market policies by the Rao government. The trade liberalisation moves by the government have brought the BJP's discomfiture into the open, with one faction favouring a *swadeshi* (national) free market that would keep the Indian economy off limits to foreign investors. At some stage people, even in the Hindu cowbelt, will begin to judge BJP state governments and thence the national party on issues of *roti, kapada aur makan* (food, clothing and shelter); *Jai Shri Ram* (Hail to Lord Ram) will not be enough.

Class-Based Parties

'Asiatic poverty' is difficult to imagine in human terms without first-hand experience. One might expect such abject poverty to be a breeding ground of radical Marxism. Instead, what seems to be crucial is the intervening variable of a widespread *questioning* of poverty as a fixed factor in social relations. Resort to direct political action to ameliorate poverty occurs when there is a shift from a condition of absolute destitution to one of relative deprivation. At this point, poverty is no longer an accepted condition, but a grievance. Recourse to extra-constitutional violence will result if the political system proves unable to remedy the grievance, or at least to bring about some alleviation of the symptoms.

Communist Parties

The communist parties of India have five interesting characteristics. Uniquely in the world, communist parties have gained and held on to power at the state level within the framework of parliamentary democracy and a non-communist regime at the national level. With origins going back to 1928, they are the heirs to a strong revolutionary–Marxist tradition in modern Indian political history. They have not threatened the core stability of the Indian state. Nor have they themselves faced the threat of liquidation by the state. But they have split and splintered into several factions. The two principal communist parties are the Communist Party of India (CPI), and the CPI(Marxist) – or CPI(M) – which split from its parent party in 1964. Five years later, several militant factions imbued with revolutionary romanticism and committed to terrorism began to splinter as well. The group that had the greatest impact was the Naxalite movement, named after the place Naxalbari (in the district of Darjeeling) where an armed insurrection was launched. The movement has been a nuisance to particular state governments (Andhra Pradesh, Bihar) rather than a threat to the Indian state.

The CPI itself tried the revolutionary path with the armed uprising in Telengana (Andhra Pradesh) shortly after independence. The insurrection was dealt with firmly by the state. Since then, the CPI, and later the CPI(M), although occasionally tempted to smash the constitution from within, have generally committed themselves to parliamentary politics. While the CPI has often been supportive of 'progressive elements' in Congress, and endorsed the 1975–7 emergency, the CPI(M) has been a staunch opponent of Congress governments and policies and entered into a successful anti-Congress alliance with the Janata Party in 1977. In economic policy, the communists favoured a more intensified policy of heavy industrialisation than that pursued by Congress. Non-communist socialist parties favoured Gandhian decentralisation and labour-intensive small-scale industrial development. In foreign policy, the communist parties took the cold war rivalry as their point of departure and supported the international class struggle against the forces of capitalism. The socialist groups concentrated instead on the role of India as an independent actor in world affairs.

Both the CPI and the CPI(M) have tended to focus their efforts in selected peripheral states rather than in the core states, let alone the whole country. Their biggest and most durable successes have come in the states of Kerala in the south and West Bengal and, to a lesser extent, Tripura in the east. Somewhat surprisingly, therefore, the communist parties are cohesive regionally but not in terms of class. The CPI(M) in West Bengal draws its support not just from agricultural labourers and industrial workers, but also from the urban middle class. There is a twofold explanation of why the socialist group of parties pursue a multiclass strategy rather than focusing on the poor and the landless. Rural classes are not sharply differentiated in India, with caste being the more salient cleavage in village society. Moreover, at the local level, politics as well as economics is still dominated by the elite and middle-caste landed gentry.

The fall of communism in the Soviet bloc presented some difficulties to India's communist parties. As news came in of the hardline coup against Mikhail Gorbachev on 6 August 1991, the CPI(M) reacted with immediate and unconcealed joy. Politburo member Harkishan Singh Surjeet described the coup as a natural corollary of Gorbachev's policies and said that the people backed the coup. When the coup collapsed, the CPI(M) stayed silent, saying that it was awaiting more detailed information before making any comments (*HIE*, 31 August 1991, p. 6). The premature ecstasy damaged the party's image of sobriety and restraint. A more important political fallout was that it created an obstacle to the consolidation of left–democratic unity in India's national politics. Other left leaders were appalled by the 'simplistic, irresponsible and immature approach' to Soviet developments that had been displayed by the CPI(M) (*SW*, 31 August 1991, p. 6). Their hasty congratulations to the coup leaders caused considerable embarrassment to the Left Front. At the 14th party congress in 1992, nevertheless, the CPI(M) reaffirmed its faith in Marxism–Leninism. But in October 1994 the CPI(M)-dominated Left Front Government of West Bengal adopted an industrial policy which admitted to a 'lack of new investments, growing sickness and stagnation' in the state's economy; welcomed foreign investment and recognised the key role of the private sector in promoting growth; and urged workers to take an interest in productivity even while protecting their rights and privileges (*India Today*, 15 November 1994, pp. 56–7).

Unlike the CPI(M), the CPI did not express immediate and uncritical support for the coup and was able to welcome the return of Gorbachev. But it was less happy with the moves to abolish the Communist Party of the Soviet Union (CPSU) and to bring down the statue of Lenin. In the CPI's view, Lenin, symbol of the struggle against exploitation, belonged not just to the Soviet Union but to the whole world (*HIE*, 7 September 1991, p. 5). In the following year, at the 15th party congress of the CPI, delegates decided to 'naturalise' communism. They concluded that the Soviet and East European communist parties had been alienated from the masses and the people and consequently crumbled in the face of an offensive. Delegates argued that the CPI had become stagnant and could be rejuvenated only if applied to the specific Indian conditions. In particular, too much jargon and theorisation was causing the party to lose touch with the masses (*SW*, 18 April 1992, p. 6). It may be that the momentous events in the former Soviet bloc have robbed the communist parties of India of an ideological base other than anti-Americanism and 'anti-marketism'.

Regional Parties

The main regional parties in India have been the Dravidian parties in Tamil Nadu, the Telugu Desam in Andhra Pradesh, the Akali Dal in Punjab, and the National Conference in Kashmir. The Asom Gana Parishad and Telugu Desam are latecomers to the group. Their distinguishing features are the emphasis on regional nationalism and cultural identity, linguistic opposition to Hindi, political commitment to greater regional autonomy and focus on state-specific issues. Although the National Conference is more firmly entrenched in state politics than Congress, the Kashmir situation has already been covered in our earlier chapter on federalism. The Telugu Desam and Asom Gana Parishad, formed in the 1980s, lack the historical and cultural depth of the Dravidian parties and the Akali Dal.

Tamil Nadu

State and national politics in Tamil Nadu have been dominated since 1967 by the two Dravidian parties, the DMK and the AIADMK. The Dravida movement is unusual for its origins, its history and its success in state politics in India. It grew out of the historic social cleavage between Brahmins and non-Brahmins in the old state of Madras. The leading landowning non-Brahmins in rural areas organised into an opposition group to resist the domination of the professional and administrative services by the Brahmins. To mobilise support for its anti-Brahmin ideology, the movement emphasised its Dravidian identity and cultural nationalism (Barnett, 1976). In the 1920s the anti-Brahmin coalition defeated Congress for control of the provincial government, but was overshadowed by Congress from the 1930s as nationalist fervour swept the country. Dravidian groups combined under the leadership of C. N. Annadurai to form the Dravida Munnetra Kazhagam (DMK) in 1949. 'Anna' had impeccable nationalist credentials, having supported independence and opposed southern secession. But he also promoted Tamil nationalism and the non-Brahmin cause, and the DMK found a ready response to its fight against the Hindi imperialism of the north.

Efforts to foist Hindi as the national language in the 1960s greatly increased support for the DMK. In the same period, the party dropped its anti-Brahmin platform and projected itself as the natural home for all Tamils. The anti-Hindi agitation was particularly useful in mobilising the Tamil youth who were fearful of their employment opportunities being curtailed if Hindi was established as the language of government. The dropping of the anti-Brahmin image was symbolised in the alliance with C. Rajagopalachari, a Congress elder statesman and the leading Brahmin politician in the state. In the 1967 assembly elections, the DMK won 138 of the 234 seats, the Congress only 50. The death of Annadurai in 1969 was followed by a split of his party in 1972 into the DMK and the All-India Anna DMK (AIADMK). Essentially the two Dravidian parties offer competing visions of Tamil cultural and political nationalism, dominate all politics in the state and forge shifting electoral and political alliances with Congress, Janata coalitions and, latterly, the BJP.

Punjab

Unlike the Dravidian parties, the Akali Dal in Punjab never transcended its ethnic origin and identity as a Sikh party to become a party of Punjabi nationalism. Its historical roots too go back to the early part of the century, when it was organised to win control of the Gurdwaras (Sikh temples). By bringing the Gurdwaras under the control of a committee elected by universal adult suffrage, in 1925 the Akali Dal demonstrated considerable popular appeal and simultaneously gained access to the patronage of substantial endowments. The Dal played an active role in protecting Sikh interests in the communal conflicts leading to partition of the subcontinent and of Punjab. But the Akali Dal has never captured the loyalty of a clear majority of Sikhs, with its core support coming from the Jat middle peasants. Scheduled caste and urbanised Sikhs continued to support Congress. Nor is the Akali Dal supported by the substantial non-Sikh community in Punjab. The Akali Dal demanded the creation of a separate Sikh state made up of Sikh-majority areas of Punjab. Instead, Mrs Gandhi accepted the call of Congress Sikh leaders for a linguistic basis which split off the Hindi speaking areas of Punjab into the separate state of Haryana in 1966. In succumbing to the demands for reorganisation of Punjab on the basis of language, Mrs Gandhi finessed religious exclusive nationalism with linguistic inclusive nationalism. The Akali Dal has failed to segment the Punjabis into Hindu and Sikh communities. But because it retains the committed support of about half the Sikhs, it continues to play a pivotal role in the politics of the state.

Much of the violent tragedy of Punjab in the 1980s was a result of efforts by the central government to marginalise a party which represents the preferences and aspirations of half the Sikhs in Punjab and many overseas Sikhs as well. At the same time, part of the reason for the failure of the Akali Dal to improve its political strength is its inability to broaden its programme into one of regional nationalism. But Punjab also offers a clear illustration of how regional parties were legitimised in direct reaction to Mrs Gandhi's drive to centralisation (Mitra, 1984). For Congress lost all claims to being a vehicle for articulating regional identity. This was to cost it dearly by the 1990s when the resurgence of ethnonationalism was a global phenomenon.

The Hindi Belt

Charan Singh's Lok Dal was unusual in India in being cohesive in regional as well as class terms, being based on the middle peasantry in the Hindi-speaking belt of northern India. Because its regional strength was in the most populous area of India, and because its linguistic unity lay in Hindi, the share of votes it attracted enabled it to claim a significant share of power in central government politics: 'the principal underlying conflict in north India [is] between the middle peasantry and all other social forces' (Brass, 1981, p. 41). Charan Singh split away from the Congress in 1964 to form the Bharatiya Kranti Dal (BKD). The main bastion of his strength lay in the Jat caste of peasant proprietors. As the class prospered with the spread of the green revolution, it was awakened to the importance of the political process in controlling the inputs of the agricultural economy: credit, high-yield varieties of seeds, fertilisers and pesticides, irrigation and tubewells, even diesel fuel. In the state elections of 1969, the BKD won more than a fifth of the vote. As Congress was paralysed by factional infighting, Charan Singh was able to form a coalition government in the politically most important state of U.P. (With 85 seats in the Lok Sabha, U.P. alone accounts for 16 per cent of the strength of the House.)

In 1977, Charan Singh joined forces with the Jan Sangh and Congress dissidents (including the veteran harijan leader Jagjivan Ram and the veteran conservative leader Morarji Desai) to form the Janata Party which won power in the national elections. The Lok Dal (as the BKD was now known) had won about two-thirds or more of the vote in Bihar, Haryana, Rajasthan and U.P., and more than half in Orissa. For this reason, Charan Singh believed himself to be the rightful heir to the prime ministership. Never quite reconciled to the choice of Morarji Desai as the Janata head of government, Charan Singh broke with the Janata in mid-1979 and had his brief moment of glory as prime minister before going down to defeat in January 1980 to Congress. The scheduled castes and tribes, as well as the Muslims, represented substantial segments of the population of U.P. They deserted Congress in 1977, but Mrs Gandhi succeeded in wooing them back to the Congress fold in 1980 in a winning coalition with the Brahmins and Rajput landowning castes. Even though the Lok Dal received considerable support in other adjacent states, Charan Singh himself remained but a state leader in U.P.

Pressure Groups and Indian Politics

The role of pressure groups in Indian politics can be described in terms of six propositions (see Fadia, 1980). First, they are yet to acquire legitimacy in the eyes of the political elite. They are regarded as being extra-constitutional and as external to the political system, rather than as genuine partners in policy-making. Second, traditional groups based on ascriptive ties of caste, language and religion continue to be more important in structuring Indian politics than occupational groups like labour, business and professional associations. Third, many apparently autonomous groups (for example, student, peasant and labour organisations) are in fact controlled by political parties, or at least serve their ends rather than the interests of their own members. Fourth, and following from the preceding propositions, pressure groups have exercised little influence over public policy. Fifth, Indian politics is dominated instead by factional coalition-building and disintegration. Finally, one consequence of the failure to integrate pressure groups into the policy process is that interest articulation is dominated by street politics. All major groups, not excluding the political parties, resort to agitational politics like marches, demonstrations, strikes, fasts and other confrontational techniques.

Conclusion

The history of India since independence shows that the legacy of nationalist struggle continues to structure the modern Indian party system. Overall, the communist parties have never recovered from the identification of the CPI with the British (because Britain was allied to the Soviet Union) against the nationalist cause during the Second World War. Subsequently, in an expression of international class solidarity over patriotism, the communist parties identified with China in the Sino–Indian conflict. The strength of the communist parties is concentrated in Kerala and West Bengal, where Congress was less dominant in the nationalist movement. The socialists were at the forefront of the Quit India movement in 1942 in Bihar and U.P., and the mantle of nationalist legitimacy has helped to preserve their influence in these core states. Congress itself was the largest, most influential and only all-India organisation fighting for independence, and this is the starting point for any explanation of its post-1947 dominance of Indian politics. By refusing to take office, the socialist wing of Congress deprived itself of leaders with experience in organising election campaigns and running government, as well as the spoils of patronage stemming from the power of office. The internal balance of Congress governments after independence was thus shaped by the momentous decisions and events before independence.

Congress, either on its own or in coalition with other parties, does manage to win a majority of seats in the national parliament that allows governments to be formed. At the same time, several opposition parties have always won substantial electoral support as well. So far at least, India's party system has not been so fragmented as to preclude the formation of stable governments, nor so centralised as to suppress electoral competition. Differences among India's political parties do not fully reflect the country's caste, class, religious, regional and linguistic cleavages.

There is an ongoing debate among political scientists as to the proper relationship between ethnic and class politics. For one group, social elites deliberately foster ethnic attachments in order to inhibit the development of class consciousness. Conversely, it may be that reductions in class cleavages lead to a rise in regional consciousness. Alternatively, an attenuation of one form of ethnic cleavage, say caste, may be accompanied by the rise of another form of 'tribal' consciousness, such as linguistic or religious. To anchor this debate to the state of Indian politics, it will be recalled that the communist parties focus on class contradictions through ownership and control of the means and relations of production; the Janata Dal emphasises caste politics by promising reservations of half the government jobs for the coalition of outcastes, backward castes and tribals; the BJP promotes Hindu revivalism; the Shiv Sena combines religious militancy with regionalism; and the Dravidian parties, the Akali Dal, the Jharkhand Morcha, and the Asom Gana Parishad are repositories of regional nationalism. These several parties are in competition with one another as well as with Congress.

In future, Congress may revert to the post-independence model of relatively autonomous state-based units forming winning but varying social segment coalitions. Their success would translate into victories for Congress at the centre as well as dominance in most of the states.

Or Congress could be reduced to the party of the centre coexisting alongside regional governments at the state level. The experience of other federal systems with parliamentary government, such as Australia and Canada, indicate some divergence between state and federal voting patterns. Against this it must be remembered that the Indian system is more strongly weighted towards the centre, and that the Indian state is more interventionist than the Australian and Canadian examples. Both factors would counteract tendencies towards federal–state divergence. Even so, the norm in the 1980s was that the party in charge of the central government held control of no more than half the state governments.

The third possibility is for the emergence of triangular contests in national politics between Congress, a left coalition and the BJP.

The fourth possibility is the emergence of an effective two-party system around the BJP and Congress at the centre. In this scenario, Congress would try to forge electoral coalitions in line with the social cleavage theory of party systems at the local and state levels, while the BJP would try to realign the party system with the overriding religious cleavage.

The most unlikely eventuality is an eclipse of Congress at both the state and national levels.

Notes

1. In an STV system, voters record at least two preferences for each vacancy. The successful candidate is required to obtain at least 50 per cent of the votes cast. This is achieved by eliminating the first preferences for the least preferred candidates in each successive round until one candidate emerges with a 50 per cent margin. The STV is the preferred voting system for most party positions requiring elections.
2. 'Ram mandir' refers to the campaign to build a temple to Ram in Ayodhya. 'Ram Rajya' is a phrase which is used to describe any era characterised by the idealised rule of Lord Ram when peace, justice and general contentment prevailed.

Further Reading

Bhatnagar and Kumar (1988). A discussion of regional political parties.

Brass and Robinson (1987). A centenary year look back at the Congress Party.

Chhibber and Petrocik (1989). Locates the Indian party system within the Western social cleavage theory.

Graham (1993). A comprehensive and perceptive study of the Jana Sangh from 1951.

Joshi and Hebsur (1987). Another centenary look at Congress.

Kochanek (1968). The authoritative study of the Congress Party under the stewardship of Jawaharlal Nehru.

Malik and Singh (1994). Traces the origins of Hindu nationalism, examines its role in Indian politics, and analyses the emergence of the BJP as a major political force.

Mallick (1994). Argues that communism survives in India, in a democratised form, because conditions favouring revolutionary change persist in Third World countries.

10

Electoral Politics

The subject of India's electoral behaviour is a complex and fascinating one. In this chapter I will seek to answer four questions:

1. What special features set India's elections apart?
2. What have been the main shifts and patterns in India's elections in the last two decades?
3. How and why is there a regionalisation of India's politics?
4. What theoretical explanations can be offered to account for India's electoral shifts?

Distinctive Attributes of India's Elections

The most striking feature about elections in India is the sheer scale of the exercise. The constitution requires that the central parliament and state legislative assemblies are to be elected at least every five years on the basis of universal adult suffrage. Since 1952 India has been the most populous democracy in the world. Lowering the voting age from 21 to 18 added another 36 million people to the electoral roll for the ninth general election in 1989: more than the total number of voters in most democracies. In 1991, at around 520 million, the Indian electorate was larger than the entire population of any country in the world save China. It was also more than double the total population of the United States, the second largest democracy in the world. As a corollary, nearly half the peoples in the world with the privilege of free elections in that year lived in India.

257

Moreover, the tenth general election of 1991 was a continuing triumph of India's election machinery. The electorate has trebled since the first elections in 1952 (see Chapter 6, Table 6.1); the number of polling stations has also trebled to almost 700 000; and there were 2.4 million ballot boxes staffed by almost four million election personnel (as well as another two million security personnel) in 1991. Voting turnout increased steadily between 1952 and 1984, but has fallen since then (see Table 6.1). Moreover, the rise and fall of the turnout has been more or less uniform throughout the country. In part the initial rise was due to the increased politicisation of the scheduled castes and tribals and a consequential increase in their numbers at election time.

The number of people seeking legislative office has been going up too (see Table 10.1). There were 8953 candidates in the 1991 Lok Sabha elections for the 537 seats being contested, or an average of around 17 candidates per constituency. One reason for the proliferation of candidates is the habit of running 'dummy' candidates in order to wean votes away from rival contestants. A more important reason may be the ease with which anyone can contest elections. The deposit required is a mere Rs 500 (Rs 250 for a state assembly, and half these amounts again for members of the scheduled castes and tribes). In recent elections, about four-fifths of candidates (including 99 per cent of all independent candidates) have lost their deposits, but the amount is not a sufficient deterrent to stop frivolous candidacies.

To hold free and peaceful elections on such a scale is no mean achievement in any country; it is a wonder in a Third World country. The responsibility for delimiting more than 500 parliamentary and over 3000 state assembly constituencies, and for organising and conducting national and state elections, was vested in an independent Election Commission. It also carries out such tasks as registering all eligible voters, recognising political parties and their election symbols, and establishing procedures for the nomination of candidates. The constitutional status of the Election Commission elevates its importance and enhances its stature. The Chief Election Commissioner is given security of tenure on par with the judges of the Supreme Court. Article 324.6 of the Constitution states that 'The President, or the Governor of a State, shall, when so requested by the Election Commission, make available to the Election Commission or to a Regional Commissioner such staff as may be necessary for the discharge' of their functions. Unlike the Western democracies, electoral registration is the responsibility of the Commission, not of

TABLE 10.1

Candidates, seats and votes in Lok Sabha elections, 1984–91

Parties	Candidates	Seats	Seats (%)	Votes (%)
1984				
Congress (I)	517	415	76.7	48.1
Telugu Desam	34	30	5.5	4.1
CPI (M)	64	22	4.1	5.7
AIADMK	12	12	2.2	1.6
Janata Party	219	10	1.8	6.7
CPI	66	6	1.1	2.7
Congress (S)	39	5	0.9	1.6
Lok Dal	174	3	0.6	5.6
Bharatiya Janata Party (BJP)	229	2	0.4	7.4
Other parties	261	31	5.7	8.3
Independents	3878	5	0.9	8.1
Total	5493	541		
1989				
Congress (I)	510	197	37.3	39.5
Janata Dal	244	143	27.1	17.8
BJP	225	85	16.1	11.4
CPI (M)	64	33	6.3	6.5
CPI	50	12	2.3	2.6
AIADMK	11	11	2.1	1.5
Telugu Desam	33	2	0.4	3.3
Other parties	1318	33	6.0	12.2
Independents	3703	12	2.3	5.2
Total	6158	528[*]		
1991				
Congress (I)	493	225	44.0	37.3
BJP	479	119	23.3	19.9
Janata Dal	317	56	10.8	11.6
CPI (M)	59	35	6.8	6.7
CPI	38	14	2.7	2.5
Telugu Desam	34	13	2.5	3.0
AIADMK	11	11	2.2	2.3
Samajvadi Janata Party	353	5	1.0	3.5
Other parties	1523	32	6.3	8.5
Independents	5646	1	0.2	4.7
Total	8953	511[**]		

Note: [*] Elections were not held in 14 constituencies; [**] elections were not held in 32 constituencies.

Sources: David Butler, Ashok Lahiri and Prannay Roy, *India Decides: Elections 1952–1991* (New Delhi: Living Media, 1991); *Elections in India* (New Delhi: Ministry of Information & Broadcasting, 1991); Robert L. Hardgrave and Stanley A. Kochanek, *India: Government & Politics in a Developing Nation* (Fort Worth: Harcourt, Brace, Jovanovich, 1993); *India Today.*

the individual voter. Rolls are prepared on the basis of house-to-house canvassing, and the lists are published in order to give an opportunity for people to check the accuracy of the electoral roll.

Fraudulent practices are not unknown, but do not affect the overall outcomes of election results. 'Booth-capturing' is particularly notorious in Bihar and, to a lesser extent, U.P. Mercenary thugs are available to the highest bidder for forcible capture of election booths, at the point of a gun if need be. Ballot boxes are then stuffed in favour of the paymaster candidate. The security officers standing guard to ensure the sanctity of the voting process are either bribed into active connivance or intimidated into passive acquiescence. Gradually the professional thugs have begun to contest elections themselves instead of hiring out their talents to others. There has therefore been a steady criminalisation of politics to match the earlier politicisation of crime. More than 300 people were killed in election-related violence in 1991, including 26 parliamentary and assembly candidates. Chief Election Commissioner T. N. Seshan asserted his authority to the point of fighting the central government through the courts in a largely successful effort to cleanse the electoral process during the state assembly elections in November 1993.

In addition, ceilings on campaign expenses are so absurdly low that the lubricant of elections is 'black money'. Businesses try to insure against plausible as well as probable contingencies by donating generously to more than one political party. Earlier, voters used to be bribed individually. This practice eased for two reasons. Candidates decided that their rupees would go farther by buying musclemen who could capture booths than by buying individual votes. Villagers for their part were awakened to the value of their vote, drawn into the political process and socialised into using their votes for their individual or collective good. Minor flaws include the unfair advantage of incumbent governing parties because the electronic media is under total state control. In the 1970s, public radio became popularly known as All Indira Radio; in the 1980s, the Doordarshan state television was similarly referred to as Rajivdarshan.

A second notable feature about Indian elections is the length of time for which they have been held. The first general election was conducted in 1952, the tenth in 1991. When one adds the number of state elections that have been held in India during this period, the total represents a stupendous laboratory for psephologists. After a study of four state elections in 1969, Ramashray Roy was already asserting that 'as far as democratic institutions are concerned, they have acquired a high degree of acceptability and legitimacy' (1975, p. 281). India's political stability has been exceptional in the Third World; its soldiers have not come riding onto the political stage; its former leaders have neither been executed nor, as a general rule, imprisoned or exiled.

A third distinguishing feature about India as a Third World democracy is that the choice and turnover of political leadership has been determined at the ballot box rather than by bullets. Lawson (1991) has refined democratic theory in the light of Fijian experience. In particular, she argues for the importance of the culture and practice of alternating governments as an essential element in the establishment of democratic politics in any country. Toleration by government of dissent and opposition is necessary but not sufficient. What is required in addition is acceptance of the opposition becoming government as per voters' preferences. On this criterion, although Fiji was found wanting in 1987, India is fully democratic (although not without flaws). After more than four decades of competitive electoral politics, India has had alternation of governments in all the states as well as at the centre (Brass, 1990, p. 64).

A fourth point worth noting about Indian democracy is that elections have been conducted on the basis of universal adult franchise from the start. The Montagu–Chelmsford Reforms enfranchised over five million Indians in 1919, the Government of India Act extended it to 30 million in 1935. The Constitution of India made suffrage universal for all men and women at age 21, with no property or literacy requirements. The system of communal electorates, bitterly opposed by Congress before independence, was abolished. Unlike most Western democracies where voting rights were extended to women after protracted debate and agitation, they were granted to all women as well as all men in India from the first general election in 1952.

Fifth, Indians revel in the excitement of elections. It is a huge *tamasha* (carnival) on a vast stage. The campaigns are colourful affairs, the political debate is engaged in passionately by millions of people and the results are awaited and analysed with intense interest. Increasing use is made of electronic technology: audiocassettes were in common employ in 1989 and videocassettes in 1991. At the same time, the persistence of widespread illiteracy gives extra importance to visual symbols differentiating the parties. In fact, the mechanics of voting are built around the symbol. Voters mark their ballot with a rubber stamp on the symbol of their candidate. At a superficial level, politics in India is concerned more with symbols than with issues. Parties contest elections on the basis of slogans – *garibi hatao* (remove poverty) in 1971, *Indira hatao* (remove Indira) in 1977, *Indira lao desh bachao* (bring Indira, save India) in 1980 – instead of argument over ideology or policy. The people know that the politicians are engaged in a battle over power as an end in itself or as a means to money. So all the parties make solemn promises to eradicate poverty, combat corruption and preserve the nation; all buy votes or musclemen specialising in the delivery of votes; and life returns pretty much to normal after the hullabaloo and *tamasha* of elections.

Sixth, the practice of defections, whose effect is to nullify voter preferences, has been developed to an art form in India, especially in the state of Haryana. In the 15 months after the 1967 elections, on average about one state government was brought down every month by being 'toppled' through defections. Because of this, politicians are commonly referred to as 'Gaya Rams' and 'Aya Rams'. (This is the idiomatic equivalent, applied to party loyalties of legislators, of here today and gone tomorrow.) In January 1980, the Haryana chief minister Bhajan Lal had himself set a precedent by defecting en masse with his cabinet to the Congress fold after Mrs Gandhi's dramatic comeback to power in New Delhi. After the state elections of May 1982, Bhajan Lal's 21-member Congress cabinet included one MLA (member of the legislative assembly) who had won on a Lok Dal ticket, another who won as a nominee of a rival Congress faction, and three who had won as rebel Congress candidates against official party candidates.

The techniques of persuasion used to encourage and discourage defections are not always subtle. They can range from political bribery (promise of cabinet posts) through financial bribery to coercion. In 1982, for example, Brij Mohan, a Lok Dal member of the Haryana state assembly, was kept under lock and key in a New Delhi hotel in order to prevent him from defecting to the Congress Party. However, he escaped by sliding down a drainpipe (*OHT*, 10 June 1982, p. 3). Then there was Lal Singh. A deputy minister in the dissolved Bhajan Lal cabinet, he was denied selection as a Congress candidate, expelled from the party when he contested against the official party candidate, and won. Taken to New Delhi as part of the entourage of Devi Lal, the rival Lok Dal claimant to the chief ministership, he was being kept in the 'safe house' of the veteran Jagjivan Ram. He managed to escape by climbing out of a window, was welcomed back into the Congress fold and promoted to minister of state in the new cabinet sworn in on

27 May. As noted by a commentator, 'the ability to grab opposition MLAs has been the prime requisite for the survival of chief ministers in the State' (Menon, 1982, p. 7).

Not surprisingly, the scale and frequency of unprincipled, faction-based defections generated considerable cynicism towards the political process. The cycle of Indian politics was commonly described as selection, election and defection. Pressure mounted on the government to impose legislative curbs on the practice. The Constitution 52nd Amendment Act, enacted by Rajiv Gandhi's government in January 1985, permits a genuine party split while prohibiting defections. The Act requires that, for defection to be permissible, at least one-third of a parliamentary party must seek to leave the party. Otherwise, defecting MPs and MLAs lose their seats. But the interpretation of the Act is solely at the discretion of the chairman of the Rajya Sabha or the speaker of the Lok Sabha or any state assembly, whose pronouncements are beyond appeal to any further individual or body. This has produced some astonishing mathematics: the speaker of the Manipur assembly ruled that 14 defecting MLAs amounted to less than one-third of a party's strength of 26 (*Newstrack* video newsmagazine, April 1991) and were therefore subject to disqualification. Such judgments reflect the dangers of nominating the speaker, a political appointee whose continuance in office is dependent upon a legislature's majority, as the sole judge of issues of law and fact of significant consequence.

Seventh, the quality press in India provides remarkably sophisticated analyses and assessments of elections. This extends to psephological predictions. On the basis of professional opinion polls and a combination of other measures developed over the years, such as the degree of unity among the opposition parties, *India Today* in particular is very good in its election coverage. In 1989, the newsmagazine predicted 195 seats for Congress; the party won 197. In 1991, the prediction was 225, the result was 227.

And finally, it is worth bearing in mind that the outcome of elections in India affects the fate of a rather large number of people. They are indeed momentous events.

India's General Elections, 1980–91

The 1980s was an especially interesting decade for students of Indian politics. It began with the ignominious collapse of the country's first experiment in coalition government and the triumphant return to power of Mrs Indira Gandhi in 1980. It witnessed the assassination of Mrs Gandhi and the transfer of the mantle of Nehru–Gandhi leadership to her second son Rajiv Gandhi. It was marked by an increasing interplay of caste, religion and regionalism with state and national party politics and the increasing resort to individual and group violence as a means of resolving conflicts. A steady induction of criminals into politics produced a corresponding politicisation of crime during the decade. Armed thugs and *goondas* were used with diminishing reluctance to intimidate and murder political opponents. The 1980s ended with the defeat of Rajiv Gandhi and the election of a second experiment in a non-Congress coalition government which lasted just eleven months.

Written off by most political commentators as a spent force in March 1977, Mrs Gandhi found herself at the nation's helm again less than three years later. She had made an orchestrated effort to run her 1977 campaign on the issue of strong leadership, but the people instead chose to vote on the theme of democracy and delivered themselves of her. Her opponents campaigned once again in 1979–80 on the issue of freedoms, but a nostalgic and forgiving electorate preferred her leadership and delivered itself to her.

The seventh general election in 1980 was India's first mid-term poll. There were three broad reasons for the failure of the sixth Lok Sabha to complete its term: a lack of performance by the Janata government, virulent factionalism within the Janata coalition and a manic compulsion to harass and humiliate Mrs Gandhi. Mrs Gandhi's eagerness for fresh elections was easily understood. Not only had the Janata failed to function as a government; not only had it sickened the people with its unseemly squabble for power; it had also relentlessly pursued Indira and Sanjay Gandhi on three fronts. A number of commissions of inquiry produced verdicts that were well-documented, well-argued and well-publicised, but bored the people with overkill. When it became clear that Mrs Gandhi could indefinitely frustrate efforts to prosecute her through normal legal channels, the government set up special courts to bring her to speedy justice. The third front of imprisonment was opened by the government bumblingly early. She was arrested on 3 October 1977 on charges that were unceremoniously dismissed by a court on the following day. In sum, the official pursuit of Mrs Gandhi dissipated government energy, entangled the courts and made a political martyr of her.

Mrs Gandhi's successors in office were not her equals in imagination, drive or the capacity to generate popular enthusiasm. They also lacked her charisma, manipulative ability and capacity for exploiting dissension among foes. If Mrs Gandhi was restlessly anxious to return to office, the Janata remained less a political party than a coalition of sectional interests, inadequately held together by rhetoric and manifestly incapable of government. For all its virtues, the Janata failed to harness political consensus to positive ends. Because the Janata men knew themselves to have been found wanting in the crucible of governmental credibility, they were afraid of the feminine ghost who stalked them and were determined to discredit her.

In this too they failed. The manner of the Janata fall was such that the public revulsion that had swept Mrs Gandhi out of office fast turned against her successors and kept another anti-Congress coalition out of office for the rest of the decade. The constant switching of allegiance that was a marked feature of the campaign in 1979 played even further into her hands. The choice for the people was not between democracy and dictatorship, but between variants of opportunism: and Mrs Gandhi at least governed with firmness and direction. Her campaign line on opponents was that they undermine the political authority so vital to the very survival of India and when I try to restore it, they call me authoritarian. Her campaign slogan, used extensively and to good effect, was *Indira lao, desh bachao* ('Bring back Indira, save the country'). The Janata manifesto repeated the 1977 promise to fight dynastic dictatorships and personality cults. It reminded voters repeatedly of the concentration of power in a small clique and the Sanjay-headed caucus during the emergency. In a sense both manifestos looked back. The Janata asked for a second opportunity to implement pledges that went into abeyance with the collapse of the Desai government, while Gandhi appealed for a mandate to continue the revolution interrupted by the Janata interlude but by less harsh means.

Of all the contenders for the prime minister's *kursi* ('chair'), Mrs Gandhi alone could lay claim to a country-wide charisma transcending all sectarian groupings. She was separated from her challengers also in her ability to enforce discipline within the party. If the Janata and Lok Dal writs did not extend to their own party members, how could they rule a country like India? The new prime minister would be required to provide political stability and take hard decisions to tackle tough problems: who besides Mrs Gandhi measured up to this demand? She was widely perceived as being able to control rising prices (the price of onions was an election issue in parts of the country), cleanse politics of opportunism, weed out corrupt civil servants and protect minorities.

The 1984 general election was more in the nature of a nation's tribute to a prime minister who had been felled by the assassin's bullet on the front line of duty than a contest between political groupings. Rajiv Gandhi symbolised stability and continuity through lineage and renewal and change by age. He tugged on the popular conscience on two strings. It was widely known that Indira's heir-apparent had been Sanjay, not Rajiv. Sanjay's death in an air accident in 1980 robbed Mrs Gandhi of a son, a political confidante and a prime ministerial successor. Rajiv was a genuinely reluctant debutante into the hurly-burly of India's politics, untainted by a history of sordid backroom deals, and for this the people marked him well. And then he was catapulted into the prime ministership by the murder of his mother by her own bodyguards on 31 October 1984. His youth, charm, grief and fortitude were again marked well by a grateful people looking for solace in their hour of trauma. When Rajiv sought their blessings in the form of an electoral mandate to cope with the threat of terrorist and separatist violence sweeping the country, they responded with genuine generosity. It took him longer than most other prime ministers to dissipate the nation's goodwill.

The 1989 Election

In 1989 and 1991, there was a pronounced anti-incumbency sentiment in most parts of the country. State governments under Congress control saw a shift towards non-Congress candidates for the Lok Sabha, and vice versa. The CPI(M), however, defied this trend in West Bengal. Much of 1989 was spent by the Congress and the opposition on resolving internal disputes. The Congress state governments were especially vulnerable to bouts of dissidence, in consequence of which the party lost its one major trump card over the opposition: the promise of stability. Intra-party disputes flared embarrassingly into the open in Andhra Pradesh, Bihar, Gujarat, Karnataka, Rajasthan, Tamil Nadu and U.P. The party hierarchy in New Delhi had to make the difficult choice between dampening the public spectacle of a party bitterly divided from within by retaining chief ministers with little popular appeal and managerial ability, or jettisoning the latter in an election year even at the cost of losing credibility as a stable administration. The incumbent chief minister in Bihar, Bhagwat Jha Azad, was replaced by Satya Narain Sinha against the initial wishes of the central high command. In Gujarat, by contrast, the troublesome Arjun Singh was displaced at the wish of the centre. (P. V. Narasimha Rao was to find Arjun Singh no less a thorn in his political side after the 1991 elections.)

Rajiv Gandhi's Congress was also under attack for failing to bring under control proliferating incidents of ethnic, religious and secessionist violence. The frequency and intensity of sectarian conflict increased at an alarming rate. There were almost two thousand killings in Punjab in 1989 alone. There was an intensification of the Bodoland agitation in Assam and of the movement for a separate Jharkhand state from adjoining districts in Bihar, West Bengal, Orissa and Madhya Pradesh. Islamic militancy, on the rise again in Kashmir, turned uglier with the perceived retreat by Rajiv Gandhi on the Babri Masjid controversy in Ayodhya (discussed above in Chapter 1). The Hindus were not appeased by Rajiv caving in and accepting the performance of *shilanyas* (laying of foundation stone) by the BJP-affiliated Vishwa Hindu Parishad (World Hindu Council) on 9 November 1989. The Muslims felt betrayed by the development and the Shahi Imam of the Jama Masjid in Delhi directed his followers to vote against Congress.

Rajiv Gandhi was himself an issue in the campaign. His greatest electoral liability was the enveloping scandal over illegal commissions (bribes) paid in the purchase of 410 155mm howitzers from the Swedish firm Bofors. Congress portrayed him as an able and efficient administrator, with a clear vision of the future, trying hard to take the country into the twenty-first century, more honest and more sensitive than his opponents to the poor and the downtrodden. Large campaign portraits of Jawaharlal Nehru and Mrs Gandhi were meant to underline the continuity and stability of a Congress government. About 80 per cent of the more than 400 incumbent Congress MPs were awarded the party ticket to make the same points. But this alienated the younger generation.

The opposition happily took up the challenge of focusing on Rajiv Gandhi, attacking him for his many sins of omission (failures of government) and commission. The Bofors field-guns issue was a major campaign theme in 1989, with the opposition successfully sowing doubts in the public mind about the extent of the prime minister's involvement. Rajiv had been defence as well as prime minister when the billion-dollar contract was awarded to Bofors in

March 1986. If he had not personally profited from the deal, they insinuated, then he was at least protecting cronies who had. For the government's handling of the scandal was marked by lies and evasions that had incurred the critical comment of the Comptroller and Auditor General (CAG) of India. The government's clumsy response was to delay the release of the report, criticise the investigation on which it was based yet stall on calls for further inquiry and debate. The net result was that the politically crucial label of 'Mr Clean' was transferred to V. P. Singh, who had resigned as defence minister in 1987 over concerns about corruption in the billion dollar deal. While the security-conscious Rajiv was faulted for his failure to reach out to the people, the relaxed Raja of Manda (V. P. Singh) was praised for his populist style of campaigning.

Among the opposition groups, the Janata Party and the Lok Dal merged in early 1988 into the Janata Dal. The National Front was formed later in the year after negotiations with other national and regional parties. But the National Front too was a house divided: V. P. Singh and Chandra Shekhar were rivals for the prime ministership should the Front win the treasury benches, while the Telugu Desam and the Janata Dal faced dissidence in Andhra Pradesh and Karnataka respectively. Several members of the Telugu Desam government, who found themselves on the fringes as Chief Minister N. T. Rama Rao asserted total control of the party, switched allegiance to the Congress. The Janata Dal government in Karnataka did not improve its public image by disintegrating in election year. Despite such problems, the National Front was able to reach agreement on electoral accommodation between its constituent units and with other opposition parties, including the BJP, with surprising speed. (But the verdict in state assembly elections in Andhra Pradesh and Karnataka was a massive rejection of the Telugu Desam and the Janata Dal.)

The victory of the National Front helped to institutionalise India's democracy, as did the victory of Congress in 1991. In the two decades from 1971 onwards, incumbent governments have been defeated in four out of five elections and power transferred peacefully to an opposition party or coalition. The culture of alternation has thus become reasonably well established. The culture was strengthened by the grace with which Rajiv Gandhi conceded defeat in 1989 and insisted that the people had withdrawn their mandate from his party, even though it was in fact the largest single party in the new Lok Sabha. The Congress Party's share of the popular vote dropped from almost 50 per cent in 1984 to just under 40% per cent in 1989, and its number of Lok Sabha seats tumbled from more than 400 to fewer than 200. Gandhi committed the Congress to the role of a constructive opposition in parliament. For the first time in independent India, a Leader of the Opposition took his seat in the Lok Sabha with an obvious and credible claim as an alternative prime minister. (Mrs Gandhi had been forced to play the role of prime-minister-in-waiting between 1977 and 1980 mainly from outside parliament.)

The fate of the National Front government (1989–90) was sealed when the 86-member Bharatiya Janata Party (BJP) contingent withdrew its support. The BJP had become restive at Prime Minister V. P. Singh's policy, announced in August 1990, of implementing the Mandal Commission's report on extending the quotas for the backward castes (see Chapter 1 above). The BJP viewed this as a threat to national unity and to its own political prospects of uniting all Hindus behind its chauvinistic banner. In September the BJP launched a campaign across the country for the construction of a temple at the site of the Babri Masjid in Ayodhya. The campaign came to a halt on 23 October with the arrest of the BJP leader Lal Krishna Advani by the Janata Dal state government of Bihar with the support of the central government. The arrest of its leader compelled the BJP to withdraw support from the Singh government. In the Lok Sabha on 7 November, the 196 MPs of the Congress Party joined the BJP and the breakaway Janata Dal group of 58 MPs led by Chandra Shekhar in voting against the government on the motion of confidence. Some of the smaller parties and independents also voted against the government.

With 58 MPs, Chandra Shekhar was able to meet the requirement of the anti-defection law that at least one-third of the parliamentary representation must leave a party, in whose name they had been elected, *en bloc*. Shekhar formed his bloc into the Samajvadi Janata Party and formed a government with the support of Rajiv Gandhi's Congress Party and a number of its regional allies. The Shekhar government won a vote of confidence in the Lok Sabha on 16 November 1990. But it lasted a mere four months, with its brief tenure being marked by controversy and suspicion. Angered by a continual series of public humiliations by Congress as the price of continued support, Chandra Shekhar resigned on 6 March 1991 and advised the president to hold fresh elections. The Lok Sabha was formally dissolved on 13 March.

The 1991 Election

The tenth general election was held in two rounds: on 20 May, and on 12 and 15 June 1991. The second round, scheduled to have been held on 23 and 25 May, was delayed because of Rajiv Gandhi's assassination on 21 May. One of the interesting features of the 1991 general election was the measurable effect of the sympathy vote for the Congress. In the first round of election, when 32 per cent of people voted for Congress, there was an overall swing of 7.5 per cent away from the party compared with the 1989 votes. In the second round of voting in June, with 41 per cent of votes for Congress, there was a 1.6 per cent swing towards the party compared with 1989. The swing back to Congress correlated with an increased voter turnout. For example, 56 per cent of voters cast their ballots in Bihar in the first phase; the swing against the Congress was 6 per cent. Voter turnout increased to 63 per cent in June, and there was a swing in favour of the Congress of 1.8 per cent (*India Today*, 15 July 1991, p. 21). According to Prannoy Roy's calculations, if elections to all seats had been held on 20 May, then the Congress would have won 190 seats. Conversely, if all seats had been contested in the second round of voting, then the Congress would have won 265 seats (*India Today*, 15 July 1991, p. 34). In fact the Congress won 225 seats. From this we may hypothesise that Congress sympathisers were more strongly motivated to cast off their apathy after Gandhi's assassination. This was especially true of Muslims and the former untouchables and other backward caste Hindus.

The 1991 election was essentially a triangular affair between the Janata Dal, the BJP and Congress. The first tried to appeal through social justice to the backward castes and through secularism to Muslims; the BJP tried to capitalise on a rising tide of Hindu political sentiment; and Congress campaigned on the platform of a stable and effective government. Compared with 1989, the Janata Dal (and Chandra Shekhar's Samajvadi Janata Party) lost ground to the other two. The Janata Dal lost more than 80 seats compared with 1989, and its share of the vote plummeted from 18 per cent to 12 per cent. The Left Front increased its tally slightly from 44 to 48 seats. Congress also won in the state assembly elections in Haryana, Assam and Kerala, and its AIADMK ally won in Tamil Nadu. The BJP won in Gujarat and U.P. But it lost ground in Himachal Pradesh, Madhya Pradesh and Rajasthan in an anti-incumbency swing in seats. (The BJP did not lose ground in popular votes, but its militancy caused a polarisation of opinion which worked against it.) The Janata Dal held on to power comfortably in Bihar.

The government formed by Prime Minister P. V. Narasimha Rao was the first minority government in India, that is, one without an assured majority in parliament. Indeed Narasimha Rao and some of his key cabinet colleagues, for example Finance Minister Manmohan Singh and Defence Minister Sharad Pawar, were not even members of parliament initially, and had to be inducted through safe Congress seats. (Pawar returned to head the state government of Maharashtra in 1993.) The prime minister's consensus-building skills were frequently required for the survival of his minority government, starting with the first vote of confidence on 15 July 1991. With no party prepared to risk the responsibility of bringing down the government, the Rao government has survived on an issue-to-issue pattern of selective voting.

The 1991 election also confirmed a trend towards realignment. In U.P., for example, the Congress share of the popular vote fell from 32 per cent in 1989 to 20 per cent in 1991: the upper-caste Hindus voted mainly for the BJP, and the scheduled castes, backward castes and Muslims for the Janata Dal. In addition to winning 119 seats, the BJP came second in another 130. In state assembly elections that were held at the same time, the BJP's share of the votes climbed from 8 per cent in 1989 to 35 per cent in 1991. The BJP was the only party to increase its votes significantly from 1989 to 1991, and it did so virtually all over the country. But it was also notable that gains for the BJP were most marked in those areas that had experienced communal tensions and riots.

Regionalisation of India's Politics

Another notable feature of electoral trends in India is the regionalisation of the Lok Sabha. Already after the first seven elections (1952–80), it was possible to demonstrate that Congress was at its strongest in the south and then west, but less successful in the core northern and eastern states as well as in Tamil Nadu in the south (Sisson and Vanderbok, 1984, p. 1093). A plausible working hypothesis would have been that in losing constituencies where the party contested elections consistently, it would gradually build up a core of dependable support and thus become institutionalised. In fact the data through 1980 indicated that the party became weaker in those constellations of districts which had been contested without success (Sisson and Vanderbok, 1984, p. 1093). In the 1991 election, the Congress performed best in the southern states, reasonably well in the western states, unsatisfactorily in the eastern states and disastrously in the northern states (see Tables 10.2 and 9.4 above).

. This obscures the fact that in some respects the party improved its performances in the north and east compared with the 1989 results. In 1989, the Congress had won only 38 of 245 seats in the Hindi-speaking states; in 1991 it picked up 59 of 214 seats (Andersen, 1991, p. 984). Paradoxically, the heavy rout in the north in 1989 helped to preserve Rajiv Gandhi's leadership of the party. The old party bosses who might have challenged him came mainly from the north, and their pretensions to leadership were severely dented by the miserable performance of the party in their home states. Congress MPs from the south by and large remained faithful to Rajiv Gandhi.

The second largest party, the BJP, is strongest in the north and west, but extremely weak in the south and east. Some parties exist only in one state each: the Telugu Desam in Andhra Pradesh, the AIADMK in Tamil Nadu. Others, although they field candidates in several states, are strong only in one or two states each: the CPI(M) in West Bengal and Kerala, the Janata Dal in Bihar and U.P. The biggest political attraction of the Janata Dal in 1991 was its firm commitment to the quota issue for the backward and other backward castes. Its victory in Bihar was due to the solid bloc voting by the Yadav caste and the support of Muslims. The latter group split in its voting behaviour in U.P. between the Janata Dal and the Congress. But the complicating factor there was the mosque–temple controversy in Ayodhya. Caste calculations were superseded by religious emotions. Mulayam Singh Yadav remained as chief minister at the head of the Samajvadi Janata Party after it split from the Janata Dal. The SJP state government, kept in office by the support of the Congress, was uncompromising in its opposition to the BJP-led move to construct a temple at the site of the Babri Masjid in Ayodhya. Police were deployed on a massive scale to thwart the temple movement in September 1990. A pro-temple rally in New Delhi on 4 April 1991 attracted a crowd of around 600 000: the biggest political rally ever in the nation's capital.

Looked at together, the 1989 and 1991 general elections suggest that the era of one-party dominance may be over. The advantages of the Congress are being challenged with considerable success by the BJP. The mantle of nationalist legitimacy for having spearheaded the

TABLE 10.2

The political composition of the Lok Sabha, 1991

State	Congress	BJP	JD	CPI(M)	CPI	AIADMK	TD	Others	Quota
Andhra Pradesh	24	1		1	1		13	1	42
Arunachal Pradesh	2								2
Assam	8	2		1				3	14
Bihar	1	5	28	1	7			6	54
Goa	2								2
Gujarat	4	20						1	26
Haryana	9							1	10
Himachal Pradesh	2	2							4
Jammu & Kashmir									6
Karnataka	22	4						1	28
Kerala	13			3				4	20
Madhya Pradesh	27	11						1	40
Maharashtra	37	5		1				4	48
Manipur	1							1	2
Meghalaya	2								2
Mizoram	1								1
Nagaland								1	1
Orissa	12		6	1	1				21
Punjab									13
Rajasthan	13	12							25
Sikkim								1	1
Tamil Nadu	28					11			39
Tripura	2								2
Uttar Pradesh	4	50	22		1			4	85
West Bengal	5			27	3			7	42

Union Territory	Congress	BJP	JD	CPI(M)	CPI	AIADMK	TD	Others	Total
Andaman & Nicobar Islands	1								1
Chandigarh	1								1
Dadra & Nagar Haveli	1								1
Daman & Diu		1							1
Delhi	2	4							7
Lakshadweep	1								1
Pondicherry	1								1
Total	226	117	56	35	13	11	13	36	545

Notes: BJP = Bharatiya Janata Party, JD = Janata Dal, CPI(M) = Communisty Party of India (Marxist), AIADMK = All-India Anna Dravida Munnetra Kazagham, TD = Telugu Desam.

Total Lok Sabha seats = 545: elected 543, nominated 2.

Seats vacant at time of this table = 36. The final total in the bottom row of the right hand column is the sum of the seats filled (507), the seats vacant (36) and the nomination quota (2).

independence struggle is being neutralised by the image of militant chauvinism; the organisational strengths of the Congress are being steadily matched by the BJP all over the country; the BJP is gradually expanding the corps of party members with actual experience of government; the tightly disciplined BJP can more credibly offer the prospect of stable government than the faction-prone Congress; and the Congress is itself jettisoning its strong socialist image. The significance of the BJP winning four state assembly elections in 1991 lay in its novelty. For the first time ever, four states were simultaneously under the government of one non-Congress party. BJP leaders are convinced that the party is on an ascending growth curve, and that the era of two-party politics may be on the horizon: the BJP on the one side and a Congress-National Front left-of-centre secular coalition on the other. At the same time, the BJP's credentials as the instrument of social cohesion are somewhat suspect because of its religious politics, and there are some signs of tactical and fundamental disagreements inside the party on the timing of constructing a temple in Ayodhya and the need to reach out to moderates by diluting chauvinism, and on the tension between economic liberalisation and fighting off international economic predators.

Another distinctively Indian electoral trait is the phenomenon of families with split political personalities. In Madhya Pradesh, for example, several members of the royal family of Gwalior enter the electoral fray on opposing sides. The rajmata (queen-mother) Vijayaraje Scindia and her daughter Vasundhara are bitter BJP opponents of the Congress; her son and king, Madhavrao Scindia, is a senior Congress Party member who has held cabinet posts in a number of Congress governments. In Rajasthan, similarly, Maharani Gayatri Devi of the House of Jaipur supports the BJP against her Congress-backed stepson the Maharaja of Jaipur Col. Bhawani Singh. When families are united within one political party, the voters do not necessarily reward the candidates for thus depriving them of political excitement. In the 1989 elections, for example, the wife of Bihar's Chief Minister S. N. Sinha, his daughter-in-law and her mother were all rejected by the people in no uncertain terms.

Theoretical Questions

The study of elections combines an interest in empirical trends with normative concerns about the workings of representative democracy.

Do voters cast their ballots on any systematic basis? What is the nature and magnitude of the impact of elections on changes in the relationship between political institutions and socioeconomic structures? Do elections enable citizens to influence public policy by exercising a choice between groups of political leaders or parties? The first and second questions entail systematic explorations of voting behaviour and electoral outcomes, while the third deals with the responsiveness and efficacy of democratic government.

Explaining Electoral Shifts

A number of different explanations have been offered for the distinctive patterns of India's electoral outcomes. Three special features of elections in India are:

- *The Splinter.* The splinter measures the effect of the number of candidates per constituency on the proportion of votes cast for the Congress Party. Until the 1971 election, the larger the number of candidates in each constituency, the lower was the proportion of votes cast for the Congress Party.
- *The Multiplier.* The splinter should be placed alongside the multiplier, which measures the relation of seats won to votes cast (Figure 10.1). This has generally worked in favour of the Congress Party. One possible explanation for this may be the tendency of those who are sympathetic to the Congress to be more likely to vote than those who support opposition parties (Goel, 1974, pp. 216–17). Opponents of Congress may well believe that their votes will be wasted. Or, since the proportion of the better educated and the higher income categories is relatively greater for the non-Congress parties, they might be less inclined to put up with the time-consuming inconveniences of voting in Indian conditions.
- *The Index of Opposition Unity (IOU).* As a corollary, when the opposition has been united, the multiplier has worked to bring about the defeat of the Congress Party (for example in 1977 and 1989). The IOU is a measure developed by Ashok Lahiri and Prannoy Roy (1984), and popularised by *India Today*, for quantifying how united or divided the opposition parties are in challenging Congress as the 'natural' party of government (Figure 10.1). In practical terms, it refers to the extent to which the opposition parties have combined to avoid their votes being splintered into nothingness.

FIGURE 10.1
The Multiplier, the Index of Opposition Unity (IOU) and Congress Party performance in elections, 1952–91

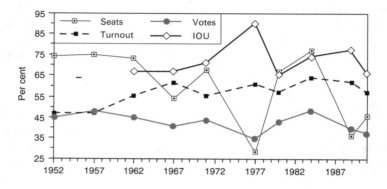

The IOU was developed for explaining the relation between seats and votes in India because of dissatisfaction with the traditional swing analysis derived from essentially two-party systems. For example, each 1 per cent change in votes has produced dramatically varying changes in the number of seats for the Congress Party, with the average ranging from 2.5 in 1957 to 27.6 in 1980. If changes in seats was chiefly a function of swings in votes, then of course there would be a more uniform pattern.

Opposition parties can unite either by forming an alliance or by entering into seat adjustments so that they do not field candidates against each other. The IOU is insensitive to the number of parties contesting an election; it is simply a measure of the strength of the opposition unity. The fewer the number of constituencies in which several parties confront one another, the higher the IOU. It is calculated as the votes of the largest opposition party as a percentage of the total opposition votes:

$$IOU = \frac{\text{Votes of the largest opposition party}}{\text{Sum of votes of all opposition parties}} \times 100$$

If there are three opposition parties, and their votes are 30 per cent, 20 per cent and 10 per cent, then the IOU would be [30/

$(30 + 20 + 10)] \times 100 = 50$. In a two-party system, the IOU is automatically 100. In a multiparty system, it may range from zero (when there are an infinite number of parties and they get equal shares of the vote) to 100 (when there is total electoral cooperation between the opposition parties).

From an explanatory point of view, a united opposition can affect voting behaviour in two ways: voter perceptions and electoral mathematics. If voters believe that the opposition parties are seriously divided, then they will remain sceptical of the ability of the opposition to offer a stable government. The perceptual element helps to convince voters that the opposition parties can offer a credible alternative government and thereby persuade voters that a vote for the opposition will not be wasted.

The mathematical explanation directs our attention to a curious fact in Indian politics. One might expect that when two or more parties combine forces for an election contest, then they risk antagonising core voters who will question the parties' commitment or conviction to party ideologies. In fact in India when two or more parties come together during an election, then the erosion in their traditional support base is only around 2 or 3 per cent. If, for example, the BJP can expect to get 20 per cent voter support in an election, and the Janata Dal another 15 per cent, then if the two parties enter into an electoral alliance their united vote will be around 33 per cent. That is, the disenchantment factor is greater with a divided opposition than with a marriage of electoral convenience.

The Congress Party vote actually declined from 39.5 per cent in the 1989 general election to 37.3 per cent in the 1991 election, yet its number of seats increased from 197 to 225. Psephologists used by *India Today* rated the IOU at 77 in 1989, declining to 66 in 1991. According to them, a 3-point movement in the IOU is the equivalent of a 1 per cent swing in popularity of the Congress Party, and both translate into 15–20 fewer or more seats in election results. A movement of 11 points in the IOU has the same effect, therefore, as a swing of 3.5 per cent. The net impact in the 1991 election therefore was the equivalent of a swing of about 1.2 per cent in favour of Congress.

The most familiar explanation of the discrepancy between the votes cast for a party and the seats it gains in parliament (Figure 10.1) is still the simple plurality electoral system also known as the first-past-the-post system. A further explanation lies in another peculiarity of the Indian political system. Unlike the situation in most Western representative democracies, durable party loyalties in India are yet to develop. They might perhaps be said to be incipient in regard to the CPI(M) and the BJP, but of few others. Because electoral support in India is typically unimodal rather than bimodal or multimodal, the mode itself becomes the free-floating vote and shifts with changing public opinion.

The exaggerated impact of relatively small shifts in votes on electoral fortunes has given rise to another distinctive concept in the Indian political lexicon, namely 'wave'. As far as popular explanations go, a pro-Indira wave brought major gains to Mrs Gandhi in 1971–2; an anti-Indira wave turfed the Congress out after the emergency in 1977; and she swept back into power atop a tidal wave in 1980. Rajiv received a huge popular endorsement on the back of the sympathy wave in 1984. No waves were discernible in 1989 and 1991; yet much of the street and drawing room discussions centred on efforts to locate the flow of any wave that might have determined the outcome.

The exaggerated impact of small shifts in voter preferences serves also to suggest greater political volatility than is actually the case. In fact there is surprising voter stability which belies the fluidity of party positions across elections. William Vanderbok (1990, p. 259) characterises this as 'a situation of contained volatility'. With the exception of the 1977 election, when for the first and only time support for Congress dipped below 35 per cent, the major party's strength has varied within a ten percentage point band (from about 38 per cent to about 48 per cent). Not just Congress, but many other parties too have their core supporters. In every election since 1957, the two communist parties combined have polled within 1.5 percentage points in either direction of 8.6 per cent of the popular vote (see Table 10.1). That is a remarkable level of consistency in voting support for any political grouping. By contrast, support for the socialist parties has been declining steadily, while that for the Jan Sangh and its successor the BJP has been growing.

Exit polls conducted by *India Today* in the 1989 general election showed another distinctively Indian characteristic: for the dominant political party, voter preferences within broad bands remain insensitive to age, gender, rural, urban, caste and religion cohorts (see Table 9.3 above). In every category of voter, the Congress Party received between 34 per cent and 45 per cent of votes. That is, every type of voter fell within a 10 per cent band – or, more accurately, within 5 per cent on either side of the overall percentage of vote for the Congress Party (39.5 per cent in 1989). Consistent with this interpretation, if the overall votes for the Congress drop, then there is a comparable movement in every voter sub-category.

A word of caution is very much in order. The reality of diversity in India affects electoral politics too. For example, one study found that while the impact of socioeconomic status on the level of political information was considerable in West Bengal, it was quite slight in Punjab. And the correlation between age and electoral involvement was found to be inverse in West Bengal but positive in Punjab (Roy, 1975, pp. 274–5).

Empirical

Political scientists are perennially interested in the extent and strength of party identification, the social bases of party support and the degree to which voters identify with candidates and parties, the measures of and reasons for political apathy and participation, the determinants of electoral outcomes, and so on. That is, the subfield of psephology embraces the complex swirl of attitudes and behaviour connected with voting, identifying and choosing candidates, and choosing and supporting leaders. Voters may identify with parties rather than candidates. This does not necessarily mean, however, that personal characteristics are not pertinent factors in their preferences. For they might be basing their voting choices on the personalities of party leaders (for example, the integrity and competence of Rajiv Gandhi in 1984) rather than on issues and policies (the need for stability in 1984).

Scientific investigations of these questions try to ensure that the methodology is sound, the sample of respondents is representative and not biased, the study is replicable by other analysts and the conclusions drawn are logically derived from the evidence collected. A further caution to bear in mind in collecting and analysing data in India is that cultural variables may affect how respondents fill out survey questionnaires. Thus there may be risks in extrapolating statistical techniques derived from market research surveys to a society intrinsically suspicious of the consumer ethic. In one study of three-phased interviews, for example, only a quarter of respondents were consistent in saying that they would vote, and actually voting (Varma and Narain, 1973, pp. 58–9). 'Casteism' is a pejorative term in India. No one likes being called a casteist, and respondents are unlikely to admit to voting on the basis of caste, and yet all the available evidence on voting behaviour attests to the enduring importance of caste solidarity in shaping voting preferences. Moreover, pleasing one's audience is regarded as a social good, and so several respondents may try to anticipate the researcher's preferences and mark their choices accordingly.

Political scientists have built up a considerable pool of data on electoral behaviour in the Western democracies. They have been particularly diligent in trying to establish the potency of class, education, ethnicity, residential environment (that is, urban or rural), religion and language as determinants of party choice. Most studies show social class and religion to be the most potent explanatory variables. Yet there remains some controversy even in regard to Western democracies, where the data collection and statistical analysis techniques are far more advanced than in developing-country democracies. For example, while Lipset (1960) gave primacy to class, Rose and Urwin (1969) found religious divisions to be the primary determinants of the social basis of political parties. A subsequent study of electoral behaviour edited by Rose (1974) found that religion accounted for the highest amount of variance in party choice in five Western democracies (the Netherlands, Belgium, Italy, Germany and Canada), occupational class in another five (Sweden, Norway, Finland, Australia and Britain). In the other two countries covered in the study (Ireland and the United States), neither class nor religion, but historical roots in a civil war, was the principal explanatory factor in partisanship.

The evidence from India would suggest that social class is a principal determinant of party choice only in the absence of other salient cleavages. The most powerful factor is to be found where religious, regional and linguistic cleavages coincide and reinforce one another, as with the Akali Dal in Punjab. The second most powerful combination is region and language, as with the two Dravidian parties in Tamil Nadu (the DMK and the AIADMK), Telugu Desam in Andhra Pradesh and the Asom Gana Parishad in Assam. Caste solidarity is also important. People may vote either for a party with which their *jati* is identified, or for a respected member of their *jati* standing for election. All this is a reflection of weak party loyalties in India compared to Western democracies. Hence the common phenomenon of people denied nomination by their party of first choice happily looking for nomination from another party. Candidates and canvassers show remarkable abilities in electoral calculations. During an election campaign, they seem to have caste, religious, personal following and party following numbers at their fingertips. It does not always prove reliable.

Another point to bear in mind in applying Western psephological findings and techniques to India is the individual–group link. In the individualist ethos prevailing in Western democracies, a study of individual preferences as rational actors makes more sense than in a society like India with a strong impulse to group identities. Individual status is a function of group identity; social status determines much of individual life opportunities; the struggle for individual power is therefore a struggle for social status, and vice versa. That is, politics in India is not just a struggle for political power among individuals or classes; it is also a struggle for social status among castes. Imbalances in the social order can be corrected through victory in the political arena. If the middle peasantry, for example, combine to vote as a bloc and form a government, then its members can seek to influence government policies on agricultural credits, subsidies and pricing policy and, by that means, increase individual and group social status.

The backward castes, untouchables and tribals make up 66.2 per cent of the population; the Muslims, Christians and Sikhs make up another 15.1 per cent (see Table 1.2 in Chapter 1). By attracting most of these 'minorities' to its aggregative fold, as well as some 'majorities', Congress reaped remarkable electoral advantages. Because of the first-past-the-post system and the multiplicity of other parties, winning just 40 per cent of the vote has been sufficient to ensure a comfortable parliamentary majority for Congress, for example in the 1967 general election. A 60 per cent support from this minorities' coalition is sufficient to win 40 per cent of the national vote. Alternatively, with half the minorities' vote, Congress needs a mere 20 per cent of the votes from caste Hindus to capture political power.

Political participation refers to the activity of citizens aimed at influencing who governs and how. There is a notable discrepancy between three measures of political participation (interest in politics, discussion about politics, and attempts to influence political decisions) and the fourth measure of voting. There are no significant differences by religion and caste on any of the four measures. But there are some variations when some of the categories are cross-tabulated. Muslim women were less likely to vote than Hindu women, and sex differences on voting were much sharper in the less literate states (Assam, Bihar, Madhya Pradesh and Orissa) than in the more literate ones (Kerala, Maharashtra, Punjab and Tamil Nadu).

A curiously Indian form of political participation is the political demonstration. A large variety of nonviolent protests has been perfected for use as a political tactic in India: the *satyagraha* (civil disobedience), invoking the mantle of Gandhian and nationalist legitimacy; *bandh* (strike); *dharna* (general strike); *gherao* (confinement of people in their office premises); *jail bharo* (filling of prisons); *rasta* (or *rail*) *roko* (road or rail blockages), *ekta yatra* (national unity pilgrimage), *ratha yatra* (chariot pilgrimage) as well as fasts, walkouts, blackflag demonstrations and so on. The politics of street protests are ways of communicating to the government, officials and people the mobilising potential and public support for a particular party or leader.

The major form of political participation is voting in elections. As we would expect, discrimination in the choice of candidates, parties and leaders increases with income and literacy levels. Earlier studies (for example Sirsikar, 1973) had found that while caste loyalties influenced voting preferences, age, occupation and income levels did not; literacy was correlated negatively with the influence of the head of the family on the voting behaviour of other members of the family; linguistic and religious voters tended to support Congress, while support for the opposition parties was strongest among the highly educated voters. Table 10.1 suggests that there is considerable continuity in voting tendencies. Survey research suggesting that party identification is weaker than candidate identification is at odds with the levels of stability in party support from one election to the next. One way to reconcile the two would be to argue that fluctuations at the micropolitical level tend to offset each other and so dampen volatility at the macropolitical level. Another possible explanation might lie in the aggregative nature of the Congress Party. In the last chapter, we noted how many opposition strands of thoughts have their counterparts inside the Congress. Many voters too may have affinity with Congress as well as opposition parties and so decide on the basis of their evaluation of the candidates' merits in any particular election.

The correlation between social characteristics and partisanship is a measure of the salience and political significance of a country's cleavages. The social cleavage theory of party systems, derived from Western models, predicts a high correlation between political parties and social cleavages in deeply segmented societies. This does not denote a deterministic model of politics, but rather a thesis that political beliefs and ideological orientations are conditioned by social group conflicts. India is an apparent anomaly, with Congress commanding substantial support from virtually all segments (see Table 9.3 above). Rajni Kothari (1964) explained this by stressing the nature of Congress as a catch-all, centrist, pragmatic party that had managed to retain the support of a broad spectrum of people who had been politically mobilised during the struggle for independence. The dominant party is the repository of the legitimacy of the state; the opposition parties can act as political pressure valves and no more.

In an interesting article, Chhibber and Petrocik (1989) challenged the assumptions of this model to argue that Congress is a coalition of state and local parties which represent different groups and interests. At the local level, the political competition between Congress and its opponents reflects the social and economic conflicts of India. Viewed from the national level, Congress is a party of consensus. Disaggregated at the local level, it is a party of special-interest groups. Chhibber and Petrocik based their findings on an analysis of data derived from the 1971 general election. The year chosen was particularly good for a rigorous testing of the social cleavage theory, in that it was the first time that the national election was delinked from state elections. If social cleavage theory was validated at sub-national levels in the 1971 general election, therefore, one could reasonably expect it be equally salient in other years.

At the national level of analysis, in 1971 Congress received majority support from all segments divided by religion, caste and class. Religion played little role in structuring the vote for Congress, caste distinctions even less, and class categories the least (Chhibber and Petrocik, 1989, pp. 198–9). But the specificity of social cleavages in India are geographically bounded. Consequently, social conflicts too are geographically specific. At the national level, caste, class and religion together accounted for only 2 per cent of the variance in vote in the 1971 general election. At the state level in the same Lok Sabha election, they accounted on average for 20 per cent of the variance (Chhibber and Petrocik, 1989, pp. 201–2).

The geographical specificity of the linkage between social cleavage and partisanship has four further points of relevance to an analysis of India's electoral politics. First, it helps to explain the adverse electoral consequences of the centralising tendency of Congress under Indira and Rajiv Gandhi. The defining characteristic of Congress was the state basis of the party, and it was destroyed by centralisation. Second, it helps to explain the failure of other parties at the national level. The Congress could transcend the territorial boundaries of ascriptive cleavages by invoking symbolic and organisational linkages to the nationalist movement which identified it with the structures of state authority throughout India. Other parties could not do this, and so lacked a comparable national framework for mobilising votes. Third, it draws our attention to the importance of the BJP's efforts to mobilise on the basis of the one social cleavage which is not geographically bounded, namely the Hindu–Muslim divide. By the same token, fourth, it helps us to understand why politics in India might be coalescing around a triangular contest between Congress, the BJP and the left alliance which too can try to mobilise support on the basis of a transregional cleavage, namely class.

Normative

Voting turnout, party membership and street activism may give us only crude measures of political participation, but they can provide gross estimates of trends. A reasonable level of voter turnout in a general election, for example, is inherently necessary to the effective functioning of a democratic political system. It has been remarked that India's elections 'constitute the largest forum of collective public activity in the world' (Sisson, 1990, p. 121). Voting turnouts in elections remains quite high, helped by the continuing belief that elections make a difference. Given the turnover of governments since 1977, this is hardly surprising. Eldersveld and Ahmed (1978, p. 6) concluded that political development has occurred in four senses: 'Citizens have become politically participant, party and electoral institutions have emerged, identification and commitment to national symbols and a national system have occurred, and the polity has expanded to the rural and social periphery.' Whatever the measure used, the most important point to remember is that politics has penetrated into the deepest recesses of village India. Political consciousness and participation have increased among all segments of the society and in all parts of the country. The major catalyst for this has been competitive multiparty elections.

   A more interesting question is the relationship between political institutions and social change. There are two types of normative theories about India's elections, the liberation and the exchange. According to the liberation theory, the practice of voting has liberated Indians from the stifling bondage of tradition, changed their attitudes towards those in positions of authority and awakened them to the power of their votes in determining the fate of political leaders. This will be the path to improved performance of the political system and enhanced quality of politicians. For democratic institutions will increase ordinary people's knowledge of governmental and administrative authority, habituate them to discussing issues of public policy and help them to relate their beliefs to their voting choices. With each Lok Sabha MP now representing an average of almost one million voters, it would be unrealistic to expect a close relationship between ordinary citizens and their MPs in the nation's capital. Yet surveys show that between one-half and two-thirds of Indian voters believe that periodic elections make the government pay attention to the people.

That is, the democratic system continues to function in India, enjoys the confidence of the dominant political elites and is steadily being entrenched in the Indian national psyche (Field, 1980). More and more ordinary citizens are becoming involved in the political process, elections are the major means of selecting leaders at all levels of the polity and power and initiative have been decentralised in a federal framework. Contrary to the gloomy assessments of modernisation theorists who had feared the overloading of fragile political institutions, the people of India have been successfully socialised into the democratic order. The exceptional outcome may be due in part to the planting and nurturing of democratic seeds by the British.

A second reason for the unusually close involvement of people in the democratic process in India may be the extensiveness of government. An interventionist state committed to social and economic development of a society mired in poverty produced an odd outcome. The government was not merely the regulator but also the provider: 'Good government is not one that governs least but one that provides the most' (Weiner, 1987b, p. 49).

The decentralisation of power and initiative may be an important reason for the rise of regional political parties. As might be expected, regional issues are relatively more dominant in state elections when there is a separation of state and national elections; but their influence can be felt even when the two sets of elections are held simultaneously. Governments that seek to exploit the general pattern must therefore accept the risk of a trend-bucking outcome. For example, the central government might calculate that it would increase its chances of winning in a particular state by holding elections in that state alongside a general election for the Lok Sabha. If however the sense of regional identity is strong, then the state-based party, in addition to winning control of the state government, might make inroads into the ruling party's seats from that state in the Lok Sabha.

As the last paragraph suggests, it is not necessarily the case that the impact of representative politics on social practices is benign or progressive from a normative point of view. The proposition that parliamentary democracy has made Indian society more open, secular and liberal needs to be investigated empirically instead of asserted axiomatically. So too does the claim that democratic institutions cannot be created in a country without the educational and economic underpinnings to sustain them. Liberal as well as Marxist political theorists make assumptions about the relationship between political institutions and socioeconomic structures that can be tested in the crucible of Indian politics, which is after all the largest laboratory of democratic elections in human history. The optimistic assessments of the early 1980s have been challenged by more recent analyses of India's growing crisis of governability. Kohli has argued that the state has indeed been stretched beyond its capacity, and that political institutions have crumbled partly because of overload and partly because of intentional subversion by the elites (Kohli, 1990).

The alternative theory of political exchange approaches the relationship between political institutions and social structures on the assumption of an essentially unchanged pattern of hierarchy. Traditional leadership remains intact, but has been forced to adapt modes of interaction by building up coalitions of electoral support. Political coalitions are formed on the basis of an exchange of material rewards and privileges in return for electoral services and resources. The basis of the exchange is the ability to fulfil one's side of the bargain. The political leader must be able to offer greater inducement than potential rivals; the professional political intermediaries must be able to deliver votes to the politicians and material rewards to followers; the voters must learn to bargain, to honour the deals struck and to punish politicians who cannot deliver, regardless of traditional and affective considerations. In this way the exchange theory can help to explain the increased responsiveness of a political system to the demands and interests of social groups.

It can also help to explain social mobility. The Yadav community in Bihar is traditionally a backward caste. Awakened to its political weight by force of numbers, the community has dominated the political process in the state since the mid-1980s. That is, the political process has been the route to social mobility.

A competitive electoral system has been instrumental in broadening the bases of political participation for most communities. Following the logic of electoral politics, political parties have been compelled to reach out to groups beyond their initial narrow band of supporters. Anti-Brahmin parties like the DMK learned to court the Brahmins in a more inclusive regional identity; urban parties like the Jan Sangh/BJP have had to reach out to the rural periphery in order to challenge the dominance of Congress. To the pressures of electoral politics then must go the credit of politicising the masses and extending the boundaries of India's political community.

There is also a debit side of the ledger of electoral politics. Parties and groups may not seek national status. They may have more to gain by emphasising and retaining solid cores of committed activists and supporters on narrow criteria.

In both cases, reciprocal causation is at work between the social structure and the political process. Social stratification is changing under the pressure of competitive electoral politics as well as social and economic change. Under a 'capillary' model of party–society relations (Hardgrave and Kochanek, 1993, p. 228), party leaderships have become more regionalised in their bases of support and more traditional in their idioms of political behaviour. As increasing numbers of social groups were politicised, so political parties were increasingly traditionalised. In turn this has produced changes in the way that social cleavages structure political partisanship.

Conclusion

The data from India suggests that at the national level, a *normal election* produces parliamentary majorities for Congress reflecting the balance of long-term political coalitions in the electorate. A *deviating election* produces occasional defeats for Congress, as in 1977 and 1989, due to short-term factors. A *realigning election* (or sequence of elections) would see a major redistribution of partisanship in the Indian electorate, such as between a Hindu-supported BJP and a secular–democratic Congress. There is also the related notion of *dealignment*, which results from the weakening of bonds between voters and parties (Hague, Harrop and Breslin, 1992, pp. 205–6). Described as a major electoral trend in Western postwar democracies, partisan de-alignment produces electoral volatility and the emergence of new parties (such as the Greens or environmental parties). As democracies mature, voters become more sophisticated. Instead of expressing a lifelong commitment to one political party, they base their electoral decisions on the performance of parties in government, a phenomenon that is labelled *retrospective voting* (Fiorina, 1981). The pronounced anti-incumbency trend against almost all parties in recent state and national elections in India is perhaps best encapsulated in this concept.

Further Reading

Butler, Lahiri and Roy (1991). The major handbook of Indian electoral data as well as methodological commentary.

Gould and Ganguly (1993). Leading North America-based scholars dissect the ninth and tenth general elections of India.

Lahiri and Roy (1984). Sets out the Index of Opposition Unity as a concept for analysing India's election results.

Lijphart (1994). A systematic and comprehensive study that describes and classifies 70 electoral systems used by 27 democracies, including India.

Singh & Bose (1987/1988). A handbook on state elections.

11

Development Theories and India's Record

We have now completed our overview of the government and politics of India. It is time to put Indian politics in the context of general debates on the meaning and conditions of development. The conceptual vocabulary of development studies is profoundly rooted in the historical encounter between the European and the non-European. Is tradition necessarily an obstacle to progress and development which must be discarded? Is modernisation necessarily all good? How much conceptual coherence is there to the term 'Third World'? The abundance of terms to refer essentially to the same group of countries reflects continuing dissatisfactions with each: backward, developing, undeveloped, underdeveloped, less developed, Third World, low income, traditional. In these days of political correctness, perhaps we should call them 'the economically challenged' or 'the industrially embarrassed'.

If we move away from attempted connotative definitions to examine the denotative list of countries covered by this rich variety of terms, then the most striking feature is the diversity on virtually every imaginable criterion. Yet there are also important shared characteristics: small, subsistence, agrarian economies dependent on a narrow range of products in international exchanges, often just one or two cash crops like coffee, cotton, rubber or sugar; low levels of life expectancy and literacy; and simplified political and bureaucratic structures. The combined, interactive effect of the developing country syndrome has been illustrated in the form of a vicious circle by Mountjoy (1978, p. 17): 'ill health = reduced working capacity = low productivity = poverty = undernourishment = ill health'.

Despite the similarities, the variations among developing countries are probably more significant than those among the developed countries. Heavy industrialisation and the rapid extension of technology into the farthest reaches of social life is more likely to generate pressures towards social and institutional homogeneity (the 'coca-colonisation' effect). Those who are the least engaged with the world's technological cross-currents are the ones best able to preserve distinctive social structures and belief patterns. In the years since the Second World War, the differences between developing countries have if anything become even wider.

Bearing in mind the lack of consensus on the meaning of development, in this chapter I want to do the following:

1. Look at economic growth as an index of development.
2. Discuss the modernisation school's approach to the subject.
3. Examine some of the major alternative indices of development that have been suggested from time to time.
4. Analyse in more detail the contributions and shortcomings of the dependency school of development and underdevelopment.
5. Evaluate India's development record since independence.

Economic Growth

In the paragraph before last, we have been describing what is known as *multifinality*, where countries with initially similar starting conditions end up at startlingly different destinations. By contrast, the concept of economic development was predicated on the assumption of *equifinality*, or the belief that no matter how divergent nations are initially, they can all be brought to converge at the end. The key unit of measurement was economic growth, and the key goal was the attainment of a high level of income through sustained economic growth. 'The crucial problem in economically advanced systems is to maintain a constant rate of economic growth' (Macridis and Brown, 1961, p. 3).

The concept of aggregate growth, using such measures as GDP, GNP or national income, dominated policy and scholarly debate through the 1960s. Development policy centred on the concept of material productivity as an indicator of economic welfare. Rostow's non-communist manifesto (1960) was especially influential. On the basis of comparative date from several countries, he argued that the most important preconditions for take-off to self-sustained growth were a rise in the rate in productive investment from 5 per cent to 10 per cent of national income; the emergence of one or more substantial manufacturing sectors as the leading sectors in growth; and a modification of the political and social institutional framework to exploit the productive impulses in the modern sector in order to make growth self-sustaining.

There were several flaws and shortcomings in the thesis. It rested on slender evidence. It was vague and imprecise, with distinct stages being difficult to identify for many countries. It was ideological, as indicated in the subtitle of *A Non-Communist Manifesto*. It was ethnocentric, with only the United States being said to have reached the final stage: development models were structured by the historically specific experience of Western countries. And of course it was to prove spectacularly premature in regard to the key criterion of self-sustaining growth.

Despite these deficiencies, it proved remarkably influential. It was seductively persuasive in communicating the idea that every country had an equal chance to achieve the good life, in pointing out a clear path to progress and in refuting Marxism. The 1960s were full of such glorious phrases as take-off, steady growth, alliance for progress and the critical minimum effort. The developed countries agreed to try to allocate 1 per cent of their GNP in official development assistance (0.7 per cent) and private financial flows (0.3 per cent). (In fact the ODA levels dropped from an average of more than 0.5 per cent of GNP in 1961 to around 0.3 per cent in 1970 and have stayed at that level.) Foreign aid would be used to short-circuit the century or so it had taken the Western countries to change from subsistence agrarian economies to highly industrialised ones. The experience and expertise of the West could be readily transferred to the rest through financial and technical aid in order to produce a more rapid social and economic metamorphism.

In time, disenchantment set in in the donor countries because of perceptions of aid simply disappearing into the development black hole. Recipient countries too were disillusioned at efforts by former colonisers to perpetuate economic, political and cultural ties through directed aid. Sometimes the solution of a surplus disposal problem – for example, food that could neither be consumed at home nor sold in international markets – was described as aid. At other times foreign aid was a disguised subsidy to home producers whose goods were not competitive in world markets.

The twin pillars of the economic order after the Second World War were the World Bank and the International Monetary Fund (IMF), established at the Bretton Woods conference in July 1944. Their prescriptions came to be attacked for:

- the application of identical remedies regardless of each country's particular circumstances;
- the support of programmes that were theoretically elegant but did not work in practice;
- the doctrinaire application of a market-oriented, free-enterprise philosophy;
- harming the poor, the weak and the vulnerable by the imposition of austerity measures;
- ignoring the views of developing-country governments while being unable to influence the views of rich governments;
- promoting programmes of investment that caused serious environmental damage.

In reaction against the IMF–World Bank orthodoxy and the perceived shortcomings of foreign aid, developing countries called for a New International Economic Order (NIEO) which would stabilise raw material prices, protect every country's sovereignty over its resources and over the operations of multinational firms on its territory, and institutionalise their access to the management of the international economic system.

The Modernisation School

The emphasis on economic growth by the development economists found an echo in the modernisation school of social scientists. At its simplest, the modernisation school argued that there is a unilinear movement of historical change from the traditional to the modern, with accompanying social, political, economic and attitudinal correlates. The ends were fixed: traditional and modern structures of society, economy and polity. The timing was variable. The path and process would mimic those followed historically by the West. In this the school reflected its philosophical antecedents in the eighteenth–nineteenth century belief in evolutionary progress (Hermassi, 1980, pp. 2–5).

The modernisation school was inter-disciplinary in its efforts to trace the complex linkages between social structure, economic activity and political institutions. In addition to borrowing from Rostow's stages of growth in economics, the school borrowed the categories of analysing 'primitive' societies from anthropology, and the Parsonian pattern variables from sociology (Organski, 1965; Russett, 1965; Black, 1966; Levy, 1966; Nettl, 1967). The analytic pretensions of the modernisation school camouflaged an arbitrary dichotomy between modern and non-modern which was an essentially ethnocentric construct. In addition to suffering from a teleological illusion, the dichotomy was also tautological: 'The man who is more modern in attitude and value acts to support modern institutions and to facilitate the general modernisation of society' (Inkeles and Smith, 1974, p. 313). It involved a philosophical position, from which followed its methodology. Certain attributes were imputed to the 'developed' countries which happened around 1960 to coincide with the Western countries; by a wave of the scholarly wand these attributes were transformed into criteria of development; these criteria, when 'objectively' applied, showed most countries to be underdeveloped; and the logical opposites of these attributes were then posited as the correlates of underdevelopment. That is, the tautology lay in defining modernisation in the image of the materially most advanced countries of the age in the 'effort to apply knowledge of European patterns of political development to the contemporary problems of nation building in the non-Western world' (Almond, 1970, p. 21). Moreover, Westernisation was held to be necessary both as an end and as a process: modernisation was 'the process of change towards those types of social, economic and political systems that have developed in western Europe and North America' (Eisenstadt, 1966, p. 1).

Borrowing from the acculturation thesis of anthropology, modernisation theory too implied that there would be a diffusion of capital and technology, and political and cultural values, from the West to the rest. Yet Mahatma Gandhi used tradition with striking effect for political ends, using the very modern political idiom of the Congress political party. The *jati* (caste), the most traditional of all idioms, has shown itself to be as effective an institution in inaugurating change as in preserving tradition (Rudolph and Rudolph, 1967). Conversely, an increasing wealth of election data shows the persistence of ascriptive, traditional variables like religion and language in determining voter preferences in the major and minor Western democracies.

All agree that India is slow to change. To modernisation theorists that was its weakness; to many Indian political scientists that is its strength. Hinduism is distinctive among complex, highly differentiated civilisations for maintaining a cultural identity that is free of a given political framework. This meant that political changes could be implemented without being impeded by religious resistance. The new political centre was developed and promoted by the Brahminical elite who were the bearers and repository of the great Hindu cultural tradition. Conversely, the establishment of new political institutions did not pose a threat to the core values of the established social order, and therefore did not unleash general instability.

Huntington (1968) challenged the optimistic assumptions of the modernisation school of a congruence between socioeconomic modernisation and political democracy. Instead, he argued, socioeconomic modernisation could overload the political system, and so lead to political decay rather than development. By redefining *political* development as the institutionalisation of political organisations and procedures, he severed its dubious links with socioeconomic modernisation. India was cited as the leading example of how low levels of socioeconomic modernisation could coexist alongside a high degree of political development.

Another distinguishing feature of the modernisation school was its reliance on dichotomous analytic constructs: development and underdevelopment, agrarian and industrial economy, tradition and modernity. The danger of constructing dichotomies is that two facets of the same phenomenon end up as mutually exclusive categories: heads and tails go together in the same coins. The modern–traditional dichotomy was especially pernicious. Fundamentalists and revivalists are strangers to traditional society. Religious tolerance was the norm in India for two thousand years. Religious violence has been a companion to 'modernisation': the moral cosmos of religion is displaced but no alternative principle is established to channel individual behaviour into socially constructive ends.

In taking the independent state as its starting point, not only did the modernisation school detach politics from the social context in which public morality is embedded. It also neglected historical and international realities. The post-1945 developing countries had higher population densities and a worsening land:person ratio than the Western countries during their period of industrialisation; the rapidly rising population also absorbed productivity gains; their trade did not comprise the dominant portion of global economic exchanges, and they had to enter world markets in competition with Western firms that had a solid market presence already; the negative terms of trade for their products militated against a strategy of export-led growth; the trade-related difficulty discouraged capital inflows for investment; the urgency of their problems required them to telescope the timeframe for development; but the attempt to force the rate of change generated resentment and created a backlash against the programmes of development. India attempted three major, interrelated and difficult transitions simultaneously: demographic, agrarian and industrial. Europe went through these transitions sequentially.

In the 1960s, some theorists, faced with an increasingly tense international situation and challenges to the state even in the West, reordered their normative priorities to emphasise order and stability over constitutional democracy. Huntington (1968) seemed to value political stability both as an end in itself and as a means for consolidating and extending public benefits. But violence, as the resort of declining rather than rising classes, can be instigated by those in power. Modernisation theorists referred to this indirectly as a 'paradox of modernization' (Welch, 1971, p. 10). The primacy of order also led to a misplaced faith in the centralisation of authority and the managerial approach to development: political modernisation is characterised by 'an increased centralization of power in the state, coupled with the weakening of traditional sources of authority' (Welch, 1971, p. 7). Visions of effective modernisation through political institutions designed to disperse power and decentralise authority were excluded at the point of definition. Yet ironically, in India the combination of loss of traditional authority and increased centralisation was to lead to a crisis of governability by the end of the 1980s (Kohli, 1990).

Sometimes the modernisation theory embraced diametrically opposite hypotheses when earlier ones were falsified. The 'melting pot modernization' theories (Newman, 1991, p. 451) had predicted that modernisation would mute ethnic conflicts as people embraced more 'modern' attitudes based on achievement, rationalism and secularism. When this failed to occur, there was an intellectual somersault. By the mid-1970s, 'conflictual' modernisation theories began to argue that economic modernisation was a sufficient condition for the rise of ethnic political conflict. Instead of being integrated by the process of modernisation, ethnic groups find themselves competing for the same scarce resources. They come into conflict because of the differential impact of modernisation on the various ethnic groups.

Even more crucially, the core premises of modernisation theories became suspect from the 1970s onwards with social upheavals and political crises in the industrialised Western countries. Clearly, they were not immune to problems of social change and institutional adaptation.

Alternative Indices of Development

As dissatisfaction grew with the assumptions and prescriptions of modernisation theory, analysts tried to think of alternative measures that would better capture the reality of development. A focus on economic growth and its correlates like urbanisation, literacy and energy consumption and so on seemed too arid. The focus shifted to the quality of life.

Redistribution with Growth

A group of scholars argued for a reduction of inequalities alongside increases in national outputs and incomes (Chenery *et al.*, 1974). They did so on the basis that, despite earlier expectations of a sequential relationship between growth and equity, more than a decade of rapid growth in developing countries had brought little or no benefit to the poorest third of the populations. The question was raised as to whether higher equity was itself growth-promoting. India, and South Asia generally, suffer from significant inequalities in ownership and control of land as well as tenancy arrangements, absentee landlordism and interlocked factor markets. Land and tenancy reforms have been intentionally flawed in conception and half-hearted in implementation.

Changes in distributional conditions can be measured either in terms of relative income shares or absolute incomes per capita. The report on development issued by the World Bank annually now routinely provides income distribution figures for all reporting countries. Comparative data show that high levels of per capita income do not ensure an absence of 'absolute poverty'. It is possible for the rich to prosper while the poor multiply. Conversely, a widening relative income can be consistent with an improvement of the poorest segments of society in terms of absolute income. That is, the trade-off may be between poverty and inequality, rather than between growth and equity. With real rates of economic growth, the number and proportion of people living below the poverty line will fall, even though an inegalitarian income distribution may remain constant or even worsen. A state-by-state analysis in India showed that the incidence of poverty was much lower in states with higher rates of foodgrains production (S. Chakravarty, 1990, pp. 137–8).

The philosophical debate around the competing conceptions of development can be organised around two alternative principles of distributive justice: maximising growth or minimising poverty (Beitz, 1981). Growth-oriented development economists argue that distributive inequalities are justified if, and to the extent that, they are necessary to maximise the rate of growth of national income. Some regard distribution as essentially a political question beyond the purview of economists. Others argue that distributive inequalities should be minimised, but consistent with attaining the maximum growth rate. That is, the only role of equality in this conception is to break deadlocks between alternative strategies of development which are indifferent from the point of view of maximising growth.

By contrast, the poverty-minimising principle would regulate growth in order to maximise the wellbeing of the worst-off groups in society. The Chenery *et al.* report (1974, p. 13) concluded that there was little empirical basis for the claim that greater inequality is inevitable with higher growth rates. But there was some confirmation of the thesis that income inequality increases initially with development before tapering off (Chenery *et al.*, 1974, pp. 13–17). There was a case for a reallocation of public resources in order to remove the physical, institutional and international constraints to alleviating poverty. In India, it was argued, 'the major constraint is rooted in the power realities of a political system dominated by a complex constellation of forces representing rich farmers, big business, and the so-called petite (*sic*) bourgeoisie, including the unionized workers of the organized sector' (Bardhan, 1974, p. 261).

Physical Quality of Life Index (PQLI)

A second group of analysts came up with the concept of the physical quality of life index (PQLI), which was a composite measure of life expectancy, infant mortality and adult literacy (Morris, 1979). Its appeal lay in its simplicity: it used an equally-weighted average of three basic indicators of development for which the requisite data were readily available for most countries. Moreover, it facilitated cross-national and longitudinal (over time) comparisons.

Basic Needs

A third attempt to find a more satisfactory concept of development than modernisation pointed to the importance of satisfying the basic needs of a population (Streeten, 1981). The focus on GNP, or GNP per capita, had confused a principal performance measure with the objective of development. Although the emphasis on redistributive growth was a major conceptual advance, it failed to address the problems of poverty eradication and social services for the poor. Of 23 million babies born each year in India, 4 million die in childbirth, 9 million suffer serious physical and mental disabilities because of malnutrition, 7 million suffer from less debilitating malnutrition, and only 3 million grow into healthy adults (*Economist*, 19 March 1983, p. 54). That is, only 13 per cent of Indians are able to achieve their full potential, and India's biggest asset, its manpower, is undermined from birth.

The basic needs approach came up with a list which included nutrition, education, health, sanitation, water supply and housing. The approach was attractive for focusing on ends as well as means. For example, literacy measures the effectiveness of the educational system and is therefore a better indicator than the number of students enrolled in primary or secondary schools, or the students:teacher ratio. Participation rates are better input measures, and government expenditures (both absolute and relative) are better indicators of government intention. But the success of government policies is better captured by the output measures.

Human Development Index (HDI)

The most recent attempt to come up with a new measure of development is the human development index constructed by the United Nations Development Programme (UNDP) under the leadership of Pakistan's Mahboub ul Haq. Again, it is a composite index of life expectancy, adult literacy and purchasing power parities. It has the merit that at least it does bring in national income as one of its three measures. But it does so on the basis of purchasing power parities (PPP).

In its 'growth-plus' perspective, the UNDP acknowledged the importance of economic growth: 'In the long run, economic growth is crucial for determining whether countries can sustain progress in human development or whether initial progress is disrupted or reversed' (UNDP, 1990, p. 3). Measures of real income are reasonably good indicators of people's command over goods and services. In another attempt to construct a plural composite measure of wellbeing, the author was surprised at how closely it correlated with national income per head (the Spearman correlation coefficient between the plural measure of wellbeing and national income per capita was 0.87). That is, poor countries do not face a 'cruel choice between the protection and promotion of human rights . . . and growth' (Dasgupta, 1990, p. 1718).

But the UNDP also acknowledged that GNP was a flawed measure of wellbeing, and its own composite index gave a snapshot of welfare as well as wealth. As Table 11.1 shows, the HDI re-ranks a number of countries with dramatic effect in comparison with the standard GNP per capita measure. Some, like China and Sri Lanka, are hugely promoted. Others, like Saudi Arabia, are hugely demoted. While many Middle Eastern countries are relegated in comparison to the GNP per capita rankings because their high income levels are not matched by life expectancy and literacy achievements, India gains 11 points.

Flaws in the Alternative Indicators

The attractions of the alternative indicators of development lay in their efforts to incorporate measures of social welfare as well as wealth creation into the concept of development. Yet there is no agreement on any of these four measures, and none of them is free of problems of theoretical definition, conceptualisation and measurement; operationalisation; data collection, reliability and comparability.

The PQLI was criticised for its simplistic methodological approach. There was no theoretical foundation for the choice of indicators and for their relative weightings (Hicks and Streeten, 1979). Its advocates could not 'prove' that their index gave a better overall measure than alternatives using a different selection of component indices or different weightings for the same components.

TABLE 11.1

The Human Development Index of selected countries (N = 140)

	Life expectancy (years, 1990)	Adult literacy (%, 1990)	GDP per capita (PPP $, 1989)	HDI	Rank by GDP per capita	Rank by HDI	Quality of life rank (N = 48)
Canada	77	99	18635	0.982	11	1	
Japan	79	99	14311	0.981	3	2	
USA	76	99	20998	0.976	8	6	
Germany	75	99	14507	0.955	10	12	
USSR	71	99	6270	0.873	38	33	
South Korea	70	96	6117	0.871	39	34	2
Singapore	74	88	15108	0.848	25	40	
Brazil	66	81	4951	0.739	54	59	
Romania	71	96	3000	0.733	53	60	
Saudi Arabia	64	62	10330	0.687	33	67	
North Korea	70	96	2172	0.654	78	75	
Sri Lanka	71	88	2253	0.651	120	76	1
China	70	73	2656	0.612	130	79	9
Egypt	60	48	1934	0.385	108	110	15
Kenya	60	69	1023	0.366	129	114	
Pakistan	58	35	1789	0.305	127	120	31
India	59	48	910	0.297	132	121	13
Bangladesh	52	35	820	0.185	150	135	

Sources: Dasgupta (1990); UNDP, *Human Development Report 1992* (New York: Oxford University Press, 1992).

Even empirically, the PQLI ignored the lack of cross-national comparability of the underlying data (Brodsky and Rodrik, 1981).

The basic needs approach failed to overcome the problems of unreliable and variable standards of measurement, differing social objectives and the inherently subjective ranking of the hierarchy of needs.

The HDI too could not escape all flaws. It measured the standard of living across countries, but not the quality of life. While political freedom and human rights are acknowledged as being important for the quality of life, such social achievements are not easily measured. Yet to ignore them is to divorce the world of the intellectual from that of the subject of the study. Dasgupta (1990) tried to construct an alternative composite index which gave equal weightings to civil liberties and political freedoms as well as income per capita, life expectancy, infant mortality and adult literacy. He produced an ordinal ranking of 48 developing countries on each of these six measures. He then used the Borda rule as his ordinal aggregator. (The Borda rule awards each country a point equal to its rank in each criterion of ranking, and then adds the scores to obtain the aggregate score for each country.) The final column in Table 11.1 is the Borda ranking for some of his 48 countries. It will be clear from that that the overall ranking of a composite index which included civil liberties and political freedoms is quite distinct from the HDI which does not include them. China, for example, moves considerably closer to India, while Pakistan falls well below it.

Thus the choice of the three indicators used to construct the HDI, and their implicit weighting, was arbitrary. The informal sector of the economy was no more reflected in PPP than in GNP national income figures, and a range of non-marketed goods and services (for example much of women's work in developing countries) were excluded at the point of definition. Similarly, neither GNP nor PPP took into account future production prospects, for example by depreciating environmental capital assets by the very activities which were being measured as contributing to the growth of national product. Nor does the HDI report explain why some countries have been so much better than others at translating economic growth into human development.

The Dependency School

The dependency school refers to a group of analyses united in a shared outlook or perspective on the predicament of underdevelopment. It changed the conceptual thrust of the development literature by insisting that the poorer countries cannot simply develop along the Western paradigm. The chief distinguishing feature of the dependency school lay in its insistence that the key variable in understanding the so-called Third World of developing countries is not their internal characteristics, but the structure of the international system and their mode of articulation to it. The 'logic' of underdevelopment can best be understood by locating it within its globally defined historical context. Today's global political economy is the outgrowth of past European expansion. Where colonialism was the product of the expansion of mercantile capitalism, dependency is the product of the expansion of monopoly capitalism. 'Dependency' refers to 'a situation in which the economy of certain countries is conditioned by the development and expansion of another economy to which the former is subjected' (Dos Santos, 1970, p. 231).

Following from this, 'the alternatives open to the dependent nation are defined and limited by its integration into and functions within the world market' (Bodenheimer, 1971, p. 158). In a dependent economy, the central determinants of economic development are imported factors of production, such as capital and technology. Therefore, growth in the dependent nations occurs as a reflex of the expansion of the capitalist core and serves the needs of the latter. Even industrialisation has three dependent characteristics: it takes place on the basis of imported capital and technology; it is foreign-controlled; and it is geared to serving foreign needs. Similarly, the mode of articulation of the periphery to the core conditions the emerging relations of production and the new social strata and classes. The points of articulation between the interests of the dominant classes in dependent countries and class interests in the capitalist core reside in their positions at the apex of their respective structures of wealth, privilege, and power, in distinct yet symbiotically related worlds. Moreover, different patterns of development embody the dominance of different combinations of class interests.

The basic dichotomy of the modernisation school between development and underdevelopment was thus replaced by a fundamental unity between them in dependency analyses. Modernisation theorists had used 'underdeveloped' to mean 'insufficiently developed'. For dependency theorists 'underdevelopment' acquired a more specific meaning, to refer to the impoverishment of some countries as a consequence of their economic exploitation in the cause of the development of international capitalism. The extraction and appropriation of surplus value from the former was necessary for the latter. For modernisation theorists, the condition of the developing countries was due to the lack of capital, expertise and other inputs that had sustained industrialisation in the West. To dependency theorists, it was the application of Western capital and power that had structured economic and social relations in colonies in the interests of international capital.

Critique

On the positive side, dependency theories were an advance upon the modernisation theories in the sense that they drew attention to vital aspects of the totality of developing countries' historical and international relationships. In the liberal theory, the wealth of nations is a function of the expansion of the market to all countries and their progressive incorporation into an international division of labour. Dependency theorists were at their most valuable in emphasising the causal connection between the development of one group of nations and the underdevelopment of another. Many Third World countries were underdeveloped not because they had been untouched by international capital, but in order to help the capitalist core to develop. Dependency theorists were particularly good in describing concrete situations of dependency, including structural socioeconomic links between national elites and international interests. Because it had originated in Latin American structural theories, the dependency school served the useful political purpose of 'indigenising' development theory: it was a declaration of intellectual independence. And at the international level, the catalytic impact of the school could be traced in the demand for a New International Economic Order. Many of the arguments and much of the vocabulary of the demand for a NIEO came from the writings of the 'dependentistas' (Hettne, 1990, p. 98).

Yet in the end the dependency theories were incomplete and fractured in description, unsatisfactory and perhaps inconsistent as explanation, and frustratingly empty in prescription. Descriptively, the dependency school was insensitive to the differential patterns and intensities of dependency relationships. The empirical meaning of underdeveloped was as empty as that of Third World, and for the same reason: both included a tremendous diversity within one catch-all concept. It is not very accurate to lump together countries like Brazil, Haiti, Tanzania and India within one conceptual category. If 'underdevelopment' has the same practical meaning as the 'developing country' concept of the modernisation school, then it is an analytical definition, not an empirical one. If the two are not the same, then, by definition, dependency theories give an incomplete account of the politics and economics of all developing countries.

At the level of explanation, not all approaches within the dependency label were successful in showing just how the social, political and economic spheres were related to one another. Conditions which gave capitalist development its specificity were assimilated into the characteristics of underdevelopment. Consequently, dependency analysts failed to distinguish properly between the characteristics of capitalist and dependent development (Lall,

1975). Most countries, developed as well as underdeveloped, import technology, are dependent on exports and contain pockets of marginalisation. Dependency theories had failed (1) to identify characteristics of dependent economies that are not found in capitalist economies, and (2) to show how these characteristics were causally related to the course and pattern of the development of dependent economies. The first failure pointed to conceptual flaws, the second meant that a catalogue of social, economic and political indicators had been mistaken as a 'theory' of underdevelopment. The explanatory utility of dependency analysis was limited also by the difficulty of deriving falsifiable propositions in Marxist and neo-Marxist theories. Empirically minded scholars tried to subject logically derived dependency propositions to rigorous testing, and came up with inconclusive results (Chase-Dunn, 1975; Holsti, 1986; Kaufman *et al.*, 1975; Weede and Tiefenbach, 1981).

The argument that dependent countries grew as a reflex of growth in the capitalist core was put to rest completely in the 1980s as the reality of the dramatic growth rates of the Asian 'tigers' finally registered in the development literature. Between 1960 and 1990, the East Asian economies produced the fastest rise in incomes for the biggest number of peoples in human history. This falsified dependency theory and could not be explained within existing development theories. Figure 11.1 shows that developing countries as a group, as well as some countries within it, have grown considerably faster than the core capitalist countries over a sustained period of time. In the 1980s, the increasing employment opportunities in the Asian tigers, particularly in the manufacturing sector, contrasted starkly with the spreading unemployment in the the Organisation for Economic Cooperation and Development (OECD) countries. The East Asian experience – buttressed by a wealth of social and economic indicators – also refutes the thesis that capitalism loses its historically progressive character in a context of dependency. One could argue that the growth of the Asian tigers is still dependent on their relations with the leading Western industrial powers. But this denudes 'dependency' of its specific meaning within the underdevelopment literature. In the redefined meaning, even the United States and Japan are dependent on the Organisation of Petroleum Exporting Countries (OPEC). It seems more accurate to argue that the capitalist centre is itself shifting eastwards.

The economic determinism of the dependency school meant that internal structures were viewed as being mechanically determined by

FIGURE 11.1
Average annual increase in GDP/capita, 1965–91

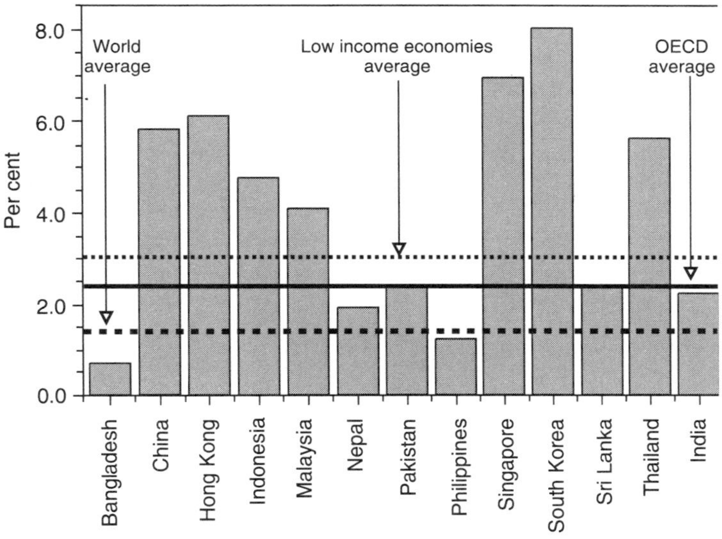

Source: United Nations, World Bank.

external ones. While indigenous elites may not have had much choice in a colonial context, in a postcolonial one they have an enlarged scope for restructuring internal relationships and rearticulating international relations. In ignoring these dynamic possibilities, dependency analyses produced accounts that were static. Peripheral economies were bound to be affected by coming into contact with the dominant capitalist system experiencing a major expansion under the impetus of the industrial revolution. Yet the historical process is characterised by a diversity in the resulting articulation, and the important task is to explain how the general trends in capitalist expansion are transformed into specific relationships between people, classes and state (Palma, 1978, p. 910). Instead, dependency analysis is 'formulistic and reductionist' (Tony Smith, 1979, p. 258). It is formulistic in that universal laws of capitalist expansion override all else, and reductionist in that the particular case has no identity independently of the general category. The dangers of formulism and reductionism were magnified because of the extrapolation of Latin

America's experience to other developing countries. The geographical proximity of Latin America to the United States, and the nature of their historical contacts, make their relationship qualitatively and quantitatively different from the relationship of other developing countries with the United States.

Tony Smith (1979) argued that dependency theorists substantially overestimated the power of the international system and underestimated the autonomy of national elites. The poor peripheral countries were not even allowed to have home-grown villains: the local exploiters were merely the agents of the world capitalist exploiters. Swainson (1980) found international capital to be dominated by the postcolonial state in Kenya. The use of state power was vital in the emergence of an indigenous bourgeoisie. The 'balance of bargaining power between host-countries and transnational corporations' (Biersteker, 1980, p. 207) is a matter for empirical research rather than *a priori* determination. Sometimes state power will prevail, at other times foreign enterprises will employ a range of defensive strategies which effectively neutralise state policy.

Dependency explanations are analytically deficient also because of their tendency to draw empirical conclusions from ideological premises. Baran (1962, p. 149) accused the British of having systematically destroyed 'all the fibres and foundations of Indian society'. He argued that instead of economic expansion and technological progress, colonial capitalism had brought economic stagnation and social backwardness. He made two further points: India's economic development would have been different if Britain had invested the economic surplus extracted from the colony back in India; and India would have found a shorter and less tortuous road to a better and richer society if it had been left to itself.

In fact the two propositions are unrelated. On the second point, moreover, Baran fails to assess the price of British India relative to Mughal India, or to set out the likely path that the Indian economy would have followed in the absence of British rule. Mughal India did not show a marked capacity for significant economic change: 'the chief reasons for economic stagnation were usually present before the British arrived, remained in place during their rule, and have stayed there after its ending' (Tomlinson, 1993, p. 21). On balance, British rule did not destroy incipient industrialisation that had been under way prior to the arrival of the British. Instead British rule probably laid the foundations for industrial development in India after independence (Tony Smith, 1979, pp. 255–6).

FIGURE 11.2
The framework of planning

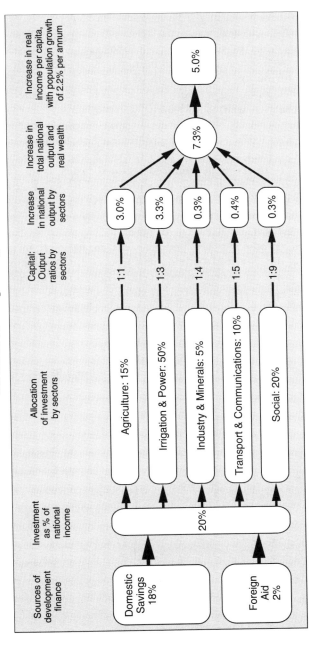

Source: Based on Colin R. Patman, 'Economic Planning: Paths to Development', in Alan B. Mountjoy (ed.), *The Third World: Problems and Prospects*. London: Macmillan, 1978, Figure 10, p. 48.

proportion through raising a given quantum of resources (domestic savings, foreign aid and borrowing). Second, each plan set out inter-sectoral priorities in terms of the proportion of resources to be invested in each sector, the capital:output ratio of each sector and the sectoral contribution to the growth of total national output by the end of the planning period. Since each plan aimed to be comprehensive as well as systematic, it set matching inter-sectoral targets, for example coal production and transport capacity for delivering the extra coal from production site to utilisation site. Third, each plan attempted to achieve a regional balance in development targets, with balanced regional justice being regarded as an important component in the wider social justice. Fourth, five-year plans were set in the context of fifteen-year perspective targets. The third five-year plan perspective for 1961–76 set the targets of a 6 per cent growth in national income, a 2 per cent growth in population (producing a 4 per cent rise in national income per capita) and the entry of 70 million new workers into the labour force. Fifth, the plans combined imperative and indicative principles. The imperative principle covered taxation measures and public enterprises, and also embraced a positive regulation of the private

FIGURE 11.3
India's 1992–3 budget plan outlay (total expenditure: Rs 484.07 billion)

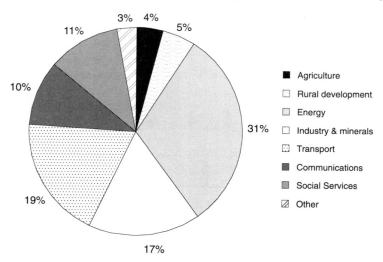

sector through industrial licensing and foreign exchange permits. For example the second industrial resolution policy of 1956 gave exclusive responsibility to the state for the development of most heavy and extractive industries, utilities and telecommunications. The indicative principles referred to the selective stimulation of branches of the private sector by fiscal and monetary instruments.

As the preceding paragraph suggests, the goals of planning have been self-sustaining economic growth; structural transformation and modernisation; self-reliance; and the elimination of poverty, unemployment and inequality. The first five-year plan envisaged detailed planning mainly in capital goods industries which the private sector, it was believed, would not be able to create. 'Command capitalism' came with the second five-year plan. A new industrial policy statement introduced the concept of the commanding heights of the economy to India in 1956. The concept was borrowed from the literature on Soviet planning. Three sets of dichotomies underpinned the strategy of economic development in both countries: central planning versus market anarchy; socialist versus private ownership of the means of production; and egalitarian versus class-based income distribution.

The alternative strategies facing Indian policymakers in the 1950s differed in the choice of who was to produce what; the role of central government; the balance of power between central, state and local governments; and India's strategic autonomy in world affairs. Prime Minister Jawaharlal Nehru and Planning Commission chairman P. C. Mahalanobis shared a socialist belief in an interventionist state and an aristocratic disdain for American-style consumerism. Their strategy was to transform India into an industrial giant. The Mahalanobis grand design of the second five-year plan opted for the primacy of large-scale heavy industry over agriculture. Growth was to be achieved by the allocation of productive resources to the production of capital goods. The rate of growth would accelerate with an increasing proportion of national output being saved and reinvested. Conversely, investing scarce resources in agriculture or consumer goods would divert investment from the capital goods sector and thereby inhibit long-term growth. Imports would be curtailed through tariff, quotas and bans; exports would not be needed as a principal engine of growth for a country of India's size. Resource-poor countries with small domestic markets can grow only by selling abroad. India was resource-rich with a large domestic market.

In pursuit of the second five-year plan, 17 major industries were nationalised and a regime set up to control, direct and guide the management of virtually the entire industrial sector. By the end of the 1980s India had 225 public sector enterprises (or, in the Indian jargon, PSUs – public sector undertakings) (Heston, 1992, p. 116). Elements of the planning regime included: direct controls, licences, guidance on location (in 'backward areas') and production (for example the textile industry had to meet a quota of cheap cloth), and a prohibition on factory closures even if profits turned to losses.

Planned agricultural development was based on public investment in irrigation, research and extension, price support and procurement subsidies, and provision of credit at concessional rates of interest. Industrial development would result from a parallel public investment in basic capital goods industries and infrastructure, especially power and transport. Agricultural and industrial growth and equity would be promoted through a judicious mix of market mechanisms and plan stimulus. A frontal assault on poverty was launched in the fifth five-year plan (1974–9). A new basic needs approach tried to improve village quality of life by investing in human resource development activities by providing basic infrastructure and amenities like rural roads, housing, nutrition, safe drinking water, and elementary and adult education. At the same time, the basic needs approach also aimed to improve the condition of the individual directly by providing wage employment.

The achievements of planning were genuine and substantial. There was a high level of domestic savings, a broad and diversified industrial structure was created, self-sufficiency was achieved in foodgrains production and a large pool of skilled labour was created. The attainment of a resilient food security that can withstand adverse weather conditions is in marked contrast to the recurring pattern of famines during the British Raj.

In comparison with stagnation in the fifty years before independence, India has not fared too badly. It broke the pre-1947 economic stagnation, raised national income per head and strengthened the economic infrastructure. India's economy grew thrice as fast in the 1950s and 1960s as during the British Raj, and faster than the rate of British growth during its comparable stage of development in the eighteenth and nineteenth centuries. The public sector was instrumental in transforming an exploited plantation economy into a vibrant and diversified industrial power in a remarkably short period of time. It may also be the case that state-directed planning has enabled the private sector in India to grow strong enough to find the extensive public sector the main impediment to its further profitable expansion (Maitra, 1993, p. 6). High domestic savings meant that the resources for growth were found at home, so avoiding the double burden of a crippling government debt and an unrepayable foreign debt. In just forty years, infant mortality was halved, life expectancy nearly doubled and adult literacy almost trebled (Table 11.2). The considerable social improvements may not have reached the poorest Indians. Even so, today a much larger proportion of Indians has access to health and education benefits which before independence had been restricted to the privileged elite.

TABLE 11.2

India's Quality of Life indicators, 1901–91

	1901	**1921**	**1941**	**1951**	**1978**	**1991**
Infant mortality (per 1000 live births)				183	132	90
Life expectancy (years)	20	21	31	32	51	60
Adult literacy (per cent)	6	8	15	17	29	48

Sources: Tomlinson, 1993, p. 4; *World Development Report*, annual volumes.

More recent results however have been economic stagnation, structural rigidity and backwardness, desperate international infusion of capital to stave off defaults and the persistence of poverty and inequality. India's record has been a failure by the standards of its own targets and the needs of its people. Its long-term growth rate pales into insignificance in a comparative context (see Figure 11.1 above). While South Korea and Singapore have left the poorer countries farther and farther behind, India has remained firmly anchored around the low income economies' average from start to finish (Table 11.3). The extent of poverty has barely been dented. In 1990, 410 million Indians (compared with 120 million Chinese) were still below the poverty line. India's achievements are less than impressive on virtually all measures. For example, World Bank and UN data show that India's 1991 infant mortality rate of 90 deaths per 1000 live births was much higher than those of East Asian countries (Brunei 9, China 38, Hong Kong 7, Malaysia 15, Singapore 6, South Korea 16, Thailand 27).

TABLE 11.3

India's continuing relative poverty, 1976–92

	GNP/capita (US $)		Rank by GNP/capita	
	1976	**1992**	**1976 (N = 125)**	**1992 (N = 132)**
Low income economies	150	390	–	–
India	150	310	108	115
Singapore	2700	15730	36	18
South Korea	670	6790	64	27

Source: World Development Report.

In sum, India achieved capital accumulation and technical change under planning, but these were not matched by improvements in productivity and welfare. Under Indian conditions, a net increase in social welfare requires labour to achieve sustained increases in productivity, employment and returns above subsistence. Four decades of state-guided development had given India slow growth, rising unemployment, growing dependence on imported capital goods and technology and an ailing economy. In international economic exchanges, policy failures were reflected in a falling share of world exports, a depreciating currency and an inability to export sophisticated manufactures.

Limited initial benefits to the poor had been accepted as a short-term cost of the Mahalanobis grand design which opted for the primacy of large-scale heavy industry over agriculture. In fact the costs proved durable. Heavy industry grew more slowly than anticipated, rates of savings and investment were not as high as had been assumed, agricultural performance was unimpressive and rapid expansion of employment failed to materialise. In the end the socialist mixed economy faced collapse because of internal contradictions. The overall goal was massive and rapid industrialisation. This required a shift in resources from the agricultural to the industrial sector. But 70 per cent of the people lived in the countryside and were dependent on the farming sector, so attempts to help the poor meant directing increasing resources to the rural economy. Helping the weak rather than the strong also required state support for small, labour-intensive farms over bigger capital-intensive ones.

A complicated mix of mutually undercutting policies eventually created an impossibly labyrinthine command economy. One set of instruments took resources out of the farm economy to feed the industrial strategy, another channelled funds back into the farms to reduce poverty. In 1991, the state bill for food and fertiliser subsidy was a whopping US $3.2 billion (Srinavasan, 1992). Ironically, the biggest beneficiaries of the fertiliser subsidy were the rich farmers and the fertiliser producers. Ironically too the massive subsidy still left India's farmers paying about 10 per cent to 25 per cent higher prices for their fertiliser than world market prices: for the subsidy was not enough to offset the protection-driven inefficiencies. Additional, opportunity costs included lack of state investment in infrastructural development (irrigation, primary education and roadways linking farm producers to their markets).

Explaining India's Economic Shortcomings

There are six different lines of argument that could account for the failures of planning. First, it could be argued that the poor performance was due to exceptional circumstances: fickleness of weather, wars (1962, 1965 and 1971), oil shocks (1970s and 1980s), and so on. Such an explanation is difficult to sustain over a long period of time and also in a comparative context.

A second response would be to argue that some of the disappointment with India's economic results is rooted in lack of understanding of the exceptionally low base from which India began in 1947 (see Mellor, 1979, pp. 94–9). On the debit side, the economy was characterised by intense and pervasive poverty, a dominant but stagnant agricultural sector, an export sector dominated by commodities and a transport network built for maintaining colonial control. The century before independence saw little improvement in rates of capital and labour productivity, and low levels of crop yields, industrial productivity and human capital formation. On the credit side of the ledger were size and the human and natural resource base.

The attempt to trace the cause of the poor economic performance in colonialism points to the wealth drain from India to Britain. Functioning indigenous sources of economic growth and power were displaced by British agents and networks. In the modern sector, Indian entrepreneurs were deprived of the chance to lead a process of economic development. In the traditional sector, the welfare and distributional effects of coercive foreign competition and commercialisation of agriculture were negative. With Britain, India ran a persistent trade deficit in goods and services which was paid for by a surplus in the current balance of trade account with the rest of the world. By the end of the last century, India was the largest market for British goods, the supplier of half of the British empire's military manpower, a significant recipient of British capital and a major employer of British civil servants (Tomlinson, 1993, p. 13). British nationalists argued that India's payments were less than the increased wealth resulting from British capital and services. Indian nationalists responded that India's growth was retarded because the British removed all investible surplus above subsistence from the colony to the imperial centre.

A third explanation would locate the failures of planning in defective machinery and faulty implementation. Such an explanation would not question any of the basic assumptions on which planning was built. The obstacles to economic development in India can indeed be identified within prevailing theories of growth: insufficient investment capital, inadequate domestic and export markets, unproductive farming sector, lack of skilled labour, obsolete technology, infrastructural inadequacies and so on. A more clearly political explanation of this type may be that while the task of formulating plans is done competently enough by the Planning Commission at the central government level, there is considerable slippage in implementation at state level over which the commission has little control.

When planners blame the ignorance and unresponsiveness of farmers, then it is time to question the wisdom of the planners. If the cause of failure is the refusal of the villagers to respond to the planners' signals, then failure is attributable to the social distance between village reality and planning headquarters. The desire for a continuously higher standard of living may not be uniformly shared, or there may not be a nationwide social consensus on economic values as postulated by planning officials.

A fourth possible answer would be to blame planning failures on faulty conception: the neglect of sociology and politics in a technocratic emphasis on formal planning. In terms of modernisation theory, perhaps there were major bottlenecks to economic development in the form of social and cultural impediments: lack of entrepreneurship, traditional pattern variables in a cleavage-ridden society which stressed ascription over achievement and conspicuous consumption over sensible savings. Deepak Lal (1988) has written of the 'Hindu Equilibrium' to explain the persistence of low growth in India, including a traditional Hindu contempt for merchants and markets. Hindu society, he argues, faced four long-run constraints: labour shortage, political decentralisation, climatic variability, and a cultural disdain of merchant activity. Certainly attitudinal transformation is required so that the creation of wealth can be made an honourable pursuit. Prime Minister V. P. Singh, for example, referred even in the 1990s to a 'wealth line' above which people should not be permitted to possess unproductive assets like jewellery and unused land, as well as a poverty line below which people should not be allowed to fall (*The Economist*, 23 June 1990, pp. 21–2).

Yet Lal's thesis is not entirely convincing. His aggregate analyses ignore significant regional variations in determinants and outcomes. Seeming continuities over time on a large canvas disguise cross-cancelling fluctuations from one time and place to another. In Indian village cultivation arrangements, economic imperatives have often overridden the constraints of morality and law (Stokes, 1978, pp. 234–6). The unity of South Asian economic history belies the thesis that the low-level equilibrium is a uniquely *Hindu* phenomenon. Nor are culturalist explanations easily sustained by comparative histories of a number of Asian societies. Still others argue that modernisation theory itself distorted India's development priorities with its pervasive emphasis on growth and catching up. This diverted the attention of Indian planners from reducing inequalities at home to bridging the per capita income gap internationally.

Fifth, one could argue that failure has been due to the neglect of political economy at the national or international level. A noted Indian economist traced the cause of 'retardation' of poorer countries to the domination by the advanced capitalist countries of the producers and exporters of primary products (Bagchi, 1982). The historically progressive role of capitalism was lost in the colonies because its dynamism was harnessed to serving the needs of the metropolitan economy. The laws, political institutions and social structure were created to meet metropolitan needs for cheap labour and captive export markets. Another Indian economist explained the low-level equilibrium trap of slow growth in terms of a deadlocked contradiction of interests between the three dominant classes of industrial capitalists, big farmers and white-collar public sector professionals (Bardhan, 1985). The degree of market penetration, the character of the markets and the nature of the involvement of various economic groups of producers and consumers are major determinants of production conditions. Yet many of the capital, commodity and labour markets are interlinked, with the availability of land, credit and employment often being concentrated in the same small group of agricultural landowners and industrial entrepreneurs (Tomlinson, 1993, pp. 27–8).

Alternatively, neo-Marxists would argue that the national economy was too closely tied to international capital and served the needs of the latter. Operating a mixed economy after independence led to distortions to serve external needs. Only a socialist economy could have redistributed incomes and the means of production between different occupational groups and economic sectors in line with a preferred strategy of development. That is, Soviet-type targets were not achievable without Soviet-style methods. The bankruptcy of the Soviet model was not to be shown in its totality until the 1990s. The model was admired in a misunderstood form by Nehru (misunderstood because he failed to appreciate the full horrors of the Soviet strategy in the 1930s), and it continued to influence the ideology of planning in India until the end of the 1980s.

The sixth and final answer is that planning is bound to fail because it ignores market forces and the price mechanism in favour of a command economy. An apocryphal Indian political commentator put it so: 'Take a pinch of fantasy, add some daydreams, garnish with wishful thinking, serve with optimistic assumptions sauce, and there you have one of our Five Year Plans'. Or as *The Economist* (4 August 1990, p. 22) remarked of Mongolia: 'Only central planning could ensure that meat is hard to come by in this vast country of rolling, grassy steppes, where livestock . . . outnumber the people (roughly 2.2m of them) ten to one.'

The newfound awareness of the limits of government and central planning was matched by an increased acknowledgment of the importance of markets and incentives. The Rao government took over the reins of power in India in 1991 at a time of an emerging new global consensus on economic development policy: a non-inflationary macroeconomic policy built around modest budget deficits and prudent monetary policy, greater openness to trade and foreign investment and greater reliance on market forces as efficient allocators of resources. Rapid and sustained economic growth has been the result of the right mix of economic policies: sensible monetary and fiscal management; the use of the price mechanism to reflect market realities in making production, location and consumption choices; interest rates that reflect the true cost of capital; openness to imports and foreign investment as the instrument for achieving efficiencies; and a realistic exchange rate. So completely did the new consensus overturn the old orthodoxy that it has been dubbed a counter-revolution in development theory and practice (Toye, 1987).

As Figure 11.4 shows, India is not a trading nation. At 17.2 per cent, its trade dependency is almost half the world average of 31.7 per cent (1991 figures). It has one of the most protected economies in Asia. The contrast with the East Asian tigers is especially stark. Tariffs have been but one of several instruments buttressing the policy of a closed economy. The policy damaged consumers, producers and exporters alike. It was self-defeating because each problem seemed to beget state intervention, and each intervention created a fresh problem. By erecting frontier protection and fortifying it with an

FIGURE 11.4
Trade dependency (exports + imports as percent of GDP)
of selected Asian Countries, 1991

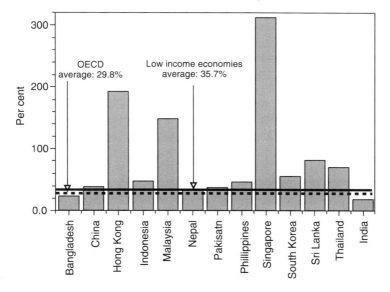

Sources: United Nations, World Bank.

array of policy instruments, the Indian government forced its people to pay more for the goods that they wished to consume and its producers to allocate resources on the basis of false prices. Import-substitution policies dampened India's exports as well. The lack of international competition took away the edge from exporters' incentives to strengthen their competitive position in world markets through improved productivity and enhanced efficiencies. As protection drove up the price of inputs, the cost competitiveness of Indian manufactures steadily deteriorated. And import controls raised domestic prices higher than prevailing international levels. Protection became a tax on exports and a subsidy to domestic suppliers. Firms therefore found it more profitable to sell at home than abroad, and exporters were given an incentive to switch from overseas markets to the home market.

The neoclassical consensus has returned to the idea that all economies can achieve growth and development if they are prepared to adopt free-market and open trade and investment policies. Gunnar Myrdal (1968, pp. 895 ff.) had postulated a causally interconnected relationship between productivity and incomes, living standards, and labour inputs and productivity. India's low-level equilibrium was marked by low labour productivity, low per capita income and archaic production techniques. An import-substituting policy of self-sufficiency had effectively perpetuated this low-level equilibrium. The efficiencies generated by free-market competition, foreign trade and investment will combine to increase the productivity of land, labour and capital.

One of the first acts of the Congress government headed by Prime Minister P. V. Narasimha Rao was to announce liberalisation measures and a new industrial policy in August 1991 that by Indian standards were quite radical. The balance of payments crisis of 1991, coupled with the dramatic worldwide trend towards market reforms, convinced many Indians that their country had little alternative to modernising its industrial and export structure and entering the world economy. Finance Minister Manmohan Singh decided that the nation could not forever remain captive to fear of the East India Company. In an interview in early 1992, Narasimha Rao argued that economic liberalisation had become inevitable and essential to help prepare India for the complex and competitive economic environment of the twenty-first century (*Euromoney Supplement*, April 1992, pp. 10–11). Budget and trade announcements have been aimed at ensuring simplicity, stability and export promotion. In a speech in

Calcutta on 29 June 1993 that was interpreted as an epitaph on Nehruvian socialism, Rao said that government investment should focus on health and education; giant industrial projects could be left to the private sector.

If the stifling regulatory regime could be lifted and the dead hand of the state removed, then India could exploit its superb base for rapid and substantial industrial expansion. The country has an enormous pool of sophisticated scientists and technicians, and an untapped reservoir of entrepreneurial talent. The policies of self-reliance followed by Jawaharlal Nehru and his successors have provided India with the capacity to grow quickly. The resources are not lacking in India: entrepreneurs, gross domestic savings of around 20 per cent of GDP, capital formation of more than 20 per cent and a people capable of punishingly hard work. But the potential of these 'comparative advantages' has been constrained by imported Soviet-style inefficiency in the public sector, built with Soviet assistance, that pervades the whole of a sluggish economy.

The economic reforms paid early dividends. During the 1980s, foreign investment into India averaged a meagre $150m per year; the liberalisation policies helped to push the figure up to $2.2 bn from July 1991 to the end of March 1993. India's GDP grew by a modest 1.2 per cent in 1991–2, by 4.2 per cent in 1992–3 and was forecast to grow by more than 5 per cent in 1993–4. The finance minister expected industrial growth of around seven percent in the fiscal year 1993–4. The budget deficit had shrunk from 8.3 per cent of GDP in June 1991 to 4.7 per cent two years later. Inflation had fallen from a peak of 17 per cent in August 1991 to 6.1 per cent by mid-1993. For the year ending 31 March 1994, exports surged by 20 per cent while imports declined by 7 per cent, trimming the trade deficit from $3.31 bn in 1992–3 to $1.04 bn in 1993–4. Foreign exchange reserves had risen to $13 bn by March 1994 (they had stood at around one billion dollars only in the spring of 1991), reflecting the higher export earnings and foreign investment. These are remarkable achievements, particularly when we remember that India lost a major export market with the disintegration of the Soviet Union and had made the rupee fully convertible on trade accounts.

The 1993 budget was designed to propel India into the global market. In an interview published in *The Economic Times of India* on 4 March 1993, Singh promised further reforms over the next 12–18 months, including cuts in subsidies, decontrol of oil prices, further liberalisation of exchange controls and the introduction of a labour policy. The 1994 budget, announced on 28 February, cut maximum customs duty, corporate tax and the top income tax rates; rationalised indirect taxes; and made the rupee convertible for current-account transactions such as travel and education abroad. The lack of an 'exit' policy has impeded the restructuring of wealth-destroying public sector industries and the closing of loss-making enterprises. The finance minister hopes to create a climate in which redeployment, retraining and in extreme cases even retrenchment will become acceptable. The focus of India's economic agenda will now shift from stabilisation policies to structural reform. Three things remain to be done: labour market and industrial relations reform; farming sector reform, including the removal of price-distorting subsidies, additional infrastructural investment, and the abolition of state-monopoly marketing boards; and percolation of the reforms and the new business-friendly ethos to the lower-level bureaucracy and state governments. The danger now for India is that slow growth in industrialised countries is creating protectionist trends. If the reforms of economic policy under way in developing countries and transition economies are to yield their full promise, then access to world markets through an open, nondiscriminatory, multilateral trading system is absolutely critical.

Further Reading

Bhagwati (1993). Argues that India's disappointing record in generating growth stems from a distrust of growth as an instrument of poverty alleviation.

Chakravarty (1987). A good discussion of India's planning machinery and process.

Frankel (1978b). An influential study of India's attempt to bring about rapid economic growth and reduction in socio-economic disparities without violent social change.

Hettne (1990). An interdisciplinary survey of social science theories of development in different historical and geographical contexts.

Oldenburg (1993). The latest in an established series designed to provide reliable and timely updates on political, economic and foreign policy trends.

Palma (1978). An excellent exposition and critique of dependency and underdevelopment theories.

Roy and James (1992). A collection of papers by well-known India specialists on the politics and economics of the country, mainly in the 1980s.

Somjee (1991). An attempt to ground development theory in the experiences of 'emerging countries'.

Stern (1993). Argues that India's institutions are undergoing rapid and profound changes that are adaptive to the continuity and vitality of the underlying social system rather than disruptive of them.

Tomlinson (1993). Examines the debates over imperialism, development and underdevelopment, and sets them in the context of historical change in agriculture, trade and manufacture, and the relations between business, the economy and the state.

12

India as a Liberal–Democratic State

'Government' and 'politics' are among the central concepts in political science. Some of the accompanying core concepts remain essentially contested: state, sovereignty, power, authority, legitimacy as well as politics itself (see Hague, Harrop and Breslin, 1992, pp. 6–20). This book has provided an introduction to the government and politics of India. 'India' in this context refers to the *state* of India: an abstract yet powerful notion that embraces the total network of authoritative institutions which make and enforce collective decisions throughout the country. The modern state is the most substantial manifestation of political power that has been progressively depersonalised, formalised and rationalised. That is, the state is the medium through which political power is integrated into a comprehensive social order. The state embodies the political mission of a society, and its institutions and officials express the proper array of techniques that are used in efforts to accomplish the mission.

Liberalism and Democracy

As a concept, liberal democracy is both descriptive and normative. It embraces a set of political institutions (popular elections, accountable government, majoritarian decisions), and a set of principles (civil liberties, legal equality, rule of law and so on), which the institutions embody. The fusion of liberalism and democracy is historically contingent rather than logically necessary. The liberal pole is individualistic and calls for liberty; the democratic pole is collectivist and calls for equality.

In Western societies, the democratic franchise came after the liberal society and the liberal state were firmly established. In the postcolonial countries, democracy could not be installed as an adjunct of the liberal state, for the latter itself had not been established. In these societies, the rhetoric of democracy often involved, and the logic of the empirical reality occasionally implied, opposition to establishing the liberal capitalist state. A liberal democratic political framework superimposed upon such a society can result in what may be termed a 'dual polity'. The economic cornerstones of liberalism have been private property and a market economy; the political cornerstones are political freedom and a market polity. The dual economy is produced where a modern market economy coexists amidst a much larger traditional, that is non-market, economy. But a traditional culture can be as little attuned to political competition as to economic. The market polity of a competitive political party system may, therefore, fail to take root, and comprise instead just the 'top dressing' of a political system. Contradictions generated by the coexistence of a market and traditional polity within one political system may lie dormant initially but mature over time.

State nationalism too originated in Europe. The state used its institutions and resources to promote national identity in order to consolidate and legitimise itself by manipulating these powerful new symbols. The campaign was so successful that national self-determination became a shorthand for the idea that nationalism requires the creation of a sovereign state for every nation. The nation-state became the focus of cultural identity. Yet the relationship between 'nation' and 'state' too has been historically contingent rather than logically necessary.

India was 'the first great post-colonial state' (Lyon, 1991, p. 18). The difficulty for most postcolonial societies was that state-building and nation-building had to be embarked on simultaneously. If 'postcolonial' is to mean something other than post-independence, then it must entail some enduring legacy of British rule for the state that came into being in 1947. For India, part of the colonial legacy included the rudiments of statehood. The British Indian state was geared to serving the needs of the metropolitan power. The Indian state differs from both the bourgeois and the communist model: it is not the end-product of an industrial revolution led by the bourgeoisie nor the product of a revolutionary capture of power by the peasantry or the proletariat. But the British did help to create a middle class that was socialised into power-sharing through competition and collaboration.

The logic of independence movements gives yet another impetus to the assault on the liberal state. The struggle for independence encourages the formation of a mass movement and a dominant, aggregative party. The self-image of the Congress Party at the time of India's independence was that it transcended sectarian and regional interests and was the guardian of the national interest. With independence, these parties are transformed into one-party, or one-party-dominant, systems. They perceive the need to forge a new political and national identity as an essential task. But the process in turn demands a strong ideological leadership at the head of a mass movement. The ideological content can be at variance with liberal beliefs. In particular, individualistic civil liberties and property rights are seen to cut across equality of human rights and freedom on a societal scale (Macpherson, 1966, p. 59).

The framers of India's constitution could have left the choice of the governing ideology to emerge as the outcome of normal electoral processes. Instead they chose to prescribe the basic norms that would control and guide political decisions in the form of core constitutional principles (Sudarshan, 1990, p. 45). But this introduced a measure of dissonance in the framework governing India's political institutions. The basic structure is derived from the Anglo-American liberal tradition. But the chapters on fundamental rights and directive principles imported European ideas of the state as an integrating and legitimising concept which sets out the basic values of the political community. The state embodies the public interest. Although separate from civil society, it 'steers' society in the right direction. The directive principles in particular ensured that the constitution was 'programmatic', inviting 'teleogical rather than textual interpretation of its provisions' (Sudarshan, 1990, p. 48). The restraints on the state's power, provided by a distinctive intellectual and social tradition in Europe, had to be exercised by the judiciary in India.

The judiciary forbore from doing so during the period of Congress Party dominance. In the 1967 elections, Congress was under attack simultaneously from the right for its assault on property rights and from the left for its retreat from socialism. The *Golaknath* verdict of the Supreme Court, rejecting parliament's right to abridge fundamental rights, was delivered on the eve of the 1967 elections. The election results severely undermined Congress dominance in several states as well as in the union parliament. When the court also invalidated Mrs Indira Gandhi's bank nationalisation and abolition of privy purses policies in 1970–1, the prime minister sought a popular mandate to remove judicial obstacles to her programme of social justice. The court expressed its distrust of party politics and attempts to use state power for personal and party gains by articulating a new 'basic structure and framework' of the constitution doctrine in the *Kesavananda* verdict in 1973. By appointing the dissenting judge from that decision as the Chief Justice, Mrs Gandhi inaugurated her programme to collapse the judicial order into the political order.

State and Society

'The whole dream of democracy', wrote Gustave Flaubert, 'is to raise the proletariat to the level of stupidity attained by the bourgeoisie' (in Barnes, 1984, p. 85). There are many in India who argue that the operation of parliamentary democracy has been an essentially disillusioning and dispiriting experience. The dominant state ideology as expressed in the constitution came into conflict with prevailing values and posed a threat to the controllers of symbols and norms of traditional social order. Liberalism emphasises individual rights; both Hinduism and Islam elevate the community over individuals. Democracy is predicated on the essential equality of fellow-citizens; the Hindu social order is built around the notion of human beings divided into fundamentally unequal castes.

'State-building' has been viewed in the theoretical literature as essential to political and economic development, or alternatively, for Marxists, as an integral element in the class struggle. In development theory the state was viewed as autonomous, homogeneous, in control of economic and political power, in charge of foreign economic relations, and possessing the requisite managerial and technical capacity to formulate and implement planned development. In reality in many developing countries the state was a tool of a narrow family, clique or sect that was fully preoccupied with fighting off internal and external challenges to its closed privileges. In most of the literature, development has meant a strengthening of the material base of a society. A strong state would ensure order, look after national security and intervene actively in the management of the national economy. Yet the consolidation of state power can be used in the name of national security and law and order to suppress individual, group or even majority demands on the government, and to plunder the resources of a society.

Three theoretical strands in particular are worth mentioning for explaining the relationship between group struggle and state power (Brass, 1991, pp. 247–52). Their most crucial difference lies in whether they view the state as being an autonomous force, a neutral arena for conflict resolution and an impartial distributor of privileges; or an agent for a collectivity that has captured the levers and symbols of state power and uses its instruments to perpetuate domination over other groups.

Pluralist Democracy

The pluralist theory of democracy views democratic public policy as the outcome of struggle between organised groups for control of the state. In this theory, stability is the outcome of cross-cutting cleavages: when individuals belong to multiple groups, the disruptive consequences of group conflict are attenuated. Conversely, though, in the theory of pluralism, where groups are homogeneous and individuals belong to mutually exclusive functional associations, social conflict is intensified. Originating in the American political context, the theory is open to the criticism that it ignores the differential group access to policy-making even in the industrial democracies; and that it is irrelevant to absolutist, authoritarian and otherwise controlled states.

With a tradition of deference to authority, a social order based on hierarchical status and hereditary distribution of functions, and a population characterised by poverty, illiteracy and fatalism, India should have succumbed to authoritarian rule shortly after independence. The continued functioning of democratic institutions defies the sceptics. The belief that the political structure is determined by social and economic structures rests on the assumption that political institutions cannot be autonomous of the social order in which they operate. Attempts to transplant democratic principles and processes from Europe to India would therefore produce stress in the host country's social order.

Yet the theoretical literature abounds with apparently contradictory findings on the relationship between political systems and socioeconomic variables. The modernisation theorists examined the social conditions for the establishment and maintenance of democratic systems. Some argued that there was a direct correlation between democratic stability and such indices of modernisation as per capita income, industrialisation and literacy (Lipset, 1959). Others found only a low relationship between democratic performance and socioeconomic development (Neubauer, 1967). A recent cross-national study of 125 countries over a 25-year period (1960–85) concluded that it is still not possible to identify any systematic net effects of democracy on economic growth (Helliwell, 1994). Yet historically at least democracy is rooted in the growth of capitalism. In the post-1945 developing world, no anti-capitalist country succeeded in establishing a durable democracy, but even many countries that chose the capitalist route to development failed to move to democratic governance. On the other hand, while economic success may not necessarily bring democracy, economic failure necessarily threatens the survival of democracy.

Some cross-national correlational analyses failed to find any significant relationship between political democracy and egalitarian or redistributive policies (Jackman, 1975; Wilenski, 1975). In a carefully crafted construction of correlations between economic, social and political variables, Dasgupta and Weale (1992, p. 128) concluded that political and civil liberties are positively and significantly correlated with real national income per capita and its growth, declining infant mortality rates and rising life expectancy rates. These were of course statistical results, where causation cannot be inferred from correlation. But correlation can be used to weaken the force of arguments to the contrary. Citizens cannot choose to live under a 'good' authoritarian regime. Should they find themselves saddled with a bad authoritarian regime, they would not find it easy to rid themselves of the burden. Moreover, lacking competition in a free political marketplace, authoritarian regimes have no market incentives to correct their errors and increase their appeal to citizen consumers. By contrast, political competition in a pluralist democracy provides built-in incentives for error correction.

Marxism

The second theory of state is Marxism, which holds that the existence of two or more classes involved in economic relations of dominance and subordination is necessary for the existence of a state. Threats to the social order and the stability of the state result from an intensification of the class struggle. The dictatorship of the proletariat signifies the capture of social and political power by one class; class antagonisms disappear as there is only one class; and the state as the instrument and embodiment of the rule of one class over another withers away.

Yet the autonomy of the state is a troublesome concept precisely because the state is very vulnerable to pressures by ruling and non-ruling classes and groups alike. The state is an abstraction. It is different from government ministers who prescribe state policies; from legislators who act as power-brokers between groups and classes, on the one hand, and law-makers and bureaucrats, on the other, for the distribution of patronages; and from the bureaucracy which implements state policies by using the instruments of state power. Marxist analyses are guilty of anthropomorphism in vesting the abstract entity of the state with independent will and purpose. Decisions are taken by individual ministers or bureaucrats. The pattern of their decisions may be shown empirically to serve the interests of a particular class. But the state does not thereby become an autonomous actor.

Marxists locate the cause of underdevelopment in international capitalism. There are of course ills of capitalism. But a demonstration of flaws in capitalism is insufficient to prove that the capitalist mode of development is the wrong choice for India. For this several further arguments would be necessary. First, one would need to show that, on balance, the ills are greater than the benefits of economic growth.

Second, one would need to argue that the increased inequalities are less tolerable to a social conscience than lower levels of wealth for all sectors. Suppose that, initially, the bottom fifth of the population has only one-tenth the average income of the top fifth. Suppose further that after ten years of high growth under capitalism, real income doubles for the bottom fifth and trebles for the top fifth of a population. The richest 20 per cent would now be fifteen times better off then the poorest 20 per cent; but the latter are twice as well off than they were ten years previously. In other words, the process of wealth-creation may well increase the distance between social classes even while it brings real benefits to all classes.

Third, one would need to show that poverty and inequalities would not have been exacerbated under alternative models of development. That is, the choice may not be a static one but a dynamic one. *Even if on balance* capitalism brings greater ills than gains to society as a whole, it still needs to be demonstrated that the net loss is greater under capitalism than other genuine alternatives. This is where the now known experiences of communist countries in the former Soviet bloc are so relevant. Hence too the claim that capitalism has brought more economic and social progress than any other mode of economic organisation known to man (Crook, 1993, p. 48).

Non-Marxist class analysts argued for the critical role of a strong urban bourgeoisie in the growth of parliamentary democracy (Moore, 1969). Neo-Marxist scholars explained the breakdown of democratic regimes in terms of dependent development: local elites had to act repressively in order to drive wages down and attract foreign investment in the drive to capital accumulation. Anti-Marxists argued that attempts to suppress the natural drive to property acquisition leads to coercion and impoverishment. A political order which gives free rein to the impulse produces an expanding property-owning class which is a necessary (but not sufficient) condition for the development of stable democratic institutions.

Plural Society

The third theory of state is that of the plural society, a social order in which institutionally segmented groups coexist in one political unit without significant intermingling, and political power is monopolised by one cultural group (Furnivall, 1939; Smith, 1974). The most salient feature of the postcolonial state is not its previous history of conquest by an alien culture, but the persistence of cultural incompatibility of its plural parts. This nullifies efforts to forge bonds of common citizenship and instead leads one group to use the state as an instrument of domination over other groups (Smith, 1974).

Ethnic nationalism rests on the assumption that nations are made up of ascriptive groups who differentiate themselves by ethnicity. 'Ethnonationalism', as it is now referred to, uses ethnic identity as the basis for social relations and political mobilisation. It may be argued, however, that ethnic identity is the product rather than the cause of political mobilisation. The political significance of ethnicity is also contextual in the sense that individuals define themselves as members of ethnic groups in order to extract resources that are dispensed by the state on the basis of such self-identification. Alternatively, such identification may be a form of self-defence against perceived group persecution, as with the Sikhs and Kashmiris in India.

The Congress Party played a historic mission in integrating state and society. Begun as an organisation of westernised elites in 1885, under Mahatma Gandhi's leadership the party became a mass organisation by incorporating the peasantry and the proletariat. The struggle for independence placed a premium on a broad social base for the nationalist party; the need for a broad social base led to efforts at balancing competing interests; and the attempt at balance produced policies of class conciliation rather than sharpened class antagonisms. Congress dominated the Constituent Assembly which drafted the constitution of independent India. The party in turn was dominated at the time of independence by lawyers, landlords and businessmen.

The Constitution of India encapsulates the nature and mission of the Indian state. It establishes the rules of the struggle for political power in the country, specifies what the state may strive for, but also sets limits to state power in order to check it from acting arbitrarily. The point is that the Constitution of India does not represent a consensus on fundamental values and agreement on procedures. The conflict of values, ostensibly settled authoritatively in the constitution, is in fact still contested fiercely in the political arena. Success in the struggle will depend in part on the ability of elites to mobilise people in large numbers around symbols and values that can be used as political resources against those who control the administrative and judicial institutions of state power (Brass, 1991, p. 274). We saw this to be true in regard to the control of gurdwaras (Sikh temples) in Punjab. The emerging competition between the Congress and the Bharatiya Janata Party (BJP) shows that while the former would prefer to have religion removed from the competitive political arena, the BJP is courting religious authorities because they can provide additional symbolic support in the struggle for political power. Most fundamentally (in terms of the numbers of people involved), the invasive intensification of caste consciousness in India today confirms that it is a society yet to develop stable relationships between the principal political institutions and the core social groups.

India's Democracy

Much of the discussion of the state tends to be polemical, designed to assert the superiority of one system over another or the historical inevitability of the demise of the state. Despite the polemics, the use of coercive power to maintain a specific social order, and the social organisation of the economy at a particular level of productive and distributive efficiency, are prime aspects of the state (Fried, 1968, pp. 147–8). Any particular state may also have a distinctive relationship with religion, ranging from a secular state that separates the realm of the statesman from that of the prophet, to a theocratic state which collapses the first into the second.

One advantage of testing theories of democracy against India's experience is that cleavage-ridden and poor India appears to deviate from the predicted patterns in so many theories rooted in social and economic variables. Yet, on the face of it, the task of any satisfactory democratic theory should be to explain the success of democracy in India, not to explain it away as an exception to the rule. Given the size of the country and the longevity of its democratic institutions, India should be the starting point for formulating and testing a theory of democracy in a developing country.

Myron Weiner (1987a, p. 19) has argued that 'Tutelary democracy under British colonialism appears to be a significant determinant of democracy in the Third World.' There were three components of the British model. (Weiner writes of two components only, assimilating the third point into the first two. I believe that the importance of the third component warrants its separation into an independent factor.) First, the British created bureaucratic structures (civil service, judiciary, police, army) underpinned by an ideology that legitimated the role of state authority in maintaining social order through prescribed procedures and the rule of law. The appointment and conduct of officials were also governed by rules. Second, the British introduced, instilled and progressively expanded the principles and institutions of representative government. Third, in regard both to the bureaucratic structures and representative institutions, the British incorporated progressively larger numbers of 'natives' into the process of government. By the time that the British departed, they were able to leave behind political parties that had learnt to participate in competitive elections, and an educated elite that had been socialised into the norms and procedures of democratic governance. The end result was that while there was considerable difference between political parties over substantive policies, 'the extent of consensus on procedures – for choosing candidates for elections, for the conduct of the elections themselves, for norms of conduct for elected officials – is striking' (Weiner, 1987a, p. 20).

The successful establishment of democracy in India was built on the assets bequeathed by British rule. Congress was transformed from an elite into a mass party. It acted as the conduit for the articulation of popular demands on the well-established bureaucratic structures.

The satisfaction of voter demands in turn strengthened the social bases of the ruling party. Yet the existence of alternative parties with well-developed organisations and programmes exerted the discipline of a 'free market' in politics. At the same time, the party system in India did not develop along the ridges of one overriding cleavage. The most salient all-India social cleavage is that between Hindus and Muslims. One reason why the state has been able to survive despite enduring low-intensity insurgencies in Assam, Kashmir and Punjab is that these are geographically confined to certain regions. The Muslims are dispersed all over the country. The rise of the BJP, and the prospects of an effective Congress–BJP two-party system, raise the spectre of party competition based on communal appeals. This might create the conditions for civil conflict and the destruction of civil society.

The relationship between Hindus and Muslims in India is closer to the theory of the plural society than pluralist democracy. The two groups belong to different religions, worship in rigidly separated temples and mosques, have identifiably different occupational spreads, read different vernacular newspapers and rarely intermingle socially in common recreational clubs. This is why Hindu–Muslim conflict is endemic, intense and pervasive; brings civil politics into collision with primordial loyalties; and corrodes the integrative potential of the state.

One problem distinctive to Indian democracy is that of sycophancy. In June 1993, one state chief minister was weighed against gold-plated silver coins with his face engraved on the obverse side. The coins were a tribute from a junior minister in his cabinet. A few weeks later, a 160-page book – which took all of five days to write – was published in praise of the chief minister with a colour photograph of him on the cover and a postage-stamp-sized photograph on the top left corner of every page (Amar Kumar Singh, 1993). A commentator noted that 'The book oozes sycophancy and unadulterated flattery' (Narayan, 1993).

A second problem is that of dissidence. In Bihar, for example, it has become rare for any one person to complete a full five-year term as chief minister. On the surface, the second tendency might seem to contradict the first. In fact both are manifestations of the same phenomenon, namely fickleness. Rank and file politicians are loyal to no cause, ideology or persons. Instead, they are loyal to the office and to the office-holder in a position to dispense the most generous patronage.

There are three deleterious consequences that flow from this. First, there is general political instability. This is true even with the same party remaining in power. A chief minister often has to spend as much time on political self-preservation as on policy matters. Second, those who come laden with gifts of silver are also full of expectations of full cost recovery (and more) as a result of being in office. That is, financial corruption is the other side of financial sycophancy. Third, because of the political instability, no person can presume to be in office for any length of time. Whatever profits are to be made must therefore be made speedily.

The net result is that one of the country's most resource-rich provinces is one of the poorest in terms of income, wealth-creation and productive economic activity. 'Whatever index of prosperity and development you choose, Bihar comes triumphantly at the bottom' (Dalrymple, 1993, p. 45). In 1993, at least 33 of Bihar's state legislators had criminal records (Dalrymple, 1993, p. 45). The criminalisation of the political process includes what is called 'booth capturing'. The first known instance of ballot-rigging was recorded in Bihar in the 1962 national elections. Since then it has become the norm. The booth-capturing armies do not discriminate between ideologies, castes and parties. They are pure mercenaries. When contacted, they will obligingly inform prospective employers of their past efforts and success rates. Booth capturing makes politicians beholden to armed criminals and establishes an unholy nexus between them. In the 1990s, great swathes of Bihar's countryside are controlled by the private armies of politicians, landlords and Maoist militias called Naxalites.

The 1975–7 Emergency

Fox Butterfield, the *New York Times* correspondent in China, commented that except for the brief aberration of the 1975–7 emergency, India

has maintained its political freedom; there have been no unchecked Public Security Ministry, no street committees, no network of forced-labor camps, no persecution of whole groups of people because they were intellectuals or had relatives who had once been landlords, no destruction of libraries and universities. (Butterfield, 1982, p. 447)

A blanket of repression was cast over India by the emergency. About 110 000 people were arrested and imprisoned without trial. The emergency period was the most substantial assault on the liberal democratic nature of India since independence. It called into question virtually every aspect of Indian democracy that we have discussed in this book. The extent of powers claimed by the state under emergency laws is best captured in the words of the Attorney-General of India. He argued before the Supreme Court in December 1975 that 'Even if an executive officer were to deprive a citizen of life or personal liberty by way of settling some personal score, the citizen would not have any remedy so long as the emergency . . . lasted' (*Indian Express*, 17 December 1975). For this reason, it is worth examining in some detail the theoretical issues thrown up by the emergency.

In the liberal Lockean tradition the chief threat to freedom lies in the tyranny of government. So authority of government must be circumscribed. In the newer countries, however, authority is in scarce supply and great demand, thereby producing stress in the political system. Authority to be curbed must first exist (Huntington, 1968, pp. 7–8). The requirement therefore is not to restrain political power, but to make it effective. Postcolonial governments have often come into conflict with constitutional provisions that seek to safeguard individual rights by restricting the authority of government. Strong leaders especially are not easily reconciled to their desire to act in the national interest foundering on constitutional barriers. Yet one of the major purposes, if not the central one, of any constitution is precisely to act as a check upon those in whom authority of government has been vested for a delimited term. Freedom for the citizen = restraints upon the rulers.

However, should the rights of the many be sacrificed to the privileges of the few? A limited state functions to protect individual rights to life, liberty, and property, but cannot act as the 'guarantor' of equal rights and opportunities for everyone. The liberal ideal of the state functioning in a purely supportive or regulative capacity fails to acknowledge indirect impediments to individual activities, as embodied particularly in property relations. Liberalism as a system of thought permits the legal titleholder to interfere with the tiller freely disposing of the produce of his labour. In doing so, liberalism contains within itself a moral endorsement of private property in favour of the landlord. Is not the lack of access to the means of life and labour a denial of liberty?

The postulates of arguments developed along the above lines are often correct, but not the conclusions drawn. Liberal democracy aims at attaining equality through liberty. It is not possible to invert the relationship in practice. The notion of 'real freedom' is a terminological 'sleight of mind' that artificially collapses liberty into equality without overcoming the problem, namely, that there exists no objective means of determining which of the two is the more important. A search for equality may take the democrat and the liberal along separate paths. A commitment to freedom however necessarily anchors democracy to liberalism.

The liberal–democrat differences on equality recall Berlin's distinction between negative and positive liberty (Berlin, 1969). Even in the market equilibrium concept of pluralist democracy, there is insufficient heed paid to the fact that the poorer sections of society lack *effective* (political) demand. The qualification is particularly significant in a country such as India, where the poor constitute a majority. The political market is characterised by imperfect competition, for it is oligopolistic. The suppliers of political goods (that is, political parties) can control 'prices' and to an extent even manufacture demand (Macpherson, 1977, pp. 87–9). The market is also oligopsonistic. A citizen wishing to enter parliament has little real choice but to work through the existing political parties. There can be little doubt that disparities in resources give unequal access to influence over decision-makers and unequal opportunity to become a decision-maker. Political equality is thus clearly dependent upon socioeconomic equalities. That is, formal rules and structures may not be sufficient conditions of democratic equality. Nevertheless, they are still necessary conditions.

Egalitarian slogans targeted at civil liberties too mask rather than overcome the philosophical dilemma. In much of the Third World the prevailing situation is often best described as neither bread nor liberty. There is an unbridgeable gap in logic between arguing that liberal democracy presents peculiar obstacles to economic growth, and the claim that other forms of government will perform better on this score. If liberal democracy is prone to being congenitally ineffectual, the alternative may well be chronic instability and disintegration – not economic miracles.

It is also difficult to see how the masses could be guaranteed that concentrated and unfettered authority will be used to pursue national wellbeing and not private gain. What is to prevent the absolute power being guided by an ideology to the left of self-interest or to the right of self-importance? The sins of the leadership are visited upon the subjects in any type of regime: but at least under a liberal system there are institutional checks to the damage that may be inflicted, and under an accountable system the citizens have the choice and the means to return their leaders to private lives. The risks of power relationships being frozen at the existing levels of inequitable distribution are thereby lessened.

Nor is there any logical or historical reason to believe that an authoritarian government will be more successful than a 'soft' democratic state in carrying out a programme of institutional change in society. The obstacles to change constitute practical political constraints on compulsion regardless of regime type. Alternatively, if the masses can be carried with government-initiated programmes of reform, then the legitimacy deriving from democratic rule can help both to break the power of local elites and to absorb the weakening of traditional authority structures (Frankel, 1978a). The point is not that there are no serious objective and subjective hurdles. Redistributive and transformative efforts may well run into obstacles at the ideological, organisational, electoral, governmental and bureaucratic levels (Kohli, 1980). The point rather is that the alternative types of government can offer no better assurances of negotiating these hurdles successfully. The argument boils down to a Churchillian essence: what, in realistic terms, offers better prospects at less cost?

Equally, attacks upon freedoms from the opposite flank involve manipulations as well. The emergency was justified not simply in terms of lighting the path to 'real' freedoms, but also in the language of defending democracy against itself. Liberty is based in law, but neither liberty nor law can obtain, it was argued, in conditions of disorder. Once again, however, it is not possible to invert the relationship between law and order. Law is a prerequisite of order, not the other way round. To transpose the relationship is to invite turning the law enforcers into law breakers, as happened during the emergency in India. With the suspension of civil liberties, the Lieutenant-Governor of Delhi was able to instruct the police that 'every bad character, known or unknown (*sic*), should be immediately arrested' (*Times of India*, 1 July 1975).

In reality, the emergency was flawed from the beginning because it was born in sin. It was too transparently a measure of personal protection to carry conviction as an instrument of national salvation. The emergency was also faulty in its execution, in that it was selectively applied against personal political enemies. And the suspension of democratic processes cut off the supply line of political oxygen to the government in the form of voter disaffection. Officials were able to bulldoze hutment settlements and attain sterilisation targets through compulsion because there were no elected representatives to check their excessive zeal.

If any national leader in India can be accused of having demonstrated authoritarian tendencies, it is Mrs Gandhi during the emergency. Yet the total picture shows that even she was committed to adversarial politics within bounded rules. In voting Mrs Gandhi out in 1977, Indians showed that while they can put up with much economic injustice, they would not tolerate tyranny. In accepting defeat gracefully, Mrs Gandhi confirmed that the norms of democratic transition of power had been internalised at the highest levels of India's political elite. Indeed she was careful throughout the emergency to justify her actions within the framework of the Indian constitution, thereby demonstrating the extent to which the rule of law has been embedded as a constraint on arbitrary government. By contesting and winning the 1980 general election, she further showed a willingness to exploit the constitutional channels for regaining power.

The result of the elite commitment to democratic governance has been the development of the infrastructure of democratic society: well-organised groups that compete through established norms and procedures; a number of trade unions that compete for the loyalties of workers and have organisational links with different political parties; an independent, robust and critical press; an autonomous university system; a constant exposure to and interaction with the evolution of the values of civil society elsewhere in the world; and so on. That is, the operation of democratic institutions over a period of time gives rise to popular attitudes supportive of, and social classes parasitically dependent on, democratic procedures.

The events of 1977 also underscore the genuineness of India's democracy. It satisfies the following six conditions of democracy: universal adult suffrage; free and fair elections underwritten by such procedures as secret ballot, open counting and absence of fraud and intimidation to an extent that affects the outcome of elections; the right to organise competing political parties with alternative platforms of public policy; periodic holding of elections at legally prescribed intervals; the choosing of the principal policy-makers through competitive elections: the elected government should be accountable to the people, not a mere figurehead for the military, bureaucracy or an oligarchy; and the vacating of office by the ruling group when it loses elections, with no punishment of defeated candidates and parties.

On the positive side, crises provide learning experiences for political elites. The electoral verdict on Mrs Gandhi's Congress was so severe in 1977 that no future prime minister will contemplate that option with sanguineness. In the final analysis, constitutional clauses can promote democratic governance only to a limited degree. The survival of a liberal democratic state depends more crucially on the commitment of political leaders to democratic norms and values, on the socialisation of political elites into the procedures of democratic bargaining and accommodation, and on elite decisions in both ruling and opposition parties at critical historical junctions.

Market Democracy

The emergency represented the most serious challenge to the political credentials of India's democracy. The first substantial challenge to the socialist–interventionist state established since independence has come with the moves towards a more market-friendly economy in the 1990s. Most development economists can be divided into two groups: those who trust unregulated markets to deliver the public good of development and those who put their faith in government intervention. The obvious success of East Asian economies has been used by both sides to bolster their case. These countries have succeeded in breaking the Asiatic poverty trap. The benefits of their growth have been surprisingly evenly distributed. Within one generation, the material conditions of life were transformed even for the unskilled workers. Interventionists argue that the key to the success of the Asian dragons has been selective trade protection and an enlightened industrial policy. Free marketeers point out that by the standards of the Third World, the dragons have had 'small' government, open trade regimes, competitive exchange rates and low inflation.

While neoclassical explanations do not ignore the role of the state, their major preoccupation is with the provision of public goods; the maintenance of macroeconomic stability; and realistic trade, exchange rate and pricing policies that permit firms to exploit comparative advantage. Markets that are permitted to work freely produce outcomes which maximise social as well as individual benefits. That is, both the distributive and productive outcomes of free markets are beneficial. Conversely, the costs of intervention include productive and distributive inefficiencies, and also new kinds of efficiency costs such as rent-seeking (to be discussed below). Excessive intervention is the cause more than the result of market failure. The goal of government intervention should be to nudge the relative prices of goods and factors to approximate those that would prevail in a free market. In such conceptions, targeted industrial policies discourage efficient resource allocation and encourage unproductive rent-seeking behaviour by firms.

Taking issue with neoclassicism, Robert Wade (1990) postulates an alternative governed market theory of Taiwanese success wherein the government encourages both high levels of investment and a sectoral composition of investment which is different from that which would prevail in a free market. In effect, government-initiated industrial policies lead the market. Wade provides a detailed catalogue of state intervention: financial and fiscal instruments for guiding resource allocation decisions and the pervasive role of state-owned enterprises.

'Structuralists' had argued that the degree of imperfection in developing-country markets was so great that they were less socially efficient in allocating goods and services than industrialised-country markets (Colclough, 1991, p. 2). The colonial state in India catered to its own administrative interests that were different from the demands of the colonial masters in Britain and the needs of the subject people in India (Tomlinson, 1993, p. 217). One of the legacies of British rule to the people of India was a strong state. The type and extent of economic growth and development in independent India was conditioned by the nature of the markets that (1) decided how to generate surplus over subsistence and (2) allocated the surplus between capital, labour and the state. The main distributor of goods and services was the state. The model of planned heavy industrialisation favoured the few owners of scarce resources like land, capital and power, rather than the numerous owners of the plentiful resource labour. This led to a vicious circle of labour-intensive, low wage, low productivity processes in both agriculture and industry, under-employment of labour at subsistence wages and a depressed demand for basic wage-goods. The East Asian examples suggest that an abundance of low labour is not an insurmountable obstacle to development. With the right policy mix and investment in technology and human capital formation (education and public health), labour can be rewarded through high productivity increases, high utilisation rates, rising real wages and rising effective demand. It was not the inheritance from the colonial state, nor a lack of alternatives, but the ideology and competence of the dirigiste state that perpetuated underdevelopment.

The licence-raj model of development adopted after independence gave rise to the *rentier* state. Bureaucratic controls formed an integral part of a 'rent-seeking society' (Krueger, 1974) in which the owners of scarce assets like land and capital, or scarce privileges like import licences, were simply rewarded for their ownership. In a free market, they would have been forced to earn a return on their assets and privileges through efficiency and productivity gains. In a *rentier* state, profits become a function of maintaining scarcities, limiting the number of rent-holders and blocking alternative channels for access to the scarce assets. Bhagwati (1993) argues that India's persistent low productivity is explained by extensive bureaucratic controls over production, investment and trade; inward-looking trade and investment policies; and an inefficient, over-extended public sector. Together, these created a *rentier* instead of an entrepreneurial economy. The economic outcome is under-utilisation of industrial capacity, inefficient allocations of foreign exchange and investment capital, blocked land reforms and a generally corrupt polity that severely inhibits the possibility of development. The political outcome is a stable exchange relationship between bureaucrats, politicians and a narrow circle of propertied and favoured groups. The net welfare loss resulting from government intervention is greater than the welfare gain realised from correcting market imperfections.

This is not to imply that the state should have played no role at all in economic development after 1947. Two hundred years of foreign rule had left India with an underdeveloped economy and market institutions. The economy was neither ready nor capable of being readied for take-off. There was some justification for the philosophy of economic development adopted at independence. Keynesian interventionism had triumphed against the adversities of the great depression, and the Marshall Plan had reinforced faith in the visible hand of government. Comprehensive planning was viewed by Nehruvian socialists as the answer to pervasive market imperfections. Markets were therefore set aside in favour of the government running public sector industries and disdaining imports. Gradually, however, the view has prevailed that imperfect markets work better than imperfect governments. The interventionist state has produced failures on a massive scale in Africa and Latin America as well as India. By contrast, economically liberal and liberalising regimes have witnessed growth spurts in China, Taiwan, South Korea, Hong Kong and Singapore in East Asia and Chile in Latin America. In the real world, governments are frequently incompetent, frequently corrupt, and sometimes, as in India, both. The result of inappropriate and corrupt state policy has been ineffective and rent-seeking use of scarce resources coupled with a neglect of infrastructure and human capital formation.

In India, traditional thinking about 'development economics' had led the government to such broad and deep involvement in economic management that it will take years to roll back the state. But a start was made in the 1991–4 budgets. As in Eastern Europe and the former Soviet Union – where interventionism was taken to its most ambitious extremes – in India too it is the government itself which is the most forceful critic of the bad old ways and wishes to set the country on the path to market reforms as fast as political realities permit.

Yet the debate over the boundaries between the space which may properly be inhabited by the state and private space which is closed to the state is not limited to the liberal virtues of free enterprise and the vice of economic meddling by governments. Rather, it is a question of striking the right balance between markets which deliver freedom and prosperity and communities which sustain cultural and social values. Much of the animosity among Indians towards the American way of life is sourced in a mistaken conflation of the vices of American libertarianism with economic liberalism. Culture and morality need not be dictated by consumer preference. The examples of Japan and Singapore show that it is possible to combine belief in a free market with support for communitarian values.

In some sectors the state will continue to have to assume the main responsibility: in providing the indispensable legal and political context, ensuring that law and order prevails, protecting property rights, creating the necessary infrastructure, dispensing primary health care and education and providing every citizen with a minimum insurance against life's disasters. Collective action is inescapable and uncontroversial to deal with some economic ills caused by market failure. Externalities can stop free markets from bringing about outcomes sought by individuals, for example a clean environment: here the state must indeed step in on behalf of society.

In turn, neointerventionism has abandoned the pursuit of replacing the market with the state. Instead, it seeks to guide the market towards the attainment of economically and socially desired objectives. The use of the price mechanism is supplemented by the utilisation of non-price methods to give a directional thrust to key industries, modernise and broaden the technological base by strengthening links with foreign firms and, most importantly, channel investment into productive sectors and industries. Factor advantages in labour and land costs are insufficient to offset the competitive disadvantage of starting operations against firms already established in the international marketplace. Industry assistance may still be required to guide targeted sectors while subjecting them to competitive performance tests.

To be successful, neointerventionism must rest on two principles: strategic planning for trade and industry and continuous recalibrations in response to market signals. For example, selected industries could be identified as potential high performers by *international* standards. The government could put in place a range of measures to provide state help to targeted parts of these industries and subject to specified conditions like productivity gains, export performance and increasing use of local componentry. Furthermore, the second principle, of openness to market feedback, would require a constant monitoring of the gap between the domestic and international price of the item being manufactured with state assistance. If the gap has widened after a stated interval of five or ten years, then imports of the item could be liberalised through increased quotas and lowered tariffs. The important implication of such a strategy is that while domestic producers are receiving government help or subsidy, they are not shielded from the competitive pressures of the international market.

Contemporary Challenges to Indian Democracy

By the end of the 1980s, the state was in crisis in all three worlds (Hettne, 1990, pp. 27–8). In the industrialised West, the welfare state had been the main instrument of political legitimacy since the 1930s. The shift from Keynesian orthodoxy to an 'economic rationalism' that viewed the state as a problem rather than a solution produced considerable social dislocation. The socialist state faced a crisis of legitimacy arising from declining living standards. In the ultimate irony of an erroneous Marxist reading of the march of history, it is the

Soviet communist state that withered away in 1991. In many Third World countries, the state remained an intellectual construct of Westernised elites and came under threat from ethnopolitical movements. In all three worlds, the very identity of the state has come under assault from international flows of goods, services and ideas that ignore geographically-bounded territory. Moreover, as the state has increased the number and scope of its activities, policy has been progressively disjointed from politics. The increasing separation of the machinery of government from popular control has produced a corresponding crisis of democratic accountability.

State actors have also come under increasing challenge from sectarian and social movements inside their borders. In its external setting, sovereignty means the legal identity of the state in international law, an equality of status with all other states, and the claim to be the sole official agent acting in international relations on behalf of a society. In its internal manifestation, sovereignty refers to the right of the state to make authoritative decisions of government with regard to all people and resources within its territory. The old development paradigm viewed the assertion of ethnic identity as a problem to be solved during the process of nation and state-building. Today the rise of ethnonationalism appears to be a fairly common phenomenon, as does 'mobilisation from below' on a number of issues like the environment and the nuclear threat. Social movements network across state borders and express solidarity with one another against their respective home governments. This is accompanied by the rise of regionalism, where a region becomes the focus of economic, cultural and political identity. In the real world, therefore, there are variable degrees of stateness and sovereignty is relative; but this fails to detract from the postulated ideal-type.

The Indian state has been facing challenges on many fronts. It is threatened by the forces of casteism, religion, regionalism, globalism and the 'privatisation' of the state. In a major study of Italy, Putnam *et al.* (1993) argued that stable democratic governance is a function of a high level of 'civic community': patterns of social cooperation based on tolerance, trust and widespread norms of active citizen participation. India has been witnessing rising intolerance, erosion of trust and greater willingness to participate in the politics of group exclusion. The gravest threat to India's democratic order and civic governance lies in the fragility of Congress as the party of government and the fragmentation of the others as parties of opposition (Weiner, 1987b, p. 75).

India is under assault as a secular state from the rising tide of Hindutva forces represented by the BJP in the arena of party-political competition. The Supreme Court of India came to the defence of the secular nature of the state in an important verdict on 11 March 1994. In upholding the 1992 dismissal of four BJP provincial governments, the court ruled that religion and politics cannot be mixed. Any state government that pursues unsecular policies or unsecular courses of action, the court continued, acts contrary to the constitutional mandate and may be dismissed under Article 356 of the constitution. This is a good example of the institutions of state acting in defence of the integral nature of the state. The Supreme Court's well-established doctrine of the 'basic structure' of the constitution can also be interpreted along these lines.

The liberal facet of the Indian state has been under challenge from resurgent castes seeking ever-expanding programmes of preferential policies at the expense of individual rights. Moreover, as the state has itself become the biggest prize because of its asset as the prime distributor of resources, it has been losing its distinctive integrative role that allowed it to mediate in group conflicts. Violence through confrontations on the streets and on the farms have become increasingly commonplace, displacing conflict resolution through allocative and distributive public policy in parliamentary forums.

The advance of the market in the 1980s and 1990s has been accompanied by a retreat of the state. The forces of globalisation have made it more difficult for all states to achieve distributive compromises that accommodate and attenuate class, communal and regional conflicts. Increasing penetration of states by transnational flows undermines the decision-making autonomy of states. The national autonomy of the Indian state too has been steadily eroded under the impact of globalising forces. The same trends of market forces have also led to a virtual abandonment of the long-established Nehruvian consensus on a socialistic and interventionist state.

The impersonal nature of the state was under its greatest strain under the personalising–centralising thrust of Mrs Gandhi. Not being the product of a rising bourgeoisie, the state of independent India did not act like the executive committee of the bourgeoisie. Instead, it engaged in multiple roles – accommodation, extraction, production and repression – requiring state intervention in order to mediate a variety of social conflicts (Mitra, 1991, p. 396). The Congress Party's integrative role was ended with the conversion of the party into an instrument for perpetuating the personal rule of Mrs Gandhi. Given autonomy, local elites act as the linchpin of the modern state and traditional society (Mitra, 1991, p. 410). District-based factional politics in the Congress was the idiom through which the party mediated local authority structures into the national state. The centralising tendencies set in train by Mrs Gandhi ensured that local conflicts were transmitted upwards all the way to New Delhi, so that Congress became the mechanism for centralising and exacerbating conflicts instead of attenuating and reconciling them.

The resilience of Indian society is a function of a complex social repertoire of local elites; the stability of the Indian state requires that it be accommodative, constraining the behaviour of actors engaged in a transactional network of political bargaining. In the European conception, the modern state exhibits three principal virtues: political power is depersonalised, standardised and integrated into the greater social whole (Poggi, 1990). The 'privatisation' of state institutions (Sudarshan, 1990, p. 53) under Mrs Gandhi was completed in the emergency. State institutions lost their autonomous ability to arbitrate and reconcile conflicting interests, and the state itself lost the capacity to provide a legitimising ideology around which the different sectors could coalesce into a coherent and purposeful whole.

The identification of the state with a person led logically to subverting the state into a coercive apparatus which inflicted state violence on groups clamouring for political and economic power-sharing. The colonial state had succeeded in consolidating itself by linking its authority structures to the elite entrepreneurial network (Sisson and Wolpert, 1988). Similarly, the Marxist government of West Bengal has consolidated its hold on power through systematic authority links between the state governments and the districts (Kohli, 1990). It is local elites who engage in political mobilisation through allocative and redistributive policies as part of the competition for political power. Stability and resilience for the Indian state might depend on elites being genuinely responsive to local demands, and on the state re-establishing structural links with local authority elites. The dynamics of mobilisation will then keep pace with the rate of political institutionalisation.

Against all this, India is notably resilient. The democratic and federal credentials of the Indian state remain essentially intact. The persistence of India's democracy refutes a number of conjectures about the prerequisites and preconditions of democracy: per capita income thresholds, a dominant middle class, adult literacy, political institutionalisation before mobilisation, absence of deep and abiding social cleavages and so on. It may be attributable to the many legacies from the colonial state that were identified in Chapter 2, as well as to the absence of a 'natural majority' in Indian society which impels those who would aspire to power into continual coalition-building (Mitra, 1992, p. 10). It is attributable also to the success of the state in localising group conflicts that it cannot immediately solve: the persistent low-intensity insurgencies in Assam, Kashmir and Punjab have not destroyed the political centre.

That there are shortcomings in the workings of India's democracy cannot be denied. Liberal democracy cannot be predicted as the political outcome on the index of an exploitative capitalist class, civic culture or level of socioeconomic development. It is not then to be wondered at that the reverse should prove equally true: liberal democracy can no more cause economic growth than itself be a function of economic prosperity. This is not to deny that there are costs associated with each category of government, including liberal democratic. For example, in pointing to the masked coercion in the historical development of capitalist democracies, Moore's work (1969) served the useful purpose of correcting distortions in comparing the costs of the differing routes to industrialisation. Moreover, attacks against liberal democracy are frequently misdirected in that they assimilate the abuses of the system to its necessary concomitants. Perhaps the most important lesson to be learnt from objections to democracy is that it cannot be self-guaranteeing.

Some of the very symptoms of the frailty of India's democratic polity – the myriad forms of public protest, such as caste violence and political insurgency – are simultaneously indices of the assertiveness of upwardly mobile political groups being recruited into the political centre through distinctively Indian political idioms. A case in point is the rapid rise of the Bahujan Samaj Party (BSP) as the champion of the *dalits* (the oppressed): the BSP is now a coalition partner in U.P., the country's most populous and politically most important state. It is precisely the democratic nature of India's state that has been most effective in providing political and social mobility to ever-expanding numbers of individuals and groups and consolidated the legitimacy of the state as the authoritative intervener in group conflicts. For the struggle for political power among social groups is carried out substantially in the electoral arena, and the most widely accepted outcome of the struggle for political power is electoral triumph. India confirms that state institutions and structures do matter. They do not simply reflect social relations, but can help to shape the political outcomes of social conflicts.

Democracy imparts procedural legitimacy to the struggle for political power. In the Western industrial democracies, agreements had been reached on the great issues of distributive allocations, and on the merit of settling the remaining issues through the authenticated collective procedures. In India, failure to realise the distributive values enshrined in the constitution has caused an erosion of substantive legitimacy despite the continuance of procedural legitimacy which still authenticates the collective decision-making process. In the words of Sir Karl Popper, 'anybody who has ever lived under another form of government – that is, under a dictatorship which cannot be removed without bloodshed – will know that a democracy, imperfect though it is, is worth fighting for and, I believe, worth dying for' (Popper, 1988, p. 25).

Further Reading

Colclough and Manor (1991). An interesting collection of essays which questions neoliberalism and restates the case for a modified form of the traditional approach to development.

Frankel and Rao (1989/1990). Studies by distinguished social scientists of relations between state and society.

Helliwell (1994). Using data from 125 countries over the period from 1960 to 1985, argues that it is not possible to identify any systematic effects of democracy on subsequent economic growth.

Kohli (1990). Argues that a combination of centralisation and powerlessness has produced a crisis of governability for the Indian state.

Rudolph and Rudolph (1987). Addresses the familiar question of the enduring sources of political centrism in a country that should be vulnerable to political extremism. The answer is provided by means of an extended essay on the paradox of a weak–strong state and a rich–poor economy.

Vanaik, Achin (1990). A Marxist analysis of the state of India's democracy.

References

Abbreviations used:
HIE   Hindu International Edition (Madras)
SW   Statesman Weekly (Calcutta)
OHT   Overseas Hindustan Times (Delhi).
TOI   Times of India

Adelman, Irma and Cynthia Taft Morris (1973), *Economic Growth and Social Equity in Developing Countries*. Stanford: Stanford University Press.
Afshar, H. (ed.) (1987), *Women, State and Ideology*. London: Macmillan.
Ahmed, Helel Uddin (1994), 'Bureaucrats Out', *Far Eastern Economic Review*, 7 April, p. 30.
Akbar, M.J. (1985), *The Siege Within*. Harmondsworth: Penguin.
AICC (1991), *Constitution of the Indian National Congress*. New Delhi: All-India Congress Committee.
Almond, Gabriel (1970), *Political Development: Essays in Heuristic Theory*. Boston: Little, Brown.
Ananth, V. Krishna (1993), 'The Reservation Rigmarole', *HIE*, 25 September.
Andersen, Walter K. (1991), 'India's 1991 Elections: The Uncertain Verdict', *Asian Survey* 31 (October), pp. 976–89.
Andersen, Walter K. and Shridhar D. Damle (1987), *The Brotherhood in Saffron: The Rashtriya Swayamsevak Sangh and Hindu Revivalism*. Boulder: Westview.
Anon (1991), 'Drifting towards Disaster', *Indian Express*, 6 January.
Apter, David (1965), *The Politics of Modernization*. Chicago: University of Chicago Press.
Austin, Dennis and Peter Lyon (1993), 'The Bharatiya Janata Party of India', *Government & Opposition* 28 (Winter), pp. 36–50.
Austin, Granville (1966), *The Indian Constitution: Cornerstone of a Nation*. London: Oxford University Press.
Badhwar, Inderjit (1992), 'Narasimha Rao: From Meek Inheritor to Power Player', *India Today*, 30 June, pp. 24–7.
Bagchi, Amiya Kumar (1982), *The Political Economy of Underdevelopment*. Cambridge: Cambridge University Press.
Banerjee, D. (1989), 'Indian Army's Officers Training Establishments', *Asian Defence Journal*, February, pp. 16–20.
Baran, Paul (1962), *The Political Economy of Growth*. New York: Monthly Review Press.

Bardhan, Pranab (1974), 'Annex – India', in Hollis B. Chenery *et al.*, *Redistribution with Growth*. New York: Oxford University Press, pp. 255–62.

Bardhan, Pranab (1985), *The Political Economy of Development in India*. Delhi: Oxford University Press.

Bardhan, Pranab (1988), 'Dominant Proprietary Classes and India's Democracy', in Atul Kohli (ed.) *India's Democracy: An Analysis of Changing State–Society Relations*. Princeton: Princeton University Press, pp. 214–24.

Barnes, Julian (1984), *Flaubert's Parrot*. London: Picador.

Barnett, Marguerite Ross (1976), *The Politics of Cultural Nationalism in South India*. Princeton: Princeton University Press.

Basu, Amrita (1992), *Two Faces of Protest: Contrasting Modes of Women's Activism in India*. Berkeley: University of California Press.

Basu, Durga Das (1993), *Introduction to the Constitution of India*. New Delhi: Prentice–Hall of India.

Baxi, Upendra (1980), *The Indian Supreme Court and Politics*. Lucknow: Eastern Book Company.

Baxter, Craig (1969), *The Jana Sangh: A Biography of an Indian Political Party*. Philadelphia: University of Pennsylvania Press.

Bayley, David H. (1969), *The Police and Political Development in India*. Princeton: Princeton University Press.

Bayley, David H. (1983), 'The Police and Political Order in India', *Asian Survey* 23 (April), pp. 484–96.

Beitz, Charles R. (1981), 'Economic Rights and Distributive Justice in Developing Societies', *World Politics* 33 (April), pp. 321–46.

Benn, S. I. and R. S. Peters (1959), *Social Principles and the Democratic State*. London: George Allen & Unwin.

Berlin, Isaiah (1969), *Four Essays on Liberty*. Oxford: Oxford University Press.

Bernstein, H. (ed.) (1973), *Underdevelopment and Development*. Harmondsworth: Penguin.

Béteille, André (1971), *Caste, Class, and Power: Changing Patterns of Stratification in a Tanjore Village*. Berkeley: University of California Press.

Bhagwati, Jagdish (1993), *India in Transition: Freeing the Economy*. New Delhi: Oxford University Press.

Bhargava, P. K. (1984), 'Transfers from the Center to the States in India', *Asian Survey* 24 (June), pp. 665–87.

Bhatnagar, S. and Pradeep Kumar (eds) (1988), *Regional Political Parties in India*. New Delhi: Ess Ess.

Bienen, Henry S. (1978), *Armies and Parties in Africa*. New York: Africana.

Biersteker, Thomas J. (1980), 'The Illusion of State Power: Transnational Corporations and the Neutralization of Host-Country Legislation', *Journal of Peace Research* 27 (August), pp. 207–21.

Biersteker, Thomas J. (1990), 'Reducing the Role of the State in the Economy: A Conceptual Exploration of IMF and World Bank Prescriptions', *International Studies Quarterly* 34 (December), pp. 477–92.

Björkman, James W. (ed.) (1988), *Fundamentalism, Revivalists, and Violence in South Asia*. New Delhi: Manohar. Contributions on communal politics and religious violence.

Black, Cyril E. (1966), *The Dynamics of Modernization*. New York: Harper & Row.

Bodenheimer, Susanne (1971), 'Dependency and Imperialism: The Roots of Latin American Underdevelopment', in K. T. Fann and Donald C. Hodges (eds), *Readings in U.S. Imperialism*. Boston: Porter Sargent, pp. 155–81.

Bopegamage, A. (1971), 'The Military as a Modernizing Agent in India', *Economic Development and Cultural Change* 20 (October), pp. 71–9.

Bose, Tarun Chandra (ed.) (1987), *Indian Federalism: Problems and Issues*. Calcutta: K. P. Bagchi.

Boserup, Esther (1970), *Women's Role in Economic Development*. London: Allen & Unwin.

Brass, Paul R. (1965), *Factional Politics in an Indian State: The Congress Party in Uttar Pradesh*. Berkeley: University of California Press.

Brass, Paul R. (1981), 'Congress, the Lok Dal, and the Middle Peasant Castes: An Analysis of the 1977 and 1980 Parliamentary Elections in Uttar Pradesh', *Pacific Affairs* 54 (Spring), pp. 5–41.

Brass, Paul R. (1982), 'Pluralism, Regionalism, and Decentralizing Tendencies in Contemporary Indian Politics', in A. J. Wilson and Dennis Dalton (eds), *The States of South Asia: Problems of National Integration*. London: C. Hurst, pp. 223–64.

Brass, Paul R. (1990), *The New Cambridge History of India IV.1: The Politics of India since Independence*. Cambridge: Cambridge University Press.

Brass, Paul R. (1991), *Ethnicity and Nationalism: Theory and Comparison*. New Delhi: Sage.

Brass, Paul R. and Francis Robinson (eds) (1987), *The Indian National Congress and Indian Society, 1885–1985: Ideology, Social Structure, and Political Dominance*. Delhi: Chanakya.

Brodsky, David A. and Dani Rodrik (1981), 'Indicators of Development and Data Availability: The Case of the PQLI', *World Development* 9 (July), pp. 695–9.

Brookfield, Harold (1975), *Interdependent Development*. London: Methuen.

Buckley, Walter (1967), *Sociology and Modern Systems Theory*. New Jersey: Prentice–Hall.

Butler, David, Ashok Lahiri and Prannay Roy (1991), *India Decides: Elections 1952–1991*. New Delhi: Living Media.

Butterfield, Fox (1982), *China: Alive in the Bitter Sea*. New York: Times Books.

Calman, Leslie J. (1992), *Toward Empowerment: Women and Movement Politics in India*. Boulder: Westview.

Cammack, Paul, David Pool and William Tordoff (1988), *Third World Politics: A Comparative Introduction*. London: Macmillan.

Cassen, Robert (1994), *Does Aid Work?* Oxford: Oxford University Press.

Chakravarty, Nitish (1990), 'Mission to Woo the Grassroots', *HIE*, 14 July, p. 9.

Chakravarty, Sukhamoy (1987), *Development Planning: The Indian Experience*. New York: Oxford University Press.

Chakravarty, Sukhamoy (1990), 'Development Strategies for Growth with Equity: The South Asian Experience', *Asian Development Review* 8, pp. 133–59.

Chanda, Ashok (1965), *Federalism in India*. London: George Allen & Unwin.

Chari, P. R. (1977), 'Civil–Military Relations in India', *Armed Forces and Society* 4 (November), pp. 3–28.

Chase-Dunn, C. (1975), 'The Effect of International Economic Dependence on Development and Inequality: A Cross-National Study', *American Sociological Review* 40 (December), pp. 720–38.

Chawla, Prabhu (1983), 'Injudicious Moves', *India Today,* 15 December, pp. 54–5.

Chenery, Hollis B., Montek S. Ahluwalia, C. L. G. Bell, John H. Duloy and Richard Jolly (1974), *Redistribution with Growth.* New York: Oxford University Press for the World Bank and the Institute of Development Studies, University of Sussex.

Chhibber, Pradeep K. and Subhash Mishra (1993), 'Hindus and the Babri Masjid: The Sectional Basis of Communal Attitudes', *Asian Survey* 33 (July), pp. 665–72.

Chhibber, Pradeep K. and John R. Petrocik (1989), 'The Puzzle of Indian Politics: Social Cleavages and the Indian Party System', *British Journal of Political Science* 19 (April), pp. 191–210.

Cohen, Stephen P. (1976), 'The Military', in Henry C. Hart (ed.), *Indira Gandhi's India: A Political System Reappraised.* Boulder: Westview, pp. 207–39.

Cohen, Stephen P. (1988), 'The Military and Indian Democracy', in Atul Kohli (ed.), *India's Democracy: An Analysis of Changing State-Society Relations.* Princeton: Princeton University Press, pp. 99–143.

Cohen, Stephen P. (1990), *The Indian Army: Its Contribution to the Development of a Nation.* New Delhi: Oxford University Press.

Cohen, Stephen P. (1991), 'Asian Political Leadership', in Robert H. Taylor (ed.), *Asia and the Pacific,* Vol. 1. New York: Facts on File, pp. 965–85.

Colclough, Christopher (1991), 'Structuralism versus Neo-liberalism: An Introduction', in C. Colclough and J. Manor (eds), *States and Markets: Neo-Liberalism and the Development Policy Debate.* Oxford: Clarendon Press, pp. 1–25.

Colclough, Christopher and James Manor (eds) (1991), *States and Markets: Neo-Liberalism and the Development Policy Debate.* Oxford: Clarendon Press.

Coulter, Philip (1975), *Social Mobilization and Liberal Democracy.* Lexington, MA: Lexington Books.

Crick, Bernard (1968), 'Sovereignty', in David L. Sills (ed.), *International Encyclopaedia of the Social Sciences,* Vol. 15. London: Macmillan, pp. 77–82.

Crook, Clive (1993), 'The Future of Capitalism', *The Economist,* 'The Future Surveyed', 11 September, pp. 48–53.

Crossette, Barbara (1991), 'India's Soon-to-Be-Ex-Premier Likes It That Way', *New York Times,* 18 April.

Dalrymple, William (1993), 'State of Terror', *Good Weekend (The Age, Melbourne)* 14 August, pp. 43–6.

Dandekar, V. M. (1987), 'Unitary Elements in a Federal Constitution', *Economic and Political Weekly,* 31 October, pp. 1865–70.

Das, Dilip K. (1992), *Korean Economic Dynamism.* London: Macmillan.

Das, Veena (ed.) (1990), *Mirrors of Violence: Communities, Riots and Survivors in South Asia.* Delhi: Oxford University Press.

Dasgupta, Partha (1990), 'Well-Being in Poor Countries', *Economic and Political Weekly,* 4 August, pp. 1713–20.

Dasgupta, Partha and Martin Weale (1992), 'On Measuring the Quality of Life', *World Development* 20 (March), pp. 119–31.

Datta, Abhijit (ed.) (1984), *Union–State Relations*. New Delhi: Indian Institute of Public Administration.

Datta-Ray, Sunanda K. (1990), 'Making of Martyrs: Why India Needs Farooq Abdullah', *SW,* 3 February.

Datta-Ray, Sunanda K. (1991a) 'Keeper of the Law: Scope for Presidential Action', *SW,* 22 June.

Datta-Ray, Sunanda K. (1991b) 'State of Disunity', *SW,* 14 September.

Desai, A. R. (ed.) (1979), *Peasant Struggles in India*. New Delhi: Oxford University Press.

Desai, Neera and Maithreyi Krishnaraj (1987), *Women and Society in India*. Delhi: Ajanta Publications.

Desai, P. D. (1992), 'Reforms in Administration of Justice', unpublished paper delivered to the Indo–British Legal Forum by the Chief Justice of the Bombay High Court.

Dos Santos, Theotonio (1970), 'The Structure of Dependence', *American Economic Review* 60 (May), pp. 231–6.

Dua, Bhagwan D. (1983), 'A Study in Executive-Judicial Conflict: The Indian Case', *Asian Survey* 23 (April), pp. 463–83.

Dua, Bhagwan D. (1985), 'Federalism or Patrimonialism: The Making and Unmaking of Chief Ministers in India', *Asian Survey* 25 (August), pp. 793–804.

Dumont, Louis (1970), *Homo Hierarchicus: An Essay on the Caste System*. London: Weidenfeld & Nicolson.

Dwivedi, O. P. and R. B. Jain (1985), *India's Administrative State*. New Delhi: Gitanjali.

Easton, David (1990), *The Analysis of Political Structure*. New York: Routledge.

Eckstein, Harry (1966), *Division and Cohesion in Democracy: Study of Norway*. Princeton: Princeton University Press.

Eisenstadt, S. N. (1966), *Modernization: Protest and Change*. New Jersey: Prentice-Hall.

Eldersveld, Samuel J. and Bashiruddin Ahmed (1978), *Citizens and Politics: Mass Political Behaviour in India*. Chicago: University of Chicago Press.

Elkin, Jerrod F. and W. Andrew Ritezel (1985), 'Military Role Expansion in India', *Armed Forces and Society* 11 (Summer), pp. 489–505.

Embree, Ainslee T. (1990), *Utopias in Conflict: Religion and Nationalism in Modern India*. Berkeley: University of California Press.

Engineer, Asghar Ali (1992a), *The Rights of Women in Islam*. London: C. Hurst.

Engineer, Asghar Ali (1992b), 'Sitamarhi on Fire', *Economic and Political Weekly,* 14 November, pp. 2462–4.

Fadia, Babulal (1980), *Pressure Groups in Indian Politics*. New Delhi: Radiant.

Fadia, Babulal (1984), *State Politics in India,* 2 vols. New Delhi: Radiant.

Fadia, Babulal and R. K. Menaria (1990), *Sarkaria Commission Report and Centre–State Relations*. Agra: Sahitya Bhawan.

Fay, Peter Ward (1994), *The Forgotten Army: India's Armed Struggle for Independence 1942–1945*. Michigan: University of Michigan Press.

Field, John Osgood (1980), *Consolidating Democracy: Politicization and Partisanship in India*. Delhi: Manohar. An optimistic assessment that India has achieved and is sustaining a functioning democracy.

Fieldhouse, D. K. (1967), *The Theory of Capitalist Imperialism*. London: Longman.

Finer, S. (1976), *The Man on Horseback: The Role of the Military in Politics*. Harmondsworth: Penguin.

Fiorina, M. (1981), *Retrospective Voting in American National Elections*. New Haven, CT: Yale University Press.

Foster-Carter, A. (1976), 'From Rostow to Gunder-Frank: Conflicting Paradigms in the Analysis of Underdevelopment', *World Development* 4 (March), pp. 167–80.

Frank, A. G. (1966), 'The Development of Underdevelopment', *Monthly Review* 18 (September), pp. 17–31.

Frankel, Francine R. (1978a), 'Compulsion and Social Change: Is Authoritarianism the Solution to India's Economic Development Problems?', *World Politics*, 30 (January), pp. 215–40.

Frankel, Francine R. (1978b), *India's Political Economy, 1947–1977: The Gradual Revolution*. Princeton: Princeton University Press.

Frankel, Francine R. and M. S. A. Rao (eds) (1989/1990), *Dominance and State Power in India: Decline of a Social Order*, 2 vols. Delhi: Oxford University Press.

Fried, Morton H. (1968). 'State: The Institution', in David L. Sills (ed.), *International Encyclopedia of the Social Sciences*, Vol. 15. London: Macmillan, pp. 143–50.

Furnivall, J. S. (1939), *Netherlands India: A Study of Plural Economy*. Cambridge: Cambridge University Press.

Galanter, Marc (1990), *Competing Equalities: Law and the Backward Classes in India*. Berkeley: University of California Press.

Gallagher, John and Ronald Robinson (1968), *Africa and the Victorians: The Climax of Imperialism*. New York: Doubleday.

Ganguly, Sumit (1991), 'From the Defence of the Nation to Aid to the Civil: The Army in Contemporary India', *Journal of Asian and African Studies* 26 (January–April), pp. 11–26.

Ghosh, S. K. (1981), *Women in Policing*. New Delhi: Light and Life.

Ghoshal, U. N. (1959), *A History of Indian Political Ideas*. Madras: Oxford University Press.

Goel, Madan Lal (1974), *Political Participation in a Developing Nation: India*. Bombay: Asia.

Gopal, Sarvepalli (1979), *Jawaharlal Nehru: A Biography*. 3 vols. London: Jonathan Cape.

Gopal, Sarvepalli (ed.) (1991), *Anatomy of a Confrontation: The Babri Masjid-Ramjanmabhumi Issue*. New Delhi: Viking.

Gothoskar, Sujata (1991), 'Pushing Women Out: Declining Employment of Women in the Organised Industrial Sector', *Manushi* 65 (July–August), pp. 10–20.

Gould, Harold and Sumit Ganguly (eds) (1993), *India Votes: Alliance Politics and Minority Governments in the Ninth and Tenth General Elections*. Boulder: Westview.

Graf, Violette (1992), 'The Muslim Vote', in Subrata Kumar Mitra and James Chiriyankandath (eds), *Electoral Politics in India: A Changing Landscape*. New Delhi: Segment, pp. 213–40.

Graham, Bruce (1993), *Hindu Nationalism and Indian Politics: The Origins and Development of the Bharatiya Jana Sangh*. Cambridge: Cambridge University Press.

Grant, James P. (1986), *The State of the World's Children, 1986*. New York: UNICEF.

Grewal, J. S. (1990), *The New Cambridge History of India II.3: The Sikhs of the Punjab*. Cambridge: Cambridge University Press.

Gupta, Amalendu Das (1990), 'BJP in Perspective', *SW*, 24 March, p. 12.

Gupta, Anand Swarup (1979), *The Police in British India 1861–1947*. New Delhi: Concept Publishing.

Gupta, D. C. (1982), *Indian Government and Politics*, 5th edn. New Delhi: Vikas.

Hague, Rod, Martin Harrop and Shaun Breslin (1992), *Comparative Government and Politics: An Introduction*, 3rd edn. London: Macmillan.

Hale, Sylvia M. (1989), 'The Status of Women in India', *Pacific Affairs* 62 (Fall), pp. 364–81.

Hanson, A. H. and Janet Douglas (1972), *India's Democracy*. New York: W. W. Norton.

Hardgrave, Robert L. (1992), 'After the Dynasty: Politics in India', *Current History* 91 (March), pp. 106–12.

Hardgrave, Robert L. and Stanley A. Kochanek (1993), *India: Government and Politics in a Developing Nation*, 5th edn. Fort Worth, TX: Harcourt Brace Jovanovich.

Hariharan, A. (1983), 'Levelling Down, All the Way', *Overseas Hindustan Times*, 28 April.

Hart, H. L. A. (1961), *The Concept of Law*. Oxford: Clarendon.

Hart, Henry C. (1976), *Indira Gandhi's India: A Political System Reappraised*. Boulder: Westview.

Hartley, Keith *et al.* (1993), *Economic Aspects of Disarmament: Disarmament as an Investment Process*. Geneva: United Nations Institute for Disarmament Research.

Hasan, Mushirul (1995), *Legacy of a Divided Nation: India's Muslims Since Independence*. London: C. Hurst.

Heeger, G. A. (1977), 'Politics in the Post-Military State', *World Politics* 29 (January), pp. 242–62.

Heginbotham, Stanley J. (1975), *Cultures in Conflict: The Four Faces of Indian Bureaucracy*. New York: Columbia University Press.

Heginbotham, Stanley J. (1976), 'The Civil Service and the Emergency', in Henry C. Hart (ed.), *Indira Gandhi's India: A Political System Reappraised*. Boulder: Westview, pp. 67–91.

Helliwell, John F. (1994), 'Empirical Linkages between Democracy and Economic Growth', *British Journal of Political Science* 24 (April), pp. 225–48.

Hermassi, Elbaki (1980), *The Third World Reassessed*. Berkeley: University of California Press.

Heston, Alan (1992), 'India's Economic Reforms: The Real Thing?', *Current History* 91 (March), pp. 113–16.

Hettne, Björn (1990), *Development Theory and the Three Worlds*. Harlow, Essex: Longman.

Hewitt, Vernon (1989), 'The Congress System is Dead: Long Live the Party System and Democratic India?', *Journal of Commonwealth and Comparative Politics* 27 (July), pp. 157–71.

Hicks, Norman and Paul Streeten (1979), 'Indicators of Development: The Search for a Basic Needs Yardstick', *World Development* 7 (June), pp. 567–80.

Hoffmann, Steven A. (1981), 'Faction Behavior and Cultural Codes: India and Japan', *Journal of Asian Studies* 40 (February), pp. 231–54.

Holsti, Kalevi J. (1986), 'The Horsemen of the Apocalypse: At the Gate, Detoured, or Retreating?', *International Studies Quarterly* 30 (December), pp. 355–72.

Huntington, Samuel P. (1968), *Political Order in Changing Societies.* New Haven, CT: Yale University Press.

Hussain, Mushahid (1991), 'Indian Army's Changing Profile', *Regional Studies* (Islamabad), 9(3), pp. 3–19.

ICSSR (Indian Council of Social Science Research) (1975), *Status of Women in India: A Synopsis of the Report of the National Committee on the Status of Women (1971–74).* New Delhi: Allied Publishers for the ICSSR.

Inkeles, Alex and David H. Smith (1974), *Becoming Modern.* London: Heinemann.

Iyer, Justice V. R. Krishna (1990), *Human Rights and Inhuman Wrongs.* Delhi: D. K. Publishers.

Jackman, Robert W. (1975), *Politics and Social Equality: A Comparative Analysis.* New York: John Wiley & Sons.

Jackman, Robert W. (1976), 'Politicians in Uniform: Military Governments and Social Change in the Third World', *American Political Science Review* 70 (December), pp. 1079–98.

Jacobs, G. (1985), 'India's Army', *Asian Defence Journal*, September, pp. 4–27.

Jaffrelot, Christophe (1994), *The Hindu Nationalist Movement, 1925–1993.* London: C. Hurst.

Jain, Devaki (1990), 'Development Theory and Practice: Insights Emerging from Women's Experience', *Economic and Political Weekly* 25 (7 July), pp. 1454–5.

Jain, R. B. (ed.) (1983), *Public Services in a Democratic Context.* New Delhi: Indian Institute of Public Administration.

Jancar, Barbara Wolfe (1978), *Women Under Communism.* Baltimore: The Johns Hopkins University Press.

Janowitz, Morris (1977), *Military Institutions and Coercion in Developing Nations.* Chicago: University of Chicago Press.

Jaquette, Jane S. (1982), 'Women and Modernization Theory: A Decade of Feminist Criticism', *World Politics* 34 (January), pp. 267–84.

Jayakar, Pupul (1992), *Indira Gandhi: A Biography.* New Delhi: Viking/Penguin.

Jayawardena, Kumari (1986), *Feminism and Nationalism in the Third World.* London: Zed Books.

Jeffrey, Robin (1994), *What's Happening to India? Punjab, Ethnic Conflict and the Test for Federalism.* London: Macmillan.

Jha, Prem Shankar (1993), 'Narasimha Rao's Lonely Battle', *HIE*, 20 March, p. 9.

Joshi, Ram and R. K. Hebsur (eds) (1987), *Congress in Indian Politics: A Centenary Perspective*. Bombay: Popular Prakashan.

Kapoor, Coomi (1984), 'The Supreme Court: The Conflicts Within', *India Today*, 15 November, pp. 96–9.

Kapur, Ashok (1993), 'State Service: The Steel without a Frame', *SW*, 6 March, pp. 10–11.

Kashyap, Subhash C. (1969), *The Politics of Defection*. Delhi: National Publishing House.

Katyal, K. K. (1991), 'Hard Options for President', *Hindu Weekly*, 16 March.

Kaufman, R., H. I. Chernotsky and G. S. Geller (1975), 'A Preliminary Test of the Theory of Dependency', *Comparative Politics* 7 (April), pp. 303–30.

Kay, Geoffrey (1975), *Development and Underdevelopment: A Marxist Analysis*. London: Macmillan.

Khator, Renu (1991), *Environment, Development and Politics in India*. Lanham, MD: University Press of America.

Kishwar, Madhu (1991), 'The Assassination of Rajiv Gandhi', *Manushi* 63–64 (March–June), pp. 2–5.

Kochanek, Stanley A. (1968), *The Congress Party of India: The Dynamics of One-Party Democracy*. Princeton: Princeton University Press.

Kochanek, Stanley A. (1974), *Business and Politics in India*. Berkeley: University of California Press.

Kochanek, Stanley A. (1976), 'Mrs. Gandhi's Pyramid: The New Congress', in Henry C. Hart (ed.), *Indira Gandhi's India: A Political System Reappraised*. Boulder: Westview, pp. 93–124.

Kohli, Atul (1980), 'Democracy, Economic Growth, and Inequality in India's Development', *World Politics* 32 (July), pp. 623–38.

Kohli, Atul (1985), *The State and Poverty in India: The Politics of Reform*. Cambridge: Cambridge University Press.

Kohli, Atul (ed.) (1988), *India's Democracy: An Analysis of Changing State-Society Relations*. Princeton: Princeton University Press.

Kohli, Atul (1990), *Democracy and Discontent: India's Growing Crisis of Governability*. Cambridge: Cambridge University Press.

Kothari, Rajni (1964), 'The Congress System', *Asian Survey* 4 (December), pp. 1161–73.

Kothari, Rajni (ed.) (1967), *Party Systems and Election Studies*. Bombay: Allied.

Kothari, Rajni (1970), *Politics in India*. Boston: Little, Brown & Co.

Kothari, Rajni (1976), *Democratic Polity and Social Change in India: Crisis and Opportunities*. Bombay: Allied.

Krueger, Anne O. (1974), 'The Political Economy of a Rent-Seeking Society', *American Economic Review* 63 (June), pp. 291–303.

Kukreja, Veena (1991), *Civil–Military Relations in South Asia: Pakistan, Bangladesh and India*. New Delhi: Sage.

Kumar, Dharma (1992), 'The Affirmative Action Debate in India', *Asian Survey* 32 (March), pp. 291–302.

Lahiri, Ashok K. and Prannoy Roy (1984), 'Assessing Swings in Multi-Party Systems: The Indian Experience', *Electoral Studies* 3 (August), pp. 171–89.

Lal, Deepak (1988), *The Hindu Equilibrium – vol. 1, Cultural Stability and Economic Stagnation*. Oxford: Clarendon.

Lall, Sanjaya (1975), 'Is Dependence a Useful Concept in Analysing Underdevelopment?', *World Development* 3 (November), pp. 799–810.

Lawson, Stephanie (1991), *The Failure of Democratic Politics in Fiji*. Oxford: Clarendon Press.

Levy, Marion J. (1966), *Modernization and the Structure of Societies*. Princeton: Princeton University Press.

Lewis, Primila (1979), *Reason Wounded: An Experience of India's Emergency*. London: Allen & Unwin.

Leys, Colin (1975), *Underdevelopment in Kenya: The Political Economy of Neo-Colonialism, 1964–1971*. Berkeley: University of California Press.

Lijphart, Arend (1977), *Democracy in Plural Societies: A Comparative Exploration*. New Haven, CT: Yale University Press.

Lijphart, Arend (ed.) (1992), *Parliamentary versus Presidential Government*. Oxford: Oxford University Press.

Lijphart, Arend (1994), *Electoral Systems and Party Systems*. Oxford: Oxford University Press.

Lincoln, Abraham (1919), *Speeches and Letters of Abraham Lincoln, 1832–1865*, ed. by Merwin Roe. London: Dent.

Linz, Juan J. (1991), 'The Two Faces of Democracy', *Dialogue*, 2/1991, pp. 21–7.

Lipset, Seymour Martin (1959), 'Social Requisites of Democracy: Economic Development and Political Legitimacy', *American Political Science Review* 53 (March), pp. 69–105.

Lipset, Seymour Martin (1960), *Political Man: The Social Bases of Politics*. Garden City, NY: Doubleday.

Lipset, Seymour Martin and Stein Rokkan (1967), 'Cleavage Structures, Party Systems and Voter Alignments: An Introduction', in Lipset and Rokkan (eds), *Party Systems and Voter Alignments: Cross-National Perspectives*. New York: Free Press, pp. 1–64.

Lively, Jack (1975), *Democracy*. Oxford: Basil Blackwell.

Lyon, Peter (1991), 'The First Great Post-Colonial State: India's Tryst with Destiny', in James Mayall and Anthony Payne (eds), *The Fallacies of Hope: The Post-Colonial Record of the Commonwealth Third World*. Manchester: Manchester University Press, pp. 17–43.

Lyon, Peter and James Manor (eds) (1983), *Transfer and Transformation: Political Institutions in the New Commonwealth*. Leicester: Leicester University Press.

McAulay, Peter (1993), 'Civilian Police and Peacekeeping: Challenges in the 1990s', in Hugh Smith (ed.), *Peacekeeping: Challenges for the Future*. Canberra: Australian Defence Studies Centre, Australian Defence Force Academy, pp. 33–40.

McKinlay, R. D. and A. S. Cohan (1976), 'Performance and Instability in Military and Non-Military Regime Systems', *American Political Science Review* 70 (September), pp. 850–64.

MacMillan, Margaret (1969), 'The Indian Army since Independence', *South Asian Review* 3 (October), pp. 45–58.

Macpherson, C. B. (1966), *The Real World of Democracy*. Oxford: Clarendon.

Macpherson, C. B. (1973), *Democratic Theory*. Oxford: Clarendon.

Macpherson, C. B. (1977), *The Life and Times of Liberal Democracy*. Oxford: Oxford University Press.

Macridis, Roy C. and Bernard E. Brown (eds) (1961), *Comparative Politics*. Chicago: Dorsey.

Maddison, Angus (1971), *Class Structure and Economic Growth: India and Pakistan since the Moghuls*. London: Allen & Unwin.

Maheshwari, S. R. (1992), *Problems and Issues in Administrative Federalism*. New Delhi: Allied.

Maitra, Priyatosh (1993), *Mahalanobis Planning Model – Revisited*. Dunedin: University of Otago, Economics Discussion Paper No. 9313.

Malhotra, Inder (1989), *Indira Gandhi: A Personal and Political Biography*. London: Hodder & Stoughton.

Malik, Yogendra K. and V. B. Singh (1994), *Hindu Nationalism in India: The Rise of the Bharatiya Janata Party*. Boulder: Westview.

Mallick, Ross (1993), *Development Policy of a Communist Government: West Bengal since 1977*. Cambridge: Cambridge University Press.

Mallick, Ross (1994), *Indian Communism: Opposition, Collaboration, and Institutionalization*. New Delhi: Oxford University Press.

Manchester, William (1983), *The Last Lion: Winston Spencer Churchill; Visions of Glory: 1874–1932*. Boston: Little, Brown & Co.

Mandal, B. P. (1980), *Report of the Backward Classes Commission*, 2 vols. New Delhi: Government of India Press.

Manor, James (1988), 'Parties and the Party System', in Atul Kohli (ed.), *India's Democracy: An Analysis of Changing State–Society Relations*. Princeton: Princeton University Press, pp. 62–98.

Manor, James (1991), 'India', in David Butler and D. A. Low (eds), *Sovereigns and Surrogates: Constitutional Heads of State in the Commonwealth*. London: Macmillan, pp. 144–70.

Manor, James (1992), 'BJP in South India: 1991 General Election', *Economic and Political Weekly*, 13–20 July, pp. 1267–73.

Manor, James (ed.) (1994), *Nehru to the 1990s: The Changing Office of Prime Minister in India*. London: C. Hurst.

Mansingh, Surjit (1991), 'State and Religion in South Asia: Some Reflections', *South Asia Journal* 4, pp. 293–311.

Mathur, Kuldeep (1992), 'The State and the Use of Coercive Power in India', *Asian Survey* 32 (April), pp. 337–49.

Mazumdar, Vina (1976), 'The Social Reform Movement in India from Ranade to Nehru', in B. R. Nanda (ed.), *Indian Women: From Purdah to Modernity*. New Delhi: Vikas, pp. 41–66.

Mehta, Bhanu Pratap (1991–92), 'India's Disordered Democracy', *Pacific Affairs* 64 (Winter), pp. 536–48.

Mellor, John W. (1979), 'The Indian Economy: Objectives, Performance and Prospects', in J. W. Mellor (ed.), *India: A Rising Middle Power*. Boulder: Westview, pp. 85–110.

Menon, N. C. (1982), 'Principles of Power', *Overseas Hindustan Times*, 17 June, p. 7.

Milliken, Max and Donald Blackmer (1961), *The Emerging Nations*. Cambridge, MA: MIT Press.

Misra, B. B. (1976), *The Indian Political Parties: An Historical Analysis of Political Behaviour up to 1947*. Delhi: Oxford University Press.

Misra, B. B. (1986), *Government and Bureaucracy in India, 1947–1976*. New Delhi: Oxford University Press.

Misra, K. P. (1980), 'Paramilitary Forces in India', *Armed Forces and Society* 6 (Spring), pp. 371–88.

Mitra, Chandan (1984), 'Pride Hurt in Punjab – II: Politics of Region and Religion', *SW*, 29 September.

Mitra, Subrata Kumar (ed.) (1990), *The Post-Colonial State in Asia: Dialectics of Politics and Culture*. Hemel Hempstead: Wheatsheaf.

Mitra, Subrata Kumar (1991), 'Room to Maneuver in the Middle: Local Elites, Political Action, and the State in India', *World Politics* 43 (April), pp. 390–413.

Mitra, Subrata Kumar (1992), 'Democracy and Political Change in India', *Journal of Commonwealth & Comparative Politics* 30 (March), pp. 9–38.

Mitra, Subrata Kumar (ed.) (1994), *Subnational Movements in South Asia*. Boulder: Westview.

Mitra, Subrata Kumar and James Chiriyankandath (eds) (1992), *Electoral Politics in India: A Changing Landscape*. New Delhi: Segment.

Mitta, M. (1993), 'Diluting Mandal: A Tightrope Walk', *India Today*, 30 September, p. 15.

Moore, Barrington (1969), *Social Origins of Dictatorship and Democracy: Lord and Peasant in the Making of the Modern World*. Boston: Beacon.

Morris, Morris D. (1979), *Measuring the Condition of the World's Poor: The Physical Quality of Life Index*. Oxford: Pergamon.

Morris-Jones, W. H. (1957), *Parliament in India*. London: Longman.

Morris-Jones, W. H. (1971), *The Government and Politics of India*, 3rd edn. London: Hutchinson.

Morris-Jones, W. H. (1978), *Politics Mainly Indian*. Delhi: Orient Longman.

Morris-Jones, W. H. (1979), 'The West and the Third World: Whose Democracy, Whose Development?', *Third World Quarterly* 1 (July), pp. 31–42.

Mountjoy, Alan B. (1978), 'The Third World in Perspective', in A. B. Mountjoy (ed.), *The Third World: Problems and Prospects*. London: Macmillan, pp. 13–22.

Mukherjee, Alok (1989), 'The Devolution Debate', *Frontline*, 4–17 March, pp. 20–2.

Myrdal, Gunnar (1968), *Asian Drama: An Inquiry into the Poverty of Nations*. London: Pelican.

Nanda, B. R. (ed.) (1976), *Indian Women: From Purdah to Modernity*. New Delhi: Vikas.

Nandy, Ashis (1989), 'The Political Culture of the Indian State', *Daedalus* 118 (Fall 1989), pp. 1–26.

Narayan, Hemendra (1993), 'A Book of Praise for Laloo', *SW*, 7 August 1993, p. 5.

Nath, Trilok (1978), *The Indian Police: A Case for a New Image*. New Delhi: Sterling.

Nayar, Baldev Raj (1966), *Minority Politics in the Punjab*. Princeton: Princeton University Press.

Nayar, Kuldip (1984), 'The Law and Order Problem', *The Tribune* (Chandigarh), 4 October.

Nayar, Kuldip (1992), 'A Devalued P. M. after 500 Days', *SW*, 28 November, p. 7.

Nayar, Gen. V. K. (1992), *Threat from Within: India's Internal Security Environment*. New Delhi: Lancer.

Nehru, Arun (1993), 'Pampering Minority Hawks Won't Work', *The Indian Express* (New Delhi), 3 January.

Nehru, B. K. (1979), 'Western Democracy and the Third World', *Third World Quarterly* 1 (April), pp. 53–70.

Nehru, Jawaharlal (1960), *The Discovery of India*. London: Meridian.

Nehru, Jawaharlal (1961), *India's Foreign Policy: Selected Speeches, September 1946–April 1961*. New Delhi: Government of India, Ministry of Information and Broadcasting.

Nettl, J. P. (1967), *Political Mobilization: A Sociological Analysis of Methods and Concepts*. London: Faber.

Neubauer, Deane (1967), 'Some Conditions of Democracy', *American Political Science Review* 61 (December), pp. 1002–9.

Newman, Saul (1991), 'Does Modernization Breed to Ethnic Political Conflict?', *World Politics* 43 (April), pp. 451–78.

Noorani, A. G. (1990), *The Presidential System: The Indian Debate*. New Delhi: Sage.

Noorani, A. G. (1992), 'President's Rule: Nagaland Step Unconstitutional', *SW*, 18 April, p. 12.

Noorani, A. G. (1993a), 'Rao's Credibility Shattered on Article 356', *SW*, 16 January 1993, p. 11.

Noorani, A. G. (1993b), 'Split Mind: The Speaker & the Defection Law', *SW*, 3 July, p. 10.

Noorani, A. G. (1994), 'Human Rights in Kashmir', *Frontline*, 15–28 January, pp. 44–8.

Nossiter, T. J. (1982), *Communism in Kerala: A Study in Political Adaptation*. Berkeley: University of California Press.

O'Brien, P. (1975), 'A Critique of Latin American Theories of Dependency', in I. Oxaal, T. Barnett and D. Booth (eds), *Beyond the Sociology of Development*. London: Routledge & Kegan Paul, pp. 7–27.

Odetola, Olatunde (1982), *Military Regimes and Development: A Comparative Analysis in African Societies*. London: George Allen & Unwin.

Ohmae, Kenichi (1993), 'The Rise of the Region State', *Foreign Affairs* 72 (Spring), pp. 78–87.

Oldenburg, Philip (1987), 'Middlemen in Third World Corruption: Implications of an Indian Case', *World Politics* 29 (July), pp. 508–35.

Oldenburg, Philip (ed.) (1993), *India Briefing 1993*. Boulder: Westview.

Oommen, T. K. (1990), *Protest and Change: Studies in Social Movements*. New Delhi: Sage.

Organski, A. F. K. (1965), *The Stages of Political Development*. New York: Knopf.

Özbudun, Ergun (1987), 'Institutionalizing Competitive Elections in Developing Societies', in Myron Weiner and Ergun Özbudun (eds), *Competitive Elections in Developing Countries*. Durham, NC: Duke University Press, pp. 393–422.

Packenham, Robert A. (1992), *The Dependency Movement: Scholarship and Politics in Development Studies*. Cambridge, MA: Harvard University Press.

Padgaonkar, Dileep (1991), 'Shekhar in Good Form: Congress Ambivalence Must End', *TOI* (Patna), 11 January.

Pal, R. N. (1983), *The Office of the Prime Minister of India*. New Delhi: Ghanshyam Publishers. Traces the evolution of the role of the prime minister.

Palkhivala, Nani (1983), 'Centre–State Relations: The Unwritten Rules', *India Today*, 31 August, pp. 34–5.

Palkhivala, Nani (1993), 'Are We Misusing the Judiciary?', *The Illustrated Weekly of India*, 2–8 January, pp. 8–9.

Palma, Gabriel (1978), 'Dependency: A Formal Theory of Underdevelopment or a Methodology for the Analysis of Concrete Situations of Underdevelopment?', *World Development* 6 (July), pp. 881–924.

Palmer, Monte (1989), *Dilemmas of Political Development: An Introduction to the Politics of Developing Areas*. Itasca, Ill: F. E. Peacock.

Panandiker, V. A. Pai and Arun Sud (1981), *Emerging Patterns of Representation in the Indian Parliament*. New Delhi: Centre for Policy Research.

Paranjape, H. K. (1990), 'Planning Commission as a Constitutional Body', *Economic and Political Weekly*, 10 November, pp. 2479–81.

Park, Kyung Ae (1993), 'Women and Development: The Case of South Korea', *Comparative Politics* 25 (January), pp. 127–45.

Pathak, Rahul (1992), 'The Judiciary: Crumbling Citadel', *India Today*, 30 June, pp. 51–7.

Patman, C. R. (1978), 'Economic Planning: Paths to Development', in Alan B. Mountjoy (ed.), *The Third World: Problems and Prospects*. London: Macmillan.

Pearson, Lester B. *et al.* (1969), *Partners in Development: Report of the Commission on International Development*. New York: Praeger.

Perlmutter, Amos (1977), *The Military and Politics in Modern Times*. New Haven: Yale University Press.

Phadnis, Urmila (1989), *Ethnicity and Nation-Building in South Asia*. New Delhi: Sage. An influential study of ethnic identities and movements.

Poggi, Gianfranco (1990), *The State: Its Nature, Development and Prospects*. Stanford: Stanford University Press.

Popper, Karl (1988), 'The Open Society and its Enemies Revisited', *The Economist* (London), 23 April, pp. 23–6.

Potter, David C. (1986), *India's Political Administration, 1919–1983*. Oxford: Clarendon.

Powell, G. Bingham (1982), *Contemporary Democracies*. Cambridge, MA: Harvard University Press.

Prasad, Anirudh (1984), *Centre and State Powers under Indian Federalism*. New Delhi: Deep & Deep.

Praval, K. C. (1987), *The Indian Army after Independence*. New Delhi: Lancer.

Puri, Balraj (1981), *Jammu and Kashmir: Triumph and Tragedy of Indian Federalisation*. New Delhi: Stirling.

Putnam, Robert with Robert Leonardi and Raffaella Nanetti (1993), *Making Democracy Work: Civic Traditions in Modern Italy*. Princeton: Princeton University Press.

Pye, Lucian W. (1962), 'Armies in the Process of Political Modernization', in John J. Johnson (ed.), *The Role of the Military in Underdeveloped Countries*. Princeton: Princeton University Press, pp. 69–89.

Pylee, M. V. (1965), *Constitutional Government in India*. Bombay: Asia.

Pylee, M. V. (1992), *India's Constitution*. New Delhi: S. Chand.

Quigley, Declan (1993), *The Interpretation of Caste*. Oxford: Clarendon.

Radcliffe, Sarah and Sallie Westwood (eds) (1993), *Viva*. London: Routledge.

Rai Chowdhuri, Satyabrata (1992), 'Yes, Minister: The Iron Grip of the Civil Service', *SW*, 5 December, p. 10.

Reddy, G. Ram and G. Haragopal (1985), 'The Pyraveekar: 'The Fixer' in Rural India', *Asian Survey* 25 (November), pp. 1148–62.

Robinson, R. and J. Gallagher (1961), *Africa and the Victorians: The Official Mind of Imperialism*. London: Macmillan.

Rose, Richard (ed.) (1974), *Electoral Behaviour: A Comparative Handbook*. New York: Free Press.

Rose, Richard and Derek Urwin (1969), 'Social Cohesion, Political Parties and Strains in Regimes', *Comparative Political Studies*, 2 (April), pp.7–67.

Rosenthal, Donald B. (1977), *The Expansive Elite: District Politics and State Policy-Making in India*. Berkeley: University of California Press.

Rostow, W. W. (1960), *The Stages of Economic Growth: A Non-Communist Manifesto*. Cambridge: Cambridge University Press.

Roy, Ramashray (1975), *The Uncertain Verdict: A Study of the 1969 Elections in Four Indian States*. Berkeley: University of California Press.

Roy, Subroto and William E. James (eds) (1992), *Foundations of India's Political Economy: Towards an Agenda for the 1990s*. New Delhi: Sage.

Rudolph, Lloyd I. and Susanne H. Rudolph (1964), 'Generals and Politicians in India', *Pacific Affairs* 37 (Spring), pp. 5–19.

Rudolph, Lloyd I. and Susanne H. Rudolph (1967), *The Modernity of Tradition*. Chicago: University of Chicago Press.

Rudolph, Lloyd I. and Susanne H. Rudolph (1981), 'Judicial Review *versus* Parliamentary Sovereignty', *Journal of Commonwealth & Comparative Politics* 19 (November), pp. 231–56.

Rudolph, Lloyd I. and Susanne H. Rudolph (1987), *In Pursuit of Lakshmi: The Political Economy of the Indian State*. Chicago: University of Chicago Press.

Russett, Bruce (1965), *Trends in World Politics*. New York: Macmillan.

Ryan, M. P. (1975), *Womanhood in America: From Colonial Times to the Present*. New York: New Viewpoints.

Saffiotti, H. (1975), 'Female Labor and Capitalism in the United States and Brazil', in R. Rohrlich-Leavitt (ed.), *Women Cross-Culturally: Change and Challenge*. The Hague: Mouton, pp. 59–94.

Saha, B. P. (1992), 'Police in Chains', *SW*, 4 July, p. 11.

Saksena, N. S. (1987), *Law and Order in India*. New Delhi: Abhinav.

Sankhdher, M. M. (1980), 'Case for a Presidential System', *Overseas Hindustan Times*, 27 November.

Sarkaria (1988), *Report of the Commission on Centre–State Relations*, 2 vols. Nasik: Government Printer.

Sartori, Giovanni (1965), *Democratic Theory*. New York: Praeger.

Sathe, S. P. (1989), *Constitutional Amendments, 1950–1988*. Bombay: Tripathi.

Sayeed, K. B. (1967), *The Political System of Pakistan.* Karachi, Oxford University Press.

Seervai, H. M. (1990/1991), *Constitutional Law of India: A Critical Commentary,* 2 vols. Bombay: Tripathi.

Sen, Amartya K. (1981), 'Public Action and the Quality of Life in Developing Countries', *Oxford Bulletin of Economics and Statistics* 43 (November), pp. 287–319.

Sen, Sankar (1991), 'Police and Public: Walls of Misunderstanding', *SW,* 21 December, p. 12.

Sen Gupta, Bhabani (1989), *Rajiv Gandhi: A Political Study.* New Delhi: Konarak.

Shah, Ghanshyam (1990), *Social Movements in India: A Review of the Literature.* New Delhi: Sage.

Shankar, Jogan (1990), *Devadasi Cult: A Sociological Analysis.* New Delhi: Ashish.

Sharma, Navneet (1994), 'Simmering Discontent Sparks Off Exodus in Army, Navy', *SW,* 29 January, p. 3.

Sharma, P. D. (1981), *Police, Polity and People in India.* New Delhi: Uppol Publishing House.

Sharma, P. D. (1984), *Police and Political Order in India.* New Delhi: Research.

Shourie, Arun (1987), *Religion in Politics.* Delhi: Roli Books International.

Singh, Amar Kumar (1993), *Pride of Socialistic Consciousness: From the Plough to the Chief Minister's Residence.* Patna: Bharat Granth Academy.

Singh, Khushwant (1966), *A History of the Sikhs,* 2 vols. Princeton: Princeton University Press.

Singh, Khushwant (1984), 'Is It All Over?', *Probe India,* July 1984, p. 36.

Singh, K. S. (ed.) (1982), *Tribal Movements in India.* New Delhi: Manohar.

Singh, Mahendra Prasad (1981), *Split in a Predominant Party: The Indian National Congress in 1969.* Delhi: Abhinav.

Singh, Mahendra Prasad (1992), 'India: Searching for a Consensus by Amending the Constitution?', *Governance: An International Journal of Policy and Administration* 5 (July), pp. 358–73.

Singh, Tarlok (1974), *India's Development Experience.* London: Macmillan.

Singh, V. B. and Shankar Bose (1987/1988), *State Elections in India, 1952–85,* 5 vols. New Delhi: Sage.

Sinha, S. K. (1980a), *Of Matters Military.* New Delhi: Vikas.

Sinha, S. K. (1980b), *Higher Defence Organisation in India.* New Delhi: United Service Institution of India.

Sinha, S. K. (1991), 'Stemming the Rot: Change to Presidential System', *SW,* 11 May.

Sirsikar, V. M. (1973), *Sovereigns without Crowns: A Behavioural Analysis of the Indian Electoral Process.* Bombay: Popular Prakashan.

Sisson, Richard (1990), 'India in 1989: A Year of Elections in a Culture of Change', *Asian Survey* 30 (February), pp. 111–25.

Sisson, Richard and Stanley Wolpert (1988), *Congress and Indian Nationalism: The Pre-Independence Phase.* Berkeley: University of California Press.

Sisson, Richard and Ramashray Roy (eds) (1990), *Diversity and Dominance in Indian Politics,* Vol. 1. *Changing Bases of Congress Support.* New Delhi: Sage.

Sisson, Richard and William Vanderbok (1983), 'Mapping the Indian Electorate: Trends in Party Support in Seven National Elections', *Asian Survey* 23 (October), pp. 1140–58.

Sisson, Richard and William Vanderbok (1984), 'Mapping the Indian Electorate II: Patterns of Weakness in the Indian Party System', *Asian Survey* 24 (October), pp. 1086–97.

Sivard, Ruth Leger (1985), *Women . . . A World Survey*. Washington, DC: World Priorities.

Smith, M. G. (1974), *The Plural Society in the British West Indies*. Berkeley: University of California Press.

Smith, Tony (1979), 'The Underdevelopment of Development Literature: The Case of Dependency Theory', *World Politics* 31 (January), pp. 247–88.

Snyder, Margaret (1990), *Women: The Key to Ending Hunger*, The Hunger Project Papers No 8, August.

Somjee, A. H. (1991), *Development Theory: Critiques and Explorations*. London: Macmillan.

Sowell, Thomas (1990), *Preferential Policies: An International Perspective*. New York: William Morrow & Co.

Spear, Percival (1957), *India, Pakistan, and the West*, 4th edn. New York: Oxford University Press.

Srinivas, M. N. (1962), *Caste in Modern India and Other Essays*. Bombay: Asia Publishing.

Srinavasan, Kannan (1992), 'India Should Take a Saber to Its Defense Budget', *Asian Wall Street Journal*, 23 March.

Stepan, Alfred (1974), *The Military in Politics: Changing Patterns in Brazil*. Princeton: Princeton University Press.

Stepan, Alfred and Cindy Skach (1993), 'Constitutional Frameworks and Democratic Consolidation: Parliamentarianism vs. Presidentialism', *World Politics* 46 (October), pp. 1–22.

Stern, Robert W. (1993), *Changing India: Bourgeois Revolution on the Subcontinent*. Melbourne: Cambridge University Press.

Stewart, Frances (1985), *Planning to Meet Basic Needs*. London: Macmillan.

Stokes, Eric (1978), *The Peasant and the Raj: Studies in Agrarian Society and Peasant Rebellion in Colonial India*. Cambridge: Cambridge University Press.

Streeten, Paul (1981), *First Things First: Meeting Basic Needs in Developing Countries*. New York: Oxford University Press.

Streeten, Paul and Shahid Javed Burki (1978), 'Basic Needs: Some Issues', *World Development* 6 (March), pp. 411–21.

Subramaniam, S. (1994), 'Ending the Lathi Raj: Corrective Action to Remove Flaws in Police Act', *Indian Express* (Bombay), 8 February.

Sudarshan, R. (1990), 'In Quest of State: Politics and Judiciary in India', *Journal of Commonwealth & Comparative Politics* 28 (March), pp. 44–69.

Swainson, Nicola (1980), *The Development of Corporate Capitalism in Kenya 1918–1977*. London: Heinemann.

Thakkar, Usha (1992), 'The Women's Vote', in Subrata Kumar Mitra and James Chiriyankandath (eds), *Electoral Politics in India: A Changing Landscape*. New Delhi: Segment, pp. 199–211.

Thakur, Ramesh (1976), 'The Fate of India's Parliamentary Democracy', *Pacific Affairs* 49 (Summer), pp. 263–93.

Thakur, Ramesh (1977), 'The March 1977 Indian Election', *Queen's Quarterly* 84 (Autumn), pp. 420–32.

Thakur, Ramesh (1980), 'The Return of the Helmswoman', *Queen's Quarterly* 87 (Winter), pp. 693–708.

Thakur, Ramesh (1982), 'Liberalism, Democracy and Development: Philosophical Dilemmas in Third World Politics', *Political Studies* 30 (September), pp. 333–49.

Thakur, Ramesh (1992), 'India after Nonalignment', *Foreign Affairs* 71 (Spring), pp. 165–82.

Thakur, Ramesh (1993a), 'From the Mosaic to the Melting Pot: Cross-National Reflections on Multiculturalism', in Chandran Kukathas (ed.), *Multicultural Citizens: The Philosophy and Politics of Identity*. Sydney: Centre for Independent Studies, pp. 103–41.

Thakur, Ramesh (1993b), 'Restoring India's Economic Health', *Third World Quarterly* 14, pp. 137–57.

Thakur, Ramesh (1993c), 'Ayodhya and the Politics of India's Secularism: A Double-Standards Discourse', *Asian Survey* 33 (July), pp. 645–64.

Thakur, Ramesh and Carlyle A. Thayer (1992), *Soviet Relations with India and Vietnam*. London: Macmillan.

Thakur, Ramesh and G. Antony Wood (1989), 'Paradise Regained or Paradise Defiled? Fiji under Military Rule', *International Studies* 26 (January–March), pp. 15–44.

Thapan, M. L. (1993), 'Need to Dispense with Politicians', *SW*, 27 March, p. 10.

Thomas, Raju G. C. (1978), *The Defence of India: A Budgetary Perspective*. New Delhi: Macmillan.

Thomas, Raju G. C. (1986), *Indian Security Policy*. Princeton: Princeton University Press.

Tilly, L. A. and J. W. Scott (1978), *Women, Work, and Family*. New York: Holt, Rinehart, and Winston.

Tomlinson, B. R. (1993), *The New Cambridge History of India – The Economy of Modern India, 1860–1970*. Cambridge: Cambridge University Press.

Toye, J. (1987), *Dilemmas of Development: Reflections on the Counter-Revolution in Development Theory and Policy*. Oxford: Basil Blackwell.

Tummala, Krishna K. (1992), 'India's Federalism under Stress', *Asian Survey* 32 (June), pp. 538–53.

UNDP (United Nations Development Programme), *Human Development Report*. New York: Oxford University Press, annual since 1990.

UNIFEM (United Nations Development Fund for Women) (1989), *Strength in Adversity: Women in the Developing World*. New York: United Nations.

UNO (United Nations Organisation) (1985), *The State of the World's Women 1985*. New York: United Nations.

Vanaik, Achin (1990), *The Painful Transition: Bourgeois Democracy in India*. London: Verso.

Vanderbok, William G. (1990), 'The Tiger Triumphant: The Mobilization and Alignment of the Indian Electorate', *British Journal of Political Science* 20 (April), pp. 237–61.

Varma, S. P. and Iqbal Narain (1973), *Voting Behaviour in a Changing Society*. Delhi: National Books.

Varshney, Ashutosh (1991), 'India, Pakistan, and Kashmir', *Asian Survey* 31 (November), pp. 997–1019.

Varshney, Ashutosh (1993), *The Myth of Rural Powerlessness: Town-Country Struggles in India's Development*. New York: Cambridge University Press.

Verma, R. R. (1992), 'Crime & Law: Does Defying Society Pay?', *SW*, 18 July, p. 12.

Verney, Douglas V. (1985), 'The Role of the Governor in India's "Administrative Federalism"': A Comparative Perspective', *Indian Journal of Public Administration* 31 (1985), pp. 1243–68.

Vogel, Ezra F. (1991), *The Four Little Dragons: The Spread of Industrialization in East Asia*. Cambridge, MA: Harvard University Press.

Wade, Robert (1985), 'The Market for Public Office: Why the Indian State Is Not Better at Development', *World Development* 13 (April), pp. 467–97.

Wade, Robert (1990), *Governing the Market: Economic Theory and the Role of Government in East Asian Industrialization*. Princeton: Princeton University Press.

Wallace, Paul (ed.) (1985), *Region and Nation in India*. New Delhi: Oxford University Press.

Wallace, Paul (1990), 'Religious and Ethnic Politics: Political Mobilization in the Punjab', in Frankel and Rao (eds), *Dominance and State Power in India*, vol. 2, pp. 416–81.

Wallerstein, Immanuel (1979), *The Capitalist World-Economy*. Cambridge: Cambridge University Press.

Watkins, Frederick M. (1968). 'State: The Concept', in David L. Sills (ed.), *International Encyclopedia of the Social Sciences*, vol. 15. London: Macmillan, pp. 150–7.

Weber, Max (1957; first pub. 1922), *The Theory of Economic and Social Organisation*. Berkeley: University of California Press.

Weede, Erich and Horst Tiefenbach (1981), 'Three Dependency Explanations of Economic Growth: A Critical Evaluation', *European Journal of Political Research*, 9 (December), pp. 391–406.

Weiner, Myron (1965), 'India: Two Political Cultures', in Lucian Pye and Sydney Verba (eds), *Political Culture and Political Development*. Princeton: Princeton University Press, pp. 199–244.

Weiner, Myron (1967), *Party Building in a New Nation*. Chicago: University of Chicago Press.

Weiner, Myron (1978), *Sons of the Soil: Migration and Ethnic Conflict in India*. Princeton: Princeton University Press.

Weiner, Myron (1987a), 'Empirical Democratic Theory', in Myron Weiner and Ergun Özbudun (eds), *Competitive Elections in Developing Countries*. Durham, NC: Duke University Press, pp. 3–34.

Weiner, Myron (1987b), 'India', in Myron Weiner and Ergun Özbudun, (eds), *Competitive Elections in Developing Countries*. Durham, NC: Duke University Press, pp. 37–76.

Weiner, Myron (1989), *The Indian Paradox: Essays in Indian Politics,* (ed.) by Ashutosh Varshney. New Delhi: Sage.

Weiner, Myron and John Osgood Field (eds). (1975–77), *Electoral Politics in the Indian States: The Impact of Moderation,* 4 vols. Delhi: Manohar.

Weiner, Myron and Mary F. Katzenstein (1981), *India's Preferential Policies: Migrants, the Middle Classes, and Ethnic Equality.* Chicago: University of Chicago Press.

Welch, Claude E. (1971), 'The Comparative Study of Political Modernization', in C. E. Welch (ed.), *Political Modernization: A Reader in Comparative Political Change,* 2nd edn. Belmont, CA: Duxbury Press, pp. 1–16.

Welch, Claude E. (1976), 'Civilian Control of the Military: Myth and Reality', in C. E. Welch (ed.), *Civilian Control of the Military: Theory and Cases from Developing Countries.* Albany: State University of New York Press, pp. 1–42.

Wheare, K. C. (1951), *Federal Government.* Oxford: Oxford University Press. A dated but classic account of federalism.

Wiatr, Jerzy J. (1985), 'The Military in Politics: Realities and Stereotypes', *International Social Science Journal* 37(1), pp. 97–109.

Wilenski, Harold L. (1975), *The Welfare State and Equality: Structural and Ideological Roots of Public Expenditures.* Berkeley: University of California Press.

Wolpert, Stanley (1977), *A New History of India.* New York: Oxford University Press.

Wolpin, Miles D. (1986), *Militarization, Internal Repression, and Social Welfare in the Third World.* New York: St. Martin's Press.

Wood, John R. (1975), 'Extra-Parliamentary Opposition in India: An Analysis of Populist Agitations in Gujarat and Bihar', *Pacific Affairs* 48 (Fall), pp. 313–34.

Wood, John R. (ed.) (1984), *State Politics in Contemporary India.* Boulder: Westview.

World Bank (1993), *The East Asian Miracle: Economic Growth & Public Policy.* New York: Oxford University Press.

Newspapers and Journals

Frontline (Madras). A fortnightly newsmagazine published from Madras that has some excellent feature articles on political, military and international affairs.

HIE. Hindu International Edition (Madras).

India Today (New Delhi). Probably India's most influential newsmagazine in English, published fortnightly.

Manushi: A Journal about Women and Society.

Sunday (Calcutta). A weekly newsmagazine published by the Anand Bazaar Patrika group in Calcutta that offers some penetrating and insightful analyses.

SW. Statesman Weekly (Calcutta).

TOI (Times of India). The most widely-read English language daily in India.

Index